The Hotelkeeper's Son

The Hotelkeeper's Son

Atlanta and Beyond

A Memoir

Jerald Lee Watts, M.D.

THE HOTELKEEPER'S SON: ATLANTA AND BEYOND
Copyright 2020 by Jerald Lee Watts, M.D.

This memoir is a work of creative nonfiction.
Some names are changed to maintain privacy or are composites to make a point or lessen unnecessary storytelling. Any real names used, or persons recognized, implies singular respect and or affection for that person by the author.

ISBN: 978-1-09831-844-4

Written and Published in the United States of America by the author,
JERALD LEE WATTS, M.D.
Peachtree City, GA 30269
jerald.watts@yahoo.com

OTHER BOOKS BY THE AUTHOR

PROMISES KEPT
ISBN: 978-4401-6807-9 (PBK)
ISBN 978-1-4401-6809-3 (EBOOK)
COPYRIGHT 2009 JERALD LEE WATTS, M.D.

MILITARY MEDICINE AND COLD WAR
ISBN: 987-1-4917-4409-3 (PBK)
ISBN: 978-1-4917-4410-9 (EBOOK)
COPYRIGHT 2016 JERALD LEE WATTS, M.D. FS, USAFRES.

Both from
iUniverse Publishers 2015
WWW.IUNIVERSE.COM
1663 LIBERTY DRIVE BLOOMINGTON, IN 47403
1-800-AUTHORS (1-800-288-4677)

Dedicated to my grandchildren:

Marcus Francesco Paoletti
Kathryn Miller Watts
Carter Dillon Watts
Amanda Kathryn Burns
Charlotte Elizabeth Burns
John Andrew Champion
Josephine "Jo Jo" Grace Burns

ACKNOWLEDGEMENTS

Thanks to so many folks that have made this Atlanta
memoir writing journey
a wonderful adventure.

Thanks to Rebecca Watts (no relation, but I should be
proud to claim her) for her critical and supportive
editing. She made this writing voyage enjoyable and
rewarding as I recalled so many Atlanta and other
friends along the way.

Thanks to Ellen Hunter Ulken for her help in
reviewing the manuscript
and for her continued encouragement.

In Atlanta research and in all my writings I have used
references and photographs from the Kenan Research
Library of the Atlanta History Center, the Emory
Woodruff Archives, Georgia State University Archives
and profited from the Peachtree City Library Writing
Circle and the numerous seminars of the Georgia
Writers Association and wish to express my deep
appreciation to each.

In reviewing my medical and surgical practice and my
brief, but interesting, stint in the military,
I wish to thank so many colleagues and airmen who
have helped me along the way and those patients who
have honored and allowed me to participate, even in a
small way, in their care. Ultimately, they are what my
practice of medicine and surgery was all about.

Table of Contents

Atlanta, early morning viewed from Grady Hospital

1960

PART ONE

ATLANTA:
SELECTED STORIES

ATLANTA:
A LITTLE HISTORY

A great city from a tiny railroad terminus

*They drove a spike into the ground in wooded
North Georgia.
They called the place Terminus.*

MOST FOLKS THINK of Atlanta as a city of dogwoods, long
flowing green lawns, majestic homes, and in the business districts,
towering glistening buildings. Atlanta is thought of as a city with
wonderful coffee shops, delicious restaurants, major athletic
events, the Cyclorama, the Atlanta Symphony, and the Southern
town historically associated with Margaret Mitchell's *Gone with
the Wind*. It is also thought of as the cradle of the 1960s Civil Rights
Movement led by Reverend Martin Luther King, Jr., and his
followers. Atlanta has all that and more.

The first white settlers came to the area in 1821 after the Creek
Indians were removed and a state lottery offered land lots of 202.5
acres in the unsettled region. The winners of the lottery–eligible
free white males, 18 years or older–were known as "fortunates."
Each had paid $19 to the lottery. A special consideration was given
to veterans. Hardy Ivy was said to be the first resident to settle.
However, some debate suggests that Richard Todd was the first
who bought land, Lot #17 for $100 from William Zachary of
Columbia County, Georgia, in 1822. He is said to have built a
house in 1823 while Hardy Ivy built a house in 1833.

Atlanta's real history began at the end of a railroad line at the
western end of the Western & Atlantic Coastal Railroad. Terminus
was born when the railroad, which crossed two Cherokee and
Creek Indian trails, was authorized by the Georgia State legislature
in 1836.

In 1837, Albert Brisbane, the assistant to Colonel Stephen Harriman Long, an Army topographical engineer on leave of absence to work with the Western & Atlantic Railroad, drove a spike into the ground where Marietta Trail and Peachtree-Whitehall Road intersected. This "zero-mile post" marked the town.

Initially, many wells were dug and years later, in the 1880s, they dug a deep village well at Five Points, near the zero-mile post, to furnish water to the growing new railroad town. This first western extension of a rail line to Terminus would ultimately connect Chattanooga with Augusta and the seaboard at Savannah for the anticipated interior commerce of the state of Georgia.

Whitehall Street ran south and west of Five Points, a road that extended beyond the stagecoach rest stop, a white-washed, wood house built by Charner Humphrey, appropriately known as "White Hall Tavern." This location marked the last stop for coach passengers who would change stages for points south, Macon, and the state Capitol at Milledgeville. Future railroads figured prominently in transportation and in the defense of Atlanta some twenty-five years later during the War Between the States.

Subsequent to the development of the railroads, Atlanta and its population grew from a rough and tumble frontier town, or a town described by one author of "shanty shacks of railroad workers and prostitutes," as construction along the railroad assured its ultimate commercial importance. Workers built wood frame buildings and planked sidewalks to protect the inhabitants from the muddy sludge of the unpaved streets. The expanding commerce began with a *boom*.

The entrepreneurs and builders descended upon the village of Terminus and its name was changed to "Marthasville" to honor the first-born female child of Governor Wilson Lumpkin of Georgia. A new and forward-looking appellation, "Atlanta," was ultimately given to the new town (1845) with great hopes for expansion and prominence. No one really knows where the name was derived. Some claim that J. Edgar Thompson, an engineer, suggested the name. It stuck and now the melodic name Atlanta represents the South's most vibrant city.

Some folks noted that Governor Lumpkin's daughter's middle name was Atalanta and perhaps this was a subtle suggestion for the name "Atlanta."

According to Atlanta author, Elise Reid Boylston, the interior population differed from the "old Tide Water or Coastal polished and cultured aristocratic folks." They were more Bourgeois, more hospitable and unpretentious and in the mid–1800s lived comfortably in large frame houses (earlier in simple rough-hewn log structures) and not Mansions as did the coastal population.

A hundred years after its settlement, during the mid–1930s, Atlanta was a progressive city. Sixty-five years earlier the Civil War had left it ruined and in ashes after the "Siege" and the burning of the town by both the Confederate retreating soldiers and the Union Army of General William T. Sherman. The streets in 1930 still followed the cow paths and the old Indian trails. Peachtree Street followed the prominence of a small hilly ridge extending north from Five Points out to a site called "Buck's Head." Here the road split at a point where a "Buck's Head" was attached to an old oak, (some say a village store) hence the name "Buckhead." Peachtree Road extended northeast and Roswell Road extended more northerly toward the settlement of Roswell.

"Everything in Atlanta is called Peachtree," someone once remarked. "Why is that? And where did the name come from?" They further commented, "We see cherry, dogwood, pines, and oaks, but we don't see many peach trees."

Historians say that there was an Indian camp along the Chattahoochee River where the Native Americans obtained "pitch" from the pine trees used to seal their canoes. The term "pitch tree" was allegedly misnamed to be "peachtree" therefore the name is commonly used in Atlanta.

However, in 1782, a letter from John Daniel refers to a rendezvous of Coweta Creek Indians "at Standing Peachtree." Many (North) Creeks later sided with the British during the War of 1812 and the state of Georgia constructed a fort at Standing Peachtree. The area was designated as a Post Office in 1825. Thus, the name "Peachtree" was established from Standing Peachtree during the late eighteenth century.

The intersection of "Five Points" divided Atlanta into North Side and South Side. The South Side roads followed a southwesterly direction by the old stagecoach stop. In the late 1800s, the area known as West End was developed as an early suburb out in the country from Atlanta. This was one of the initial suburbs to have horse or mule-drawn trolley transportation. Years later, Mr. Joel Hurt (1889) initiated electric "Street Cars" on the newly developed Edgewood Avenue, out toward another new development, Inman Park. The street cars with overhead electric wires and steel rail tracks replaced the horse or mule–drawn trolleys.

Joel Chandler Harris' Home, The Wren's Nest
West End – Atlanta, Georgia
(Photo by author)

In West End, Joel Chandler Harris bought a home from George Muse, an early clothier, called Snap Finger Farm and later known as The Wren's Nest. Harris's neighbors gave his home the "Wren's Nest" name because the wrens persisted in building their nests in his mailbox. He had accepted the insistent residents and received his mail at his front door. Joel Harris, a journalist, wrote for the *Atlanta Constitution*, during the period that Henry W. Grady, author of *The New South*, was editor.

The Uncle Remus stories of African American folklore were brought to this country by slaves from Africa and the Caribbean and handed down orally from generation to generation. Harris collected, edited and published the tales in African American ethnic dialect. Beloved by generations, trickster Br'er Rabbit, Br'er Bear, and Br'er Fox, and their shenanigans are described by the benevolent and ancient African American, the fictitious "Uncle Remus."

The old Decatur Road ran east from Five Points. The road figured prominently in the "Battle of Atlanta." It is depicted in the celebrated Atlanta Cyclorama, a diorama of painting combined with scale models which illustrates the Battle of Atlanta in the summer of 1864. The Cyclorama was previously located in East Atlanta's Grant Park, named after the Confederate Colonel Lemuel P. Grant, who designed the defense and fortifications about Atlanta. He gave the land to the city for the park. In early 2016 the Cyclorama began the process of moving to a newly constructed building at the Atlanta History Center on West Paces Ferry Road.

Almost seventy years after slavery was abolished, Atlanta was still a city of segregation of the races, White and Colored, the Jim Crow Era. It seems improbable now, to many citizens, that such a society could exist. Those of us born in the 1930s or who were young and lived during those years had little understanding of why one group of persons sat in the front and one group in the back of the bus or streetcar, or in divided sections of the railroad station, went to separate schools, used separate public bathrooms, drank from separate water fountains, and entered and exited separate doors. Most did not question this, but these were the inequalities of living in the deep South in the first half of the twentieth century.

The Atlanta that I knew was a "White" society with a "Colored" or African American subculture. Economically, the prominent White society extended from the "elite" of the North Side–Ansley Park, Buckhead, and Driving Club–to upper middleclass West End and East Atlanta and sections south of downtown. Influence and affluence varied among white Atlantans from bank executives, politicians, professionals, business owners, police officers, and factory workers.

The Colored community necessarily developed their own society within a society. The black ministers and the black churches became the center of the religious, social, and political activities. Fortunately, Atlanta was blessed with Atlanta University, Morris Brown, Morehouse, Clark College, and Spelman, all primary education centers of collegiate learning for the black population of the South. This University system gave a firm foundation to the Black Agenda, that of rising to sustain leadership, not only in the African American community but also in the post -1964 integrated Atlanta.

During Atlanta's International Cotton Exposition of 1895, the extraordinary African American educator and scientist Booker T. Washington spoke to the crowds. He subscribed to the political and social ideology of the day, that of developing blacks independently, intellectually, and financially to gradually take their proper place in society by fiscal as well as intellectual achievement. His theory was not one of immediate racial integration but of parallel development. Many black citizens, however, felt he was too tolerant of the "Status Quo." Some referred to him, as an "Uncle Tom," acquiescing to the segregated "Jim Crow" laws. They demanded more aggressive entitlement to the prescribed rights of every American citizen guaranteed by the Constitution, white or black.

Despite President Lincoln's Emancipation Proclamation and the end of the War Between the States, African Americans were free only in name as White political dominance limited the advancement of the black man in a white South.

The Reconstruction period had done little for the Black Southerner. He or she remained in political bondage, enduring segregation or "slavery without chains."

African American education was marginalized; and employment was limited to labor and more menial jobs in the city. Domestic help, janitorial service, common labor, city blue collar, and lesser jobs were the only jobs offered to persons of color. Even at the United States Federal Army facility of Camp and later Fort

McPherson, the military services were segregated by race. It was not until after World War II that President Harry S Truman "integrated" the Military.

In 1954, the United States Supreme Court ruled in *Brown v. Board of Education* that segregated schools, "Separate but equal" was "anything but equal." Integration began, however, not without trembling of the local political ground.

Under the leadership of Mayor William B. Hartsfield and Ivan Allen, Jr.; Chief of Police Herbert T. Jenkins; and – within the wings of the Coca Cola Company's boardroom – business magnate Robert Woodruff; along with Civil Rights leaders Rev. Martin Luther King, Jr. and Ralph David Abernathy; women like Hellen Bullard, and *The Atlanta Constitution's* editor, Ralph McGill, Atlanta pursued peaceful racial integration without riots or mayhem. Atlanta was not going to be another Birmingham.

The recollection of one of my favorites, Reverend Hosea Williams, stirred the conscience of many white Atlantans. A local "character," Williams served in the United States Army as a soldier in an all African American unit under General George S. Patton in France and Germany, fighting for the freedom of the whole nation. He had been awarded a Purple Heart for injuries received in combat.

Hosea Williams returned home to Atlanta and "could not drink water from the fountain" of the people he had protected with his own sweat and blood.

With all its faults and frailties, Atlanta has risen not only from the ashes of Civil War, but from the tragedy of slavery and the spectacle of segregation with the strength of its symbol, the Phoenix, to a new social and higher moral plane. Atlanta has grown from a point where men drove a spike into the ground, dug a well, and laid a railroad line into the South's most vibrant metropolis.

CHILDHOOD IN ATLANTA
1930s
A time when Atlanta was safe and kind

In June 1934, I was brought home to a couple awaiting the addition of a child, a son. To my new family, I was a wish come true. Nanny, my grandmother, my Aunt Fanny, and my mother Dorothy had come to fetch me.

Along Peachtree Street various trees were in full foliage and azaleas were fading. The air was warm and pleasant and the city traffic along the shaded streets flowed with a Southern drawl.

After picking me up and before getting into the car, Dorothy nudged her sister-in-law Fanny and pointed toward the young woman standing at the end of the porch smoking a cigarette. "That is the one." Fanny glanced toward the young woman that was leaning on the porch watching the whole scene unfold. Then the woman turned and slowly moved away from the rail back into the building with a slight glance over her shoulder. The screen door closed. She was gone.

I was handed gently to my Nanny who sat quietly in the back seat of the black 1934 Chevrolet. Soon the car was in motion and we were on our way. I would make the trip home nestled safely in my grandmother's arms.

Dorothy, the only woman in the family who could drive, started the motor, shifted the floor gears, let out the clutch, and we slowly backed out of the drive and into the afternoon Atlanta traffic.

The car edged its way west on North Avenue to Peachtree Street. I became an official Atlantan. We mixed with the traffic noise and the clanging of the streetcar trolleys, taking care not to slip on the shiny trolley tracks, yet avoiding the big grayish-green, steel streetcars as they continued to ring their bells to clear the tracks. It was my first ride up Peachtree Street, a street I would learn to love.

We drove south on Peachtree and ascended the hill to its crest where the old Victorian Governor's mansion stood for so many years. In 1923 the property on Cain (now Andrew Young International Boulevard) and Peachtree streets, one of the highest points downtown, was leased by the State of Georgia to Mr. Cecil Cannon, the builder of the new Henry Grady Hotel.

After the Great Stock Market Crash of 1929 and during the Depression, my dad Harvey worked at the Henry Grady Hotel when so many of Atlanta's men were unemployed. The Henry Grady was advertised as "Atlanta's newest, most modern, fire-proof hotel with five hundred-fifty rooms and five hundred-fifty baths, hot and cold running water." They advertised a fan in every room.

We stopped in front of the Henry Grady Hotel, under the big marquee. The hotel doorman hurried across the sidewalk to open the car door. He looked inside the car then turned about and rushed into the hotel lobby, his long red doorman's coat tails flying. The doorman returned, leading my dad to the car where he visited with us for a few minutes.

We continued past the Roxy and Capital Theaters, Davison-Paxon Company, and the Winecoff Hotel, that was said to be the tallest hotel in Atlanta. It, like the Henry Grady, was advertised as "fireproof." We began approaching Five Points. We passed Lowe's Grand Theater where in a few years the movie *Gone with the Wind* would make its World Premiere in December 1939. (Margaret Mitchell, a native Atlantan, authored the book of the same name.) For now, however, the journey was simply to get me, the new baby, home. Dorothy pulled into the drive on Lawton Street, bumping over the pavement edge and came to a gradual stop. Nanny handed me to Aunt Fanny and the troop of happy women climbed the brick steps to the porch. There were no balloons nor bells nor whistles, yet everyone was glad to be home.

I was carried to my parent's bedroom. Wee Toy, a Boston Bulldog stood in the door. She was not sure about the new arrival.

It smelled human and not at all like the puppies she had recently lost. She scampered away, back to the closet where she had delivered her litter of puppies only to have them die. She had stayed hidden in the closet for many days after the loss of her brood.

I had a fresh new baby crib, my own little nest. It would be many more days before Wee Toy accepted this interloper. She gradually began to slip out of the closet and lie under my cradle. She assumed the position of foster mother and henceforth would be my guardian and protector.

Harvey had worked all day at the hotel. At dusk he rode the electric streetcar home to claim his new son.

My first few weeks were problematic. I did not take milk or at least did not keep it down. Shortly after completing a bottle I would spit it up, projecting it like a faucet spewing milk everywhere. Since I was not nursing, Dorothy thought changing from cow's milk to goat's milk might help. They tried a wet nurse, but without success.

Doctor John C. Blalock, my mother's doctor, followed me medically at the Central Presbyterian Church Children's Clinic. I continued to lose weight, "a failure to thrive." While admitted to Georgia Baptist Hospital my pediatrician, Dr. Sam Perry and the other physicians thought the problem was pyloric stenosis. This condition was said to occur most commonly with first born males. The Ramstedt operation was suggested, a surgical procedure that splits the offending tight muscle around the stomach. I was too weak for that operation or any operation and while hospitalized received blood transfusions.

In the 1930s, a blood transfusion was a major and sometimes a dangerous undertaking. The recipient patient would lie on a stretcher or table and the donor would lie alongside. Blood would be drawn from the donor's veins into a sterile double stopcock cylinder syringe. The blood would then be directly injected through a tube into the recipient's vein. I was the recipient. Mr. Joe Vining, a friend of the family, had my blood type and he volunteered to be the donor. He claimed me partly as his own since his blood now "flowed in my veins."

A young intern on the staff of Georgia Baptist Hospital suggested a high sugar condensed milk for calories and nutrition, so *Eagle Brand* milk was diluted with water and I tolerated it and slowly gained weight. I avoided the pyloric surgery and recovered within six months.

My family suffered dreadfully during those early difficult months. I could not sleep nor eat and cried constantly, likely from unimaginable hunger. My crying kept everyone awake. Harvey was reported to have asked, "Can't we take him back?" Perhaps he was joking, perhaps not. Many years later, I understood.

My mother was exhausted. She was up day and night trying to feed me. One night she was rocking me in a chair. She fell asleep and her cigarette set the nearby curtains on fire. With flames racing up the curtains, she awoke just soon enough to put out the fire before we both perished.

Relatives said that I survived through the sheer determination of my mother. She is quoted during that long siege as saying, "God and I will not let this child die!"

It was over half a century later before I learned I was adopted.

Natural Mother, Kathryn Lumley, as a young woman
(Photo from Lumley family)

JUST HOW DID THEY MEET

A kid always wonders

At some stage in every kid's young life they want to know, "Just how did they meet?" They ask their mothers or dads. Usually, girls seem to be more interested in that stuff than boys, but occasionally, a boy also wonders.

I was about four or five when I heard Sarah Ann, the girl next door, telling Sylvia, the child who lived next door on the other side, how her parents met. *That's girl talk,* I thought. Then I ventured to ask my mother as I was sitting on the floor playing, "Mama, where did you meet my daddy?"

"That's a funny question," she responded. "What made you ask that?"

"Oh, Sara Ann told Sylvia that her mama and dad met at a roadhouse. What's a roadhouse?"

My mother is said to have laughed and explained that a roadhouse was where "young people meet to eat and dance and have fun."

"You know, your daddy and I have taken you with us when we've gone out to eat and dance. Do you remember Carawana Lodge?" she asked. "The last time we took you there you fell asleep in the dining booth and we had to pick you up and carry you home. One time you were so sleepy you lay down on the dance floor. We had to stop dancing and bring you home."

I heard that story all my young life, but I didn't remember it ever happening.

"Well, I'll tell you how your dad and I met," she said. "I grew up in the little town of Pine Bluff, Arkansas, and your dad grew up in the big city of Atlanta. I was working with your Aunt Edna in a lieutenant governor's political campaign headquarters in Little

Rock and your dad was visiting his brother Jimmy. You know that Uncle Jimmy was a successful boxer and your dad helped him when he had those boxing matches in Little Rock. Anyway, I met your dad one night at dinner at a friend's house." She picked me up from the floor, sat down in her rocker and leaned back, rocking as she continued her story.

"My mother always told me to watch out for those big city boys, but I didn't listen to her after I met your dad. I thought he was so handsome and strong with those dark brown eyes and dark hair. My sisters and I were all fair-skinned and he was something to look at," she mused. "Anyway, we dated, and he came down to Pine Bluff to meet my family and my sisters. They all loved him at first sight; and I believe my daddy thought he had just found the son he always wanted. Yes, they hit it off and before I knew it, we were married in Little Rock in September 1928.

"The next year he lost his job because of the Wall Street stock market collapse and I had to go home to Arkansas for a while. We had no money. When your uncle Wayne gave him a job at the hotel I came back to Atlanta and we started all over." By that time, I was asleep in her arms and I guess I never heard the rest of her story.

Dorothy, my mom, was an attractive slender young woman with fair skin, brunette hair and hazel gray eyes. Her photographs reveal a woman with lovely high cheekbones and a slender straight aristocratic nose. Her family name was Perdue, and was said to be French, a line from the "Oath named family, Pour Dieu," and said to have emigrated from Angers, France (Pays-de-la Loire), in the late eighteenth or early nineteenth century.

[The name Perdue is Medieval English, but of Norman French origin. It is old French "for God," a subset of the oath names.]

There were three Perdue sisters and my Uncle Wayne, at age ninety, once told me as he reminisced, "Those three sisters were the best-looking sisters in Pine Bluff, Arkansas, and they knew it."

Dorothy and her husband Harvey survived the Great Depression, but the depression altered America's notion of financial invincibility. It crushed the spirit of many families who had always been able to care for their own without outside or government help.

America changed. America's victory in the First World War was over a decade past. The wild Roaring Twenties, a time when everything was great and glorious, ended as the sobering thirties began. The early 1930s was also a time of worldwide economic depression. National economies collapsed. Working people no longer had jobs.

There was not enough money in circulation to buy food or coal for heating, or money for rent or home mortgages. Families stood in government soup lines to obtain food and lost their homes and property. Many lost their dignity. The country was destitute. My dad once told me, "Bud, there were folks on the street corners selling apples for a nickel each, just trying to make a living."

The post–Depression era of the late thirties brought a sobering of the financial market, employment, and the reality of how important it was to have a job that could support a family. America had changed and I was born and reared during that period of economic and social change.

What I didn't know until over fifty-four years later was that I was born in Atlanta to a young mother who could not keep me, perhaps because of the social stigma or rigid mores of the day. I was given up for adoption. The surgeon who had previously operated on Dorothy told her she would not be able to bear children. He is said to have arranged the adoption.

The event that allowed me to learn that I was adopted occurred when my wife and I were planning a trip to Europe. Noting that my passport had expired I contacted the passport division and was told I would have to have my original birth certificate to renew the passport. I headed to Atlanta from Gainesville where I then lived, and at the Fulton County Records office the young lady identified me by my driver's license and in a short time presented me with a certified copy of my birth certificate. I glanced over it and noted on the line where parent's names are recorded that in parenthesis was the word "foster." I wondered about this and after returning home I showed the certificate to my wife. "What does that mean?" I asked.

"Oh my, that means that these people are not your real–your natural parents."

I was stunned and couldn't believe it. Soon I was on the phone calling family members. They told me, after first denying any knowledge of the event, that my mother's instructions were that if I ever learned of my adoption that I was to be told, "Your natural mother was a nurse and your natural father was an Atlanta doctor, a surgeon."

When I heard that, my first thought was, *How theatrical!* Searching for an answer led to Atlanta's Fulton County Courthouse. There I discovered in the files, after considerable legal wrangling and maneuvering, some of the information I was seeking. I found the original official legal requests for adoption, the temporary probationary papers, and the final decree of adoption.

Typed and written in long hand, in the adoption papers was my natural mother's signature. She was, as I had been told, a graduate nurse and I was left to guess the name of my alleged father. Under Georgia law the putative father of a child, born out of wedlock, had the right to withhold his name from the birth certificate.

A couple of years later one of Dorothy's surviving brothers-in-law confessed the family secret and implied that the same doctor that had treated my adoptive mother, Dorothy, and had procured me for adoption was in fact my natural father. That avenue has never been pursued.

(Unfortunately, the in-laws are now all dead and there is little documentation, so I have left the dog to lie.)

Little did I know that the ashes of the person said to be my father were interred in the churchyard of the St. Philip Cathedral in Atlanta where I was an active member during the 1980s and early 1990s. I never met him. On occasion I've ventured into the memory garden and quietly meditated as if I were talking to him.

YOUNG ROMANCE

"Always liked girls…"

Her name was Sara Ann. I still remember her well. She lived next door. She was little but beautiful with blue eyes and silky blonde hair, held back with a shiny silver hair clip.

On sunny mornings I looked outside to see if Sara was about. When we were together, I was happy.

I'm sure all the boys liked her, too. Sarah was my special girl. She would light up, skipping toward me. She seemed to always be smiling. That was her way, giggling, too. We used to meet when no one was around, just us. We were a pair.

I was not so big, but I protected her from dangers. She was daring but I tried to keep her safe. When she skinned a knee, I was there to console her.

She would give me a big hug when no one was looking, and I hugged her back. We were not shy and often held hands. I knew I would marry Sarah. I loved her so, even more than my dog.

Years later, I heard the song, *Sue City Sue…* "I'd trade my horse and dog for you." I didn't have a horse and I thought I could keep my dog. So, all I had to give was my love and she took it.

One day a big truck pulled up to Sara Ann's house and loaded up her family's furniture and she was gone.

I never saw her again. I never forgot her. She was so beautiful.

Young Romance
(Photo from author's collection)

BEECHER STREET

A Street for childhood memories

His name was Peter, but they called him Petey Pund. He lived a few doors up the street from my house in a big red brick house. We lived on one side of a one-story yellow brick duplex. Our neighbors, the Buchanan family lived on the other. Two French doors inside divided the units in half. Each side had a kitchen and separate bath and one or two bedrooms. It was a middle-class neighborhood. Our families were employed and paid our bills on time. Many of the neighbors were renters and did not own their own homes. The families were mostly young Atlantans starting their families.

I was five years old. When my mother was away I "minded" Louise, our housekeeper, as if she were my surrogate mother.

Petey was five years old too, but Petey did not mind her.

"She's not my maid," he boasted.

When he visited from up the street, we played inside the house and outside in the small yard. On the day in question, it rained. We played on the brick porch with a low brick wall enclosing the porch. To the side of the porch was the concrete drive about four to six feet below. Petey insisted on walking on the banister above the wall.

Louise came out on the porch to check on us and Petey had climbed up on the porch banister. "Get yourself down from there!" Louise yelled at Petey and he reluctantly climbed down. She went back into the house. She slammed the screen door and Petey climbed back on the wall.

"I don't have to mind her," he yelled defiantly.

"Yes, you do," I shouted back at him in my trembling, high-pitched voice.

"Not so," he answered, now determined to do as he pleased.

"We'll see," I announced. I grabbed him by the pants leg and tried to pull him back. We tugged, each pulling and suddenly he disappeared over the wall into the drive.

I ran to Louise, "Petey just fell!" I cried to her.

Louise rushed out the front door, down the front steps, across the grass into the drive to the crumpled child. He lay unconscious in the drive, his head bleeding. He didn't move. "Lord, he's dead," she screamed.

She picked up the limp body and ran next door with him to our neighbor's house, screaming all the while, "He's done dead, Lord, I believes he's done dead."

Our neighbor, Mrs. Richon appeared at her door. She pushed the screen door open and took Petey in her arms. She was a real nurse. She took one look at him and calmly spoke, "Not yet, not yet, Louise."

I trailed behind, tears running down my cheeks, terrified, but like our neighbor, Joel Chandler Harris' Br'er Fox, I was "laying low."

When my mother came home, she asked, "What happened? Were you two boys fighting?"

"No, mama," I sobbed. "Petey was up on the wall and wouldn't come down like Louise told him."

"Did you push him?" she demanded.

"I pulled him," I answered, now crying uncontrollably.

She must not have believed me for I got a real bad switching. It was not until later, when Louise calmed down, that my mother realized that I was simply obeying our Louise's instructions. Then my mother sat down and cried over the switching.

Petey was taken to Grady Hospital where he stayed for over a week. My mother took me to see him. The hospital was scary, long dark halls and the smell of sickness and disinfectants that burned my nose. I remembered having visited my dad at Piedmont Hospital, but it didn't smell the same. Petey had a big white gauze bandage wrapped around his head, just as my dad had had some months before when the neurosurgeons operated on him. I could see blood on the bandage. My mother took me back daily with flowers that I picked from our yard for him.

After he came home his mother kept his room dark as night. It was frightful to visit in the gloomy room with all the shades pulled and I felt shivery when I went into the room. I still feared he might die and I would be blamed. His mother and I cried together. Before I left, his mother always gave me a big hug. "Sometimes good friends have accidents," she said. Yet, it didn't make me feel better. I still thought it was my fault.

Years later, 1952, as friends, Petey and I graduated Brown High in the same class.

THE GRADYS AND CHARLIE

We were like "Huck and Jim."

The next time I dealt with the Grady Hospital was when old Mr. Charlie was sick. Charlie lived in our basement. That must have been about 1938 or 1939, because I was a small boy and Charlie helped Louise look after me when my mother was away.

Mr. Charlie was colored. That is what Black or African Americans were called in those days. Charlie tended our coal furnace and our neighbor Captain Richon's coal furnace. For that job, Charlie was given a place to stay, food and a small salary, "spending money," he called it. Charlie was an older fellow with thin, graying hair, and a scruffy, whiskered, worn face. He was thin and had a slight stooped posture that made one sure he had stoked furnaces forever.

When I was a child, I loved Charlie and felt he was part of our family. I regularly went down the basement stairs to sit with Charlie. There in the cool basement he had an old iron bed, wire springs, a mattress and a tattered quilt, a couple of chairs, a lamp that hung from the ceiling with a single bright bulb and an old pot belly stove that he used for heat and cooking. He used coal for heating which he said was better than wood. For some reason, however he usually used wood for cooking. When I asked him what he was doing, he always had the same answer, "I'm just fixing my little something to eat."

Some of his cooking smelled awfully strong, enough to burn your nose. "It's fried," he would say. He cooked his meat in an iron skillet until it smoked before he would take it off the potbelly stove. His cooking was always "smoky." He said, "When I'm cooking, I use fatback for my beans." I could smell the beans cooking all the way upstairs. It smelled stronger than my mother's cooking. At night my mother would take a big plate of dinner to Charlie.

One night, Charlie came down with pain in his side and stomach. My dad and Captain Richon and his wife Mildred, who was a registered nurse, figured it must be appendicitis. Later that night they drove Charlie in our Chevy sedan downtown to Grady Hospital. Why they took me with them, I shall never know.

There were two Gradys. One was "White" and the other "Colored." Charlie went to the Colored side. All the doctors were white, but some of the nurses were colored. They said they had a nursing school at Grady for "Colored girls," and I thought they would be as smart as Mrs. Richon, who taught both "white" and "colored" nursing students at Grady.

When we took Charlie to Grady, we waited along with him in the Colored waiting room. Sometimes Whites were allowed to stay with their Colored help, but White children usually had to stay in the White waiting room. This time we all were allowed in the waiting room for Coloreds and inside the clinic along with Charlie.

If we were thirsty, we couldn't drink out of the Colored fountain because we were told we might turn colored. I never believed that but was afraid to try. My little Colored friends from Bush Mountain wouldn't drink out of the White fountains because their mamas told them they would turn white like ghosts.

The doctors said Charlie was "mighty sick" and would have to have an operation to drain his appendix. They suspected it was ruptured.

The Grady doctors told my dad and Captain Richon to go on home. They would call us if Charlie got sicker. We didn't know whether Charlie had any family or not, because he never said.

"Just so they don't do a 'topsy,'" he had said to my dad and Captain Richon. He didn't want a "topsy" if he died. I didn't know what a "topsy" was but knew it wasn't good if Charlie didn't want one. "Sometimes," Charlie said, "when Colored folks died and didn't have any family the Gradys would do a 'topsy' or give their bodies to the medical school to study on." Charlie didn't want that either.

The Grady "Colored Emergency Room" was a busy place that night. It seemed like many folks were either sick or got hurt or stabbed while fighting and drinking I saw one come in with a knife still in his side. His shirt was covered with blood. "It was a accident," he told the doctors. *Strange accident,* I thought.

It didn't smell too good and the buildings were old at the Gradys. There was lots of smoke and lots of yelling and lots of confusion. Those folks who weren't smoking cigarettes were chewing and spitting, sometimes on the floor. One fellow in a long white coat and a white cotton hat was mopping up the mess.

Saturday was a bad night. Some of the patients had tubes in their noses and some had tubes in their arms. "Most of them who stay in the hospital are real sick," my dad said, "they don't keep folks if they're not real sick."

There were many police officers around too, all White. There were no Black police officers in Atlanta until many years later. I saw those policemen bring in folks with handcuffs on and some policemen just held them up by the back of their britches, and even lifted them up when they had trouble walking.

A few days later my dad and Captain Richon went back downtown to Grady to see about Charlie and they said he was doing okay. They didn't say anything else about that topsy. I thought, *Well, he didn't get one after all.*

The doctors at The Gradys kept Charlie for nearly a month. When they let him come home Mrs. Richon and my mother looked in on him. Mrs. Richon was a Northern lady and spoke kinda funny, but I knew she was a real nurse. I thought she knew all there was to know about medicine and everything about most things.

30

Once, when I fell in the yard and rammed a big rusty nail through the palm of my hand, she was the only one I would allow to pull the nail out of my hand with the biggest pliers I ever saw. She could teach a person how to give shots by sticking the syringe needle into an orange. I wondered who had skin that was as thick or tough as an orange.

"Colored" Grady Hospital – built in 1906 to replace a prior building of the old Atlanta Medical College.

This building contained the segregated emergency,
outpatient, pediatric, medical, and surgical clinics
as well as medical and surgical wards.
It also had a separate ambulance entrance.
(Courtesy of Georgia State Archives)

After Charlie came home, my mother fixed him a new bed with a new mattress, new sheets and a new blanket and quilt. She told him, "We have a young boy who'll do the stoking of the furnace until you get all well."

Charlie was glad to have that boy to help him. However, he did say, "That boy will have to go when I get better." And he did. The boy lived over on Bush Mountain where most of the Colored people lived who worked around West End.

Bush Mountain was right through our back yard and up a long wooded path, about a mile long. A person could walk right to our neighborhood to work if he or she lived on Bush Mountain. On rainy days we would drive over to Bush Mountain to get Louise, our housekeeper.

Louise was stout so she was happy when she didn't have to walk through the woods to work. She was tall with coal black hair with a smattering of gray, which she pulled and tied back behind her head. She often wore a straw hat with a wide brim and a red ribbon but never a bandana on her head as some folks did. She never wore an apron but had a long white cotton coat with real pockets that she loved to wear when she was cooking or cleaning.

Louise lived in a great big, gray, wooden house with a crowd of other "Colored folks," "cousins," she said. In the yard outside the rambling house was a huge black iron kettle where they did their washing. They boiled the water with large logs on fire under the kettle, stirred the clothes with a long broom handle, then hung the washing out to dry on a long cord line that stretched along the side of the house between two heavy wood poles in the side yard.

Sometimes I could stay with Louise and her cousins and all those "chirun" as she called them. It seems we played the same games, hopscotch, threw rocks, rode bicycles, played hide and seek—often under the big house—but we could never ride together on the streetcar. I wondered why the white streetcar conductor would make the colored people sit in the back of the trolley car and us white folks got to sit in the front. While riding from the end of the car line to the Cascade Theater we mostly had to sit separately except when the housekeeper rode with us. But sometimes the conductor would let me sit in the back with my Colored friends.

The back of the streetcar was more fun. A kid could sit in the unused conductor's seat and look out the back windows at night when the conductor up front had his curtain pulled around his seat to protect him from the bright lights inside the trolley. Those were the trips from downtown on the Peachtree or Whitehall to Beecher Street run.

Louise was a good person, but she drank liquor. We had what my dad called "tonic." Louise would slip the bottle out of the cabinet, pour herself a little glass full and pour water into the bottle so no one would know. My dad figured out what was happening. One evening he came home from work and discovered the problem. Louise thought he would be mad, but he called Louise into the kitchen. "Louise if you want a drink just have one and don't dilute the Tonic." He sat two little glasses on the white porcelain tabletop, poured the spirits into the two jigger shot glasses and handed Louise one, "Now, let's have a snort together."

After that, sometimes at the end of the workday, Louise would ask my mom, "Can I have just a little nip before I go home?"

When Charlie came home from Grady, Mrs. Richon regularly came over and changed Charlie's bandage. She let her daughter Sylvia and me watch. She said, "As long as the pus comes out and doesn't stay inside Charlie, he will be all right." I noticed Charlie's skin was older looking and more wrinkled since he came home from the hospital. The brown had turned gray. His hands were large and bony with wrinkled skin as if he always had his hands in shriveling water. His hair was grayer and white like "crinkly" steel wool and his scrawny beard covered his face so only his thin, oval lips, and big brown eyes peered out of his old sad being.

After his illness, Charlie claimed he moved like an old dog. "Lord, I'm too tired to die, but too sad to live." He didn't talk much except when he was fixing his "something to eat." That was mostly a serving of that strong-smelling stew on his tin plate. He sat on his cane back chair, ate off a tilt-top table by his wood stove in his dark room. Charlie had an overhead light with an electric bulb but at night he preferred his kerosene lamp with a tall, smoky glass chimney. "It reminds me of when I was a boy," he said. His iron bed with wire springs, a new mattress, and his new sheets and quilt was placed closer to the coal furnace to keep warm.

It was quite a while before Charlie could return to his job of tending to the coal furnaces at our house and the house next door.

After he recovered, he kept the coal bin full of coal. Each morning he would rise early and stoke the furnace and we would smell the irritating soot then feel the warmth over the iron grate floor vents.

Charlie got better and that young boy went back to Bush Mountain. Though much older, the boy and I remained friends and sometimes he came back, and we played together in the yard and shot my B.B. gun, mostly from the house into the far back yard, but not toward Suzie's pen.

Besides stoking the furnace, Charlie tended and fed Suzie and tried to keep her in her pen. Sometimes she got out and the neighbors would call and tell my mother or Charlie to come and get Suzie out of their flowers or garden. We got Suzie when she was so little that she slept in a little box on the back porch. I sometimes played with her in the kitchen when my mother was gone.

Suzie got so big that we had to give her away. We gave her to our grocer, Mr. Brand. The deal was, half of Suzie for his market and the other half for Charlie. After we gave her away the "man" brought her back as bacon and pork chops, but we gave our share to Charlie because we couldn't bear to eat bacon or pork chops that came from our Suzie.

Charlie and I would sit out back on the basement steps and he would tell me stories of his life and about how his daddy was afraid and ran off when General Sherman came through Atlanta during the "War Between the States." Charlie said he could remember but I bet his mother told him all those stories. He said, "One of the Yankee soldiers, in his dusty blue coat rode his gray horse right up to our porch and said, 'You folks are all free now, so git on with it.'"

Charlie's daddy told the Yankee, "We got no place to go."

"So, we just stayed where we were," Charlie said.

One day I saw on a big sign board by the old fire station down on Lee Street, one of those "IRON MAN" stokers for coal furnaces from Campbell Coal Company. The advertisement showed a metal robot with a shovel stoking the coal furnace. I was worried that my dad might get one of those for our furnace. I didn't want to trade Charlie for one of those Iron Men. I knew he couldn't talk to me or tell me stories like Charlie could.

It was a long time before I saw Grady Hospital again. I never saw Mr. Charlie after 1940. The Army transferred the Richons and we moved away.

MY DAD'S DOCTOR

An Atlanta Institution

My dad's doctor, Edgar F. Fincher, was a prominent neurosurgeon in Atlanta from the late 1930s until his retirement in the 1960s. He is often remembered as one of the Piedmont Hospital doctors that cared for Capt. Eddie Rickenbacker, after Rickenbacker's 1941 Eastern Airliner crash near Atlanta, in the Morrow, Georgia woods. Capt. Rickenbacker was a famous American Ace pilot during the First World War and the founder of Eastern Airlines.

Doctor Fincher was for many years the attending surgeon at Atlanta's Piedmont Hospital and the Professor of Neurological Surgery at Emory University Hospital. His surgical duties also took him to the United States Federal Prison on Boulevard Avenue in Atlanta where he operated on prison inmates.

On one occasion, Dr. Fincher was operating at the Federal Prison, known jokingly in Atlanta as the "Gray Stone Apartments." The prison inmates largely staffed the operating room. He was notorious for being a temperamental, bigger than life surgeon. One day he was performing a craniotomy (opening the skull), operating on the brain, and throwing the used bloody surgical sponges all over the floor.

The inmate orderly kept moving the sponge bucket in an attempt to help Dr. Fincher. However, Fincher kept flinging the used and bloody sponges to the floor. Repeatedly, the orderly moved the sponge bucket. He asked Fincher, "Please try to hit the bucket." Dr. Fincher kept on missing.

The orderly asked one last time, "Doc, please try to hit the bucket." After much exasperation the inmate reached into the sterile operative field and placed his heavy hand on the surgeon's shoulder and whispered quietly to him, "I'm in here for killing a guy for less than this."

It is said that Dr. Fincher never missed the sponge bucket again.

Old Piedmont Hospital and Nurses Home
on Capital Avenue and Crumley Street in South Atlanta
In 1957 Piedmont Hospital moved to their location on Peachtree Road.
(Photo by author, 1960)

DOCTOR OR JESUS

It was hard to know the difference.

I first met Dr. Ed Fincher was when I was a child, four or five years of age. For months in 1938 or 1939 my dad had suffered severe headaches. During many nights I heard him groaning with pain. One night I awoke and saw him walking the floor holding an ice pack to his forehead. His headaches were so severe that he developed partial blindness. One eye was more affected than the other. He went to several Atlanta doctors without relief, despite taking heavy medications.

He was referred to the neurosurgeons. Their tentative diagnosis was a tumor of the brain. In 1938 and '39 this diagnosis had a poor if not fatal prognosis. Because of his symptoms, the physicians and surgeons felt that a diagnostic procedure should be performed to determine if there was a brain tumor and whether surgery would help.

My mother could not sleep because of her fears. She said that she prayed for a sign to tell her if he had a brain tumor and if he would live.

Some years later she related, "One night I dreamed that a glowing figure appeared in the early dawn light at our two front bedroom windows. The figure had a beautiful face. I asked if my husband would die? The mystical figure smiled and shook his head from side to side as if to say, 'No.'" She added, "I awoke suddenly in a cold sweat and no one was there. I pondered on this dream until the surgeons insisted on an operation, a diagnostic craniotomy." She confessed that she had never before told anyone of the dream.

My dad was admitted to Piedmont Hospital, then located on Capital Avenue and Crumley Street in Atlanta. Dr. Fincher performed a pneumoencephalogram. This required drilling circular holes in the skull with a trephine to allow injection of air into the brain cavity and then using primitive X-rays to contrast the air and brain tissue.

My dad was brought back from the OR by stretcher, all covered with a pristine white sheet and returned to his dark room. The rooms were always kept dark. It was believed that the light would somehow injure the patients and increase the patient's headaches. He was drowsy but not asleep. He mumbled to my mom, "They kept me awake and I had to answer questions during the operation." It made me shiver to listen and I shrunk with fright to the side of the room when I saw that his head was completely wrapped in white bandages.

My fear did not abate as I sat close beside my mother, clutching her hand, awaiting the doctor's arrival. The heavy door slowly creaked open, light from the hallway disturbed the quiet dark room. In the doorway with the bright light surrounding him in his white scrub gown, stood the most awesome person I had ever seen. Dr. Fincher was nearly six feet tall, had a bulldog face, wore rimless glasses and on this occasion his serious face slowly changed to a reassuring smile that suggested to us that everything had gone well. He glanced down at us in the dark room then he motioned his nurse to turn on a small light. In the brightness of the reflected little light, I thought he was Jesus and he might well have been as he gently said, "Your husband is going to be all right. He tolerated the surgical procedure without any problems and my X-ray films show no sign of a brain tumor."

He added, "There appeared to be scar tissue about the optic nerve and we feel we released those adhesions. That probably caused his loss of sight. I think those scar adhesions resulted from a prior head injury, not from a tumor." He stood for a moment then commented, "We don't know how much vision he may recover, but we hope the headaches will be relieved. We'll just have to wait and see."

"Thank you, Dr. Fincher," my mother responded. I said nothing. I was still awed by this person who seemed larger than life. He took my mother's slender, slightly trembling hand and held it for a minute as she again expressed her gratitude for his care of her husband. Fincher slowly turned and his nurse stepped gingerly to the lamp switch and turned off the room light then followed him out into the bright hall. The door closed and we were all alone again in the dark scary room.

Many years later I was a senior medical student. I stood beside Dr. Ed Fincher at the surgical scrub basin of the operating rooms at Emory University Hospital as we scrubbed our hands for the morning's work. He didn't seem so huge at that moment, but I knew I was standing in the shadow of a great, giant of surgery. Perhaps I still thought he was Jesus.

FIRST SURGERY

It was just a small case.

The kitchen served as the operating room. She laid her out on the white porcelain table spread with newspapers. "Hand me that eyedropper." Dutifully, I did what she asked. She reached into the kitchen cabinet and brought out a bottle of bourbon. "This should do it," she whispered. "Quiet."

I stood watching in amazement as she dipped the eyedropper into a small bourbon-filled glass and dripped it down the patient's throat. "What are you doing?" I asked. She didn't answer. It should have been obvious; she was putting Hennie to sleep. "Will she wake up?" I asked.

"Not for a while, at least until we're through."

Hennie's eyes fluttered as she became quiet. She was no longer agitated. She no longer moved. "She's asleep, so we can start. Hand me the razor, now the Mercurochrome. Don't spill it," she murmured. I reached over to the kitchen counter. I handed her the little bottle of red Mercurochrome. She doused it on a soft rag and began to prep the shaved neck. "Do you want to help?" she asked.

"Yes, ma'am," I answered.

"Stand right there. Yes, by the table. Don't let her fall off."

"Yes, ma'am," I whispered, amazed at the sight of the patient lying still and not moving at all. "She's really asleep, isn't she?"

"Yes, the whiskey always works. This is the only anesthesia that we used to have. It works quite well." She took the sharp razor blade and opened the skin carefully. "This tumor mass is blocking her throat, so we'll have to cut it out. Did you notice how hoarse and crackly she sounded?"

I shook my head, not sure what she meant.

There was a little bleeding as the dissection continued, using tiny, shiny, steel scissors on the delicate tissue. The small fuzzy, lumpy, mass was removed and placed into a clean glass bowl. "I think we've got it all. Hand me that dropper again. I think she's waking." She dipped the dropper into the glass and dripped several droppers full into the open throat of the patient. "Now let's sew her up."

I handed her a spool of black sewing thread and she carefully threaded the needle after licking the tip of the thread and passing it through the eye of the silver needle. "Hold her head still so I can sew."

"Yes, ma'am," I said. I held the patient's head still.

"We're all done!"

"What are you going to do now, Mama?" I asked.

"Soon as she wakes up we'll take her off the table and put her in her own nest." I was five years old and had just assisted my mother in my first successful surgery. Hennie soon awoke. She survived the big operation, but she always cackled a bit differently from all the other chickens in our yard.

1938 THROUGH THE EARLY 1940s

A mid-century reflection

In 1938 through the early 1940s, Atlanta was a blossoming city of three-hundred thousand. The streetcars ran right down the middle of the main streets on heavy, recessed, steel rails with thin overhead electric wires that netted the city like spider webs. The cars ran from Buckhead, Avondale, and the four corners of the city to West End. One might transfer downtown at Five Points and continue in all directions.

A one-nickel car token (later a dime or two shiny tokens for 15 cents) and a dated, pink or blue transfer paper slip, torn from his pad by the streetcar conductor would get a rider all over the city. The little transfer slip was torn at an angle that showed the limited time allowed between transfers to eliminate abuse of avoiding another fare, should the rider elect to remain too long in one place in the city.

Inside the trolleys, colorful commercial advertisements were posted along the upper walls of the cars, above the glass windows, touting the benefits of shopping at Rich's, Davison's, Klein's, and even the Kay Jewelry Company that advertised on the WSB radio station with the song, "It's O K to Owe Kay 'til payday, It's O K with Kay."

The trolley cars had caned, straw-back seats that would be turned about as the trolley, on a single track at the end of the line, reversed the direction of the big gray and green cars. The conductor had to get out of the car, pull down the trolley arm, which connected with the overhead electric trolley power lines and reattach the opposite end trolley arm to reverse the street car's direction.

Along with most of the folks in the city, domestic workers often rode the trolley. It was understood that the cost of transportation was added to the salary. In the late 1930s, the average domestic worker's daily salary was somewhere near two dollars-fifty cents to three dollars plus "car fare." The average worker supporting a family made about five dollars a day or twenty to thirty-five dollars for a five or six-day work week.

After our housekeeper moved, she rode the streetcar across town. She transferred at Five Points then caught the Peachtree/Whitehall to Beecher trolley. Cascade and Beecher intersection was the southwest end of the streetcar line.

Louise got off the streetcar at Cascade and Beecher and walked the couple of blocks to our yellow brick house on Beecher

Street. If it was raining, my mother drove to the car stop to pick her up.

The social order in the South in the late '30s demanded that the Colored and White people enter separate doors. It was an immutable fact of Jim Crow segregation laws governing the states south of the Mason Dixon line. It applied even going into homes, yet at our house, our housekeepers entered through the front. I didn't understand why all maids didn't come in through the front door until later when my mother explained that Southern social pressures demanded segregation. In fact, our housekeeper had the only extra key to the front door. In such a safe neighborhood, we never locked our doors except when we were out of town.

CASCADE AND BEECHER

It was our own little village.

The area beyond West End into Cascade Heights was a "village unto itself." Here near the intersection of Cascade and Beecher Streets were two drugstores, two grocery stores, two gasoline stations, a Woco Pep (later Pure Oil) station, and a Texaco station, and Mr. Herd's Auto Repair Shop, a shoe repair shop, Beale's laundry, a bakery, an ice cream shop, a five and dime store, two beauty parlors for ladies and a men's barber shop. We even had a dentist upstairs one flight over Brand's grocery, located on one of the corners. Brand's store was the competitor to the larger A&P (Atlantic & Pacific) store at the middle of the block. The only item Brand's could not compete with was the Eight O'clock coffee sold at the A&P.

Near the intersection stood a gray frame house that was converted into a small Baptist Church. There, as a four or five-year-old, I attended Sunday school. The house was torn down for a Piggly Wiggly Market in 1940 after a new church was built a few blocks away.

From his drug store, Doctor Steagar served the area for many years. His was the oldest drug store. In those days, the pharmacist often cared for the common illnesses of the community. The medical doctor was rarely called upon for simple illnesses. The local drug store pharmacists would diagnose and send out their own medical concoctions for most conditions. Their medications varied from paregoric to Pepto-Bismol to "Leeches" for bad bruises. They practiced a form of general medicine and were rarely if ever second-guessed by the local physicians.

The pharmacists lightened the doctor's load. Doctor Steagar was the "over the counter doc." He would send out, by his little green Austin delivery truck, stomach medicines, gargle solutions, sedatives, headache powders and legitimate prescribed drugs.

The Corners at Cascade and Beecher Streets intersection
Atlanta, Georgia – 1940s
(Courtesy of Atlanta History Center)

Dr. Steagar's shop had a glass front counter of various sundries, gifts, and perfumes. A big seller was *Evening in Paris* which, as kids, we thought was the perfume of the ages and bought it for our mother's birthday or Mother's Day. It came in a little blue bottle wrapped up in a cellophane covered cardboard box with a small lace handkerchief included. Whether the mothers used it or not, I have no idea, but I still remember how as youngsters we were impressed with the brand.

I can picture Dr. Steagar: a short, balding, chubby fellow, standing smartly in his open white jacket, pens and pencils extending from his breast pocket, and his dark-colored tie swinging over his tummy as he held the phone receiver on his shoulder, taking orders, writing it all down, and scribbling out prescriptions with his free hand. When this procedure was complete and the prescription ready, he would send the medicine or item ordered out of the store by Clarence, his faithful delivery driver.

Clarence drove about in a little Austin delivery truck. Clarence also made his rounds collecting money to be bet on "the bug." "The bug" was an illegal gambling lottery that based winning numbers on the last three or four digits of the final stock market report that appeared each afternoon in the Atlanta Journal. The three or four numbers could be bet in the exact order of anticipated appearance or could be bet "in the Box." That meant the numbers selected in any order would produce a winner, but the win would not be as great as selecting the exact sequence of the numbers. The "numbers game" predated current legal state lotteries, and during the late '30s was in the hands of the vice element of the city.

Most of the maids played the bug, but occasionally housewives would have the maids make bets for them. The players would dream numbers, ask fortunetellers for numbers, and devise all sorts of methods of forecasting the winning combinations. Clarence picked up the bets and gave the bettor a slip of paper with a copy of their selected numbers and a date. Clarence would make his "mark" to authenticate the bet and then keep a copy for himself.

If by some miraculous chance they won, Clarence would quickly appear to pay them the "piddling" winnings in crisp new dollars. Word of the winner would circulate freely in the neighborhood by the domestic help and residents. This news increased the betting for the next few days. Some winnings exceeded a couple of weeks' salary. The usual bet was less than a quarter. The bug racket flourished into the '40s when it became more difficult to "run the numbers" because of increased police enforcement. Before this time the city police simply turned a blind eye or were on "the take" themselves, protecting the perpetrators. Only a few churches ever complained about the gambling.

Before 1940, Hays' Drug Store opened. Doctor Hays was a tall, thin faced, white haired pharmacist. Unlike Dr. Steagar, he wore a short white tunic with a high buttoned collar, which seemed to choke him when he turned his skinny neck to check the store or watch the soda jerk at the black marble soda fountain. He was always peering over his glasses that sat on the end of his long nose when he heard the fountain's cash register ring up a sale.

His store was located across the street from Steagar's with a shiny black and white tile exterior and large glass windows on two sides of the building, larger than Dr. Steagar's. It occupied the Southwest corner of Cascade and Beecher Streets.

Steager's Drugs had the largest neon sign that could be seen from the streetcar as the stores loomed in the distance. The streets formed a five points intersection. Steagar's Drug Store was geographically a peninsula with Cascade on one side and parallel Westmont Avenue on the other. The front of the store faced perpendicular to Beecher Street or the oncoming streetcar line.

To the children, old Doctor Hays was a grouchy fellow and reminded us of Ichabod Crane. He wouldn't allow children to read comic books on the shelves unless they bought something from his soda fountain. Dr. Steagar had no problem with the kids reading the comic books hidden behind the counter, out of the way and out of customers' sight. To take them out into the store and sit at the small wire tables, however, required a purchase from the soda fountain.

On Halloween, the kids readily soaped Dr. Hays' windows, but never Dr. Steagar's. We all loved old Dr. Steagar.

The Woco-Pep gas station, a granite and brick building with a high-pitched roof. was located across from the drug stores. It reminded one of a little Hansel and Gretel playhouse. The station had two gas pumps, one for regular and one for ethyl, a higher octane and leaded gasoline.

Gasoline was rationed during the Second World War. During the war, "A" stamps or coupons were issued and "A" stickers placed on the car's front windshield. The auto was allowed minimal gas, perhaps two or three gallons a week. The "**B**" sticker and stamp book allowed more gas to the "essential citizens," those with military or defense-related jobs or local doctors who made house calls. When the local supply of gasoline allowed, the regular customers could get "**B**" stamps worth of gas on "**A**" stamp gas coupons. The attendant would just add a little more to the tank. It was easy to let the pump run a little longer.

The station was a form of accepted "black market" in the neighborhood. All the residents turned a blind eye since they were all benefiting from the little extra gasoline. I learned later that the problem was not a shortage of gasoline, but rubber for military tires and the gas rationing limited the driving and the wearing out of the available tires.

During the war all families also had ration books which contained government stamps to be exchanged for the scarce food items deemed essential for the war effort.

Across the street from the filling station, Mr. Brand's store would slip extra sugar, meat and other items on the rationed list to his regular customers. Mr. Brand had more customers than the A&P, the chain grocery that since it was a corporate business had to abide by the closely monitored government rules.

Behind Mr. Brand's store were wire cages with live chickens that could be sold without rationing stamps since they were privately raised. A customer could select his or her own hen or a fryer and watch as the store clerk turned his back and chopped off the chicken's head. Then he would pluck the chicken and wash it in scalding water, weigh, then wrap the chicken in white paper. Sometimes blood still dripped through the paper on the way home.

The floors were covered with sawdust to keep from slipping on the wet and bloody floors in the meat and poultry section. Mr. Brand allowed credit, but the A&P was a cash operation. Mr. Brand was faithful to his customers. We all loved Mr. Brand. After the war he invested his profits in the lumber business and during the post war building boom that business became one of the largest lumber companies in Atlanta.

The one thing Brand's could never compete with was the Eight O'clock coffee down the street. My mother often took me into the A&P and I loved to stand by the grinder simply to smell the wonderful aroma as the coffee was ground. The A&P also had the best cookies in the neighborhood. You could lift shiny, metal tops, reach into the small glass bins and pick up a hand full and have them weighed, sacked and be on the way home before you knew it.

Our little neighborhood had it all. Who needed big Atlanta, when we had all we ever wanted at the corners of Cascade and Beecher?

Sadly, that has all changed as Atlanta has grown and many neighborhoods have declined with big box stores and shopping centers spread throughout the city gobbling up the small businesses.

DECEMBER 7, 1941

"A date that will live in infamy."

It was a chilly Sunday in December and I was seven years old. Earlier in the day my dad had frantically called home. "Dorothy, turn on the radio," he said to my mom.

I didn't understand her expression when she heard the news blaring from our upright Philco radio. "Oh, my God," she said. "It's happened. We're at war!"

I stared at her from the floor where I was playing with my Lincoln logs.

"What do you mean, mom?" I asked.

"It's the Japanese," she said. "Oh my," she mumbled.

The Atlanta Constitution and *Atlanta Journal* newspapers had been filled with stories about the Nazi Germans invading Poland to their east and invading France and the low countries on their west and the bombing of England, but we were not expecting anything like that in our country.

Once, a fellow with a funny accent visited our house selling and servicing our Hoover vacuum cleaner. My mom got into a discussion about world events with him. He boldly said to my mom, "Well, I think Hitler is doing the right thing in Germany and Europe."

"What do you mean?" my mom [curiously] asked.

"Well, they are just defending their country."

My mom was taken aback and after he left our house, she called my dad. Many of the FBI agents stayed at the downtown Henry Grady Hotel when on temporary assignment in Atlanta. My dad wasted no time telling one of them about my mom's experience. I heard my mom and dad talking. He told her the FBI guys had taken the fellow in for questioning.

This Japanese business was new to me and I learned that a "cowardly Japanese sneak attack" had occurred at our Pacific Navy Base at Pearl Harbor. They had bombed our big ships in the harbor and the army barracks and air base as well as civilian installations, killing many soldiers, sailors, and unarmed civilians.

That evening my mother and I met my dad downtown for supper at the hotel. There I saw men standing anxiously around in the smoke-filled hotel lobby and outside on Peachtree Street under the hotel Marquee. "Where is Pearl Harbor?" one fellow asked. A tall man with a northern accent quickly explained, "Pearl Harbor is in the Hawaiian Islands and we own those islands, in fact that's part of America."

Suddenly, we knew this meant real war. The following day President Franklin Roosevelt addressed the nation and the assembled Congress and sternly announced, "As of December the seventh, our nation has been at war with the empire of Japan." He called, "December 7, 1941, a date which will live in infamy."

A day or so later, Germany and Italy declared war with the United States of America, and we were at war with the mighty Axis Powers of Japan, Germany and Italy, on two fronts, in Europe and in the Pacific.

In his speech, Mr. Roosevelt added, "We will gain the inevitable triumph—so help us God."

The following year was a fearful and dark time for us as a family and for America. In the Far East, the Japanese expanded their empire throughout the Pacific, first attacking the Philippine Islands, the British and Dutch controlled East Indies, and largely controlling our source of natural rubber from the East Indies. The Japanese captured many other islands in the Pacific.

It was not until April 1942 that the "Doolittle Air Raid" gave our nation a breath of fresh air in the war. Twin engines, Army Air Corps B-25 bombers flown from the Navy aircraft carrier USS Hornet bombed Tokyo and, though doing little real damage, provided a propaganda lift to America. When the movie news reels described the air raid over Tokyo the audiences roared with cheers and clapping. When newspaper reporters asked President Roosevelt where the American bombers came from, he answered, "Shangri-La."

In June 1942 the American navy won a great and resounding victory in the naval air and sea battle of Midway Island in the Pacific over the Imperial Japanese fleet. The tide of war turned for America. Unknown to the public, our Military Intelligence had decoded secret Japanese communications and plans in the Pacific. Our forces were able to anticipate the presence of the Japanese Imperial fleet and its aircraft carriers, destroying most of them in the air/sea battle.

Our country was empowered by the shifts in the military events. We were soon on the offense against the European Axis powers, Germany and Italy in the North African campaign with invasions of North Africa, Sicily, then Italy.

A huge War Bond campaign was held in the city, headed by author Margaret Mitchell, for a new U.S.S Atlanta light cruiser after the loss of Atlanta's third namesake cruiser in November 1942 in the Pacific Theater's Guadalcanal campaign.

Even as a child, I carefully followed the events of the war. We all had maps on the walls of our rooms with tiny flags used to spot military movements of the opposing armies. On the Homefront we participated in blackouts and emergency exercises simulating bombing air raid attacks on our city. Volunteer Civil Defense monitors were selected, mostly older fathers and other men not in the service. Defense captains were assigned in our neighborhoods and mock air raids performed. Many of us served as victims and were triaged and treated for imagined or simulated injuries, often using the local grammar school yards as meeting places for the local Home Defense exercises.

The schools collected scrap metal and we gathered as much as we could find, scouring basements, attics and garages. Mothers saved cooking grease, said to be used for explosives. Some of us even sacrificed our old bicycles, swing sets, pots and pans, and I remember sad but bright eyes as some rolled their old Kitty Cars to the scrapheaps. Aluminum was a big item for we knew it would be used for military airplanes and we could visualize our contributions being used against the dreaded enemies.

OKLAHOMA
1943-1944

War time and a mission.

During the summer of 1943, my mother and I headed west to visit her sister in Oklahoma. From the old and smoky Atlanta Terminal we boarded our Pullman car to Oklahoma City. Our journey was uneventful until our train was stopped without warning somewhere in north Alabama and pulled over to a side track. We wondered what the delay was all about.

The train conductor apologetically announced, "Folks, we are pulled over so a military train can get by." During World War ll, even civilians shared in the discomfort of homeland inconvenience. I watched outside with my nose pressed against the train's big glass window as a fast-moving train with flatcars and boxcars rushed by.

On the flat railroad cars were loaded big tanks covered with canvas tarps. Their long gun muzzles ominously protruded from the canvases. Huge army fuel trucks also were chained down to the flat cars. There were khaki-painted boxcars with "Danger High Explosives" painted in big red letters on their sides.

"Those boxcars are from the Redstone Arsenal in north Alabama," the train conductor said. "They are headed east to the Atlantic coast for shipment overseas to North Africa and Europe where our soldiers are fighting."

We arrived late in Memphis because of the delays. It was not uncommon for the trains to be delayed by incidents such as the one we had experienced. The war effort had priority over any civilian activity or travel.

The huge steam engine billowing dark smoke pulled into the Memphis train station. We climbed down from our train car and ran as fast as we could to our next-scheduled gate. I was holding my mom's hand and she pulled me along to the nearby track's entrance to catch our Oklahoma City connection. When we arrived at the gate it slammed closed. The gate operator mumbled, "Sorry, Ma'am, the train tried to wait but had to leave to be near on schedule. You know, there's a war on!" In the distance we saw a big, bright-lighted round sign on the rear club car that read, "Rock Island Rocket." We watched, as it got dimmer in the distance and finally was only a speck of light.

"Well," my mom said, "we're stuck in Memphis."

"That Rock Island train is the last one out to Oklahoma until tomorrow," announced the gate conductor. Our bags were shipped through, so we had only the clothes on our backs, a small overnight bag, and a toothbrush each. No telling where our bags were, somewhere in transit.

"Now to find a place to stay," my mom said. We lined up in a phone line behind a crowd of tired folks who were complaining about the traffic. I remembered what the gateman had said, "You know there's a war on." The phones were busy with service men – soldiers and sailors, and marines – trying to call home before they went off to their duty stations or overseas. They hoped for just one call home. After a long wait, my mother got to a telephone and put in all the change from her purse to call my dad in Atlanta. She hoped that since he was in the hotel business, he could find us a hotel room in Memphis.

We sat in the busy smoke-filled station, the acrid smell of the smoke assaulting our breathing and we watched the tired soldiers, sailors, and other travelers as they hurried to catch their trains. The loudspeaker boomed out the destinations of departing trains in a loud resonance of sounds. I loved to hear the melody of the announcer's voice as he bellowed out, "Now departing, train for Chattanooga, Atlanta and New Orleeens…" I loved the sound when he announced, "Just arrived from Milwauk'eeee and Chicagooo at train gate four." There was nothing like sitting in a railroad station listening to the "sing-song" train station announcer.

Within an hour, my mother managed to get back into a phone line and reach my dad. "Good news," he said. "Only one room left in the city. Here is the address. Get a cab and tell them when you arrive that I have made all the arrangements. Be sure you give them my name. The room will be held till you get there."

"Call me back when you get settled," he told my mother.

"Yes, we will," she answered.

Taxi cabs were hard to get, but with an attractive mother and a little child in tow one pulled right up. "Where to, Ma'am?" the tall gray-haired driver asked as he opened the cab door for my mother.

She gave him the name of the hotel, right downtown. "How about your luggage, Ma'am," he asked?

"Don't know," she said, "it's all shipped through except this little overnight bag."

"Yes, ma'am," he drawled. He drove us downtown to a swanky hotel.

I looked up at the tall hotel, almost as tall as the Henry Grady. My mom paid and thanked the cab driver. The husky hotel doorman, dressed in his braided, black coat, tipped his cap and opened the huge glass door to the hotel. "Welcome to Memphis, ma'am" he said. "No bags?" he asked.

"No bags," my mother answered, "just us."

At the check-in desk was a tall and distinguished older clerk. He had a neatly trimmed mustache that quivered as he said, "Ma'am, I think this is the only room left in Memphis tonight. We spoke to your husband from the Henry Grady in Atlanta and he made the arrangements. We hope you like it. I must warn you however, that it's the Bridal Suite, if that's okay."

"We'll take it, thank you," my mom answered.

I hardly knew what a Bridal Suite was and there I was, age nine and in the Bridal Suite with my mom.

We arrived in Oklahoma after our unscheduled stay in Memphis and picked up our waiting luggage. My mother's sister Elizabeth met us in Oklahoma City. We drove in her 1939 Chevrolet to Lawton and Fort Sill, Oklahoma. As we crossed the Canadian River, I looked down from the high river bridge and all I saw was white sand and brown grass.

"Oh, yes, it dries up in the hot summer," said Aunt Elizabeth.

Fort Sill was the largest Field Artillery school in the United States during World War ll. Elizabeth and her husband both worked on the base. She worked as a secretary for one of the regiment commanders in the Artillery School. Her husband, Claiborne, was too old for the Army and he, too, worked for the Department of the Army. There were many civilian employees on military bases, which relieved the soldiers of jobs not related directly to the war itself.

Elizabeth had one son, Johnny, my cousin. He was twelve and I was nine. I had never spent much time with my cousin Johnny, so our summer in Oklahoma was a get acquainted experience for both of us. We were surrounded by the military and the war. We lived and breathed it. Since there were such shortages of almost everything, Johnny and I made our play guns out of broomsticks and cut pieces of wood to make model rifles and handguns. We made a special type of handgun that had a clothespin on the handle. We could pull a piece of sliced up automobile inner tube down the shaft of the barrel and attach it to the spring clothespin on the handle to use as a rubber band shooter. We played war all summer outside in the yard.

Because of the housing shortage everyone was encouraged to rent rooms to young soldiers and their families. Elizabeth rented a bedroom to a young lieutenant and his pregnant wife. They were a lovely couple. My mom said the young lieutenant was almost a child, like Johnny and me. He would play with us as if he was just another kid. He helped us collect army patches and insignias. He once said that he didn't mind buying captain bars or even major leaves, but when Johnny and I wanted general stars, the clerk really looked suspiciously at him at the BX (Base Exchange). After he finished his Artillery training, he was sent to North Africa and Italy to fight the Italians and Germans. (The invasion of Sicily occurred in July 1943 and Italy in September 1943.) He never came back. I never knew what happened to his wife and child. War is tragic.

Meanwhile, Johnny and I were struggling on our little allowance and thought we could work and make more money to buy some of the things beyond our financial reach. What was better to do than yard work? Some of the older boys did it so why couldn't we? Johnny was more imaginative than I was. He was older, so he was the leader and I would be the follower and helper.

We got a few jobs cutting grass and trimming hedges and raking yards. The summer in Oklahoma was so hot and dry that the base and town were on a water-rationing program. It amounted to almost no watering at all. The local police patrolled the streets to be sure no one was watering on the wrong days. Since there wasn't much water, there wasn't much grass. Our possibilities dwindled, though we did have a few customers in the immediate neighborhood.

On one of those typically hot Oklahoma days, we worked for an old woman nearby. We cut what grass there was to cut and trimmed what bushes the drought had not burned away. By mid-day we were so hot and tired that we sat down under a shady bush to consider our options. All we had to do to finish was to rake under the bushes. In those days no mulching was done. Under the bushes had to be raked clean down to the ground dirt. Looking back, that is surely a poor way to manage bushes, but that was the yard rule then.

We were so tired that we went to her door and rang the bell. We explained that we were so hot and tired, could she pay us for what we had done? "We are just too hot to do the rest of the raking," we said.

She opened her screen door, looked out over the yard at our work. She glanced down at us as we stood sweating. "Sorry boys," she curtly said, "I won't pay you till all the work is finished." She closed the screen door behind her. Without a word we turned around, quietly gritted our teeth, stepped slowly off her porch, picked up our rake and pushed our clanking lawn mower home. I wanted to cry, but my cousin elbowed me and whispered, "Don't let that old lady see you cry." We were two hot and disappointed little boys.

We told our mothers our plight. We listened to what they had to say. Both parents agreed. My mother said, without emotion, "When you start a job, boys, you should always be prepared to finish it."

Elizabeth joined in and they both said, "And you should never work for that old bitch again!" We didn't know what an "old bitch" was, but it sounded right to us and we never did work for her again.

LITTLE SOLDIER BOY:
GEORGIA MILITARY ACADEMY
1943–1944

A young little soldier or maybe not?

At some time in every little boy's life he wants to be a soldier. Not just the uniform, but the heroic and glamorous spirit of the military invades every little boy's heart. For some it is transient and for others it is not. As a child, the advent of the Second World War was all consuming. It was an all-out war and on the home front we all thought we could contribute to the war effort, even if that meant merely training for such eventualities. Of course, for young boys it was a pipe dream. The American flag-waving propaganda machine enlisted our young spirits in the glory of defending our country. Fortunately, we never saw the realities and the horror of war unless we had fathers or brothers who did not return from that war. For me, as a child the dream was transient. As an adult I served in the military as my duty required, but that is another story.

Unbeknown to me during our Oklahoma visit, Aunt Elizabeth and her husband were having domestic problems. They decided to send my cousin Johnny to military school. I looked at the slick, glamorous military school catalog and thought I ought to consider military school myself.

My mom and I weighed the possibility, talked to my dad by phone and decided that I would go to the military school with my cousin. Why not? This War was serious business.

To serve in some way was the patriotic thing to do. As twelve and nine-year-olds, Johnny and I were too young to go into the Army, yet we decided we should prepare ourselves to defend our country against all enemies – or something ridiculous like that.

When I studied the catalogue for Georgia Military Academy, I absorbed each photograph of marching boys and real guns held high. I was convinced that was the life for me. After all, my cousin would be there to look after me. We had become big buddies during the summer of 1943. We were ready to face the world.

When my mom and I returned to Atlanta, we visited the GMA campus. We met the teachers, visited the classrooms and had a conference with the school superintendent, Colonel William Brewster. He was a tall, husky, imposing older man. (I later learned he was a West Point graduate.) My mother felt he was an excellent teacher and that I should do well in his school. We discussed the fact that I would be living on the campus as a boarding student, away from home during the week and could come home on some weekends. How exciting it would be, I thought.

In early September, Johnny and his mom arrived from Oklahoma. My mom and dad drove us to the campus. After a short introduction program for the parents and students they showed us to our quarters. Johnny and I were gathered with the other boys and we were cadets before we knew it.

The first few days and nights were indeed exciting with many new faces, some more friendly than others. Some of the big boys grinned menacingly, knowing that we were all fresh, vulnerable, and scared kids.

Johnny was assigned a room at the far end of the hall, away from my room. His end of the dormitory was for the twelve-year olds. I was placed with the younger boys. My part of the dormitory was a converted gray, two-story wooden Victorian house. The added hall connected our house to a more recently built brick dormitory, at the rear of the large house.

This was the Junior School building, that included the upstairs dorm and first floor classrooms and study halls for both day students and boarding students. I soon learned that the school was socially divided by the day students, "the day cats" and the boarders, the "night dogs."

Our housemother, "Mother Whitaker," an elderly grandmother type, perfect for the job of mothering those of us who were younger and away from home (some for the first time) lived at our end of the hall in a two-room apartment.

My roommates were Billy Middleton from somewhere in Florida. He was tow headed boy who had the bunk above me. He was quiet and an agreeable fellow. I liked him best of my roommates.

Billy Sinrich was a bright boy, lean and dark-haired from Thomaston or Thomasville, Georgia. I just don't recall which. Billy bunked on the opposite lower bunk. He was always up at the crack of dawn and helpful in the room duties.

Michael Smith was from West Palm Beach, Florida. His bunk was above Billy Sinrich's bunk. Michael transferred from Gulf Coast Military Academy. He was a dark-haired, average-size eight-year-old boy. He seemed already an old hand at military schools. We always had a hard time getting him up in the mornings.

After we settled in, we learned that we would have to clean our own rooms. It was quite an awakening. There was no such thing as maid service as some of the boys were used to. The duties were divided. One boy would sweep, one would dust, one would help the others make up beds and the remaining boy would check lockers and help rearrange clothes or shine shoes. We had weekly room inspections and on occasion would have surprise early morning inspections.

Our military instructor and dorm counselor, Lieutenant William Fix, lived with his wife, and small child in an apartment at the other end of the hall, where the older, rowdy Junior School boys lived. He taught math to the upper grades.

The first few days were spent getting oriented, both in our dorm and to the military routine that we would follow throughout the school year. We were given our books, assigned our classes, measured for our military uniforms, and lined up to learn to march. Everywhere a group went, the group marched, never just straggled in a bunch.

We were "marching fools," an eighth grader claimed. Once we marched five miles and back on a Saturday to the Russell

Theater to see the war news and the special production, *The Defense of Stalingrad*. The school thought it was important for us to see what a war really looked like. The Russians were our Allies and we learned from that movie how brave they were in the fierce, cold, winter (1942-1943) defending their homeland against the brutal onslaught of the Nazi German invaders.

It didn't take me long to realize that the Army might not be my calling, after all. My initial experience with military justice occurred when we had our first room inspection. Everyone had an assignment. Each performed his job except one kid who was to sweep. Well, he just didn't do it. No amount of coercion from his roommates convinced him that he should do his share.

A few minutes before Lieutenant Fix and his team of student inspection officers arrived, I grabbed the unused broom and swept as best I could. I had already done my agreed chore, that of bed making. Sheets and blankets were tucked so tight that there were no wrinkles. Our beds had to be made, "*so tight*," Lieutenant Fix said, "that a silver coin could be thrown on the bed-covering and it would bounce."

Lieutenant Fix and his inspecting henchmen entered our room in full uniform. They wore white gloves and ran their hands along door frames, beds, and lockers and even in the adjoining bathroom. Meanwhile, at the foot and head of our double bunk beds we stood at perfect attention, rigid and with eyes straight ahead.

Lieutenant Fix loudly asked, "Who swept this room?" Nobody answered. He did not ask, "Who is supposed to sweep this room," or "who is responsible for sweeping this room?" No one turned a head. We all looked at Smith, who stared straight ahead. He knew the ropes of military school. He never said a word. Lieutenant Fix again asked gruffly, "Who swept this room?"

Still looking straight ahead, I raised my hand and answered.

Fix turned to his adjutant cadet sergeant. "Get his name and give that cadet three demerits, now," he ordered. "This room has not been swept." No explanation was allowed, and I made none. The inspection crew marched out of the room behind their commander. I was almost in tears. I felt nauseated, almost vomiting.

Soon they were down the hall, out of sight and hearing range. We grabbed Smith and pummeled him for getting our room in trouble.

Three demerits meant that I would have to march the first "Bull Ring" of the season. The Bull Ring is a punishment marching tour for the students who are guilty of misconduct or failing to do a duty prescribed, or simply some infraction of the Rules. Each demerit results in one hour of marching in the parade yard.

September is still hot in Georgia and not the best time to walk the punishment tour. There was very little shade except along the outside edge of the parade field.

The punishment tours were performed on Wednesdays and Saturdays. Those were the days when the cadet should have time off. Cadets would be allowed to leave campus in supervised groups to go to the Village or local drug store, down Rugby Street across the railroad tracks to College Park for refreshments, Cokes and ice cream, and to buy comic books or other desirable items. Each of the cadets had an allowance kept by the housemother or staff counselor that limited personal spending.

That Wednesday was uniform fitting day, the day the younger cadets were to get their new uniforms, a day we had all looked forward to.

For my contemporaries and for me on the tour, there would neither be a trip to the Village nor would uniforms be issued. We would have to march in front of all our new friends.

Not my cousin, he would go to the village down Rugby Avenue, get his ice cream, his Coke and his comic books with his big seventh grade buddies. He would sit in the cool shade along the edge of the parade field and watch us march in the hot Georgia sun. They would laugh and point their fingers at us. Several of my crew cried with embarrassment as we marched. They were not allowed to wipe their tears. So, many other cadets saw us and laughed.

Our drill sergeant, an upper class seventh grader himself, saw my cousin and his twelve-year-old cohorts sitting in the shade, reading their comics, drinking their ice-cold Coca Colas, laughing and pointing their fingers.

He marched us all right up to where my cousin and his pals were sitting in their crisp new blue gray uniforms.

"Halt," he ordered. "Right face. Begin kicking dirt!"

We all kicked dirt as hard as we could directly on my cousin and his friends. By the rules, "No one may touch, obstruct or interfere with any marching unit of cadets." They couldn't touch us.

We turned in perfect order. "Left face," yelled our brave and heroic leader. We marched away, a straggly band of little ill-branded brothers.

That is not to say my cousin and his cronies didn't get even with us little guys. They did even the score, but that Wednesday was our day.

I had about enough military justice, and within a few weeks I was ready to pack my bags and go home. My cousin enjoyed every minute of his military school career while many nights I quietly cried myself to sleep. Really, what was a nine-year-old doing away from home on such a misadventure. I wondered then and still do.

Billy Middleton and I shared the double deck bunk bed that was located directly beneath a large plate glass window with essentially no insulation. The cold night air sifted through the cracks around the window frame right over us. At night the school turned off the heat so if we didn't get our showers early, we would freeze. And besides, the big boys at the other end of the hall used up all the hot water before we could get our nightly showers.

After the Bull Ring affair my floor mates decided they could trust me. I had taken the punishment tour and had not told on my roommate. I was elected floor commander of my contemporaries. Part of my job was to be sure that the younger boys brushed their teeth, were showered and clean at bedtime. It was often so cold that I only made them run through the cold water, then grab a towel to dry off, and they could honestly say they had showered.

Since we had to have our beds perfectly made, the extra army wool blanket had to be properly folded at the foot of the bed. We could never get the blankets folded perfectly enough to satisfy the room inspectors, so we rarely used the extra blanket. We didn't need any more demerits. Without the extra blanket we routinely suffered the cold, shivering during the nights from the old drafty windows.

Every night lights out was accompanied by bugle "taps" sounded from the edge of the parade ground. Out went our lights as we snuggled into our beds hugging our pillows. Some of the boys were so lonesome away from home that as "taps" played they would muffle their tears under their blankets or into their pillows. I confess, sometimes I was one of those boys.

MISDEEDS

"Guilty parties, raise your hands."

At GMA we learned discipline in conduct, in study, and in personal integrity. The school attempted to follow the military code of honor, just as the senior Military Academies followed that code.

On one occasion, some of the kids got into trouble by "unspeakable deeds of mischief." The whole Junior School was assembled in the school study hall after supper. The faculty members spoke to the students as we sat at desks and stood about in the large room. They described the mischief and asked the guilty ones to confess to their misdeeds. "We'll stay here all night until we learn who did these deeds," the instructor said gruffly.

First, they asked the guilty party or parties to raise their hands. Since no one volunteered they then said, "Close your eyes, bow or place your heads down on the desks and whoever did this mischief raise your hands." No one confessed.

Now one of the senior instructors took the floor, "Boys, we can stay here all night until we find out." Still there was no response.

"Boys, if no one confesses the whole school will be confined, that is no afternoons off, no leave, no visitors, and room confinement after classes."

Now came the hard part. "We are going to hand out slips of paper and if you did the deeds write your name on the paper, fold it so no one sees it and pass it in," one instructor announced.

Still there were no confessions. As a last resort, the instructors gave the students a chance to write someone else's name who they knew was guilty.

After two hours of confinement in the study hall and no confessions and no tattle tales, the teachers dismissed the students to return to their rooms for the night. "Think on this, boys. Speak to an instructor privately if you have any information on this issue," one of the major instructors softly announced. "Now to bed and we will meet again tomorrow night here in the study hall."

We were dismissed, now frightened that each one of us was a suspect and wondered what was ahead for us. There were suspicions, but we talked only among ourselves.

We met the following night after supper and the instructors announced that a couple of the boys confessed to the deeds and the school would return to a normal schedule. We did not know who the culprit or culprits were. It was handled administratively. We were off the hook of suspicion.

A few days later a couple of boys were absent from an upper class and they never returned. We guessed they were the guilty ones.

HUNTERS AND GATHERERS

Geography and primitive societies

Her name was Mrs. Padgett. Her husband was Major Padgett and they both taught in the junior school at GMA. A dear lady, Mrs. Padgett, was like having your own grandmother as a teacher. She was firm, yet gentle and inspiring to fourth graders.

Our geography and history textbook was big and inside the covers, both front and back had an extended map of the world in color. How I enjoyed learning about the world and its pre-historic cultures.

My favorite was the story of the hunters and gatherers and the grassland nomads. I visualized the prehistoric folk as they, in animal skins and primitive woven garments, no more than rags, foraged for berries, nuts, and fruits, and hunted wild animals with stone-tipped arrows and stone-pointed spears. I was intrigued at the thought of starting campfires with flint and stones and bits of wood.

I imagined the little villages, the wooden huts, the animal hides covering the huts and the tents that we learned about in our books.

Mrs. Padgett made it all come alive as she read to us. We learned of primitive people and the development of the geographical regions, the tundra, the deserts, the mountains, and the jungles of the world. I remember the stories of little pygmies standing by the Congo River and wondered if I would ever see anything like that in real life. I was captivated by the thought of visiting those scenes.

She explained how the structure of the round earth had huge, monstrous earth plates that moved about, forming and changing land masses and oceans to become our present world. She explained how earthquakes occurred and how mountains formed. Only in imagination could we envision the happenings as we had no visual aids or television to show us what we were learning. Our imagination was enough.

At GMA I learned to study. I had never had a study hall and the intensity of the quiet effective atmosphere of the hall helped us to learn to really concentrate and study. It put me in good stead for a future of learning. No fooling around was allowed and any misconduct resulted in loss of privileges and possibly demerits that guaranteed us afternoons with the dreaded Bull Ring marching tours.

We were taught elocution and poetry. We had to memorize the Gettysburg Address and classic poetry in order to pass the English and History courses. At the spring graduation, a speaking contest was on the agenda. Though I was not a winner of the speaking medal, the award went to a youngster, J. P. Allen III who recited "The Charge of the Light Brigade." My eight-year-old buddy's dad was lost during the war in an air combat mission against the Nazis. Sadly, he had his own tragic light brigade.

PERIMETERS, DEFENSES, AND TACTICS

They taught us the principles of military operations.

Georgia Military Academy was designated a Junior Reserve Officer Training Corps (ROTC) school. Even as youngsters, we learned military science and tactics from our Regular Army instructors. We learned precision conduct from the description of "standing at attention, heels on the same line, toes pointed ahead at a 45-degree angle" to the description of full parade. We learned to form platoons, companies and battalions.

We studied the weapons from World War I bolt action rifles to the Garand M-1 rifles to BARs (Browning Automatic Rifles) and certain types of machine guns. These were the important weapons in each unit. We studied principles of military field manouvres, setting up a "defense perimeter" and "strategic planning and operations."

On special occasions we participated in setting up military field operations, command posts and individual platoon deployment on the parade field. These exercises involved the Senior School students instructing us. We were taught to disassemble, clean, and reassemble certain weapons then in use by our military forces.

On Sundays, we paraded as battalion, company, and platoon units for visitors and, on occasion, for Regular Army inspectors who rated the various military schools. As youngsters we often prayed for rain to avoid the Sunday parades. The parades were not limited to the campus. The school participated in national holiday celebration parades in Atlanta, marching as a unit.

At the firing range of the Senior School we were taught to fire .22 caliber bolt action rifles for "record." Our record scores were calculated and posted in the junior school bulletin board. Mine was not bad.

Some would continue the ROTC programs in senior school and in college. Those who entered the military directly from high school received advancement as single-striped private first class, bypassing the buck private designation and some were entered as two-stripe corporals.

Graduates of college preparatory ROTC programs entered the military as officers, second lieutenants in the army and marines or as ensigns in the navy.

During World War II, everyone wanted to share a role. Small though our part might have been, we felt we were doing our patriotic duty.

ATHLETICS

"A moment of glory…"

GMA offered all the athletic programs available at the time including the gentleman's art of boxing and wrestling. It was part of the required activities.

As a skinny kid, I wanted to be on the Junior School football team. It was the school's wish that each cadet participate in at least one major sport other than simply the required running and field exercise programs. My chance came during a night game with the hated opponent, Riverside Military Academy of Gainesville, Georgia. As a lightweight my moment of fame would come on that chilly Friday night under the lights. I was a fourth grader playing with mostly sixth and seventh- graders. The coach grabbed me by the shoulder pads and thrust me onto the playing field. "Go get 'em," he shouted as I rushed in, taking my place in the line. I forgot to tell the referee of my replacement, so we had an extra man on the field and before I realized it the dreaded enemy ran a power play right over me.

They tell me I was unconscious and was carried off the field. I still don't remember my single act of brilliance. "You stopped him," I vaguely remember the kids saying, or perhaps I just made that up or imagined it. Anyway, I had my moment of glory that night and sat on the frosty, cold bench for the rest of the season.

QUITTER

"He may be a quitter all his life."

Friday was my favorite day. That, theoretically, was a day I could go home for the weekend. On Fridays, on the way to early morning breakfast, I sang the popular song, from the 1943 Broadway musical, Oklahoma, "Oh, what a beautiful morning. Oh, what a beautiful day, I've got a beautiful feeling. Everything's going my way." I was going home, at least for the weekend.

To my parents, I must have seemed so unhappy, that they considered withdrawing me from military school. My mother and I met with the commandant, Colonel Brewster, in his gigantic office, not unlike some general's office. It resembled a war museum with flags, patriotic banners, photos and an array of military paraphernalia.

Our older cadet friends told us Colonel Brewster had whips in his office for really bad kids. They said he roamed the campus with those two big Doberman dogs to smell out any kids who tried to run off.

I had met him with my mother when we looked the school over. Now I was under his control and only saw him from a distance and feared approaching him. I noted he did travel the campus with those big dogs and wondered if my friends were telling the truth about those other things.

The meeting with Colonel Brewster, however, was reasonably pleasant. He had no whips in his office. I looked. He did have two big dogs lying beside his huge desk. He did not bite nor did the dogs. As a matter of fact, I thought he was rather gentlemanly, certainly to my mother.

She said to him, "My son is very unhappy here and I am unhappy not to have him at home. His dad and I are considering withdrawing him from the school. We think it was a mistake to have allowed him to enter the academy at such a young age."

Colonel Brewster thought a while and carefully looked me over as I sat quietly, anxious, but mostly listening. He was surmising me up, I thought. He turned to my mother and calmly said, "You know, ma'am, I think that if you remove him from the school and he quits now, he may be a quitter all his life."

There was silence for what seemed like forever. My mother looked at me and softly asked, "What do you think?"

I was ready to go home, but after I heard Colonel Brewster's comments, I answered, "I'm not a quitter. I'll stay this year then think about next year."

That said, Colonel Brewster slowly and deliberately rose from his chair, smiled at me and with a slight nod announced, "I think you have made a right decision, young man." He led us out of his office into the crisp Georgia autumn breeze. My mother took my hand and held it tightly as we walked down the stone stairs from the old Administrative building. I was still a Cadet.

LIEUTENANT BOYETTE

Our favorite

He entered the fourth-grade classroom and pulled out his desk chair as the rowdy class suddenly stood at attention by their desks.

In unison, the class greeted their teacher, "Good morning, Lieutenant Boyette."

"Morning boys," he responded, then he mumbled, "at ease, take your seats."

We all sat at our desks shuffling our books, tablets and pencils as the instructor looked about the room, obviously counting the nine-year olds, wondering who was present and what each was up to. He pulled out his grade book and called roll.

After a few minutes we sat up straight in our seats awaiting the young teacher's instructions.

Lieutenant Boyette was finishing his second year of post high school in the graduate program. The two years provided a preparatory class for students headed for the United States Military Academies, West Point, Annapolis and other university programs. Today, one might call this a one or two-year Junior college remedial program.

He was our arithmetic instructor and served as an assistant athletic coach in the Junior School. He was about twenty, a well-built lean guy, dressed in his khaki, neatly pressed summer uniform. A single gold disc insignia on his collar told us he was a lieutenant in the ROTC instructor class. Looking back now, I wonder if he even shaved.

He was our favorite instructor. His youth made him almost like one of us or perhaps a big brother.

"What were we studying yesterday?" he asked the class.

We all looked around and probably didn't remember until one of the boys, a bright one on the front row, probably Billy Sinrich, announced, "Sir, we're on page 36 and we're still studying long division."

"I thought we were doing decimals," said Lt. Boyette.

"No sir, reviewing division," chirped one of the slower students.

"Oh, yes, long division," answered Lt. Boyette. He rose from his desk holding the blue math book in his left hand, turning pages until he was at page 36 then said, "Okay boys, we're going back a couple of pages and review what we've learned already."

He walked toward the big blackboard and with a stubby piece of chalk began to write big numbers on the board until he had filled the space to the far-right side with division problems.

"Posey," he said, "you come to the board and do the first three problems. Allen, you come and do the next three and Watts you finish the last three."

"The rest of you copy all the problems on page 34 and begin to work on those."

Sometimes he would give us our day's grade from the board and we would not have to do the full review pages from the book. It was intimidating going to the board in front of our classmates, the pressure worse than just sitting at the desk working independently on the problems.

"Don't be embarrassed when you have to stand up before the class. You learn to work under pressure," he told us. "That's what life is all about."

After we finished at the board, he checked or corrected each problem or asked each student to explain how he came to the answers.

The rest of the class had to complete the prior textbook page. After the new problems were explained and completed, they turned their work in at the end of the class period.

In the following class we would again review the prior day's work and go through the same routine during the first part of the period.

For homework we would be assigned a few pages ahead to see how we had progressed and how we could handle new work before the subsequent class. It was an attempt to see how much we could learn on our own. We were not penalized for errors in future assigned work but were drilled on recent and present problems at that work level.

A few minutes before the class was over Lieutenant Boyette would say, "Okay, close your books, boys, and put your papers up and let's talk about whatever is on your mind."

Later, I reflected on how fortunate we were to have a young teacher so involved with the students. He made our classes fun and instructive. Most of the kids did well, as Lieutenant Boyette was more patient with us than the older regular instructors who were more rigid and set in their teaching ways.

Toward the end of the semester, Boyette left the school and was inducted into the Army. One teacher thought he went into the infantry and another said it was the artillery. He sent a few letters back to the teaching staff and I understand one or two to the students. We never knew where he was ultimately assigned or whether he survived the war.

A QUIET NIGHT DISTURBED

Lights out was at 10 p.m., so we had all our studying, our showers and preparations for bedtime completed. Our shoes were shined, our uniforms hanging so we could dress quickly in the morning for battalion formation and breakfast. We snuggled in our beds and talked after the darkness descended until we gradually dozed off. Most of the kids slept soundly, though slept cold on some extreme winter nights.

One morning we awoke and our roommate, Billy Sinrich, who as recalled occupied the lower bunk across from my double decker bed, was gone. His bed was made up and his closet closed. Sometime during the night, I heard movement and a door opening and closing, but was not disturbed by the bit of noise. However, I awoke and saw moving shadows quietly easing out the door into the dim light of the hallway. Then the door slowly closed. I must have rolled over and dozed off, back to sleep.

The next morning, we asked Mother Whitaker, our housemother, "Where is Billy?'

"Oh, his folks came and got him during the night. You know it's their holiday."

We knew Billy was Jewish, but that didn't mean much to us until we realized that he got more holidays than we did. "Hey," one of my clever roommates asked, "how can we be Jewish and get their holidays off too?"

Mother Whitaker had no answer except to mumble, "Oh, well, you'll have to ask your folks. That's a family decision." Still we thought it might be a good idea to check out. I later asked my dad and he dodged the question without answering directly said, "Oh Bud, don't worry about that, just remember if you have a Jew for a friend, you have a friend for life." His observation proved correct as I had many Jewish friends in college and medical school. I never forgot his words.

As noted, most of the nights were unremarkable except one night when a sudden bright light seeped under our door and we heard several low voices that sounded like they were entering Mother Whitaker's apartment. All was quiet and one of the boys pulled the cover from over his head and whispered, "What was that noise?" We at first didn't hear anything until a muffled scream shattered the stillness of the night. Then there could be heard sobbing and low shrieks of "No, no, it can't be!"

We were too afraid to peep out our door for fear of being in trouble, so we waited, whispering to each other, now all sitting up in bed, frightened and anxious. After a while we heard the door to Mother Whitaker's apartment open, then slowly close. Someone turned the key and we could hear the door lock shut. Footsteps could be heard descending the front hall steps. It sounded like several men mumbling and moving. We could hear Mother Whitaker still sobbing. Then all was still. All was quiet. We slipped out of beds, cracked open our door and peeped into the now dim hall. "They are all gone," one of my roommates said. We slipped back into our beds but did not sleep for a while.

The following morning reveille bugle sounded, and we shuffled out of bed. Before we could get dressed Lieutenant Fix came into our room. "Boys. Did you get awakened last night?"

"Yes sir," we stood at attention beside our beds and answered in unison.

"Well Mother Whitaker had to leave for a family problem and we're not sure when she will be back. We'll have someone in your area during the night so if you have any problems then check with them.

"Yes sir," we again answered.

No one spoke to us about the night's disturbance for a few days until Lieutenant Fix gathered us downstairs in what had been a parlor room in the old house. "Boys, Mother Whitaker will be coming back in a few days, so we want you all to be very nice to her and not bother her with small problems." He went on to explain the disturbance a few days before. "You know Mother Whitaker just got back from her sons' wedding and while he was coming back from his honeymoon with his wife, they were in a car accident and he and his bride both died."

We were silent and didn't know what to say.

"When Mother Whitaker comes back, we want you to be 'specially nice and give her hugs, but don't mention her son's death. She will tell you about it in her own time." He glanced at each of us, "Understand?"

We all nodded. He then left.

We were quiet and didn't ask any questions when our housemother returned. We tried to not cause her any problems, but didn't know how to address her situation, so we said nothing. It took a long time for her to tell us the story of the tragedy that had befallen her. She was never as happy, and her door was not always open as it had been in the past. I don't know how long she remained as housemother after I left GMA.

MY DEFENDER

For the younger little guys GMA could be a rough place.

The blasting reveille bugle sounded about 6 a.m. We struggled to climb out of our bunks in the unheated building. The heat was turned on shortly before reveille, yet we got up, still in the cold on those frosty winter days. Fortunately, we had showered the night before so we could reach into our lockers and slip on our blue-gray uniforms, wool trousers in winter with wool sweaters over our gray shirts and ties. We scurried down the stairs to line up in front of the cafeteria to march in for breakfast. "All present and accounted for," our student lieutenant would answer to the company captain, himself a kid of only twelve.

Inside the cafeteria we stood at our places at attention until the blessing was said and the pledge allegiance was recited. Then we seated ourselves and began to pass the food down the table line, family style. Talking was allowed at meals though we could not leave our seats until all had finished or the signal bell sounded whereupon we all rose, stood at attention by our chairs, then marched out of the dining room by rows.

Classes started at 9 a.m. and we would report directly to class on the first floor of the brick school and dorm building. There we would join the arriving day students as they unloaded from the school buses. Sleepy kids tried to stay awake in class, but a few dozed off and had to be nudged by their buddies so that they did not get the dreaded punishment tours.

Recess between classes was the time when the bigger guys ordered the younger kids around. It was always best to have a big buddy around so that the twelve-year-olds didn't intimidate the eight and nine-year-olds. My cousin Johnny was my yard defender. In later years, I saw movies about prison yards and could identify with that society.

Forbidden though it was, it was not uncommon for boys to tussle and even come to blows on the school yard. In some cases, the boys lacked the social skills that would get a boy through life without conflicts.

Bloody noses were not uncommon out in the yard after school. Fortunately, we were taught the respectable arts of self-defense, boxing with huge boxing gloves, and coach-directed wrestling. Some bigger guys carried it to extreme by accosting the others. I had many bloody noses, though inflicted only a few.

There were derisive names applied to boys from out of state and especially "Yankee" kids. At GMA during the forties there were no African Americans, no girls, and the only real outsiders were "rich" Cuban kids who, along with the bullies, often taught the younger guys the gutter language of the street. I had never heard many of the phrases. Some kids took pride in their new chancy, expanded vocabulary.

Not many kids bothered my cousin, Johnny. He was husky and tough. He could put down any of the ruffian bullies. Though strong, he rarely got into conflicts. I always thought he was part of the good tough guys who maintained a bit of order among the students.

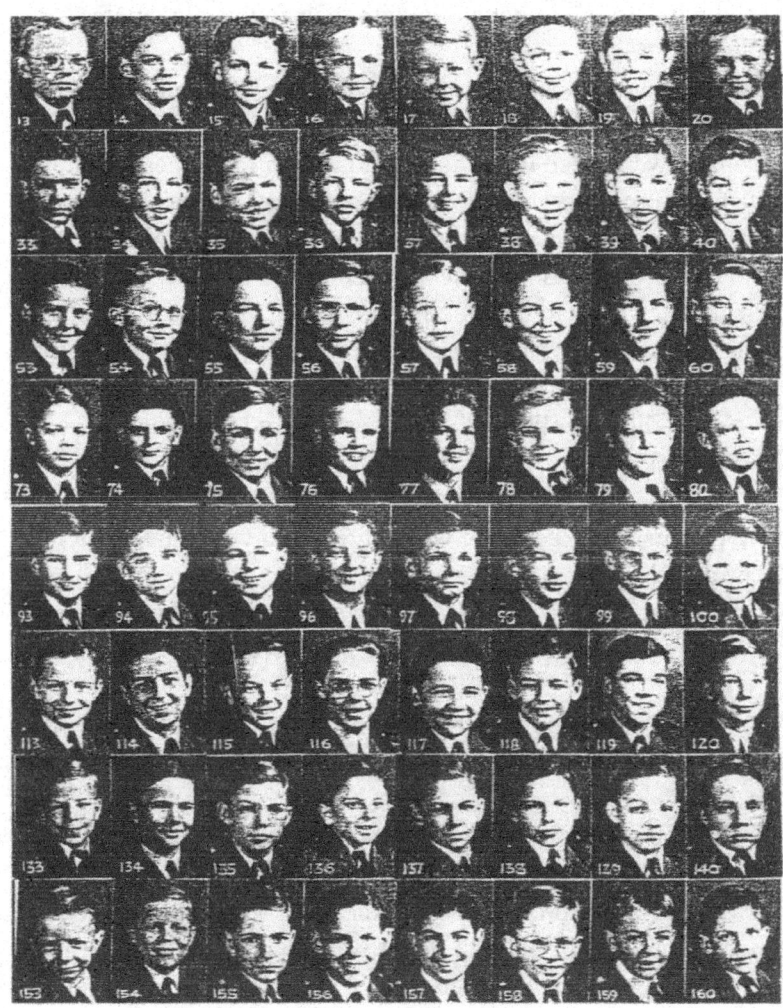

Georgia Military Academy
Part of the Junior School Roster, 1943 – 1944
(Photo from GMA in possession of the author)

I always believed those disruptive kids were from unhappy or broken homes or kids who could not be handled at home. This is not to say that they were all bad actors; they were not. Many of the kids' fathers were away fighting the war and the kids merely needed masculine supervision. Some were from families who simply wanted their child to have a better education than might be available in their towns. Most were average kids, some lonesome, and some just trying to get along with their fellow classmates.

One day out on the school yard, I was accosted by a bigger kid and it led to a fight. He soundly bloodied my nose which was not rare, but somehow, I ended up on top banging him in the head with my small fists. From nowhere I was jerked away. It was my cousin Johnny. He grabbed me and hastily ushered me behind the junior school gym, roughly shook me and demanded to know the trouble that had gotten me into the bloody–mostly my blood–conflict. Now crying, yet victorious over my hated enemy, I answered, "It's 'cause he called me a bad name."

"What did he call you?" my cousin asked, holding me away from other kids.

"He called me a son-of-a-bitch," I mumbled.

My cousin looked at me with a grin, "Do you know what that is?" he asked.

"No, but it must be bad," I answered, wiping the blood and tears from my face and nose with the handkerchief my cousin had given me.

Johnny shook his head and firmly said, "You're right. It is bad. But I better not catch you fighting again. If I do, I'm telling your mom."

To have my mom on my case was worse than a bloody nose or even the dreaded marching punishment tour.

My dad was a professional boxer in his younger days. Once, or more than once, he said, "I never want to hear of you starting a fight. However, I never want to hear of you not finishing a fight."

My cousin kept me from fighting by his threats. I learned to walk away from many conflicts and many threatening kids. At first, I felt ashamed or like a sissy for walking away but later I knew it was the right thing to do.

"Fighting only makes it worse," my cousin preached to me.

I wondered if I would ever send my young kid to a military school, yet I learned discipline and good study habits. I had a real education at GMA.

At the end of the school year in 1944, despite an ominous start, our room received The Best Kept Room Award in the Junior School, a couple of Gold Eagle academic medals. My roommates and I were promoted to single stripe private first-class students. I finished the year. I did not return. My cousin, Johnny remained and graduated from Georgia Military Academy in 1949. He attended The University of Maryland and served in the 101st Airborne Division as a Pathfinder / Paratrooper. He was the real soldier in our family.

No longer a military academy, the school is now known as Woodward Academy in Atlanta, a fine preparatory academic institution with a couple of campuses. The school now has a diversity of males, females, all faiths, national origins, and racial backgrounds.

A LITTLE JOB

"I'd get somebody bigger."

There aren't many jobs for a ten or eleven-year-old boy. I was too young for a paper route. You had to be twelve to get that job. I couldn't work bagging groceries at a grocery store. You had to be fourteen to get that job. All the neighbors did their own yards so that job was out.

I looked about and watched my next-door neighbor deliver afternoon papers to several nearby streets. Jack Slayton had an afternoon *Atlanta Journal* paper route and I wondered would he hire a helper.

We were playing outside in the woods when I broached the subject, "Jackie, do you need a helper?"

"What do you mean?" he responded. "Do you want a job?"

"Yeah, I've been thinking, and I've got a wagon and we could put the papers in the wagon, and you wouldn't have to tote that big bag of papers."

Jackie looked at me with a strange grin, "If I needed a helper, I'd get somebody bigger than you. You're too little to pull all this stuff around and besides, I can't afford a helper."

Jackie was thirteen or fourteen and a husky, medium-sized kid.

"Yeah, but I'd try," I proffered.

He thought for a minute and looked me over, sizing me up, I guessed. "Well, I can pay you a quarter a day if you really want a job, but we have to use your wagon."

I thought Jackie made a dollar or so a day. He never said exactly how much. He received a few extra papers each day from the *Journal* delivery truck. He could sell the extra papers to folks who weren't regular customers. That was incentive pay if he could sell extra papers at a nickel each and sometimes get a small tip. His route included over a hundred papers to deliver.

We started on a clear Monday afternoon after school. We waited at the corner of Cascade and Westhaven Drive, a few blocks from our house in the neighborhood. The tall, grumpy guy on the afternoon *Journal* truck dumped the string-tied paper bundles on the sidewalk along the curb and the paper boys scrambled to get their bundles and counted each to be sure the truck guy had not shorted them.

If they missed a paper or if the delivered paper was thrown into the yard or into the bushes and not on the customer's porch, they would get a "kick." Then the paper truck would have to come back and deliver a paper to the disgruntled client. A quarter or more, sometimes the whole day's pay was assessed against the paper boy and deducted from his weekly pay. We wanted no "kicks."

It was hard pulling the wagon up the steep hills but okay going down. I easily learned the correct houses to deliver the papers to, and I worked steadily with Jackie throwing the twist folded papers carefully upon each porch. We divided the sides of the streets. He was pleased with my help and paid me my quarters at the end of each week when the supervisor paid him at the pick-up stop.

Usually, Mr. Slayton drove Jackie on Sunday mornings because the papers were heavier and had to be delivered just after sunup, but one early windy, misty morning he didn't and when Jackie and I were about half through carrying the heavy Sunday papers the wheel on my little wagon twisted and broke. All the papers fell on the damp street. "Oh," we yelled as the papers scattered. We collected the papers and stuffed them into the delivery bags and carried them the rest of the route. We then dragged the wagon and the broken wheel home to my garage.

"Axle's broken," my dad said.

A day or so later after carrying the papers in the heavy, cotton shoulder bags Jackie announced that he didn't need me anymore. I was fired.

The lesson to me was that it was not my hard work ethic or my sterling personality, but my wagon that kept me employed. It's what you bring to the job market that counts.

When my dad reminded me, "Son, when you grow up, never be in a position where someone can simply walk in and fire you without a real reason." I socked it away in my memory bank. I never forgot.

A TOKEN FOR THE STREETCAR

The car fare was a dime or two tokens for fifteen cents.

"Jackie's mom called this morning. Would you like to go to the picture show with Jackie?" my mom asked.

I didn't answer and she repeated, "Would you like to go downtown with Jackie to the picture show?"

I cautiously looked up and asked, "What's on?"

"Oh, I don't know, but Mrs. Slayton says that Jackie is going, and he wants you to go with him." That would be unusual because I never went downtown with my neighbors, only to the local Cascade Theater and with other older kids on Friday night or on Saturday for the matinee and the serials. The serials were continuing episodes such as the Superman, Captain Marvel, Batman or other mystery sagas.

"Yes, ma'am, I would like to go. When is he going?"

"There's one catch," my mom quietly said.

"What's that?" I asked.

"Well, Jackie has a date and the girl's mother won't let her go unless her younger sister comes along."

"A date?" I answered.

"Yes," she paused, "do you know Jane and Jean Hudson?"

"Yes, ma'am," I answered.

"Jackie is going with Jane. Her mother says that her sister Jean will have to have a date."

"A date?" I again answered. "She wants me to be her date?"

"Yes, she's a sweet child and if you already know her that should be fine."

"Yes, ma'am, but I barely know her. She's in Mrs. Jenkins's fourth grade."

"Mrs. Slayton says she will drive you all downtown to the Capitol or the Roxy Theater then after the movie you all can take your dates to the S &W Cafeteria across the street for afternoon dinner, then ride the streetcar home. It would be nice if you will do this for your friend Jackie."

Jackie lived next door and we had a telegraph wire from my house to his positioned high and strung across our driveway. We exchanged messages by Morse code, slowly tapping our messages, writing the dots and dashes down then decoding the messages. It was our own secret communication system, more fun than talking on the telephone.

"Does Jackie want me to go or was it his mom's idea?" I asked.

"I don't know," my mom answered, "but he can't go unless you go, or someone else goes with him to take his date's sister with them."

I thought for a moment, "Okay, I'll do it."

Saturday morning came. Jackie walked over to my house and knocked on the door. I answered, ready to go, and we hurried outside and piled into Mrs. Slayton's blue Dodge sedan.

We crossed Cascade Avenue and after a couple of blocks pulled up to Jane and Jean's house. Mrs. Slayton stayed in the car while Jackie and I walked up a few stone steps and rang the doorbell. Mrs. Hudson soon peered out then slowly opened the door, "Hello boys, come right in. The girls will be down in just a minute."

We sat silently on the soft Victorian sofa and soon Jane and Jean appeared in matching dresses and soft sweaters. They shyly approached as we stood nearly at attention, hardly knowing what to say in front of their mom.

"Hi," Jackie said to Jane.

I slipped forward and politely said, "Good morning, Jean."

They giggled, looking at each other, blushing slightly, then smiled and answered, "Hi, to you, too."

Jackie and I stood mutely for a moment and both sighed, "You both look awfully nice." The girls blushed again and answered, "You look nice, too."

After a pause that seemed forever Mrs. Hudson spoke up, "Well, I guess you all should be going if you are to catch the matinee."

"Yes, ma'am," Jackie and I echoed.

She shooed us out the door with, "Have fun and be careful. Don't talk to strangers and call us if you need us."

We all four sat in the backseat as Mrs. Slayton drove up Peachtree Street to the movie house. At first the ride was quiet. Jackie and Jane whispered, and Jean held her older sister's hand. It seemed she hardly knew what to say to me.

I could feel myself shaking a little inside. I really wasn't much into dating, especially someone I hardly knew and had seen only at lunch time at school. I had barely spoken to her on the playground. I don't remember if I had ever had a real date alone before.

Mrs. Slayton spoke softly to us as we arrived at the Capitol Theater, right next door to the Henry Grady Hotel where my dad worked. She stopped the car in front of the theater. Jackie opened the car door and we squeezed out onto the sidewalk. The girls followed us. Mrs. Slayton said, "Now you all call us if you have any problems. You know the streetcar stop is just down the street by Davison-Paxon so have your tokens ready when the car comes. Do you have your money, boys?"

"Yes, ma'am, we've got our money," we answered.

We headed to the box office, paid for our theater tickets, picked up some popcorn and Cokes inside. With the help of the theater usher, we hurried into the dark theatre searching for our seats as the previews of coming attractions began.

After the movie started, I saw Jackie reach over and hold Jane's hand. She leaned toward his shoulder.

What should I do, I wondered? I could hardly watch the screen because I didn't know if I was supposed to hold Jean's hand too. I wished Jackie had told me what to do. My mom only advised me, "Behave and be nice to your date."

She smiled, "Popcorn's good."

"Yeah," I answered. We each had our own bag so there was no sharing and no chance that our hands would touch. I still didn't know whether I was supposed to hold her hand until she reached over and slipped her hand into mine as a scary scene appeared on the big screen. She leaned toward me squeezing my hand tightly and muffling a little sound of fear as the villain approached the intended victim.

The movie over, we left the theater into the still bright afternoon and crossed Peachtree Street to the S & W Cafeteria. The S & W was a popular family cafeteria in the city. It had two sides and at the rear of each were double serving lines. In the middle of each was a large porcelain-tile fishpond built up with sides about three feet tall and stone or porcelain frogs with water spouting out their mouths spewing water into the pond filled with big, beautiful goldfish. The kids always gathered about the ponds and fed the fish with little crumbs of bread.

We passed down the cafeteria line and two waiters in white starched coats toted our trays to a little table near the front windows. We had been told to give the waiter a quarter for carrying our trays, so we laid our quarters on the trays as the waiters placed our plates and silverware on the table.

I looked around and noticed several grownups looking and smiling toward our table and whispering so quietly that I couldn't hear what they were saying. Several nodded and returned to their meals.

With our best manners we ate our food trying not to spill anything. Jane and Jean seemed to enjoy the outing and were perfect little ladies. Jackie and I tried to be as gentlemanly as we could.

It was not until we left the cafeteria that a problem occurred. Jean got into the circling exit doors and would not come out. She kept twirling around and around pushing the circling doors faster and faster. I tried to get her to stop, but she just kept giggling and wouldn't come out of the turning doors. Grownups stood back, aghast that this little girl continued twirling. When she decided she had had enough she burst out onto the sidewalk, woozy and wobbly.

I knew all the grownups were watching us and I was so embarrassed that I fretted and stood close to Jackie. When the girls gathered around us, I reached into my pocket and pulled out a streetcar token and gave it to Jean. "Here's your car fare home. I'm going across the street to my daddy's. Jackie will take you home."

When I told my story to my mom, she was immediately on the telephone calling Mrs. Hudson. I don't know what they talked about, but she seemed not too happy. Strangely enough, Jean forgave me, and we became fifth grade sweethearts.

Atlanta Streetcar Service – 1940s
"The streetcar stop is just down the street by Davison-Paxon."
(Courtesy of Atlanta History Center)

SPECIAL REFLECTIONS:
BILLY

When I was a toddler, we lived on Beecher Street in the West End / Cascade area of Atlanta. My babysitter was a thirteen or fourteen-year-old youngster, Billy. He lived across the street with his grandmother. His mother and dad were divorced, and both had remarried. Perhaps they had no time for Billy. He had a home with his grandmother, and he had a second home at our house.

We moved from Beecher Street in the spring when I was five, nearly six. Billy remained with his grandmother. My mom and dad continued their contact with him.

When I was seven, Japanese Navy aircraft attacked Pearl Harbor and we were at War. Billy was seventeen and he managed to join the Army in 1942 or 1943. He likely lied about his age or had his grandmother sign permission for him to go into the service. Billy joined the Army Paratroops. We were proud of him. After Boot Camp training at Fort Benning, Georgia, he was sent to the Pacific. During the war we wrote to Billy and I religiously collected and bundled up my comic books to send to him and his Army buddies.

After the war, Billy came home to a difficult situation. His grandmother had died, and his parents had sold the house where he and his grandmother lived.

Billy had no place to go so my mom and dad took him in and made a place for him at our house. They also took in my mom's younger second cousin, Spencer Donovan, from Montgomery, Alabama, also a soldier from the war.

Billy moved into our unfinished attic. When Billy came home, he was suffering from a skin condition that had developed in the tropical South Pacific. He was treated with Gentian violet medicine, of a horrible purple color, which discolored his clothes and stained everything it touched. Therefore, Billy wore cotton pajama bottoms and a sweatshirt in the house.

Bill (far right) with his Army buddies, World War II
"Somewhere between Borneo and Tokyo"
(Photo from Bill Eskew)

In the spring of 1946, I had a fever that was later determined to be scarlet fever. Usually the homes of children with scarlet fever were quarantined with a big yellow or red sign nailed on the front door warning the neighbors of the dangerous and contagious disease, but we didn't know what my condition was until it was over. "If his hands peel, then it is probably scarlet fever," Dr. Sam Perry, my pediatrician said. A week after my fever abated my hands peeled.

Billy had a collection of Bebop, jazz and wartime music records that he dared anyone to play. During my illness my sixth-grade class marched down from my grammar school, a couple of blocks away, to visit. Some of the kids began playing Billy's records on the record player.

My mother stashed Billy on the attic steps. He looked so bad with all the spotty violet medicine painted all over him that my mother made him hide from the children. He looked like the plague.

"If they see you, they'll be terrified," my mom said to Billy. When the kids from my class started fooling around with Billy's records, he would ease open the attic door and peep at the kids. My mom would slam the door trying to hide him. This went on until at last the class left. "You can come out now," my mother announced, and Billy rushed down the attic stairs to rescue his precious records.

When he got over his tropical disease my dad gave him a job at the hotel. Billy became a bellman. A big mistake. It meant fast money, more money than he ever had before or after the Army. He and his buddies had begun to drink in the service. It became a problem. He hung out at the VFW, Veterans of Foreign Wars. There the veterans gambled, drank, and often got into fights. Many of them were receiving their discharge unemployment pay and didn't work. Some went back to school. Some were getting over the stress of the war and had severe emotional problems. Some started fights for unknown reasons. "It's all that war stress," the military doctors claimed. The Veterans Administration had no program to help these men. The problem is now described as Post Traumatic Stress Disorder and is clinically recognized; and medical and psychological treatment is at last available. There remains however, a national debate as to the proper care available at current Veterans hospitals.

My mom tried to get Billy into school with his veteran benefits, but the fast money at the hotel was too much for him to leave for a college education. Though we all loved him my mom had to ask Billy to move out.

Billy later met and married a lovely girl named Mary who changed his whole life. It was the best thing that ever happened to him up to that time. We were all delighted. After the birth of his son, he had for the first time, something that was really his own. He was healing from the war. He became a new man. We were again so proud of Billy.

During Billy's stay at our house we asked him about his military experience in the Pacific. He never opened up to us about his war experiences.

All he would allow was, "I was a sergeant a couple of times, but I kept losing my stripes. I was always in trouble, so I dug latrines from Borneo to Tokyo." So many brave veterans are still silent on those war time experiences.

OTHER VETERANS

Billy and my mom's younger cousin, Spencer Donovan were not the only young men to return from the war and become friends or "wards" to my folks. There were others who returned and had difficulty getting their acts together after military combat service. Two young sailors came into our lives in Atlanta. They were temporarily stationed at the Naval Air Station in Marietta awaiting discharge.

A point system was devised crediting certain time and military combat experience to be met before a service man could be discharged. Many were simply waiting on typically slow military processing for discharge.

Roger Burr, from Clinton, Connecticut, and Jimmy McManus from Natchez, Mississippi, had served in the navy and we met them at the Adams Park stables where they boarded their horses and we boarded my horse, Prince Junior.

I don't remember what Roger did in the navy, but I recall Jimmy was a Sea Bee (Navy Construction Battalion) on Guadalcanal (Solomon Islands) in the Pacific. We have a photo of him, shirtless in the intense jungle heat, packing a .45 caliber on his hip. In one gloved hand he held a parrot. The Sea Bees were constructing the runway for the navy and marine airplanes (Henderson Field) to fly against the Japanese as the American forces moved up the Pacific chain of islands toward the mainland, and in air striking distance to Japan.

Jimmy contracted malaria in the Pacific, and I was to see the effects of this devastating tropical disease. He had recurrent malaria attacks with high fevers and chills.

Jimmy McManus – USN Seabees
(Navy Construction Battalions), Guadalcanal,
World War II – August 1942 through early 1943
Seabees building Henderson Field
(Photo from Jimmy McManus)

During the war, folks were encouraged to rent out rooms to military personnel and Jimmy boarded in my mother's friend's house. When Jimmy had one of the malaria episodes he would sweat profusely as the fever rose to 104 degrees. He became delirious. Meanwhile, ice packs and cold towels were placed on him until the sweats and fever broke. Then the shivering chills would start, and he would have to be covered in blankets. After the episodes, all the bed clothes would have to be washed and hung out to dry.

As far as I remember, only quinine was available to treat malaria. Mother's friend Grace, though not a nurse, cared for him as if he were her own son. She had two teenage daughters who acted as her helpers in caring for Jimmy.

Our relationship was largely through the stable and our common equine interest. Jimmy and Roger were both fine horsemen.

After Jimmy was discharged from the navy he returned to Natchez. Some months later he called my folks and invited me to come and visit him and his aunt and uncle. His parents had died, and he returned to work in a civilian job for one of the local newspapers.

Alone, I rode the train in a Pullman sleeper car and arrived in Natchez in early summer. Jimmy met me at the railroad station. Since his relatives lived some distance from town, we stayed in the downtown Eola Hotel that was owned by friends of his family.

The Annual Natchez Historical Pilgrimage, the opening of the town and antebellum homes to visitors was passed, so Jimmy took me all over Natchez and allowed me to prowl around in the attics of the fashionable antebellum homes. It was exciting to visit and rummage around in old plantation houses and in the reconstructed early settlers' wooden palisade fort, originally constructed in the early 1700s to protect the new American settlers from the native Natchez Indians.

We visited his family's home and while rummaging through the attic I opened a dusty trunk and found an old Ku Klux Klan wizard robe. My mom had always said the Klan was a "trashy common bunch of bad folks," but I was told by locals that the vigilante committees such as the Klan had been the only way to control the Yankee carpetbaggers and scalawags after the Civil War.

I was not told about the intimidation and terror laid on or perpetrated against the freed black slaves and the already free blacks in the post-war the South. I was not told about the anti-Catholic and anti-Jewish sentiments of the Klan. It was enlightening to learn of this period of repression of religious and racial prejudices much later in life.

Jimmy took me to several well-known historical inns for dinner that had served many generations since the early days of settlement in the Mississippi Delta and flatlands. We traveled out into the country and to the west I saw the great Mississippi River from the heights of the Natchez Bluffs, At the time I didn't understand the significance of the local history. I didn't understand what had occurred there during the War Between the States.

By the victory in July 1863 of Union troops over the defending, starving population at nearby Vicksburg, the defeat of Confederates troops along the Mississippi River, the Union forces broke the back of the Confederacy in the Western theater of war. After these victories, the Union forces blockaded the Mississippi River as the source of reinforcements for the Confederate Army in the west.

After a couple of weeks visiting, I returned to Atlanta and though our family communicated with Jimmy McManus for years, I never saw him again.

RICHLAND ROAD

It was a boy's dream street.

Richland Road was a Mecca for boys, more boys than you could imagine. We gathered for street football, played in the vacant lots we called the woods, or went to the Cascade Movie Theater or even played golf after the regular hours on the John A. White course, one block away.

We walked two blocks and caught the jitney bus to Adams Park further out into Cascade Heights to swim, play or fish. Of course, on the way back, we were not welcome on the jitney if we had caught fish from the Adams Park Lake. "Sorry boys, you can't ride with those smelly fish," the drivers would allow. So, we walked along the side of the road for the few miles to our homes, carrying our cane poles and small fish buckets, and sometimes thumbing a ride.

The houses in our Atlanta neighborhood were built and completed just before World War II began. They were middle class two or three-bedroom homes; mostly clapboard, wood frame or brick. To have a three-bedroom brick house was "high cotton." Our house was a compromise, an asbestos-shingled house with two bedrooms and a huge unfinished play and storage area in the attic.

Our house was finished in the spring of 1940. We moved in when I was almost six years old. I was the youngest boy in the neighborhood. Across the street were the four Lamb boys. Joe, the oldest, went to the Second World War. He fought the Nazi invaders in France and Germany. He sent home German knives and other captured war souvenirs. According to his brothers he was awarded the Silver Star for gallantry for swimming the Rhine River, bringing a wounded army buddy back to safety while under German gunfire. My closest buddies were Ronald Lamb and the younger brother, Gene.

A few houses down the street was a boy named Joseph Green, my age but taller. Across from him were two brothers, the younger brother, a year older than me. The young brother and I often had conflicts that ended with serious tussles. He was bigger and could usually whip me, but I had good friends in the Lamb boys who came to my defense. On one occasion, the younger brother was whipping me, and was on top dropping grass in my face. I looked over toward his house's window and saw his mother peeping out as she slipped behind the curtain. She would stay inside if her son was winning but would come outside and break up the fight if I was on top, which was rare.

Usually, the Lamb boys rescued me and then the front porch screen door would burst open and the big brother would dart from their house and engage my defender or defenders. By this time, the younger brother and I would have made up, as kids often do. We sat on the curb watching the ruckus that we had just caused.

Those little conflicts among boys never lasted long and we would soon be pals again romping together in the vacant neighborhood lots or in the street playing ball as if nothing had ever happened.

One day my older cousin Johnny Clark, still a student at GMA, was staying at my house on his weekend off from school. We were playing jump rope in the street and Johnny was jumping as we were singing:

"One two, button my shoe.

Three four, shut the door.

Five six, pick up sticks.

Seven eight, lay them straight.

Nine ten, he's a big fat hen."

A couple of other kids and I were sitting in the grass yelling and harassing him trying to make him miss. Johnny squatted down and picked up a large rock from the street to throw at me, but I ducked and it hit one of my friends above his eye. Blood splattered from his forehead. He ran home screaming and soon his mother was on the phone calling my mother demanding she do something about that wayward child, Johnny. "You need to punish that child," she barked. "I mean do something to him."

My mother listened to her tirade for several minutes until she was full of it.

"Ma'am, I can punish him, but I can't kill him. He's just my nephew."

TO BE A SIXTH GRADER

High cotton and distant love

Grammar school ended with the sixth grade. As a sixth grader in 1946, I was a happy student. Our teacher was young and a recent graduate of Brenau College in North Georgia. To say the class was happy to have her as our teacher would be an understatement. She wore tight sweaters. We didn't know why we were so enthralled. We were too young to understand those urges, but they were there. The boys all tried to have seats closest to her desk. We all wanted to be her favorite. She was fair to all of us, but I think she loved the boys the most.

Elections in grammar school were always big occasions. Elections for patrol boy positions, class presidents, May Day Queen and May Day Court, elections for "Tip Top Student Award" (that came with a letter from the principal and a five-dollar prize) were all important happenings.

The most significant election, I thought, was the "Tip Top Student," that I won the year before in the fifth grade. By sixth grade, I was again a candidate. Surely, I would get it, I thought. Little did I know until years later that my achievement before had been gained by the slimmest margins, by a single vote and my best pal had cast that vote. Well, I thought I was in high cotton. What I didn't know was that the boll weevil was in my field.

When the votes were counted, my count was shy the winning margin. The winner was the dainty, dark-haired, brown-eyed, beautiful sixth grade girl that sat one room away from me, the girl that I could see right through the open doors between the school rooms. Her name was Joan and I had the biggest imaginable crush on her. I dreamed about just holding her hand and being near her. I changed desks from the one near our pretty teacher to one by the door. I could look right across the hall and see her at her desk during the school day. I climbed an old oak tree and carved our initials, J. W. + J. B.

Our recess and lunch periods were different, and I could only be near her during assembly or on the walk home after school. Besides, girls stuck together, and boys rarely spoke to the opposite sex. We were macho. "Let those silly girls chase us," one of my pals said. I didn't confess to my buddies, but in my heart, I still pined to know little Miss Joan better. It never came to fruition. I'm not sure she ever noticed me. We rarely spoke.

E. L. Connally Grammar School – Atlanta, Georgia
(Photo by author)

She moved away that summer and I never saw her again. She was so pretty. She probably became a movie star. I lost the tip-top student award to the girl who also took my heart.

Sixty years later I drove by the site where I had carved our initials in an oak tree and there it was, cut down and in a pile of limbs, a fitting end to the tale.

**E. L. Connally School – Sixth Grade –
Mrs. Wilcox's Class, May 1946**

First Row: Jimmy Slappey, Marion Seignous, Billy Willis,
May Queen Alice Johnson, Jerry Watts,
Ann Schneider, Warner Owens

Second Row: Stewart Watkins, Betty Jo Kelly, David Moore,
June Gaissert, Jimmy Jenkins, Joanna Smith,
Harry Whitworth, David Jenkins

Third Row: Martha Walters, Bobby Vass, Susanne Stewart,
Buddy Asbell, Patricia Vines, Tommy Scott,
Mae Brown Ridley, Jimmy Hansard, Danny Power

(Photo from school archives)

WOULD THEY TELL

My buddies and the wrath of girls

Bobby Vass was one of my best friends. We were almost inseparable in grammar school. He lived on one end of Richland Road and I lived on the other. I didn't often go across Cascade Avenue to his house, but we were pals in school. In sixth grade, the girls thought Bobby was the most handsome boy in our class and all the girls chased after him. I felt lucky to be his buddy. Some of the glitter shed a bit on me. When we chose up sides on the playground, Bobby was always picked first because he was the best athlete. I was selected somewhere in the middle, likely because I was only a "middling" athlete. If Bobby didn't choose me first, I was upset. He was just trying to make his team better. I always chose him first.

Among my several buddies, along with Bobby, was Jimmy Jenkins. They were my lieutenants on the schoolboy patrol. It was a big deal, yet I never realized how big of a deal it was until I recently read a published author as he bemoaned the fact that as a child, he was not allowed to be a patrol boy. We took it for granted and I now wonder if there were boys in my class who felt left out if they were not elected to that position. Girls were not elected to the patrol in my era.

We ran the patrol like the army. We stood our corners directing traffic like real cops. We raised our school flag with pomp and ceremony. In the afternoon, we lowered it with the same salute. We were a real operation.

Jimmy's dad was a police captain on Atlanta's Police Force. He brought Jimmy to school in a police car and stayed parked nearby until the school bell rang. We were the only school in Atlanta that had our own patrol car on site. We never had any traffic problems at E. L. Connally School. The children were always safe.

Many years later Bobby was elected Sheriff of North Georgia's Hall County and I jokingly congratulated him with, "You may be sheriff, but I'll still think of you as my lieutenant." He explained to me that many years ago I had been elected captain of the patrol by one vote, his vote. I had told him I was not going to vote for myself, so he voted for me.

E. L. Connally Boys Choir
"Angels, not quite!"

First Row: Harry Wycoff, Harold Lambert, Unidentified, David Moore, Stewart Watkins, Jerry Watts, Bobby Vass

Second Row: Tommy Scott, Don Tedder, Jimmy Hansard, Buddy Asbell, Unidentified, Bobby Keaton

(Photo from school archives)

At twelve years of age we made our own schedule, subject to the approval of the principal, Miss Avalene Morris. Miss Morris was a stout, grey-haired, commanding woman, who reminded us of Mrs. Eleanor Roosevelt. We gave her great respect, kept our distance, and appreciated her authority. Any misconduct resulted in a visit to her office and often the detention room next door. We wanted to stay out of that room at all costs.

One afternoon after school, the girls were chasing us–mostly Bobby. We hid in the thick bushes by the school building. As the girls passed, we threw rocks into the puddles of water on the gravel drive and splashed them. They screamed, "We know who you are." We laughed. They recognized us and yelled, "We're going to tell Miss Morris." That was the worst of all threats.

Bobby and I were terrified. We knew if they told, we would have to go to her office and detention. And probably lose our patrol badges.

We headed home in great despair, knowing we were going to be in trouble with Miss Morris. It was bad enough to be in trouble with our grade teacher, but to be in trouble with the principal was really bad news. What was worse was that our moms would likely be called.

We walked to nearby Cascade Avenue, a block from school. We sat on a low brick wall just thinking how to get out of this big brewing trouble.

Maybe the girls were bluffing! Maybe they wouldn't tell. While we sat on the wall, we unexpectedly saw that big blue Lincoln Zephyr automobile with Miss Morris driving. *Oh*, we thought, *we've had it.* What to do?

We hoped she wouldn't notice us, and we looked as innocent as possible. It was too late to run.

Miss Morris turned her big car into Cascade Avenue right in front of us. We sat frozen on the wall. She reached out her window and with a big smile waved her handkerchief to us. "Hi boys," she said. "Hurry on home and have a nice day."

We looked at each other. "They didn't tell," we exclaimed. We jumped down from the wall and ran home laughing until our sides hurt.

MY COUSIN LOUIS

To him I was always "Babee."

Louis Keaton was my cousin and he was deaf. My family explained to me that he was a hearing infant until he developed measles encephalitis at the age of twelve months. Soon after he recovered, they noticed he failed to respond to sound. He essentially never heard the spoken word after his illness and never learned to speak. To me that seemed impossible, yet he and I had our own communication system.

Since he was older by seven years and I was just learning to talk, there never seemed to be any difference in communicating with him as with others. In our case I learned to speak, but in a different way, on my hands to him. Most of the sign language was the standard method at the time, but perhaps we had our own secret signs and methods of understanding each other. It was so secret that when he stayed at my house and my mom made us turn out the lights at night, in bed we would grasp each other's hands and form the signs to talk after lights out.

Louis was born in Pine Bluff, Arkansas, the son of Edna and Louis Wiley, Sr. After the family realized he was deaf my grandmother Perdue and Edna took Louis all over the country to doctors to find out what could be done for his hearing problem. They took him to Johns Hopkins University in Baltimore and to The Lahey Clinic in Boston, but they found no help. "He will always be deaf," they were told by the best doctors in the country.

Sadly, his father was overwhelmed, my folks said, and he could not stand the idea that he had a "defective child". He abandoned his family and Edna brought Louis to Atlanta to stay with us until she could make arrangements for her own housing.

Thus, began my relations with my cousin. My family told me that we took to each other immediately and became buddies, he, the older, the leader and I became the follower. At seven or eight years old he became my babysitter and pal. From the beginning he would, in an abrupt attempt at speech, call me "Babee" and in fact referred to me by that name all his life.

Louis was first educated in a school for the deaf in Arkansas, then he was sent to St. Rita School for the Deaf in Cincinnati, Ohio. When I was four, I accompanied my grandmother Perdue and Aunt Edna to Cincinnati to visit him. I remember the cold snowy day we arrived in Cincinnati, driving through the railroad gate, seeing the gate rise so that we could leave the station. And driving through the heavy snow and snow drifts we arrived at the Catholic school for the deaf in the late, dark, winter afternoon.

The nuns put Edna and Grandmother in visitor rooms but put an extra bed by my cousin in his dorm. I remember they placed a little table by my bed and told me I would be treated just like the other deaf children, since I seemed to already know the sign language. They gave me my own toothbrush and said, "Now, you will be just like the rest of our boys." And so, I was.

A few years later Louis (then called Buster) moved from St. Rita School to the Georgia School for the Deaf in Cave Springs in northwest Georgia. There we could visit him more often. During the summers he came home and stayed with his mom and her new husband, Wayne Keaton and with us. It was like having my own big brother.

As we grew up, I spent more time with Buster at their house in Cascade Heights near Adams Park. During summers we hiked through the woods, climbing the huge rocks in and along the Adams Park creek, to the swimming pool beside Adams Lake. Mornings were free for kids and we had to be out before noon when they started charging. We usually headed back to his house for lunch and then often returned for the afternoon swim that cost us 25 cents each to enter the pool. Fortunately, Adams park had a lifeguard, so it was safe to swim there.

When I was four our family was having Sunday dinner at the nearby Carawana Lodge. (We still lived nearby on Beecher Street.) I wandered off into the pool. Buster was watching me but could not hear my screams as I went under water. My Aunt Edna was nearby and heard me. She frantically jumped into the pool, clothes and all, to rescue me as I sank further under the water.

My happiest young times were with my cousin. We rode our bikes in the street and I always rode first so I could listen out for cars and turn and signal him a warning. He helped me make flying model airplanes. In fact, he covered all the balsa frames as he was the best at covering the planes with paper or silk then painting the covers with airplane "dope" or paint. Years later he would make huge gas motor flying models and compete in Model Airplane Shows.

During the summers when he was home from school, we traveled the city together. It was not always easy trying to speak for and explain why I was speaking up for my tall cousin. We were like Mutt and Jeff, one tall and the other little. Once on a trolley bus, we were trying to get off and my cousin kept pulling the cord to advise the driver to open the exit door. Angry and frustrated the driver yelled and cursed at us. "Stand on the floor treadle and it will open, you damn, dumb kids," he yelled. Nearly crying with anger, I yelled back, "Don't you know he is deaf?" I could not comprehend why all others didn't understand folks like my cousin. Louis told our family, "I go with him along because he is my ears."

One problem that bothered Louis was the term "deaf and dumb." He could not understand why he was called "dumb." He would thump his forehead with a tight fist, the sign for dumb, and say, "I'm not dumb". While he was at Cave Springs School our folks noticed that when he came home on weekends, he was ravenously hungry. He was a growing boy and they thought little of it until he mentioned that at school, they were not allowed to have second servings of some food and certainly no seconds on milk. "That's strange," our moms commented.

We visited the school one weekend and my aunt had Louis (Buster) bring a few of his classmates along and my mother and aunt quizzed them about the food situation. At first, they were hesitant to tell us, but after my aunt interrogated them through my cousin's sign language. (He explained that they would not get into trouble for telling us the truth.) my aunt and mother learned that all the kids went to bed hungry.

For some of the students from impoverished rural homes, however the food seemed fine, better than they were used to. It was certainly better than their grits, cornbread and an occasional piece of "fat back" or ham. Yet the others from middle class homes vowed that the food was not enough, small servings, few seconds and a minimum of extra milk. They said they were punished if they complained.

My aunt and mom took their stories to heart, rented the Magnolia Tea Room at down-town Rich's Department store and immediately, through a luncheon, raised enough money for legal help, and contacted an Atlanta attorney. They interrogated more of the deaf students and presented their findings directly to the governor. The governor, Ellis Arnall was the first progressive governor (1943 to 1947) that Georgia had had in years. It seems that the entire school staff had been hired during the Eugene Talmadge administrations. Many if not most state jobs were tied to the political fortunes of the Georgia politicians. That era represented some of the worst and most corrupt administrations in the state's history.

Governor Arnall got right onto an official investigation and determined that the corruption started at the top of the school hierarchy. One of, if not the head of the school, had a deal with the dairy and the food contractors to pay, say $1000 for food, but to have delivered only $500 worth of food and milk, then divide the unspent funds among the sellers and kickbacks to the people in the school administration. Truly, the kids were going to bed hungry. My folks told me later that those responsible were indicted and the school head was given a choice, resign or go to jail. I never knew the whole details of the ultimate solution, except that I know my aunt and mom saw to it that the deaf students never again went to bed hungry. The school had been under the Georgia Welfare Department and was then transferred to the State Education Department.

Years passed as Lewis moved from class to class. During his last years he played end on the school's football team. He was already six feet tall and was an outstanding player. The deaf school played several hearing schools including Marist School in Atlanta. The referees not only used whistles, but flashlights to signal so both teams could see or hear the calls on the field. Some of the Marist team players claimed that the deaf boys could call signals by sign language and the Marist team had no idea what they were saying. They claimed that the deaf boys who could lip-read easily picked up Marist's signals. They wondered if that was fair!

Many of the deaf kids had come from poor rural farming homes where they had been forced to work hard in the fields. They were strong and tough players.

Before Louis finished high school, Aunt Edna and her husband (my Uncle Wayne, the friend that had given my dad a job at the Henry Grady Hotel during the Great Depression of the 1930s) moved to Washington, D.C. Louis, after graduation entered Gallaudet College, a well-known college for the deaf in Washington. When I served as a House Congressional Page in 1950, I spent many weekends at their home on Military Road, near Rock Creek Park. On Monday mornings Louis drove me, on his way to work, into the city to my 6:15 a.m. class at the page school, then located in the Library of Congress.

After college Louis applied to the Department of the Army, was interviewed and was curtly turned away and told they had no place for the "handicapped deaf." He searched around D.C. and applied to the Interior Department and got a job in Geological Survey. His section was involved in making maps from the new aeronautical photography methods developed during World War II. The planes would fly over land and photograph the landscape, just as the military had done of enemy territory and the beaches for bombing or later invasion.

On June 25, 1950, North Korean military forces crossed the 38th Parallel into South Korea and the Korean Conflict began. Suddenly we were at war again, fifteen years after the defeat of the Axis forces in Europe and the Pacific. The military did not have sufficient maps of Korea, only old captured Japanese maps that were inadequate and out of date. A military unit might be on one side of a hill or mountain range or river and have no idea what lay on the other side. The army was panicked in its desperate situation.

The Department of the Interior was called upon to map the region. American reconnaissance planes flew over Korea and the air photos were sent back to Washington where Louis and his special office staff assigned to the task, took the film and plotted the landscape and drew the topography, (using horse hair brushes or fine horse hair filaments under microscopes to draw the land contours).

Climbing Stone Mountain, 1940
Left to right: Harvey Watts, Louis "Buster" Keaton, Jerry Watts
(Photo from author's collection)

During the process and after the project was completed the maps were to be sent to the Department of the Army. Since many of Louis's friends were aware of the army turning Louis down for a job, they elected him to "personally deliver" the maps to the Department of the Army. They reminded the Army that "they did not hire the handicapped," but that these now were the guys making, for them, all the military maps.

In 1950 my cousin Louis Keaton married Mary Ann Carpenter, from Arkansas, also a graduate of Gallaudet College. Louis continued in the Geological Survey Department of the Interior, later located in Palo Alto, California. They had two hearing children. My aunt and uncle moved to Palo Alto so that they could be near their grandchildren and expose them to normal hearing family surroundings. Louis retired after many years of faithful service to our country demonstrating that many disabilities or challenges as they are now called can be overcome by diligent attention, "old fashioned gumption" and sustained effort.

TONY AND HORSEMANSHIP

My pinto pal

His name was Tony. He lived in a green pasture beside my granddad's small farm in rural Arkansas. He was not "broken," yet Tony allowed me to ride him bareback around the place while I held on to his long, flowing mane. I was twelve. He was two.

Tony was a pinto with big brown eyes, flowing mane and a long white tail. He appeared at our fence in the morning when I went to collect the chicken eggs from an old wooden shed that Granddaddy Perdue called the hen house. I first noticed him throwing his head as if to say, "This way, boy."

When I finished my chores helping my grandfather, I often eased up to the wire fence and Tony nuzzled me for an apple or a little handful of oats. I stepped up on an old tree stump, slipped over the barbed-wire fence, climbed on a shaky wooden crate and settled on his back. He would turn his head as if to say, "Are you okay?" and we sauntered across the field. He trotted gently into the nearby pine thicket. Sometimes I dismounted and walked back to the fence. He shuffled behind and pushed me with his nose. He rubbed his head along my side smelling for the apple which I often hid in my pocket.

When we arrived at the fence, I gave him the apple and he wandered off. He headed to the other side of the field toward his barn shed and water trough.

I begged my mom to buy Tony for me, but she explained, "He isn't really 'broke,' and we don't know what he would do if a saddle was put on him." She looked out the window into the yard and commented, "And besides we would have to ship him back to Georgia by freight train."

It was the end of summer and I sobbed as we pulled out of the gravel drive, shaded by the chinaberry trees, into the dusty road along a muddy pond. Tony stood at the fence throwing his head then turned and all I could see was his swishing long tail.

We headed for the main highway and the railroad station in Pine Bluff to board our train home.

"I'll find you a horse that's already trained," my mom said.

Shortly after returning to Georgia my mom found a roan gelding thoroughbred. The seller said that the horse was not big enough or fast enough for the racetrack. He had been gaited for a pleasure horse.

It was a while before he began to nuzzle up to me and I began to love that big guy as much as I had loved Tony.

My mom was an excellent horsewoman. She was taught by my grandmother Perdue, herself a fine rider. Mother rode with her friend Mildred Richon, an Army captain's wife, at the old cavalry stables of Fort McPherson outside Atlanta. From the time I was five or six, she would come home, still wearing her tall leather riding boots. "Help me get these off," she would say to me. "Pull. Pull harder." I sat on the hard wood floor and tugged and tugged until we finally pulled the dusty boots off.

We stabled my horse, Prince Junior, at Atlanta's Adams Park where a number of young Atlanta kids had horses. My mom engaged the stable manager, a crusty though prominent Atlanta trainer, "Pop" Miller, to teach me horsemanship along with several other kids about my age.

Our horsemanship classes were tough, and I began to wonder if I had made the right choice in wanting a real horse. "Pop" Miller was a firm taskmaster. He stood on the grass in the middle of the dirt ring, popping a long leather whip to keep our attention or waving a riding crop and yelling his commands, "Hands up, toes in, heels down, loosen the reins, straighten those backs."

Often, his series of commands went like this, "Now trot, walk, turn-about, now canter. Keep the right lead," he would yell as we turned our horses into, then away from the log fence surrounding the track.

Most of the kids had three-gaited or pleasure horses or ponies. He expected   real horsemanship and demanded strict observance of his instructions.

One of the early lessons "Pop" Miller taught was to learn to safely fall off the horse. I fell off so often (not always voluntarily) that I felt like a stunt rider. "It's okay to fall but when you hit the track, roll, if possible. Roll away from the horse."

My mom reaffirmed "Pop's" rules of horsemanship and scolded me if I didn't want to ride for some reason. "He's not a plaything. He's a responsibility and you have to take care of him," my mom declared. "It doesn't matter how bad the weather is, you must exercise that animal."

Once, while exercising my horse on a slushy muddy track in cold mid-winter, the horse on a canter stumbled and fell. I sailed over his head, flipped in-midair and landed on my back. Apparently, I lay there until I was conscious enough to realize that my horse was standing over me and nudging me, maybe wondering if I were alive. I was able to crawl through the mud to the log fence and was shortly found by one of the stable hands and carried to "Pop" Miller's quarters attached to the barn up on the hill nearby. I recovered within a few hours and was able to be driven home. There were no broken bones, and in a day or two I was back on my horse. "You must get right back on," my mom demanded, "or you'll never be a decent horseman."

I learned that responsibility for a huge animal was not all fun, but hard work. I shoveled manure from the stalls, provided fresh water as well as fresh straw and sawdust on the floor. We had to be sure the hay was dry and clean. If we did extra stall cleaning or grooming and washing of the other animals, we earned extra buckets of grain. Two hours of barn labor was worth a full tin bucket of grain.

There were other Atlanta adults with wonderful five-gaited American saddle-bred show horses, hunters, and harness racers (trotters) at the stable. The youngsters had to clear the ring when those folks came to ride or train their horses. That was serious and expensive business.

One day while sitting on the log fence surrounding the dirt track, I was watching my mom and Mister Milner (owner of an Atlanta textile factory) ride in the ring with beautiful five-gaited horses, all lathered up. It was magnificent to see them "racking, rack on," as their hooves thundered majestically about the ring. Sadly, I was never the rider to compare with my mother.

There was great interest in the equestrian movement in Atlanta. During our first year boarding my horse, the Adams Park Horse Show Association was formed initiating one of Atlanta's annual horse shows.

In the barn, a few stalls away, lived a dapple, gray pony named Buddy. He belonged to a petite eleven-year old girl with beautiful blonde hair and big blue eyes. Lynn was the best rider of the preteen kids and I thought she was the cutest. I loved to ride in the ring with her and Buddy. She was so elegant and poised on her little steed. We competed in a few horse shows. She won them all.

As much as I liked her, I felt shy around her. I helped her wash and groom Buddy, yet I wonder if she ever noticed me.

Lynn Renieke riding Buddy, October 1945
"She always won."
Note the Blue Ribbon attached to her pony's bridle.
(Photo from author's collection)

**Author and Prince Junior during riding lessons
Adams Park Stables
c. 1945-1946**
(Photo from author's collection)

"Pop" Miller
Adams Park Stables
1945-1946
(Photo from author's collection)

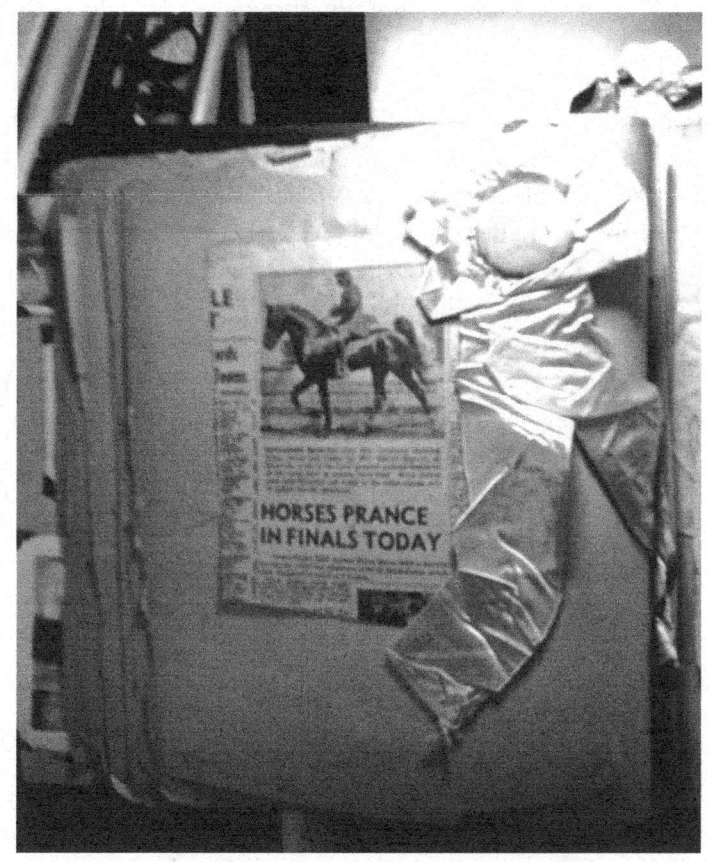

First Annual Adams Park Horse Show
Adams Park Horse Show Association
October 13–14, 1945
(Photo from author's collection)

DECEMBER 7, 1946

"Don't come downtown..."

On a cold December morning at about 7 a.m. the phone rang, waking my mom who shuffled from her bedroom and struggled to put on her house coat. She tiptoed out into the hall and picked up the receiver of the clanging phone. "Hello," she answered sleepily.

There was a silence, then my dad's hoarse voice responded, "Oh my God, Dorothy, it's horrible. Don't come downtown today." He seemed to have difficulty saying more.

"What's the matter?" she asked.

"The Winecoff is on fire." He hesitated. "The people are screaming out the windows. I saw a body fall from high up. Oh my God, it's horrible."

My mom held the phone's receiver close to her head, still not understanding what my dad was saying. "You mean it's the Winecoff on fire? How can that be?"

"Oh my, it's terrible. The firemen can't reach the upper floors and people are streaming sheets out the windows trying to get out. Smoke and flames are coming out the windows. The folks above the flames must not be able to get out."

My mom, still in disbelief, asked, "Is Nell McDuffie there? Is she okay?" Our friend, Nell was the secretary to Mr. L. O. Moseley, the general manager of the Henry Grady Hotel a block away. Nell had been his secretary when a few years before he had managed the Winecoff Hotel. She still lived at the Winecoff Hotel though she worked at the Henry Grady. My dad had many friends who worked or lived at the Winecoff. The fire was personal to him.

"Don't know," my dad answered. He was talking from the outside phone used by the Grady Hotel doorman. "There's a cop nearby and I'll ask about any folks already out."

"Don't come downtown," he said again. "It's just too awful."

The Journal and Constitution newspapers described the fire as the worst in hotel history. Our friend Nell survived the fire by crawling across a fireman's ladder that stretched between the rear of the hotel to the scorched Mortgage Guarantee Building ten feet across an alleyway along Ellis Street.

Gutted Winecoff Hotel
Weeks after the devastating fire of December 7, 1946
Corner of Peachtree Street and Ellis Street
(Photo by author, 1946)

Of the 304 guests in the hotel that night, 119 died. About 65 were injured and 120 were rescued uninjured. Among the deaths were thirty high school students on a state YMCA Club visit to Atlanta for a youth-in-government program. That night my dad lost many friends.

The Winecoff fire and the tragic Chicago La Salle Hotel fire in June of the same year prompted significant changes in North American building fire codes.

Thinking back to this tragedy I recalled that my mom and dad had filed for divorce in December of 1945. The divorce was finalized in February 1946 and my dad moved into the Winecoff Hotel.

There I visited him on weekends. After several months they reconciled and remarried on their old anniversary, September 21, 1946. I calculated that he moved out of the hotel about two and a half months before the fire.

A PERDUE FAMILY

"You're more Perdue."

My mother always told me I was "more Perdue." more like her family than the other side of the family, but I did not understand what she meant. It was only later in life that I began to understand her meaning.

My mother had two sisters, Edna and Elizabeth, and the three of them were very close. Each was a complete and versatile individual in her own right. From them, I learned integrity, and its cousins, honesty and ambition. From them I learned to laugh.

The most recent generations of their Perdue heritage began in Greenville, Alabama, where James Hilliard Perdue was the patriarch of the Perdue family to which they belonged. In Greenville's Magnolia Cemetery lie the remains of many of the Perdues to whom they lay claim.

My first visit to Greenville, Alabama, was in 1967 for the burial of Alice Kellam Perdue, my mother's great aunt, who died at age 93. At her death, Aunt Alice's body was brought home to Alabama from her residence in Pine Bluff, Arkansas. Her great nephew, Jack Perdue of Pine Bluff, accompanied her casket. She was buried in Magnolia Cemetery.

My mother died in 1960, at the age of fifty, some seven years before Aunt Alice passed away. My dad and I represented my mother at the graveside services for her dear aunt. Alice was laid to rest between the remains of her husband, John Southerlin Perdue and her mother Mrs. Mattie Kellam, born June 4, 1835, and died May 21, 1900. Mrs. Kellam was the wife of Robert Kellam of

Opelika, Ala. John Perdue had waited since 1929 for Alice to join him in eternity.

Aunt Alice and John never had children. My mother was born and grew up in Pine Bluff, Arkansas. She was always delighted when she was allowed to visit Alice and John in Pine Bluff. They treated her as their own.

Dorothy Perdue Watts
September 1928, about the time of her marriage
(Photo from author's collection)

I became interested in the names of Perdue ancestors about whom I knew little during the 1950s. My Great Aunt Laura Perdue Mahoney brought an old worn and tattered "Big Bible" from Birmingham to our house for my mother to see.

In every family there must be a family Bible that gives the history of ancestors. We often take for granted that our ancestors existed, but it is not until we touch the pages and read the scribbling therein do we realize that they really breathed, laughed and cried and we that we can almost touch them.

There, in our family Bible, in flowing hand-written inscriptions were names with dates for births, marriages, and deaths. Whole lifetimes scribbled with different inks, different scripts, written at different times, representing lives, most already gone. It was a mystery to think of each individual, not merely as a name written in the book, but names representing lives experiencing happiness, joy, sadness, grief and death.

One page with Victorian script adorning that page read simply, "Marriages." At the top of the page in "long hand" is written, "James H. Perdue and Jeanie M. Franklin were married on the 5th day of May 1857." Somewhat out of order, is the listing below the James H. notation, "Hillary Perdue, Third son of James H. Perdue and Jeanie Franklin [barely legible] and Elizabeth B. Evans were married October 15, 1878."

On another page, we read again in a different hand, "Hill Perdue and Bette B. Evans were married October 15, 1878, at Montgomery, Ala." This page also lists, "Nellie Perdue and L. G. Hill, married at Montgomery August 1, 1897." On this page is noted my grandfather, "Edward Evans Perdue and Effie Baw were married in Pine Bluff, Arkansas December 27, 1906."

At the end of the book, on a page with the fancy Victorian script title we see the simple word, "Births." Here I see my mother's name, "Dorothy Jenkins Perdue, born in Pine Bluff, Arkansas June 21, 1910."

My mother looked at that date and remarked, "It was really 1911." She held to that date until my dad corrected it when we had to select the dates for her tombstone. "She just shaved off a year," said my dad with a smile.

The final page of listings is noted in that elegant script as "Deaths." On this page we read, "Robert Perdue fourth child of James H. Perdue and his wife Jeanie M. Franklin, departed this life," No date is noted.

At the bottom of the page we sadly read, "Lilly Perdue, daughter of James H. Perdue and Jeanie M. Franklin departed this life 14 September 1871," the time of the year when the leaves were turning, dying and falling to the ground. In Magnolia Cemetery there is a tiny stone marking this child's grave, partly covered by grass and barely visible which reads simply, "Lilly Perdue."

These were my mother's people. These were the pioneers of Alabama and the Deep South. These are the folks to whom we owe a debt of life and hope. They lived their lives as best they could. Some overcame great obstacles, and some did not. Yet each has his or her own story and it is through remembering them that we celebrate their lives.

In the Magnolia Cemetery is a tombstone that reads:

He called no hours his own
Through heat and cold he
Went his way alone
He gave himself unselfish
Without measure
In service to mankind
He found his pleasure
John Aaron Kendale M. D.
May 27, 1872, – May 9, 1934

This epitaph might well have been written for ancestor, Dr. James Lewis Perdue who served Butler County, Alabama, and its rural population for so many years. He was born in 1851 and died in 1932. There are family stories of him riding in his horse carriage making many midnight calls. It being so late, Dr. Perdue would fall asleep in the carriage on the way home. His faithful horse knew the way and would trot directly home and stop at the appropriate spot for the good doctor to awaken, climb out of the carriage and go into his house for the remainder of the night.

PINE BLUFF, ARKANSAS

Before they moved to the farm, my grandparents lived in a large, rambling, clapboard house on West Barraque Street in the town of Pine Bluff, Arkansas. Pine Bluff was a railroad town and the city depended on the railroad yards for a great deal of local employment. A number of relatives lived in the town, some distant and some close cousins.

My mother's favorite, Aunt Alice, who has already been mentioned, lived near downtown along the railroad tracks that ran through the center of town. After her husband died in 1929, she opened one of her several houses as a rooming house for transient railroaders. She was a firm housekeeper and allowed no "liquor drinking" in the house, a tough rule for those rugged railroad men.

Alice and her husband, John Perdue had been founding members of the local First Baptist Church and according to my mom were front-row sitters. Though my mom said John did take a snort of liquor now and then, there was no whiskey in their cabinets. Yet, Alice in her later days regularly took a toddy in the afternoon, prescribed by her doctor. My folks were not opposed to alcohol and it was always available in our house and I suspect it was in Aunt Alice's when they visited. I suspect Alice and my folks had a toddy or so more than just in the afternoon.

Aunt Alice was a known character in Pine Bluff. She continued to drive her 1929 Dodge Brothers automobile, left to her by her husband the year he died. She drove mostly from her house to downtown for shopping. She drove in the middle of the street and everyone, including the police, recognized Ms. Perdue and moved aside when she passed by. She had promised me the old Dodge, but two clever men convinced her that they would love to have the car with the high wheelbase to travel the muddy back roads to fish. She took their wishes seriously and sold them the old car. She bought a brand new 1951 Studebaker, the most modern and flashy designed auto of the day. Folks said it was hard to tell the front from the rear, it was so modern. It stayed mostly in her garage until my dad drove it during visits, which delighted her. "Harvey, you just put so much pep in my car, I love to ride with you," she said to him.

After her husband died, a devoted childhood friend came to live with her. Miss Nettie had never married, and they lived together until Nettie passed away and was buried in her home state. Nettie was a thin, quiet, almost invisible person. She had cataracts and shuffled about the house with great difficulty toward the end of her life. I remember being a bit afraid of her with her heavy thick glasses that made her appear a bit scary to a child.

Alice remained an independent woman, who along with her faithful housekeeper, Bertha, ran the boarding house until she was ninety-three and passed away from acute pneumonia.

In the backyard of my grandparent's Pine Bluff house was an old servant's quarters where Roxy, a white haired older black woman lived. I barely remember her except that I recall her working in the huge kitchen with my grandmother and Roxy's great-tasting cornbread and fried chicken. I do recall Roxy remained a slender, very neat woman. Her voice was high-pitched, and she was quite chatty. She was always gentle in her manner to the children and grandchildren of my grandparents. She had served the family for years and now too old, she retired to the little, neatly painted white house. She spent her last days rocking on her little porch. She had no children. My grandmother and granddad cared for her until she died.

Roxy's little White House
West Barraque Street, Pine Bluff, Arkansas
"She spent her last days rocking on her little porch."
(Photo from author's collection)

"GEE-HAW COCKLEBUR"

A mule called Cocklebur

The garden measured no more than an acre or so, yet my granddad was able to raise all the vegetables they could eat – corn, beans, tomatoes, and watermelons, too. Instead of a tractor, he had an old scruffy brown mule named "Cocklebur."

The summer of 1946 or '47 I visited their farm in Pine Bluff, Arkansas. "You want to learn to plow?" my granddad asked.

I looked at my mom wondering if he was teasing or what. "He means it, would you like to learn?" my mom responded.

"Maybe," I cautiously answered.

My granddad was a railroader for the Cotton Belt Railroad and was at the point of retiring. He bought a little farm and moved from the town some five or six miles out beyond what was known as "the Dew Drop," an old roadhouse and cafe-bar, called "The Dew Drop Inn."

A dusty gravel road led from the main highway to their little farm. Along the way, near their front gate across from the farm, was a shallow pond that would play into their future adventures when my grandmother was pitched from my horse and landed in the muddy pond. That incident resulted in sending the horse to a family friend to be used by his overseer on his cotton farm.

I had helped my granddad weed, dig, hoe, and rake in the garden and had watched the mule graze in the rough-furrowed, now fallow, pasture surrounding the single-story clapboard house. That summer, having just moved in, they had no indoor plumbing and instead had a well pump on the back porch with a long pump handle for drawing clear cool water. It was unlike city water and I was told that the funny taste was sulfur in the ground.

About forty yards away, behind a low-slung barn in the field away from the garden, was a little shed known as the outhouse. It was an upscale wooden out-house, a two-seater with a Sears-Roebuck catalog for paper.

"Be careful," my granddad had said to me. "A fellow down the road got bit on his bottom by a black widow spider and he got pretty sick, so watch out before you sit in the outhouse." That admonishment and the hoeing and digging in the dusty, hot Arkansas sun, convinced me that farming would not be my chosen profession. Yet I was challenged, before giving up on farming to learn to plow behind a real mule.

We gathered the leather harness, and leather straps, fitted the tack onto Cocklebur and attached him to the single blade plow. Off he went, my granddad helping, dragging me and the plow down the deep furrow. "Not bad," my granddad nodded as he turned the plow over to me. As a-twelve-year old, the plow was bigger than me, but I hung on, yelling "gee" or "haw" as we ended each fresh row.

Though I never really felt like an accomplished farmer, I was proud that I could at least plow a straight line. "Yep, not bad for a city boy," my granddad allowed.

Granddaddy Ed Perdue on Prince Junior
We retired my horse on my granddad's small farm.
Pine Bluff, Arkansas, c. 1948
(Photo from author's collection)

WE DON'T EAT ROOSTERS

He was the terror of the yard

One summer in south Arkansas, my job was to collect fresh hen eggs every morning and bring them into the house to my grandmother, Mamaw. My problem was the huge white rooster who guarded his hens from all intruders. Each time I entered from the backporch steps I had to be wary of the defender of chicken womanhood. We didn't have a name for that dreaded enemy except, "That rooster."

The chicken yard was about thirty paces from the back porch, enclosed with a five or six-foot wire fence, yet the darn rooster managed to fly over the wire fence surrounding the enclosure. There he strutted, fluttering his wild wings and cocking his head, eycing me, first with one eye then the other, as I approached the gate to the chicken yard. When I got near, he would run at me wildly cackling, trying to nip me or throttle me with his spurs.

Usually, I was able to unlatch the wire holding the gate and enter the yard, slamming the wire gate behind me and rushing into the low wooden enclosure known as the chicken house. Inside were a couple of rows of orange fruit crates made into nests laden with straw where the hens could lay their eggs. Just beyond the nests and high up in the little shed was the chicken roost where the hens spent the night or sat cackling loudly during the day.

Outside the wire enclosure the rooster fluttered madly, trying to jump the fence to attack any intruder. He had more trouble getting in than getting out. I gathered the eggs, placed into them into my straw basket, despite his antics and the protesting hens.

When he realized he could not get back into the pen he waited patiently like a medieval assassin, squatting in the dirt ready to lunge on the intruder. Now I had to get back through the fence and scurry as fast as I could to the worn back porch steps.

After a few days, I realized that alone I was no match for that rooster. In a pile of discarded wood, I found several plaster lathing boards that measured about a half inch by two inches around and were several feet long. I stationed them along the path to the hen house so that I could more readily fight The Defender of Hens.

Sundays in the country there was always a great Southern mid-day dinner of mashed potatoes, green beans, corn, tomatoes, butter and jelly biscuits, fruit pies and, best of all, my grandmother served up deep-fried chicken. My granddad selected the fryers for the meal.

One Saturday he and I ventured out into the back yard, "You can pick out the chicken for dinner," he said to me. "You choose and we'll have it for Sunday dinner." It was not uncommon for the chickens to venture out of the chicken yard into the back, nibbling food from the gritty ground surrounding my grandparent's country home. That day I had a choice of one of many birds.

I looked about the yard and right there among the nibbling hens was that dreaded enemy, the white rooster. I pointed and gleefully volunteered, "That's the one, that white one."

My granddad glanced over to the corner of the yard. "That's a rooster son, we don't eat roosters."

Not unlike the Biblical story, Herodias' daughter, Salome received a promise from her stepfather Herod Antipas, I knew if my granddad said I could choose, he would not go back on his word. "That's the one I want granddaddy, that mean one."

He again reiterated, "But we don't eat roosters."

"Daddy Perdue, you said I could pick," I reminded him.

"You're right, I did say that," he confessed. Grimly he walked over grabbed the white rooster, lifted it up and holding it with one hand, with the other literally wrung its neck and with one pull the head was off. He dropped the victim and watched as it flitted and fluttered wildly about, blood spewing from its neck, a chicken running with its head cut off.

I licked my chops that Sunday as I tasted "fried rooster."

BIRD HUNTING

"He was a serious hunter…"

I must have been nine or ten when I hunted with my Granddaddy Perdue. He was a serious bird and duck hunter, having hunted in the rice paddies of Stuttgart, Arkansas, and the flat fields around Pine Bluff. In his earlier years, even while living in the town he had many bird dogs that lived in the yard and under the house. They preferred the cool dirt, despite a shed in the yard.

On this day, Granddaddy Perdue and I were hunting in the far back woods edging up to the plowed limits of the farm. I had my own 20-gauge double barrel shotgun and Granddaddy Perdue had a 12 or 16-gauge pump. Happily, we headed to the woods. "Keep your shotgun open and pointed to the ground. Never point it toward anyone," Granddaddy Perdue had preached. "We don't want any accidents."

Years before, when I could barely see to the top of tables, I had watched him as he brought home his game, then cleaned his birds on the old back porch. "This one's for you," he said as he tossed the dove upon the rough wooden table.

I stood nearby, fascinated, watching him. Then he began the ritual of cleaning the birds. Suddenly he began cleaning my bird and I burst out in tears and ran inside to my grandmother's kitchen, grabbed her around the skirt and screamed, "Mamaw, he's peeling my bird."

Perhaps I didn't realize that we were really going to eat them. I had obviously never connected hunting and eating. My grandmother hugged me and quietly soothed me, "Your granddad is just preparing the birds for dinner."

I'm not sure that appeased me, for I never forgot his "peeling my bird."

On the afternoon of our hunting spree, we settled into a position of crossfire near a covey of quail. "You stay here while I go over yonder and we can fire into the covey when they rise," my granddad advised. I waited quietly, checked my gun, and readied for the shot. With a disquieting loud flurry from the bushes some thirty yards away, a flock of quail arose. My granddad fired several shots and a number of birds fluttered, then fell to the ground. I stood frozen, watching, failing to fire a single shot.

My granddad, in a worried tone called out across the field, "Son, you okay?"

I didn't answer, still frozen with distress at the thought of actually killing those harmless birds.

Granddaddy Perdue quickly collected his birds, stuffed them into the hunting bag on his shoulder and eased over to where I stood motionless.

He had a strange expression. "Did your gun jam? Are you okay?" he again muttered as he approached through the prickly briars where I was hidden.

I stood motionless, now with tears in my eyes "I just didn't want to shoot those birds."

I saw a change in his expression from worry to gentle concern as he kindly reached out, took my shotgun, opened the breech, removed the shells, slipped them into his vest pocket then handed the gun back. "It's all right son, we don't have to shoot any more today."

Silently, side by side we trudged back to the farmhouse. We walked up the few steps to the porch. He laid his sack of birds on the old wooden table. We went inside. I stared up at him, "Sorry Granddad, I just couldn't shoot those poor birds."

He patted me on the head with his rough hand and quietly said, "I understand. It's all right."

He never mentioned the incident and I never hunted with him, ever again.

Many years later, after my granddad died, my cousin Johnny inherited his shotguns.

TRAGEDY HITS HOME

"He was the brightest of the cousins..."

Tragedy would hit my family when I was fourteen years old. During the summers, my mother and I often visited our Aunt Laura and Uncle Will in Birmingham, Alabama. Aunt Laura was my mom's aunt, sister to Granddaddy Perdue and later in her life she and Uncle Will adopted an infant. She named him Neal.

"Neal is adopted," my mom once confided to me. "But we love him just the same as any of the cousins." This was to ring true as years later I learned I was also adopted. I guess they loved me, too.

In 1935 Neal Mahoney and I were christened together at Woodlawn Presbyterian Church in Birmingham. We were both infants.

I always thought Neal was the smartest of my several cousins. Certainly, he was more ambitious and more determined than the rest of us. He was what some might call a young entrepreneur. From age twelve and into his early teens he raised chickens and sold their eggs, did yard work, had a paper route and saved enough money to pay for a "Whizzer Bike." This was a motorized bicycle, much smaller than a small motorcycle. Several of his friends in the neighborhood owned these bikes and often rode them after school through the neighborhood.

One afternoon while riding only a few blocks from his home, crossing a residential intersection a drunk driver ran the stop sign crashing through four youngsters, all on their motor bikes. Several were severely injured, but Neal was thrown against the road curb and sustained a massive head injury. Helmets were not required in those days. The Birmingham newspaper had an article that stated, "This youngster's youth may save his life."

It, however, was not to be. Neal died after brain surgery within a couple days of the accident. I remember my mom crying softly in our hallway as she put the phone receiver down after having learned of Neal's death.

I was not allowed to go to the funeral. I'm told my folks thought it would be too traumatic for me to attend. It was not until weeks later when I visited Birmingham and saw his mangled bike in the basement and visited the cemetery to place flowers on his grave, that I realized Neal was really gone.

The driver of the car that hit Neal was tried for manslaughter and received a long jail sentence. Many neighbors suggested that my aunt sue the man, but she said, "He has a family and will suffer enough."

It was hard for me to understand her forgiveness. I guess I never really forgave the man for taking my cousin's life.

MY DAD:
1907–1972

"It was how he played the game."

Harvey Brite Watts was born February 3, 1907, at home in Acworth, Georgia, one of nine surviving children. His father was Joseph Brite Watts and his mother was Lucy Mae Kemp.

Harvey's brothers were, Charles "Cotton" Watts, James Paul, "Jimmy," and Joseph Brite (J. B). Another male infant died shortly after birth. The last words of his mother, who died at about 93 years, were a series of mumbled words, calling out for her deceased husband and her long-dead baby. His sisters were Myrtle, Fannie, Jo, Ida Mae, and Hazel.

Harvey's mother, Lucy Mae Kemp had been reared by a maternal aunt and uncle, when her own mother and dad died when Lucy was very young. According to family history, Lucy Mae married Joseph Brite against family wishes and took her inheritance of property and houses with her.

My mother told me that Lucy Mae's family thought Joseph Brite was "not good enough" for her, and some said he squandered her inheritance. It is not uncommon for parents to feel that a man is not good enough for their daughter, but when love intervenes it may not be their opinion that matters. I do know, from my observations, they were devoted to each other. I don't know what his initial business was, but during his lifetime he became a grocer and butcher. Later, during the Depression of the 1930s, his grocery business assured food on the table for his large reassembled family.

Because of early financial difficulties, the boys worked to help the family. Harvey sold newspapers on the streets of downtown Atlanta. He remembered selling the special edition of the *Georgian* reporting the sinking of the "Lusitania." He remembered selling papers reporting the end of the First World War.

Harvey attended school until the fourth grade. After that, work kept him out of school, on and off through eighth grade. He didn't attend high school. However, he was well-read and gained a great "street smart" education. He used to say to me, "Bud, you may be a little book smart, but you're not street smart."

His older brother "Cotton" became a vaudeville actor and comedian and appeared in a couple of Hollywood movies around the late 1930s or early 1940s. He became popular as an entertainer on the Southern night club and vaudeville stage circuit, often a headliner at Atlanta night spots.

Another brother, "Jimmy" James Paul, became a professional boxer and the Southern Featherweight Champion in the late 1920s. He won the title in May 0f 1928. Harvey accompanied Jimmy as a–fill the card–boxer. He was his brother's "second" and traveled with him and the boxing trainer and manager during their younger days.

My cousin, Dr. Bill Manus, has shared many of the newspaper clippings and articles describing Jimmy's remarkable career. Jimmy was a gifted boxer, able to dodge and weave, never the gruff power boxer, but the light "hard to hit" guy. He was the original "Light as a Butterfly."

Jimmy retired from the Arkansas State Patrol Administration and was always proud of his patrol badge and the men with whom he served. My dad and I attended his funeral in Little Rock, Arkansas. As he viewed the coffin with tears in his eyes, my dad remarked, "Over two hundred fights and not a scar on his face."

Harvey B. Watts about the time of his marriage
September 1928
(Photo from author's collection)

While traveling with Jimmy, Harvey met his future bride, Dorothy Jenkins Perdue, in Little Rock, Arkansas. She and her sister Edna were working on a lieutenant governor's election campaign. The sisters lived in Pine Bluff, so he drove down to their home to meet the family. When Harvey asked Dorothy's sister's boyfriend what Pine Bluff was "noted for," he answered, "The Zebras by Damn!" which was their football team.

Dorothy and Harvey married in September 1928 and she came to Atlanta to live. Harvey worked for Atlanta's *Georgian* newspaper and was injured in an auto accident in one of the paper's vehicles when it was hit by a chicken truck "with chickens flung, flapping, and flying everywhere," according to Harvey.

With the depression of 1929 and the 1930s, Harvey was out of work and Dorothy had to return to her family in Pine Bluff and he to his family in Atlanta.

Harvey's childhood friend, Wayne Keaton was the bell captain (later referred to as the superintendent of service) at the recently opened, "Five Hundred Fifty rooms with Five Hundred and Fifty baths," Henry Grady Hotel on Peachtree Street.

Wayne gave Harvey a job as a bellman, which provided an adequate income even in the depths of the depression. There were always those travelers with enough money to stay at big city hotels. Dorothy was able to return to Atlanta and to a small rented house on Beecher Street in the West End or Cascade area.

Harvey and his brothers were athletes and followed local and national sports. Harvey played semiprofessional baseball. The Henry Grady Hotel had a baseball team that competed with numerous Atlanta company teams during the 1930s and 1940s. My cousin Louis (Buster) Keaton was the bat boy #13 and I, at age 5 years was the mascot #0. I remember some of the games and we still have a child-size blue baseball uniform with "HENRY GRADY" embroidered in gold letters on the front and a big "ZERO" on the back.

Harvey had many boxing stories. He recalled a "card" which required him to fight or hold on for three rounds to fill a vacant slot for the night. He agreed to the three boxing rounds. He accidentally caught his opponent with a sharp left hook, knocking him to the floor. The boxer cursed him in a clinch and Harvey fought the full six rounds and won the boxing match.

He and Jimmy drove to New England in the late 1920s for a national feather weight championship match. Their "T-Model Ford" stalled in New York City on Fifth Avenue. The Georgia automobile license plate with a big illustrated "peach" in the center was noted by the husky, blue-coated, Irish cop who yelled at them, "Move on boys, you're out of the Pea Patch now."

According to the family story, they negotiated the finances for the fight money with "Ned" Fitzgerald of New Haven Conn., but because of the money arrangements with the "mob," the original deal fell through. They would receive a fee in payment if Jimmy won, but no prize money. They would only receive part of the "purse" when defending the title. My dad and his brother took their training fee, bought a new car and hit the road back south, pocketing the difference.

Years later, Marie, Jimmy's wife, confided that she always felt the manager sold them out. Apparently, the northern promoters were afraid the "Southern boy" would win, so they had altered the financial incentive and perhaps paid off the manager. Who knows?

In the mid-1930s, Harvey became the superintendent of service after his brother-in-law, Wayne Keaton left the Henry Grady Hotel business to work for the Georgia Power Company, becoming their top salesman.

Harvey worked six and half days a week so after a half-day on Sunday, we often met him in town for Sunday supper at one of the downtown restaurants, Ship Ahoy, Herrin's Restaurant, S&W Cafeteria, across from the Henry Grady hotel, or at a restaurant out Peachtree Street near the Fox Theater, known as The Tavern. Later we would dine at Aunt Fanny's Cabin out in Marietta. It was a usual hangout for visiting dignitaries and movie stars visiting Atlanta. Harvey Hester, a well-known Atlanta restaurateur, was part owner and ran Aunt Fanny's.

We often attended downtown Sunday evening services at the First Methodist Church. Dr. Pierce Harris, the minister, my dad's friend, was a popular man around town. He regularly wrote an editorial column for the *Atlanta Journal*. Dr. Harris was also a well-known former baseball player, a great golfer, and his other sport was fishing – not for fish – "a fisherman for Christ" he claimed.

In all my memory, the most distressing Sunday was the Sunday night of December 7, 1941. When we met my dad, we stood outside the lobby on Peachtree Street, shocked by the news of the Japanese surprise bombing attack on Pearl Harbor.

Months later, my dad Harvey and his childhood friend "Deke" Duke went down to the Draft Board Induction Center for the Army. Deke, in his mid-thirties was accepted for the Army. He served as a combat soldier and was ultimately wounded in Europe.

Harvey, about the same age was rejected because of legal blindness in one eye, which I think was secondary to his prior auto accident. (It is likely that the prior injury was a basilar skull fracture with old hematoma and injury and scar tissue to the optic nerve.) I think his deferment and failure of acceptance for military service bothered him the rest of his life. He had always been a physically strong person.

Since Harvey's formal education was limited, he appreciated the opportunity of a good education. Numerous young men worked for him and he made special accommodations for their work hours so that they could attend college. Among those attending college were the Cawthen boys, Frank and George. My mother was concerned and upset when she once saw Frank Cawthen sitting on the bellman's bench with paper showing through the sole of his shoe. She demanded that Harvey get Frank a pair of new shoes.

Frank attended Oglethorpe University before the War and during the War he held the rank of a Navy Commander and later a Navy Captain. George also attended Oglethorpe and was listed as the youngest U. S. Army Air Corps flight instructor. On weekends he took me flying in the Army Piper Cub trainer at the old Candler Field, used by the Army Air Corps. He was reassigned to the Bomber Ferry Command section of the Air Corps, delivering bombers to the far-off military bases in Africa to be flown in the air war over the Mediterranean and Europe. He often returned to Atlanta and brought piles of foreign bills and coins, enough to begin a small coin collection.

Many of the younger boys who worked in the hotel for my dad served during World War ll. He saved their jobs until they returned from the war. Though hotel rooms were scarce in Atlanta during the war, he made sure they had complimentary rooms at the hotel when they were home on leave.

ATLANTA ATHLETICS

We missed few sporting events

Since my dad had been a fine athlete, we rarely missed local sports events during the '40s and '50s. That included, throughout the seasons, the Atlanta Crackers Baseball team, Georgia Tech and the University of Georgia football, local basketball and the boxing matches held in the downtown city auditorium.

Working at the Henry Grady Hotel, my dad always had access to sporting event tickets. Sometimes we rode the streetcar out to Ponce de Leon ballpark, across from the old Sears building. It was easier to ride the streetcar rather than try to park out by the ballpark. From the hotel we could catch the car right out front on Peachtree and Cain Streets and ride all the way to the park. We usually sat in the third base box seats so we could better see the games. When the game was sold out, we sat in the bleachers.

The Southern Association had teams from all over the South: Chattanooga, Memphis, Little Rock, Mobile and Birmingham, for example. Many of the players started their major league careers in the Association. Many ended their careers finishing up in the minor leagues. So, we were able to see both ends of the professional careers of many outstanding players.

My mom and Aunt Edna opened a little restaurant in the "551 Hotel" near the ballpark. It was called "The 551 Tea Room." Many of the visiting ball players stayed at the hotel as well as several single Atlanta players. The little hotel was owned by Mr. D. T. Cannon, the brother of Mr. Cecil Cannon who owned the Henry Grady Hotel. (The story I heard was that Mr. Cecil bought the hotel for his brother, a small, mild-mannered fellow with a lively, buxom, fiery red-headed wife.) At the hotel I got to meet many of the Cracker players. Perhaps my favorite was Lloyd Gerhart who later played for the New York Giants.

On one occasion my dad surprised me. "I want to sit on the first base side so I can watch that new kid," he said to me. The new kid was Eddie Mathews who later became a famous major league player, an inaugural Atlanta Braves player in 1966 and a member of the Baseball Hall of Fame.

Many years later, in a new stadium I would see Hank Aaron, "The Hammer" hitting his home runs.

We often attended the Georgia Tech games. Through my dad's friendship with the coaches and trainers, I sat on the sideline bench with the players. Once I met and visited with Bob Hope and his comedian and actor buddy, Jerry Colonna.

One special game I recall (perhaps the 1945 game at Atlanta) was when the Hall of Fame member, Georgia's Charlie Trippi, and Tech's All-American Paul Duke collided almost on top of me along the sideline. They injured a photographer in the same tackling collision. I remember vividly his box camera flying through the air. I always wondered if he got a photograph of the collision.

During the war, Tech had many of what were known as the Navy V-12 class, or navy officer training members completing their college education before entering active military service. Many felt that the best players came from this group of students.

Sometimes when my dad couldn't go, he would call me and tell me that his boss, Mr. Mosley the hotel manager, wanted me to go with him. Mr. Mosley's son, Buck was away at school at McCallie in Chattanooga, so I was his substitute son for the day. That was always a fine time. A hotel bellman drove us out to Grant Field, the Tech stadium. We sat in the Atlanta City Council's special box in the West stands. The bellman would return and wait just outside the West Side gate in Mr. Moseley's big black Lincoln automobile and rush us back to the hotel before the traffic became impossible around the stadium and the guests returned to the hotel.

We also went to Athens, sometimes by car and occasionally on a special football train that carried folks over to the stadium. It parked on the railroad tracks near the stadium and waited until the game was over to return us to Atlanta's Terminal Station on the Spring Street viaduct.

There was always a lot of card playing, gambling, drinking and hullabaloo on the train if Georgia won, but a quiet ride back if they didn't. If Georgia won you could hear the big, loud, victory bell ringing all over the campus on the way to the train.

When I was eight, my dad and I attended perhaps the most famous of the Georgia/Georgia Tech football games on November 28, 1942. The members of that game are historical immortals in the archives of that long and enduring contest between great rivals.

Those players were Georgia Tech's Clint Castleberry who finished third in the Heisman Trophy award in 1942, and Georgia's Frank "Fireball" Sinkwich the Heisman Trophy winner that year. Along with Sinkwich, Charlie Trippi, and Van Davis and the Georgia team defeated Georgia Tech. After Georgia's victory the team was invited to the Rose Bowl in January 1943. There Georgia defeated UCLA, 9 to 0.

Georgia Tech's Clint Castleberry joined the Army Air Corps the next year and was lost with his air crew while flying a B-26 Bomber over the desert in North Africa in 1944.

Ticket stub and Bulldogs button with ribbon
GA. TECH vs. GA.
November 28, 1942
Sanford Stadium – Athens, Georgia
(Items from author's collection)

THE HENRY GRADY HOTEL

An Icon of the city

Atlanta's Henry Grady Hotel was named for Henry Woodfin Grady, a writer, public speaker, a promoter of the South, and the editor of the Atlanta Constitution in the late nineteenth century. Henry Grady was born May 24, 1850, in Athens, Georgia. He was the son of a wealthy Georgia planter, raised in the Old South. He was a child during the War Between the States. His father died as a result of "Yankee" wounds in that war.

Grady graduated from the University of Georgia in 1868, shortly after the Civil War that so divided our nation. He was also educated at the University of Virginia from 1868 to 1869.

Years after the War Between the States, Henry Grady wrote *The New South*. According to Grady, the old South was dead, and a new South had arisen. In New York City in 1886, he spoke to The New England Society on his topic of the risen New South and influenced substantial interest in economic development, spurring financial investments in his beloved homeland.

Henry Grady was an important influence in the political arena in Georgia when the rural political powers, led largely by Populist and later staunch segregationist Tom Watson, opposed the progressive urban industrialists and the railroads.

Three years after his famous speech in New York and shortly after a speech in Boston he died, likely of pneumonia. He was buried Christmas Day, 1889 in Atlanta's Oakland Cemetery. The Henry Grady Hotel, Henry Grady High School, and the Henry Grady Hospital, bear his name.

The Henry Grady Hotel was built on the highest point of the city on Peachtree Street and Cain Street. This property was at the peak of a ridge where Native Americans had once trod on an old Cherokee and Creek Indian trail passing through the area, heading north. The Victorian styled Governor's Mansion was located on the property until 1923. The mansion was torn down and the site was leased to the Henry Grady Hotel Corporation, owned by Mr. Cecil Cannon and several other local investors.

Because the state of Georgia retained title to the property, the legislators of the state of Georgia felt they had a vested interest in the Hotel and most of them stayed at "The Grady" when the state legislature was in session. Many of the candidates for governor or other state offices had their headquarters at the Henry Grady. My dad, a great friend to the visiting legislators always claimed, "More political decisions and deals occurred on the fourteenth floor and in the Governor's Suite than over at the state capitol."

The governors "came and went." Only the Henry Grady remained the same. My dad would often call my mother to come downtown to the hotel for dinner and help entertain the members of the legislature and their wives.

It was an unusual experience to be a young child bounced on the knees of several governors. They felt right at home at the uptown "Grady Hotel." There are stories (mostly untold) concerning the "goings on" of the members of the Executive and Legislative branches of Georgia's State government.

Since Atlanta's Blue Laws prohibited open liquor bars, the downtown hotels had special "city pouring licenses" to accommodate interstate business and the legislators who wanted their "spirits," which flowed like a waterfall during the legislative sessions.

Most of the governors spent time at the Henry Grady in the specially prepared Governor's and Presidential Suites. The well-known Governor, "Bow Tie Eddy" Rivers, who "gave free schoolbooks to the children of Georgia," was Harvey's favorite governor. When discussing the vagaries of politics, he once told my dad that as governor, "You just take a little and leave a little." That sounds a little familiar today.

This was the same Governor Ed Rivers who allegedly "burned the midnight oil" on the last night of his governorship signing "Pardons and Paroles for a Price." There's not much new in Georgia politics.

Governor Eugene Talmadge usually stayed at the Piedmont Hotel in downtown Atlanta but when he did stay at the Henry Grady, Harvey used to say that you had to, "Lock up the house maids, away from old Gene."

Aware that the hotel was on state property and the legislature held the power of a future lease renewal, some politicians wouldn't pay all of their bills. Usually the representatives of the government groups paid the bills. Only Lester Maddox, when he ended his successful gubernatorial campaign, came downstairs to the front desk to personally settle his bill.

Maddox's campaign manager was the future lieutenant governor, governor and United States senator, the late Zell Miller. He was an honest man yet known as "Zig Zag Zell" for his changing political philosophies. I never understood why he left the Democratic Party that had been so good to him. He just zigged and zagged over to the Republican Party. He claimed that the Democratic party left him.

It was alleged that one major candidate, an unsuccessful candidate for governor, never paid his bill, again aware that the legislature had the power to withhold the future lease to the land.

After Cecil Cannon, the principal owner died, the Hotel Estate passed to his five sisters and the Fred and Frances Wilson Foundation. Fred Wilson, along with Gainesville attorney, Ed Dunlap and his firm (known as "four percenters" since the attorneys received 4% of the funds for servicing the loan) had handled the Federal loan assistance for the hotel during the dark days of the Depression. They rescued the hotel from bankruptcy. It was said that Georgia Senator Walter George expedited the loan.

The heirs sold the Hotel to a Chicago investment firm toward the end of the lease. The firm replaced all the furnishings and redecorated the hotel in what many felt was a garish style. I was told the stuff was bought from the Chicago family members and the Chicago investment firm financially gutted the hotel, reneged on the payments and returned the hotel to the heirs in less than desirable condition. The Henry Grady was never the same. Sounds like some modern-day promoters and investors who shall remain unnamed.

Before the expiration of the Cannon fifty-year lease, the late Mr. John Portman, the prominent Atlanta architect and builder, and his associates bought the unexpired lease on the valuable property from the heirs. He and his associates obtained a ninety-nine-year lease from the state. There they built the Westin Peachtree Plaza Hotel.

During his hotel career, Harvey progressed from bellman, to captain, to superintendent of service, to assistant manager, to corporation vice president and general manager of the Henry Grady Hotel before he retired, and the Henry Grady closed its doors forever. He was terminally ill and left his sickbed to come to the hotel and hand the staff and employees their last paychecks.

He said to them, "This hotel business has been my life. This hotel has been good to us. It has paid our salaries, fed us, and financially provided an education for many of our children. We close the doors in the black with no outstanding debts."

He died in August 1972. One Sunday morning, a few months later, the Henry Grady Hotel was demolished. It was replaced with John Portman's reflective glass Westin Plaza Hotel, then the tallest hotel, in the United States. Fortunately, my dad did not have to see the old Henry Grady come down.

He was a great dad, a real pal, a realistic and pragmatic person to admire and emulate. He was honest and met all men on an equal and level playing field. As the famous sportswriter Grantland Rice would say, "It was how he played the game."

A METRO BUSINESS

An Atlanta icon

The Henry Grady Hotel was a self-contained big business and little community. Within its red brick walls, the hotel contained its own laundry and steam press shop, print shop, kitchens, barber and beauty shops, a coffee shop, and the top entertainment spot in Atlanta. The famous Paradise Room and Dogwood Lounge offered luncheons and evening dinners and the live floor shows presented the top entertainers of the country. The Paradise Room, once known as the Spanish Room, was on a national entertainment level comparable to the Blue Room at the renowned Roosevelt Hotel, just off Canal Street in New Orleans.

In his early years, entertainer and actor Dick Van Dyke and his brother Jerry and "The Merry Mutes" entertained in the Paradise and Dogwood rooms. Other well-known entertainers and vaudeville actors also appeared. Andy Griffith reportedly got his start there. Other notables included: Ted Lewis, Dell O'Dell, Vaughn Monroe, "Cotton" Watts, Harry "Woo-Woo" Stevens, Guy Mitchell, Rudy Vallée, young Pete Fountain, and many others of note. The best resident orchestra, I thought, was the Don Grimes Band that played the Paradise Room for so many years. Many young entertainers just starting out, and older folks making comebacks, entertained in the Paradise Room.

The large banquet rooms were often used by social clubs, wedding parties, debutante balls, school banquets and various businesses. The Dixie Ball Room hosted civic meetings and greeting affairs for the Georgia State legislators when the General Assembly was in session.

Beginning in the 1960s, the "Annual Wild Hog Supper" was a regular happening at the beginning of the legislative sessions. The first supper was in the Dixie Ball Room. There the legislators ate, drank, got reacquainted and greeted new members as the January general assembly session opened. There they lined up their political gangs. It remains an annual event, though now celebrated elsewhere.

IT SEEMS I GREW UP IN
THE HENRY GRADY HOTEL

I was the son of the Hotel Keeper

For a young kid, the hotel offered many mysteries and areas of intrigue. One of my favorites was the hotel print shop located deep in the dark basement. This was where the hotel printing was done, including menus for the dining rooms, and contract printing for outside businesses. In the printing press section, I learned to set print type. I collected different colors of scrap paper for drawing and used the varied weight paper to make paper airplanes. I spent many hours fooling around in the deep basement of the hotel.

The telephone operators always enticed me. In a room just behind the lobby front desk were four operators who handled the in-coming and out-going telephone calls. On the billed calls (especially long distance) they wrote down the numbers on little slips of paper that had a red carbon copy then filed them for appropriate charges. They also took messages for the guests, which were placed in the guest mailboxes.

They taught me, even as a little kid, to use the telephone switchboards, plugging in and unplugging the telephone lines allowing the calls to go through. It was a busy place. To this day I recall the hotel telephone numbers, (Jackson) JA 4221 and JA 4222.

The Henry Grady Hotel – Atlanta, Georgia
"The hotel stood on the windy corner of
Peachtree and Cain Streets."
(Photo of postcard received by author in 1943)

Along Cain Street (now Andrew Young International Boulevard), the taxis lined up to collect passengers. Shortly after the war, returning veterans started a cab company, The Veteran Cab Company. Suddenly, the established Yellow Company had significant competition and there was a lot of rabble rousing over the parking spaces alongside the hotel. It was common for the Atlanta police to have to intervene.

The street entrance to the Grady barber shop was on Cain Street. The shop was a regular for many of Atlanta's businessmen, guests and legislators.

Mr. Slaughter, a tall, grey-haired man, was my dad's barber. He was the senior barber and had the number one chair in the shop. On Saturdays, often before Georgia Tech football games, I was sent downstairs to see Mr. Slaughter for my grown-up haircut. If he was busy, he shuffled me off to another barber.

I watched the lithe lady manicurists as they flitted around settling down by their little manicure tables to care for the older gentlemen's rough hands. They carefully lifted their hands and patted each thoughtfully and spoke softly to each customer before beginning washing, trimming and buffing their nails. I smile now when I think of their quiet, tantalizing conversations and gossip that I overheard as I sat quietly in the barber's chair or on the shoeshine stand nearby. That's where all the news about the city and state was exchanged.

My favorite friend was Mr. Henry, the shoeshine man, a spirited, short, dark-skinned, older fellow. He had a shine stand in the barber shop where customers sat as he polished their shoes.

He taught me to shine shoes. "This is how we do it, Little Mr. Harvey," he said to me. He would dip the soft rag into the polish, rub the shoes then shine them with a big shoe brush then a "buffing rag," popping it several times in mid-air as he finished. Then we would dip a toothbrush into the dark, liquid polish and trim the edges of the soles. "We're sure to make the soles edge darker," he preached. "A man is what his shoes look like," Henry said. We carefully and with reverence lined the many pairs of shoes up, ready for the bellmen to return them to their owners' rooms.

Mr. Henry lined the shoes up along the sides of the stand, he'd tell me about each owner, whom he knew well. "Those brown ones are the governor's shoes," he proudly announced, or "those are Mr. Moseley's," the hotel manager. He would point to the shoes of some state or Atlanta politician, a judge, a city councilman or banker or other prominent citizen. "Those shoes belong to Doctor Pierce Harris, he's the preacher at the First Methodist Church," Henry boasted.

"Best shine in town," he boasted. I was told that Henry was able to send all his boys to college on the money he made shining shoes at the Henry Grady in Atlanta.

When I was nine, I put the "learning" into practice as I taught my schoolmates, the kids on my hall in military school, to have the best "spit and shine" shoes in the whole Junior School.

Also deep in the hotel's basement, the bare concrete walls held the laundry and the steam press shop. There the hotel did its own laundry and contracted with many of the other downtown hotels and restaurants to do their linens uniforms, napkins and tablecloths.

In those winter days we wore scratchy long wool pants. I was often taken down the dark, dingy, concrete stairs by one of the bellmen to have my pants pressed. The main pressor was a huge dark-skinned guy who wrapped me in a sheet and sat me not far from the press as he worked while I waited to have my breeches pressed. He would lift this heavy lever arm, then bring the ironing press down to steam press the pants. It seemed the spewed steam added another hundred degrees to the already hot room. With a big smile he handed me my pants, "All done," he would proudly announce. I would give him the quarter my dad sent down with me, slip my pants on and head back upstairs.

At the Henry Grady I learned to be a people watcher. My mom and I would wait in the huge Victorian lobby for my dad to get off work. There we watched the whole world move about in mysterious ways, men and women wandering in, astounded at the hugeness of the building. Often folks were from rural Georgia – "Country come to town,"– and had perhaps never been to the big city. Some tired, unimpressed regular travelers passed through, just looking for a place to rest.

The most interesting were the single women who I much later learned were there to meet quietly, some secretly, with other guests. I was so naive that I never realized until years later that prominent Atlanta businessmen and even doctors and well-known lawyers and executives carried out secret dalliances in those downtown hotels.

From the Peachtree Street entrance, visiting guests trudged up the marble steps holding onto the brightly polished brass handrails into the main lobby, followed by spiffy uniformed bellmen carrying their luggage. Many guests were trying to keep the rowdy children in tow just long enough to get checked in. Then, after checking in, standing before the ornate brass doors of the hotel elevators, the bellmen would advise them about their luggage and take them to their assigned rooms. The female elevator operators, in dark uniforms with white lace collars and long white cotton gloves, all slender, smiling and accommodating, welcomed the guests with, "Which floor, sir?" or "Which floor, ma'am?"

Across from the check-in counter was the cigar stand or the sundry stand where newspapers, cigarettes, candy and other items of personal need could be bought. An elderly pair, Mr. and Mrs. Farnsworth ran the stand for many years, growing old and gray in the venture, yet never forgetting that they were there to please and serve the guests. They lived in the hotel, had no children and seemed to have a special place in their heart for me, always offering candy or some pleasant surprise.

Football and baseball weekends when Georgia Tech or The Atlanta Crackers had games in town were the most interesting and busiest. Before the games, men gathered, standing around smoking cigarettes and cigars, unaware of the suffocating atmosphere, loudly talking and some, over in the corners or sitting on the stuffed sofas, laying bets on the games.

After the ball games, many wandered back into the lobby, some still carried away by their team's victory or others not so happy, silently heading toward the elevators to avoid the celebrating and rowdy crowd.

Yes, the lobby was a world of entertainment for watching and eavesdropping. The Henry Grady Hotel was an Atlanta icon. Though now gone, its memory lingers in those, so few now alive, who experienced the hotel as an employee or a welcomed guest or as the only child of the Hotel Keeper.

BAPTISTS

In the beginning there was my mother who took me to Sunday School.

Though I was christened a Presbyterian in Birmingham, Alabama, with my cousin Neal Mahoney, my mother took me to a neighborhood Baptist Sunday School. The little church stood a few blocks from our home, occupying a little old gray converted frame house. They planned to build a new church. A model of it made of paper and cardboard sat on a low wooden children's table in my Sunday school room. Bricks were marked on the outside cardboard walls. Each silver dime that my little friends and I brought to Sunday school paid for a brick for the new church. When we brought our "offerings" the teacher wrote our names on one of the tiny cardboard bricks. It was wonderful to see our names inscribed on that church we were helping to build.

We moved from that little wooden house with a potbelly stove into a new and spacious sanctuary. The new church was a magnificent red brick structure; at least it was to four and five-year-olds "Dedicated to the Glory of God, A. D. 1939," the corner stone plaque said.

The new church was just across the street from my grammar school. I was in kindergarten. My folks didn't go to my church. They occasionally attended at Central Presbyterian and later evening church at First Methodist in downtown Atlanta. My dad worked seven days a week and took only a half-day off on Sunday.

I attended church school regularly. When I was old enough to go alone, I walked the couple of blocks. If it rained, my mother drove me. As I grew older, I attended morning church as well, skipping the services only occasionally to go to the local drugstore or the Teddy Bear Cafe with some of my truant buddies.

My church must have been some kind of Evangelical Baptist church since the preacher often yelled during the sermons. He would whisper to the congregation as if what they were hearing was a big secret then he emphasized that secret with a shout. To a young kid it was frightening.

I wondered how I got to be one of those sinners the preacher yelled about. I didn't lie. I didn't cheat. I wasn't old enough to worry about that demon liquor, and I certainly didn't understand all that adultery business. There had been, however some whispered complaints in our Baptist neighborhood that they were concerned about my teaching my little friends to play Blackjack and Poker.

I didn't understand why I was involved with Adam and Eve and original Sin. I didn't even know them and how was I related to them? *They must be so old*, I thought and wondered *where exactly do they live?*

What about my mom and dad? They must be worse sinners than me, because they weren't even there to hear about it. I wondered why I was there anyway. I was too afraid to ask.

When the minister asked, "Who out there in the congregation wants forgiveness of their sins?" All my friends and I, crowded in the church pews with our heads bowed low and our eyes tightly closed, held up our little hands, surely, we did not want to burn in Hell Fire. I wasn't even allowed to say that word "Hell" at home. (A memorable bit of profanity, learned from one of my buddies had resulted in a mouth wash with soap.) I dreamed once that the Devil was coming up our driveway to get us all. I couldn't get the door latched fast enough. I awoke, terrified and ran to my folks' bed and climbed in. I knew he couldn't find me under their covers. I was too afraid to tell them of my nightmare.

At twelve, I resolved that I was not to be among the damned and destined sinners and got myself baptized along with several friends. It was a lovely Easter Day when I walked down the red-carpet aisle with my buddies to be identified as members of Jesus' saved flock. I had new shoes and a special new coat, a heavenly blue. My mom and dad were there.

On the night of our Baptism, we nearly froze as we were immersed in the Baptism pool with the lighted stained glass of John the Baptist and the River Jordan right on the wall behind us. I wondered if the Jordan was as cold when John baptized Jesus.

I continued to be a faithful Baptist through high school and college, and often sang in the choir. My philosophy classes in college challenged me to reevaluate the religion I had been taught and by the time I entered medical school I had become a doubting Thomas. I still believed the major philosophy of the Christian religion, but I began to reject mindless dogma and the narrow view of life within many churches. I began to see some preachers as theatrical clowns, rather than true teachers.

NOTE: Years later, when the neighborhood integrated, the Cascade Baptist Church building was sold. It became the Second Mount Olive Baptist Church. By some strange incident the church burned (1973) and the word that I heard on the street was that the insurance payments either were not paid, or the payments had stopped and there was no fire insurance coverage. The partially destroyed building remained in poor condition until within the last couple of years it changed hands and became an Islamic meeting house (Ar–Rahman Islamic Center). I could see from the street that the cornerstone was either painted over or removed thus eliminating the inscription of the original Christian church.

"I DON'T THINK HE'S GOT GOOD SENSE"

Maybe I didn't.

I don't remember if I was thirteen or fourteen, but I sat at the dinner table that early fall evening trying to cover my mouth as I attempted to chew with a painful swollen upper lip. I could still taste the salty dried blood. My mother looked over at my dad as he passed the bowl of mashed potatoes, "I just don't think he's got good sense."

I tried to ignore the comment as my mom stared at me and shook her head. "What do you mean?" my dad asked.

"It's that football. Is it really that important?" She sighed briefly. "You know Dr. Janes says if he has to repair those braces again, he's gonna take them off and refuse to treat those crooked front teeth."

"How's that?" my dad asked, glancing across the table as I sat silent and ducking my head.

"You know he's out for football and he keeps coming home with a bloody mouth and bruises. I don't think it's worth it and I do believe Dr. Janes is tired of fixing those braces."

My dad had been a fine athlete in his younger days. He had been a professional boxer. He later became a semi-pro baseball player. I was trying to emulate him. My problem was I was not as agile nor as fast as he. There was something he had that I didn't. Try as I might I was never as good as he nor as good as some of my scruffy, childhood friends.

In the late forties and fifties, football was a sport with much less protective armor than today's vastly improved equipment. Face guards were unheard of except for boys with known musculoskeletal facial problems. We thought those who did have guards were sissies. Yet I came home many times with torn lips from elbows to the mouth when I wore braces.

Beside all that, I was not the star that I hoped to be. We practiced on what was left of a grassy field that had worn to red Georgia clay and dusty, rough ground. I struggled to push the heavy weighted "lineman's sleds" around the field. I lagged behind in the middle of the pack on the laps around the practice field. I didn't know why. It was years later that I realized that one leg didn't match the other. One foot turned out (tibial torsion) and I had to swing and rotate the leg when running which slowed me down.

As "scrubs" or "red shirts" we were used as fodder to teach the varsity squad their plays in practice. We were expendable. My job, guard and linebacker, was the best on the field. Though short and only about 138 pounds I still felt the thrill of hitting the runner hard and making those tough tackles. One hot Georgia afternoon the left end, a boy named Richard Allen (who later played quarterback for the University of Florida) and I teamed up on a young quarterback, Bobby Moore, as he swept end on a keeper.

Richard hit him high and I hit him low. After the collision we were all three laid out in the dust, half conscious. The coach rushed over yelling at us for hurting his star quarterback. The coaches gathered about our hero quarterback and left Richard and me to struggle to our feet while suffering the blistering complaints from the other members of the coaching staff.

When the list of the team roster was posted my name was not on it. I had been cut, much to my mom's delight and to my disappointment. *Well*, I thought, *I was just not tough enough.*

It was disappointing cleaning out my locker, turning in my pads and helmet with several other dejected guys who had not made the team. Our pals patted us on the back. "Maybe next year," they said.

I thought I was left out because we had hurt the quarterback, and it was not until later, I learned by X-ray, I had cracked my collar bone and I wondered if that was why it hurt so much when I attempted a head-on tackle. I wondered if the coach had noticed my difficulty in tackling. Any excuse would do but I knew in my heart that I just wasn't good enough to be on a future championship team.

Maybe I didn't have good sense after all. I kept my braces. My teeth straightened. Life went on.

HIS NAME WAS RONNIE

He was not just another kid.

His name was Ronnie Wilson. We were friends. In fact, we were buddies. The problem was that we both were competing for the same place on the lower level football team. Ronnie and I were about the same size, short, light weight but we both loved the game. It was obvious Ronnie was tougher than me. He seemed to always be where the action was, and he often ended up on the bottom of the pile. Somehow, he always threw his body into the fray without personal regard.

I was more cautious, perhaps a bit afraid, though I never admitted the fact. When the team list was posted, Ronnie's name filled the slot that we both wanted. Though disappointed, I was happy for my friend.

Together, we as eighth or ninth graders still attended the Varsity night games. Ronnie had a cow bell and together from the stands we rang it loudly when our team scored. After one game, he said, "You can take the bell home. I'll get it back next week."

"Okay," I responded, and we headed home from the night varsity win over our Atlanta opponent.

A week later I arrived at school and entered my home room. The kids were crying, and the teacher met me at the door, "Take a seat. I've bad news. It's about your friend, Ronnie." I eased into my desk seat and Miss Thompson, a tall slender middle-aged woman with tears in her eyes announced, "For you all who don't already know, Ronnie Wilson died last night."

For a moment the kids were silent, then they mostly burst into tears, "How, Miss Thompson? What happened?" they sputtered between sobs.

"We don't exactly know, but he was riding his wagon near his house in the street and was hit by a car. The police took him to Grady Hospital, but I'm told he died around midnight," she answered.

I closed my eyes and thought, *How am I going to give him back his cow bell?* Strange that was my first emotion. I had his bell and could never return it.

It seems that an older boy, a student we all knew, was driving down a hill when Ronnie dashed into the street in his wagon colliding with the boy's car. I knew exactly the street at the bottom of a shallow dip where the smoke from burning leaves often settled. I wondered if it had been smoky and the driver just didn't see Ronnie. We learned later that the driver had been drinking beer, so the law came down on him hard.

We all attended Ronnie's funeral at the Methodist church. As I sat quietly with other friends during the service, I thought, *I'm glad Ronnie got that place on the football team rather than me.* It seemed only right.

The brass cow bell hung in my room until I left for college and every time, I looked at it I thought of my friend Ronnie.

NINETEEN-FIFTIES

Sometimes I look back – Mid-Twentieth Century South

Sometimes I look back and recall the political world that I observed has little changed. The politicians use the same old rhetoric they used over half a century ago. Each "slings as much political mud" as the voting public can tolerate. There's not much new under the Georgia or national political sun.

MID-CENTURY GEORGIA POLITICS

In 1950, the Fifth Congressional District of Georgia included Fulton, DeKalb and Rockdale Counties. It was a conservative Democratic stronghold except for the central urban liberal population of Atlanta. Georgia's elections were held under the County Unit System of representation. Such laws were passed by a Georgia Convention in 1877, after Reconstruction ended, to reduce the political power of urban Atlanta. The agrarian political factions resisted the business and industrial development of the urban centers.

The smaller county, no matter how small, had two electoral votes and the larger counties had four or six county unit votes. To win the Fifth District election (Metropolitan Atlanta and Decatur) the conservative congressional candidate could carry DeKalb and Rockdale Counties and defeat the total vote of the more liberal Fulton County voters. Fulton County had six electoral votes, DeKalb had six, and Rockdale, a mostly rural and conservative, county had two. Theoretically, a candidate could have lost the total numerical vote count yet become elected.

In the 1950s the incumbent member of Congress, James C. Davis, never lost the total vote count during his tenure, though on occasion it may have been close.

Judge Davis, as he preferred to be called, even though he became a member of Congress, was from the old school of Georgia politics. He was elected after the Second World War when veterans were returning home and America was the unopposed leader on the world stage.

He remained in Congress until 1962. Georgia ended the County Unit System when Judge Griffin Bell upheld the court injunction following *Gray v Sanders* in October of that year.

Georgia continued in the throes of segregation during the Second World War and into the late 1940s and 1950s. Georgia remained a "White Supremacy" state whether anyone admitted it or not. The schools, the buses, the train stations, rest rooms, and even the water fountains were segregated.

At one time there had been white only election primaries but that had officially ended as the courts set aside such election procedures. In 1947 the Supreme Court declared the all-white primary to be unconstitutional. The Black community became more politically educated and began to understand the power of their votes.

The local Black newspaper, *The Atlanta Daily World,* had significant influence in the Black community, informing its readers of the political opportunities through its progressive message.

In 1949, "biracial voting" re-elected Atlanta's mayor William B. Hartsfield. The black population became a significant influence at the polls, no longer ignored in Georgia politics. Gone with the wind were the "poll taxes" and the "literacy tests."

Discrimination practices were hard to overcome. However, with Civil Rights advocates, Reverend Martin Luther King, Jr., and the Reverend Ralph David Abernathy, the "Movement" began to flex its voting muscle in urban Atlanta and in a few, but very few other Southern cities.

There was White resistance at every political level during those tumultuous days of social change. Yet, in the quiet back rooms of the Atlanta political power brokers – Mayor Hartsfield, later Mayor Ivan Allen, Jr., Chief of Police Herbert Jenkins, and the Coca Cola magnate and philanthropist, Mr. Robert Woodruff – the city set a new course of smooth desegregation and relative tolerance, unlike many of the other Southern cities. Mayor Hartsfield had claimed Atlanta, as a "city too busy to hate."

During the 1950s and early 1960s the Georgia Democratic Party was slow to change, and the Black voters became increasingly influential.

The Republican Party in Georgia was merely a "shadow party" with minimal visibility and even more resistant than the Democratic Party to change. They were not in the forefront of the Civil Rights Movement.

Despite shifting of population and minority influence, the majority of politicians in office were slow, probably deliberately slow, to embrace change. Consequently, they gradually vanished from the political scene.

James C. Davis remained a staid conservative Southern Democrat and it was not until 1962 that the liberal, young attorney, Charles Weltner, a grandson of Confederate General Thomas R. R. Cobb, won Georgia's Fifth District Congressional seat from Judge Davis.

Charles Weltner served in Congress until the late 1960s when the rabid segregationist, ax-handle-carrying Lester Maddox was nominated as the Democratic candidate for governor. Charles Weltner was a Democratic Representative and had signed a pledge to support the Democratic candidate for governor. He could not in good faith, with his integrity on the line, support the avowed segregationist candidate Lester Maddox. Weltner resigned at the end of his term and did not seek reelection for the Fifth Congressional District seat during that campaign. Before his death Charles Weltner became a Chief Justice of the Georgia Supreme Court. His great-great-grandfather, Joseph Henry Lumpkin had served as Georgia's first Supreme Court Chief Justice.

Lester Maddox was elected governor (1967-1971), not by the voters but by the Georgia Legislature. The Republican Howard "Bo" Calloway received the most votes of a two-way election but not the required majority. Former Governor Ellis Arnall received enough write-in ballots to split the Democratic vote. Since the vote did not produce a clear winner of Calloway vs. Maddox, the Democratic controlled Legislature preferred their Democratic candidate Maddox, over the conservative Republican businessman, Howard "Bo" Calloway, in 1966.

Zell Miller, of future political notoriety, was Lester Maddox's campaign manager. Zell Miller was later to serve as Lt. Governor, Governor and United States Senator from Georgia. His legacy is the HOPE Scholarship for young Georgians attending college in the state.

Lester Maddox proved to be a better governor than most Georgians thought he would be. He was the first governor of Georgia to actively appoint Black citizens to high state positions of responsibility.

In 1965, after Congressman Davis' political career had ended, he published a very conservative newspaper in Atlanta known as *The Atlanta Times*. He retired to his home in Stone Mountain, Georgia, where he had lived during his many years of service to his country and his state.

CONGRESSIONAL PAGE INTEREST

"Who are those boys scurrying around the House chamber?"

My association with our congressman began in 1946 after I visited my aunt in Washington, D. C. While there, I visited the usual sites of Washington and especially enjoyed my trip to the Capitol. From the visitor's gallery, I observed Congress in session. I noticed the young boys in dark suits, not much older than me, working in the House and Senate chambers. They were the Congressional pages.

There was an older gentleman in my aunt's office that served as a House Page when he was a teenager. He explained the duties and the positive experience that he had as a page. My interest quickened and I brought the subject up to my mother and dad when I returned home to Georgia. My dad mentioned that he had worked, many years before for Judge Davis who had recently been elected to Congress. He contacted the congressman's office. Thus, began the process of becoming a page.

I visited our legislator's office in Decatur and interviewed with him. I had not met him before and knew of him only through my dad. He was a tall, white-haired man – quite an imposing figure. He was pleasant and I relaxed in his presence. I realized that he was a Southern gentleman. His voice was strong and commanding, yet gentle as he talked to me and inquired about my activities, my family, and my ambitions. I knew it would be a good thing to work for him. I surmised from his strong personality that if my conduct was not satisfactory, I wouldn't be long in that job.

In 1946 the Democrats lost their majority in the Congress and became the minority party. This 1946-1948 congress was the "Do Nothing Congress," according to the Democratic President Harry S Truman. Since the Republicans were in power and since Capitol jobs or positions were controlled under the old Jacksonian patronage system, "to the victors go the spoils," only Republicans had patronage to appoint pages and certain other Capitol employees.

United States Capitol – Washington, D. C.
Viewed from the steps of the Library of Congress
First snow – Mid-Winter – 1950
(Photo by author)

Our representative had Republican friends, Congressman Clarence Brown and Senator Robert A. Taft, both of Ohio, seated in the Republican controlled House and Senate. He made inquiries, beginning in October 1947 to obtain House or Senate page patronage from Congressman Brown or Senator Taft. For a year or so letters were exchanged with Congressman Brown and Senator Taft's representatives. By the end of 1948 the November elections had turned the Republicans out of office and the Eighty-First Democratic Congress replaced the "Do Nothing Congress."

Judge Davis announced that he was able to offer me an appointment as a page in the U. S. House of Representatives. He had patronage and could offer a page job during the summer and fall of 1949, but he did not know how long Congress would be in session. The other option was to begin the new second session of the Eighty-First Congress in January of 1950. He could promise a full session appointment. We weighed the options and gratefully accepted the second session opportunity.

For the 1949 session, Davis appointed a young man, James Wesberry of Atlanta. Jim Wesberry's father, the minister of Morningside Baptist Church in Atlanta, had served as the temporary House Chaplain. Doctor Wesberry was also a friend of Judge Davis.

HOUSE PAGE APPOINTMENT

"Anticipating Washington..."

For several months I prepared for the journey to Washington, not sure what to expect. My mom and I talked about making a dry run to Washington. That seemed too expensive. I would have to wait and jump right into the job.

I learned from the congressional office that Page School would begin at 6:15 a.m. each morning. I would carry four subjects, English, Spanish, Algebra and Science. At the end of the morning classes we would walk from our school in the Library of Congress across the lawn to the Capitol for our day's work. Usually, we had to run to get there on time.

When on duty in the House or Senate chamber we dressed in blue serge suits with white shirts, black or dark blue ties, black socks, and black shoes. The Supreme Court Pages wore historical style knickers, rather than regular trousers.

Congress did not provide page housing. We had to find our own. Our congressman's administrative assistant, Mr. Bill Edens, made the arrangements for me to board in a three-story red brick row house at 305 New Jersey Avenue S. E. where several other pages lived.

Mr. And Mrs. Collitan, the proprietors, lived in a first-floor apartment with their young son. Mrs. Collitan was sort of a housemother though she had no official designation. The location was one block south of the "New" House Office Building (later named the Longworth Building). The row house has since been demolished.

The Christmas of 1949 came, and I planned to be in Washington before New Year's Day. I hoped to be prepared to begin work a few days before the Congressional session began. During the last week of December my mother accompanied me by train to Washington. We visited my aunt and uncle who lived on Military Road near Rock Creek Park.

Shortly before New Year's, my mom and I visited our representative's office and met the staff and from there we were taken to the Door Keeper's Office. The Door Keeper of the House of Representatives was the well-known Mr. William "Fish Bait" Miller from Pascagoula, Mississippi. Mr. Miller had been Door Keeper for a number of years when the Democrats were in power and was a fixture about the Capitol. He was in charge of all the patronage jobs, including the pages, police, and almost everything else about the House side. He was known as a "Yellow Dog Democrat."

When we were announced by his secretary, he appeared quickly to greet us and took us directly into his inner office. My mother, a rather attractive woman, seemed to lighten his demeanor and he became all Southern charm. He could not have been more hospitable.

"Fish Bait" Miller was a short (some might say chubby man)– had thin graying hair, a round face, small mouth, and piercing blue eyes, magnified through silver-rimmed, round thick glasses. He was wearing a gray seersucker suit, starched but frayed around the edges. He was pleasant, yet excitable with an air of the typical busy bureaucrat. His main job was to keep the congressional members happy, solving any problem that arose which might make a member uncomfortable. He gladly and unabashedly served at their command.

To me he was courteous and pleasant, but I knew that I would be under his authority. He offered us each a Coke. My mom demurred and he said that he would only "offer once." We then accepted and all enjoyed Coca Colas, the favorite drink of Atlanta. Our visit was congenial, and we were out of his office in about half an hour. I was never again in his inner office. He did, however, inquire as to the health of my mother when I had occasion to be in his presence on the House floor.

HOUSING ACCOMMODATIONS

Before New Year's Day, I moved my stuff into 305 New Jersey. Mrs. Collitan was tall, with light freckled skin and bright dyed red hair. She wore a colorful cotton print dress with a belt pulled tightly about her waist. She greeted my mother who had wanted to meet the house mother so if there was ever any need for Mrs. Collitan to call, she could feel free to communicate on a personal basis.

I was assigned the downstairs front room, that formerly had served as a front parlor in the red brick Victorian home. The room was large and sunny, with a bay window facing the front of the house, an eastern exposure. My bed was to be in the Southwest corner beside the closed off fireplace. Mrs. Collitan asked about my luggage and things. I answered, "I am fixing to bring them in."

When she heard "fixing to" she smiled and said, "I'm sure that your roommate will be delighted to room with another Southerner. He is from Texas."

I found my side of the room, put away my belongings and made my bed. We returned to my aunt's for dinner. I would move into "305" the next day.

My first roommate was James "Buddy" Glover from Linden, Texas, a husky boy, taller than me with a loud voice, not unlike many Texans I have known. I immediately liked him. His humor, I learned, was bizarre but tolerable even in close quarters. Buddy had been a page for over a year and had special duties. He exhibited an air of seniority over the newer pages.

His patronage came from Democratic Representative Wright Patman from his hometown in Texas. Buddy was assigned to the House Republican side and worked occasionally in "Documents" and in his representative's office. He was known as a sporty dresser.

Buddy was also the social butterfly of "305." Since he had seniority over most of us, he was called upon to be the page representative when it came to escorting famous guests about the Capitol. One high-water mark was his privilege, a year or so later, to escort Miss Tallulah Bankhead around the Capitol.

Her grandfather was Senator John Hollis Bankhead (1907 to 1920). Her father, William B. Bankhead was Speaker of the House. Her uncle, Sen. John H. Bankhead, was the late Senator from Alabama and she was a movie star, famous in her own right.

Miss Bankhead's uncle had passed a Senate resolution mandating that black bean soup would be served daily in the Senate dining room. During her visit, Buddy not only escorted her about the Capitol, but also dined with her in the Senate dining room, of course, sipping Black Bean soup. I was told he was untouchable for days, maybe weeks.

"305" was similar to a fraternity house. We were all pages or young employees at the Capitol, all on some kind of political patronage. We were teenaged boys from all over the country. My uncle Wayne called us "the parasites on the public debt."

A PAGE IN CONGRESS

A page's job varies according to the part of the government to which he is assigned. There are House Pages, Senate Pages, Supreme Court Pages and pages that have varied duties as special employees in the Document Rooms and pages assigned to Special Committee Rooms.

After Page School the House Pages report to work between ten o'clock and eleven o'clock in the morning. They report to the House Chamber for bench duty, to the cloak rooms for phone duty, or the door Pages report just outside the chamber doors to greet congressional constituents or visitors who have come to see their members of Congress.

The bench pages, generally between fifteen and seventeen years of age, are assigned to be in the chamber during the active business session. They are available to run errands for the legislators between the chamber, offices, and committee rooms. They may be required to fetch documents or deliver messages.

Some of the older more experienced pages stay on as employees, often as phone pages. Their relationship with the members of Congress requires more maturity. They relay sensitive messages to and from the legislators and their offices and require more sophistication than the average younger page possesses.

The Senate pages' duties were similar to the House pages, except they stayed closer to the rostrum in the chamber and had more personal contact with the senators as the senators called on them directly by voice or hand signal, without the use of electronic communications. In the House we had a light board, which produced a flash from the button at the representative's seat in the chamber. Since there are more representatives than senators it is much more difficult to locate a House member than a senator.

The Supreme Court Pages performed similar tasks as the House and Senate pages. They were messengers for the Justices, the clerks, and their auxiliary court staffs.

Their chamber work was performed behind the elevated Justices' bench and seats. They were hardly seen by the public. There was a rule, now changed, that the Supreme Court pages could not be taller than the height of the justices' seats. They were to be invisible.

The outstanding privilege of being a page is the opportunity of seeing just how our government operates and participating in that government in a small way.

Congressional House Democratic Page Bench – 1950

First Row: Jerry Watts, J. Thomas, James Platt, Dan McKinnon,
Joe Young, Edwin Pitman
Second Row: Jim Munfort, Stanley Bohrer, Oliver Furlong,
James Hearn, Jim Richardson, Jimmy McElwain, J. Cozar
(Photo from Capitol Page School Annual – 1950)

THE PRESIDENT ADDRESSES CONGRESS

State of the Union

Excitement filled the capitol that morning. We scurried around checking the House Chamber to be sure all documents were in place. The senators, the House members, the Supreme Court judges, the heads of the administration, and military commanders along with sundry other government officials would begin to filter into the House Chamber well before noon.

Mr. Turner Robertson, the Democratic Chief Page, lined up the boys and gave us our instructions. "Be quiet and keep out of the way, boys," he nervously ordered. "Watch out for any member who needs help and be sure you take care of them."

Shortly, Mr. William "Fishbait" Miller, the House Door Keeper, darted through the chamber and the cloak room making sure that everything was ready for the president's arrival. He then met the assembling crowd that would accompany President Harry S Truman into the chamber.

Meanwhile, I was out on a HOB (House Office Building) errand and in a trot headed for the tunnel connecting the House Office Building and the Capitol. Just as I jogged near the lower entrance to the capitol doors, I was blocked by two tough-looking guys in black suits and dark glasses, carrying hand radios. "Hey, stop kid!" one of the guys yelled while the other grabbed me by the coat sleeve. "Where do you think you are going?" he asked. I was stunned. It was my third day on duty, and I had no idea that we were supposed to stay out of the tunnel. I had missed the instructions about where the pages were allowed.

The men eased me against the wall, and I wondered what in the world I had done. A minute or so later a senior page, perhaps authorized to be in the tunnel rushed up to the guys. "Hey," he muttered. "It's okay, he's one of the new pages."

"But he doesn't have any ID," the guy in the dark suit proffered.

"Yes sir," the older page said and showed the man his ID card, attached to his coat by a short string. "I know this boy. He probably forgot to get his ID."

The tough guy retorted, "We're FBI and you better get this kid to where he belongs."

"Yes sir," my defender answered. "I'll usher him up to the chamber, get his ID tag, and be sure he doesn't get into more trouble."

Safely back at the page benches, I explained my encounter to the chief page. "Didn't your overseer give you an ID this morning?" he asked.

"No sir, I must have been out on a call," I answered.
"See Furlong and he'll give you one," said Mr. Robertson.

Just before noon, the noisy chamber quieted down. All eyes turned to the main aisle and entrance directly across from the speaker's dais. The doors flew open. The short anxious Door Keeper led a procession of politicians into the chamber, faced the speaker's rostrum and in a booming Southern voice announced, "Mr. Speaker, the President of the United States."

My heart fluttered with excitement when the crowd on the House floor and all the folks in the galleries rose and roared with applause as President Harry S Truman entered the chamber, shaking hands, and waving to the members along the center aisle and to the galleries as he headed for the white marble rostrum to address the Second Session of the Eighty-First Congress in Joint Session.

**President Harry S Truman
addresses the Second Session of the 81st Congress,
January 3, 1950.**
Note young House pages standing along the chamber wall.
(Photo from House document "The Capitol")

THAT OTHER BENCH

Democrats vs. Republicans

We were all on Democratic patronage but were assigned both to the Democratic and Republican House benches. However, there were those who were brainwashed by their side of the chamber. Since the Democrats were in power during the 81st Congress we felt that the minor party was just that, the minor and inferior party. Our Chief Page was a middle-aged fellow, Mr. Turner Robertson, while on the Republican side, a younger man, Joe Bartlett was Chief Page.

My good friend, Jim Wesberry, also from Atlanta was assigned to the Republican bench as was John Illges, a Columbus, Georgia, boy. Though in school it didn't seem to matter, on the floor we were competitors and served what we thought was a different clientele.

The Republican representatives always seemed stuffy and pompous and our guys almost always seemed like most folks at home. The Republicans opposed everything our Democratic president and House members believed, at least their speeches and debates sounded like that.

To me, many of the politicians, old and fat, in vests and suits with gold chain watches, seemed to mimic the newspaper cartoons. Of course, I never mentioned my secret impressions. Yet, when they spoke in the well, I could just about figure out who was speaking or at least which side of the aisle they came from.

While working, we spent time sitting quietly on the leather benches in the back corners of the house chamber. We moved closer to the overseer who sat in the angle of the benches at a small oak table. Atop this table was a worn, wooden box with tiny lights. Lights blinked when a congressman on the floor wanted a page.

We glanced down across the chamber to check how busy our Republican friends were and made hand signs at each other. By osmosis each side became an advocate for their party. Though competitors, we were still friends.

Sometimes Joe Bartlett (Republican chief page) would come over to the Democratic side to talk to our chief page or to inquire about any problems. We usually had nothing to say to the dreaded political foe. Joe was actually a very accomplished guy, having served first as a page then in the Marines. After my term, he returned to the Marines for active duty during the Korean War. He ultimately retired as the Clerk of the House and as a Reserve Marine Corps brigadier general. Not many folks had a record like that. Our chief, Mr. Robertson, a truly nice fellow, continued his service as chief Democratic Page until 1971 when he retired to Florida.

Among both benches were local boys who lived in the D. C. area or over in Virginia or north in Chevy Chase, Maryland. Several of the out-of-town boys lived in the same row house at "305." Some of the Republican bench pages lived in the other small hotels or rooming houses about the capitol.

CAPITOL PAGE SCHOOL

"You Southern boys do wear shoes, don't you?"

The Capitol Page School remains an accredited Washington, D. C. high school under the supervision of the District of Columbia School Board. For a long time, it was held in the dingy basement of the Capitol and was later moved to the top (3rd) floor of The Library of Congress, across the East lawn from the capitol and south of The Supreme Court. The school has since moved to newer accommodations. I am told the old page school upstairs now serves as a training school for the Capitol Police Force.

THE

*Best wishes to my friend
Jerry Watts.
James C. Davis, M.C.
5th District Georgia.*

*Best wishes to the Best Page —
or at least the best I've met yet —
Clare D. M'Kenna
15th Cong. District*

Congressional

Capitol Page School

Library of Congress

1 9 5 0 Washington, D. C.

Capitol Page School Annual – 1950

During my tenure in 1950, the classes were held from 6:15 in the morning until 11:00 to allow the pages and special employees to attend school before reporting to duty at the Capitol, the Supreme Court building, and to the offices of the United States House of Representatives, or the United States Senate building.

During the school day, there was a single morning break of about twenty minutes. A small private employee café in the building accommodated the Library staff and students of the Page School.

School attendance was expected of the regular employed pages, those who were employed for a full term of Congress. Other short-term pages attended according to their own individual schedules and their home school board's requirements.

School problems were handled through the individual page's Congressional office. Discipline within the school was handled within the school, but the appointing Congressional office was keenly aware of any discipline or academic problems.

The Page School was managed like any other school except that the school educated a group of students who had special time restraints related to their work schedules.

It was not unusual for the Senate Pages to remain in the Senate Chamber for extended hours into the night. After nights such as these the student was not required to attend class the next day. Special arrangements were made for "make ups."

During my stay in Washington, before recent modifications in the attendance rules, the Senate pages were expected to be in class even after a long night session. There was, however, no discipline problem if they fell asleep in class. The class simply moved on.

House pages were rarely subjected to prolonged night sessions because no *filibusters* were allowed on the House floor. The House ran on a rigid and fixed time schedule. The Supreme Court pages were on an even tighter schedule than either the Senate or the House.

There was a hierarchy in the school, as in most schools, especially when it came to the younger or newly arrived students. A few of the pages had regular appointments that might keep them working at the Capitol or Congressional offices for several years. However, most of the page positions were for short intervals and the longest were usually for a single Congressional session.

It was not only well-heeled or prominent families who obtained appointments for their children, but some were hardship cases. A member of Congress might appoint a young person to a job for financial reasons. I know that some sent money home.

Stories abound of young street boys, historically in the 1800s, hanging around Congressional offices until a member of Congress noticed them and appointed them to page jobs.

When I arrived at Page School I was treated courteously, yet as one of the new boys, I would have to prove myself to the established crowd. My fellow Southerners and I were "looked down upon" as if they thought we had all come from the red clay counties. They doubted if we even wore shoes. Some claimed that they were surprised to see us out of overalls.

In the algebra class we learned that the Southerners were about fifty pages behind, even though we used the same textbook. Our teacher, a tall willowy blonde explained, "You boys will have to catch up on your own." There was no way we could do that without considerable help. My cousin, a student at the University of Maryland, began to help me at night but the other new Southern students and I realized that we couldn't sit in class, fifty pages behind and do the current work, take the tests, and catch up at the same time. We could expect no help.

We protested, walked out of class, stacked our algebra books on our principal's desk and asked for help. Mr. Orson Trueworthy, the recently appointed principal, though a genuinely proper guy, could not force the teacher to help us. He said, "I cannot force the staff to correct the deficits of the South's school systems."

We all withdrew from the class, cutting off our noses to spite our faces. For three nights a week, to get our algebra requirements, we had to ride the trolley car to the public District of Columbia Night School in the Southeast part of the city.

It was apparent that the tall willowy blonde teacher was more interested in schmoozing with the older senior students than teaching us. Our problem was that we still had to face her for science class. We made a pact that we would study hard and make the best grades in the school. When the Southern delegation led the Page School academically, they finally noted we "all wore shoes."

PAGE SCHOOL PROM

"an unusual chauffeur…"

The school participated in outside activities and before I arrived the classes had visited the Bethesda Naval Air Station. Our extra-curricular activities with the school during my tenure, however, were limited. I do recall the Page Spring Prom at the Shoreham Hotel out toward Chevy Chase. "You need to ask your congressman's daughter before anybody else," an older page advised. So, I did and was delighted to take the lovely Southern belle, Mary Martin Davis to the Ball.

I couldn't drive so her dad offered to take us to the Prom. I looked out the window of "305" as a big black Packard automobile pulled up. A tall distinguished-looking, white-haired man in a white linen suit and a dress straw hat stepped up the walk and rang the bell. I rushed to the door, corsage in hand and was ushered to the big shiny car. I opened the back door, handed my date the flowers, then flushing with embarrassment, slipped inside and eased across the seat. Her dad drove from the curb and steered the big Packard out Connecticut Avenue.

Under the Shoreham portico the doorman in his long red coat with braided ornaments and brass buttons opened the door and Mary Martin and I stepped lively into the lobby. Her dad followed and remained quietly in the lobby reading the newspaper and visiting with congressional friends until the Ball ended. He led us to the car as the doorman again opened our door and we drove back to "305." That was the only time I was ever chauffeured by a Congressman.

CAPITOL CHARACTERS

Wonderful Characters

There were some wonderful "characters" about the Capitol. My favorite was a crotchety, old fellow, named "Percy," who ran the House "member's only" elevator. Pages could ride the elevator if it was not full of Congressmen or Congresswomen but could not ride during the roll calls when the members were scurrying back to the chamber to vote. Then the elevator was exclusively for members.

There was nothing "Old Percy" loved more than kicking the pages off his elevator. Percy was a sixty-plus ruddy-faced fellow with scruffy thinning gray hair. He always wore a gray-striped seersucker suit and the most ridiculous ties imaginable. Other pages said he "tipped the bottle too much."

The mischievous pages loved to give Percy a bad time with juvenile antics. In retrospect, we were pretty mean to harass the old fellow. If two or more pages were on the elevator, they would mumble just loud enough for Percy to hear them. "Where do you think Percy got that beautiful tie?" There would be silence.

Finally, one of them would ask, "What a tie! Where did you get that beautiful tie, Percy?"

His standard answer was, "Congressman gave it to me, boy!"

When congressmen were on the elevator, they would all smile or quietly snicker. The inside joke was that the many congressmen would select their worst, loudest, most obnoxious ties and give them to Percy. He felt obliged to wear them, since they had been given by the congressmen, as Percy had boasted.

Lobbyists are not new phenomena. They come out of the woodwork on most important legislative days. As Door Pages, we stood outside the Congressional chamber doors, received all visitors who were in the Capitol to see their congressman or congresswoman for whatever purpose.

The huge hallway outside the House Chamber was called the Lobby, hence the name, I suppose, given to lobbyists. This is where many of the true lobbyists came in the early days. They used to stand around with hats in hand. Now they seem to have more access with the huge political packs (PACs) and likely meet more privately.

In my time as a page, lobbyists–representing organizations, businesses, unions, and even the military–had real business with the members. My favorite was an elderly gentleman who appeared weekly with a new scheme to present to various members of Congress.

He was old, short and chubby, had stringy unkempt gray hair, a shaggy gray beard, and dressed in shabby clothes, wore thick steel-framed glasses and carried a worn brown leather satchel stuffed with protruding tattered papers.

He would walk right up to the "door page," get as close to his face as possible, glare through his thick glasses and spew the name of the congressman he wanted to see.

"Well, just fill out this card if you will, please," the page would ask.

The lobbyist would take the card, scribble some illegible information on the card and hand it back to the page to take into the chamber to give to the named congressman.

"Who shall I say is calling?" was the standard question the page would ask, since no one could ever decipher the writing.

"Just tell him, Billy Whiskers is outside to see him!"

"And what organization do you represent, sir?" the page would ask with a silly smile, anticipating the usual response.

"I represent the poor people, and they can't organize," Billy Whiskers always answered.

Some of the pages cruelly mocked him but he was indeed my favorite character. I was pleased that most of the congressmen would receive Billy respectfully and listen to his stories and supplications. Billy Whiskers was a compelling individual pre-dating the time when Common Cause and the social lobbyists became so prominent.

Different pages had different duties. The basic page duty involved staying in the House Chamber, available to respond to the needs of the congressmen such as running errands or procuring documents to be used on House floor debates.

There were what we called, "good Congressmen and not so good Congressmen" (never bad Congressmen). A page was to "be seen, not heard," the older Chief Page, Mr. Turner Robertson, told us, as if we were children. Each page had his idea about the individual representatives. Most were courteous and kind to the pages and we respected and admired them.

During my 1950 tenure, my favorites were: Mr. Harold Patton of Arizona and Mr. John Trimble of Arkansas (both of whom used to sit down on the page bench beside us just to chat); Mr. John F. Kennedy of Massachusetts, who had such a friendly and bright office staff reflecting the humor of its member; Mr. Hale Boggs, the gentleman from Louisiana who used to bring his young children onto the floor; Mr. John Boykin, a husky, jolly fellow from Mobile, Alabama had a big sign in his office, *"Everything is Made for Love."* Others were, Mr. Dewey Short, perhaps the best and most dynamic orator in the chamber from Missouri, known by the members as the "Orator of the Ozarks;" Mr. Charles Bennett (a page favorite) from Florida; Mr. Hugo Sims, from South Carolina; and of course my own Congressman Davis, plus my best friend Dan's dad, Mr. Clinton D. McKinnon of California.

One day early in the session, while standing by the page bench, a heavyset, gray-haired congressman grabbed a passing young fellow with a crew cut and gruffly commented, "Young man, I want you to run over to my office and pick up some papers and bring them to me on the floor and be quick about it."

Stunned the young fellow pulled away from the congressman's grasp and answered, "But sir, I'm Congressman Hugo Sims from South Carolina." The pages on the page bench could not keep from snickering as the old congressman shook his head in disbelief and answered, "But you're so young, son."

Congressman Hugo S. Sims, 81st Congress, had served in the 101st Airborne Division and received the Distinguished Service Cross and Silver Star for combat heroism in Europe during WW II.

Some congressmen were surly, feeling their importance. Some of the representatives had been there too long. They thought they owned the government. How did they keep their jobs, we wondered? Today it seems nothing has changed.

There was one congressman from North Carolina who I thought ought to go back to plowing in the field, for he had no place in Congress. One day I was working as a door page and a lovely constituent family appeared in the lobby. They had come to the House chamber. They wanted to see their congressman.

The said congressman was relaxing in the cloakroom. I went into the cloakroom with the little white visitor's card and advised the congressman that a constituent family waited outside to see him. He put on his thick glasses, looked at the card and sullenly told me, "Tell them I'm tied up and will be out shortly." He stuffed the card into his vest pocket.

"Yes, sir," I said and returned to the lobby door.

After two additional visits to the cloakroom, I told him that, his visitors were still waiting. Again, he said, "Just tell them I'm still tied up." He was in fact reclined on a couch reading the newspaper, *The Washington Post.*

"Sir, they have been here a long time."

He looked at me and sarcastically asked, "Well, what do they look like?"

Now exasperated at his tone, "Just regular folks," I answered.

"Well, how are they dressed?" he asked.

"Sir, they are dressed as well as you are," I answered, now further exasperated at his attitude. He glared at me, got up off his behind, adjusted his tie, put on his coat and frowning dispassionately at me walked out to the lobby.

"Where are they, boy?"

I led him over to his visitors, carefully identified them then introduced them to the congressman. He was all smiles, "Mr. Gladhand," as if they were long lost relatives. I couldn't believe it. I had done my job. I turned away and quietly returned to my position by the Congressional door in the lobby.

Of course, I was reported to the chief page for insolence. I was called to my congressman's office. I thought I was in big trouble. There I described the incident to my congressman, Judge Davis. He contemplated my story for a moment, leaned back in his big leather chair, smiled and said, confirming my impression, "Don't worry, that old fellow ought not to be in Congress anyway. I've never thought much of him. I will speak to the chief page and the door keeper." That ended the problem.

Occasionally, our Congressional offices called the chamber and ask us to show visitors about the Capitol. We were our congressman's tour guides. We enjoyed showing our guests, mostly hometown folks, the special secret places of the Capitol: the whispering marker in Statuary Hall that echoed one's voice from one side of the old House Chamber through the arched dome to the other, our first eaves-dropping site. Interesting to some was the room adjacent to the old chamber where, in 1848, John Quincy Adams was taken when he suffered a fatal stroke while at his desk in the old chamber. (He had returned to Congress in 1829 after serving as President from 1825 to 1829.) I understand it is now a ladies' powder room named after Louisiana's late congresswoman, Mrs. Lindy Boggs, the widow of Congressman Hale Boggs and mother of the late journalist Cokie Roberts.

We enjoyed showing the basement tomb, always a favorite, designated originally for the presidential repose of George Washington, the secret stone stairs descending with the scrapes on the walls that we described as British bayonet marks from when the British burned the Capitol (1814) during the War of 1812.

We often ended our tour at the bronze statue of Will Rogers by reminding them that Will Rogers wanted to be placed facing the House Chamber entrance doors so he "could keep an eye on those boys in Congress."

We always showed the Capitol visitors Georgia representatives in Statuary Hall, the old House Chamber. Near the hallway to the present House Chamber was Alexander Hamilton Stevens, the Vice President of the Confederacy and not too far away was Dr. Crawford W. Long, the first to use ether in Jefferson, Georgia, for general anesthesia. Doctor Long's statue now stands in the room below the dome. Some say there was too much weight for Statuary Hall to hold all the state statues.

The page's week was not always nose to the grindstone. We did have time on weekends for venturing away from the Capitol and discovering the Washington sites of interest. We visited the museums and attended the old Washington Senator's baseball games and the Annual Congressional baseball game and other events in the city. On some weekends, I enjoyed spending a bit of time reading in the old Folger Shakespeare Library near the Capitol. Some actually attended church.

Many of the boys lived in rundown hotels near the Capitol since we had no dormitory accommodations. A favorite place was the old Dodge Hotel, where some young Capitol employees resided or hung out. (A story written by the journalist, Chris Matthews, in his delightful book, *Hardball* describes some interesting stories of the old Dodge Hotel.) We ate our meals either in the Capitol or in the neighborhood. Our favorite weekend dining was an upgrade at old "Rectors," located at 149 B Street. We took our morning coffee and sweet rolls in the Library of Congress snack bar during our only morning class break. No meals were served at our lodging at 305 New Jersey Avenue.

One night after studying, we decided to go up to B Street for a late snack. John Allen Crook, of Union Springs, Alabama, Jim Bethshares from Humboldt, Tennessee, and I covered our pajamas with our raincoats, not bothering to change clothes. We had been told not to go out alone at night, so we ventured into the back door of the nearby Cannon House Office Building. We passed the security guard with no trouble (a George Washington University law student asleep on the job). When we returned, the work shift had changed and two cops, one in plain clothes, stopped us and interrogated us. They turned us over to their sergeant who said, "Obviously, you boys are disturbed, wearing pajamas out on the streets at night, so we'll have to take you over to Saint Elizabeth's for a psychiatric exam."

Oh, we thought, *what will we tell our congressmen? They'll probably send us home.* Following due warning, the cops let us go. After we turned the hall corner toward the exit, we heard the cops belly-laughing.

Sometimes our job sent us on errands for our state delegations. My congressman gave me a petition to carry around and have the Georgia delegation sign in protest for some policy President Truman had proposed (probably a "left wing civil rights" edict that was opposed by Southern politicians at that time). Several dutifully signed and I was quickly out of their offices until I entered Mr. Carl Vinson's office. Mr. Vinson was Chairman of the House Armed Services Committee.

Mr. Vinson was a slender, older, gray-haired fellow who trucked no foolishness, though a genuinely kind man. His male secretary led me into the inner congressman's office. There another man stood, tablet and pen in hand, taking dictation from the congressman. Those guys stood for dictation. Sitting was not allowed. It was like a military command post. The small Mr. Vinson sat behind what I thought was a huge aircraft carrier for a desk. His office was decorated with flags and photographs in what was otherwise a conservative spartan room.

When I presented the typed petition to sign, he looked over glasses suspended on the tip of his nose and dropped it on his desk and retorted, "Hell, son, I can't sign this. I don't need no trouble with the President. Where do you think we get all our goddamn money for the military?" Then he spat a chunk of dark tobacco some four feet to land perfectly in a shiny, polished brass spittoon.

Mutely I stood at attention and responded sheepishly, "Yes, sir, I'll tell Judge Davis."

"Right, boy, you do that!" With a half-smile he nodded to his secretary. I was ushered out of his office in a flash.

(In 1982 the aircraft carrier, The USS Carl Vinson was delivered to the United States Navy. I could not but think of his desk when I read the article.)

ACROSS THE LAWN

Running through the snow to work

Some of the pages had never seen snow. That winter morning, we awoke to an overcast sky and the first snow of 1950. Several inches covered the street by the Library of Congress and the lawn to the Capitol. We carefully trudged through the fresh snow in the dark to class.

One Florida boy, Frank Ennis, stood with his mouth open out in the weather looking up and tasting the cold flakes of snow as they drifted down from the gray clouds. He yelled with delight as he skidded and stumbled, sloshing through the mysterious white stuff to class.

We kept a close watch out the windows as the snow increased. By the time the bell rang, sending us off to work, the snow had deepened in just those few hours. Outside we scurried into the Library drive to cross the Capitol lawn. Our despot page overseer, a high school senior hurried ahead knowing he would be the target of every bench page. Oliver ran as fast as he could, but the younger pages pummeled him with snowballs, until he was yelling obscene verbs and nouns toward us. He escaped into the Capitol building, dusted the snow and yelled warnings back at us.

When we all reassembled around the Democratic page bench, he had chores assigned to each of his attackers. "Hey, you," he blurted out to his prime targets, "you get all the SOBs today and no breaks for any of you." An "SOB" was a long distance run to the far away Senate Office Building (not the favorite call). The only good thing about that assignment was that we might be able to ride the Senate underground train. (The House side did not have a train.) Nevertheless, we felt we had won the day.

FOOT DRAGGING
IN THE DOCUMENT ROOM

He loved harassing the pages

Johnny, a short stocky guy, who moved about like a slow turtle, ran the document room on the House side, just off Statuary Hall. He loved to hassle pages, making them wait to the point of absolute frustration.

The page would be sent to the document room to get a needed bill or law, or Hearing Report. "Hurry back," the Congressman often requested. The page overseer would usher the page out of the chamber with a little piece of paper from a ledger time pad with the time marked and the document number required.

Upon arrival at the document room window, the harried page would be ignored. Then, the clerk would saunter up to the window and complain that the pages always were in too much of a rush and they were harassing him while he searched for documents. He had that bureaucratic care-less swagger that never seemed to hurry.

In the Capitol it could be epidemic, not only in the record room but in other areas where the guys or gals had simply been there in boring jobs too long. We knew what a drag some of the clerical jobs must be. They were hanging in there for years until they could draw their federal pensions.

These folks did not make our lives any better. We would run back through Statuary Hall into the House Chamber. The overseer would check and record our return time. If we were not back from our errand when the overseer thought we should have been, he often denied breaks during the day's session or gave us extra assignments.

Usually, we were finished by 6 p.m. and we could leave for supper and head to our respective pads for the night. Even though we were off duty, several of us attended the D. C. public night school three times a week to get all of our required credits.

CHOO CHOO TO KENTUCKY

"...I can drive him..."

Mr. Turner Robertson, the Chief Page, came over to the page bench where I was sitting. He stood in front of me with an inquisitive expression. "You have a car, don't you?"

"Yes, sir," I answered, wondering why he should want to know. Maybe I had parked in the wrong place and was about to be scolded. My pal Dan McKinnon had placed his dad's Congressional windshield sticker on his A-Model so he could park on the Capitol Drive and caught hell when the Capitol cops realized the old Ford was obviously not a congressman's car.

Mr. "R" quietly asked, "Would you take a congressman to the railroad station today in your car?" He paused for a moment, "Mr. Morton from Kentucky has to catch a train home before the session ends today and his staff can't take him. He wants to leave directly from the floor."

"Yes, sir, I can drive him. My car is parked down on New Jersey and I can bring it up to the House portico and pick him up. I'll need a few minutes to get it though."

"Okay, good, I'll let him know," Mr. Turner responded.

Mr. Turner then spoke to the page supervisor, Oliver Furlong, "Don't send him off the floor, so he can be available to take Congressman Morton to the station."

Mr. Morton was a Republican and I was on the Democratic bench and I wondered why the Republican side didn't offer him a ride. Some of the older boys over there had cars.

An hour or so later Mr. Robertson eased over to the page supervisor and told him to send me out to get my car. "Meet Mr. Morton at the Portico by four o'clock. His train leaves at four-thirty," Furlong said to me.

I was under the portico only a couple of minutes until Congressman Morton rushed down the stone steps, "You the boy driving me to the station?" he asked.

"Yes, sir," I responded as I got out of my car to get any bags or stuff that he might have. He had only his bulky briefcase full of official papers and he opened his door and threw it into the back seat of my little '40 Plymouth coup.

"Nice little car," he said.

"Yes, sir, bought it with my own money, saved this year."

As we drove off, he urged me, "Hurry, son, we've got only a few minutes."

When we approached the station along the side street, we noticed several street barriers blocking most of the entrance. He leaned over toward me and commanded, "Just go around those." He pointed his fingers.

Suddenly, from nowhere a burly D. C. cop appeared, frantically waving his arms and yelling, "Stop! Stop, you can't go in there."

"Go on," the congressman said. "Don't mind him." He again pointed toward the barriers.

"But, sir," I mumbled.

"No damn buts' son, just keep going," he urged.

We cruised right through the opening in the barriers and in my mirror, I could see the cop huffing and puffing running after us yelling, "Stop, I said stop!" Then I noticed he had his hand on his pistol handle while waving his opposite hand in the air, "Stop, stop!"

We slowed and pulled up to the side entrance to the terminal station and the cop hurried, huffing and puffing toward my car, still holding on to his holstered gun as he approached the car.

Mr. Morton got out of my car and waved his briefcase at the police officer. "I'm Congressman Morton and I've got to catch a train."

The officer stopped, leaned over to catch his breath, put his hands on his knees and then breathlessly yelled back, "Yes sir, go right in."

Mr. Morton nodded, "Thanks for the ride, son." He disappeared into the huge terminal, clutching his brief case and rushing to catch his train home to Kentucky.

The officer turned toward my car and leaned his hand on my car fender, catching his breath he said, "Damn son, wish I had known that fellow was a congressman. If you had just stopped!"

"Yes, sir," I responded. "I just did what he told me to do."

"Right, I understand."

"How about riding me back to the barriers?" he asked.

"Sure," I responded. "Hop in."

When the cop got out, I noticed Mr. Morton had left me a five-dollar bill on the seat, about half a day's pay.

Note: Congressman Thurston Morton, a Republican, represented Kentucky in the House of Representatives from 1947 until 1953. In 1956 he was narrowly elected to the U. S. Senate and served until he resigned in 1968. Morton along with 84% of his Republican contemporaries, supported the Civil Rights Act of 1964.

IT MUST HAVE BEEN YOU GUYS

We were known to be buddies

Mr. Turner Robertson stood by the page bench, "I want to see Dan and Jerry for a minute," he announced.

Dan and I glanced at each other. "He wants to see us," I whispered to my friend.

Dan murmured, "What for?"

Mr. R led us into the cloak room by the telephone booths and said, "Boys, I've got a complaint about you two." He was not happy.

"About us?" we said in fear of what we were accused of. We had no idea what he was talking about.

"It's Mr. Powell's office that's made the complaint," said Mr. Robertson. "It's actually his secretary that has made the complaint," he added.

Adam Clayton Powell was a controversial representative from Harlem, New York. His father was a Baptist minister of The Abyssinian Baptist Church in Harlem and the young Powell assumed the leadership of his father's church in 1941. He was first elected in 1944 to congress. Mr. Powell was not the most popular man in the House.

We knew the person Mr. Robertson was talking about. She must have weighed three hundred pounds at least and we knew she hated the pages. It was common knowledge that Mr. Powell was rarely in the chamber and in fact was rarely in Washington. "He spends most of his time in Bimini," said one page. "That's why he keeps his door locked and our knocks go unanswered. He's simply not there."

I had seen the secretary slowly open the door long after a page had knocked and there had been no answer. She would shuffle out into the hall, all three hundred pounds and try to pick up the packages and letters and messages we necessarily left beside the door on the floor.

She would waddle, twist and attempt to squat to reach down and pick up the stuff. It was like watching a big circus tent descend to the floor. If we were still in the hallway we would hurry back and help her, but most of the time we had already left when she decided to come out of the locked office. Even when we helped, she was still grumpy.

"The other day one or both of you left the mail at their door and when the secretary came out, I'm told you hid down the hall and laughed when she tried to pick up the mail," our boss accused.

Dan and I were known to be buddies, but we would never be guilty of such an incident. We were too scared of losing our jobs. Dan's dad was a congressman and we knew we would catch hell from him for such a stunt and I would likely be in trouble with my congressman, even if it were Mr. Powell's office. My congressman, a sober, strait-laced fellow was no fan of Powell's antics and negligent work ethics.

Eventually a kid from Kentucky admitted that it might have been him, but if so, he was laughing at something else and not at the secretary.

Note: Mr. Turner Robertson began his employment at the U.S. Capitol in 1947, serving in several patronage capacities. He was first appointed Chief Minority Page by then-Minority leader, Sam Rayburn and later Majority Chief Page when in 1948 the Democratic victories in congress retook the majority position. Mr "R" served until 1971 and retired with the gratitude of the congress and its members. He was a fine example for all young pages to emulate and was important to many lives that served under his direction as Democratic pages, those last twenty years of his chief position.

Congressman Powell was an early activist in Civil Rights promotion but his negligent conduct in the Congress resulted in the House excluding him from taking his seat in the 90th Congress following allegations of political corruption. He later ran for office and was re-elected but did not take his seat. (The Supreme Court subsequently ruled in his favor stating that the Congress erred in failing to seat a duly elected representative.) His increasing absenteeism was noted and in 1970 he was defeated for re-election. He returned to Bimini. Mr. Powell died in Miami after an extended illness in 1972.

House Democratic Page Bench -- 1950
"It must have been you guys."
Left to right: Jim Platt, Jerry Watts, Dan McKinnon
(Photo from author's collection)

YELLING IN THE CHAMBER

Dissatisfaction with the pages

The debate in the House chamber could become fiery rhetoric. However, most of the time the atmosphere was business-like, with the relentless droning voice of the Clerk of the House, reading the bills to be considered, interrupted occasionally by the congressmen on the floor interjecting comments or introducing amendments to the bill being read.

Occasionally members would be loudly chatting among themselves until the acting speaker banged his gavel to get order. "Will the gentleman from Ohio cease his conversation with the gentleman from Tennessee." Then the monotone reading of the bill in question would resume.

Most of the members were reasonable in their requests for the pages to carry out the duties of taking messages or calling their offices or picking up documents from the record room for use on the Floor.

Rarely did a member express dissatisfaction with an errant page openly on the floor of the house. If he or she were not happy with a page's performance, he or she would readily and quietly, notify the Chief Page of the respective political party of their concerns or complaints.

One afternoon an elderly member of the North Carolina delegation became enraged at some minor error committed by a bench page. This old fellow had been in the Congress, we thought, since George Washington. In fact, as a past chairman of the powerful Ways and Means Committee, he had made a deal with President Franklin Roosevelt in 1935 when FDR was trying to pass his several national social proposals.

In exchange for his support of the Economic Security Bill, a bill that would subsequently be renamed the Social Security Act (while still in committee), the congressman demanded that the Blue Ridge Parkway be relocated. He demanded that the parkway be completely in North Carolina instead of a portion going into Tennessee, thus ending at the North Carolina Cherokee Indian Reservation.

The parkway was relocated, and the important Social Security Act was passed. The Act was a cornerstone of President Roosevelt's New Deal.

On this day, Mr. Doughton stood unsteadily in the chamber waving his arms, yelling and cursing the "damn dumb pages" who had slighted him in some way. The speaker banged his gavel for the elderly member to cease his shouting and sit down. Several concerned members and the Sergeant at Arms rushed to the gentleman and held him securely and ushered him into the cloakroom.

We were stunned. We had never seen such an outburst on the floor of the House. Within minutes the speaker banged for silence and the reading of the Bill resumed.

Mr. Robertson hurried over to our page bench, "Act like nothing has happened, boys."

Note: What the pages didn't realize was that Mr. Robert Doughton had honorably served the state of North Carolina and his country since 1910 and had simply served beyond his age and ability to normally function in his political arena. He remained in Congress until 1952. Mr. Doughton, an honorable man, died in 1954.

"A COMMUNIST IN SOCIALIST CLOTHING"

He rarely smiled.

He was a thin, slump-shouldered, wiry fellow. He wore wrinkled dark suits, was be-spectacled with thick lens glasses which hung on the tip of his sharp nose. He rarely smiled. When he entered the Chamber, each member watched to see where he would sit. If he sat on the Democratic side of the chamber aisle, a few Republican members would softly clap. If he seated himself on the Republican side, the same slight applause would be heard from the Democratic side. The Speaker ignored his presence and simply failed to respond to the noise of his political foes.

"He's a damn communist," they said. It was not good to be considered a communist when the Cold War was heating up.

Rarely would anyone sit beside him. On occasion, Franklin D. Roosevelt, Jr., of New York would ease down in the seat close by. "Birds of a feather," some members and pages whispered.

Mr. Vito Marcantonio was an Independent or Socialist, most reckoned. He was not popular with the members. We never knew which side of "the aisle" he would select for his seat, Democrat or Republican. We especially didn't know which page would be responsible to his office. As far as I can recall, I never went to his office. Nevertheless, he faithfully represented his district of New York and its people.

As Gerald Meyer wrote in his essay in **The American Radical**, "What made Vito Marcantonio utterly unique among all the other congressmen was his insistence that the Communist party was an 'American political party operating in what it considers to be the best interests of the American working-class people.'"

"He was vilified by the American press. His running solely on the American Labor Party line, universally identified him as Communist controlled."

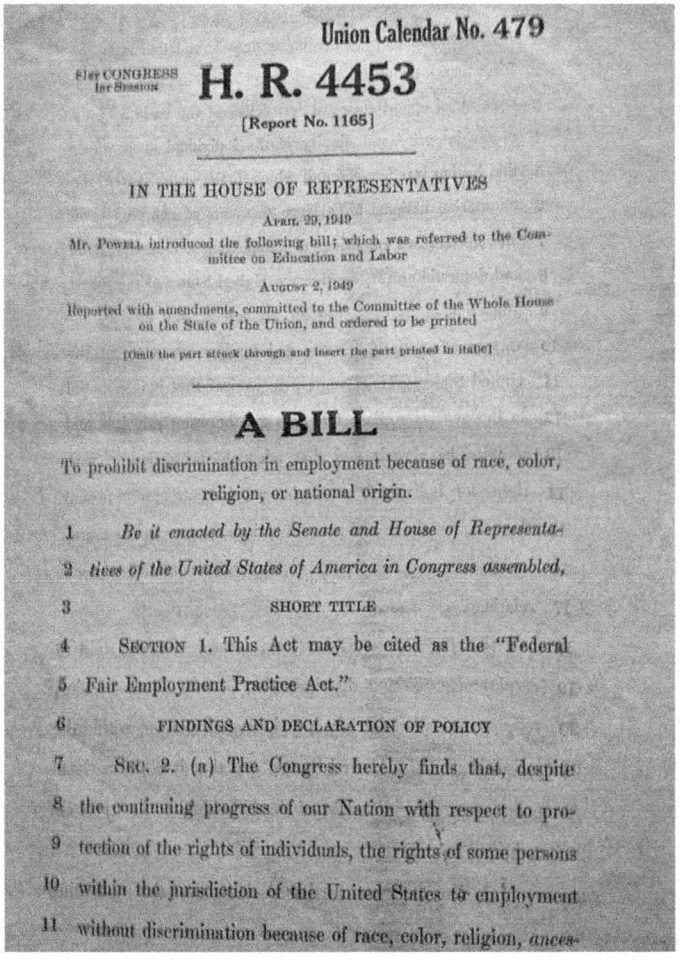

H. R. 4453 was an early legislative effort, to prohibit discrimination in employment because of race, color, religion, ancestry, or national origin.

Despite his left political credentials, he faithfully represented his district of New York and its people, an extremely liberal and mixed ethnic segment of the country.

Vito Marcantonio was among the first to introduce legislation into Congress that would protect the freedom of all to employment without discrimination as to race, color, religion, or national origin. The legislation which he supported, the Fair Employment Practice Commission (FEPC) or Act was designed to protect the civil rights of all Americans. President Roosevelt had signed Executive Order 8802 in June 1941, prohibiting discrimination in Federal Agencies. Later FEPC legislation was offered for all employment, not just federal employment.

Marcantonio said at the debate about the FEPC bill (January 1950) on the House floor, "What is involved is not the freedom of anyone to employ whom he pleases... What is involved is the tyranny of anyone to refuse to give employment to any person because of race, color, or creed..."

Note: Vito Marcantonio accused President Truman of not supporting the social issues that Marcantonio defined in his many harsh House floor speeches.

In his orations on the House Floor concerning China, Korea and Viet Nam, Marcantonio opposed any financial intervention in Taiwan calling it a corrupt government and supporting China's revolution as a cleansing of tyranny and corruption. He also opposed the financial support and military aid to South Korea, stating that the South, below the arbitrary 38th latitude, resisted unification of "all of Korea" which he supported.

Nevertheless, upon his death, he was mourned by thousands of his ethnically diverse minority district. He had declared, "I have stood by the fundamental principles which I have always advocated, I have not trimmed, I have not retreated, I do not apologize, and I am not compromising." Though we may not agree with Mr. Marcanonio on many issues we must respect his sincerity in his beliefs.

A NIGHT IN CONGRESS

"Founding Fathers…"

In February of 1950, an early version of the Fair Employment Practice Act bill was debated in the House of Representatives. My representative, a Conservative Democrat from Georgia, hotly debated Representative Adam Clayton Powell, a Liberal Democrat from Harlem, New York, on the House floor.

The House runs on a more rigid schedule than the Senate, therefore the House is rarely in session at night. This night was different. The bill was debated late into the night. Near midnight the House remained in session. The House floor pages were allowed to leave the chamber for short breaks. I took my break and wandered down to the dome of the Capitol where there were leather benches.

I passed by the bronze statue of Will Rogers in the hall between the House chamber and Statuary Hall, as his likeness stood, slouched with his head tilted toward the House chamber, "keeping an eye on those boys in Congress."

I continued on passing through Statuary Hall where each state had immortalized one or more of their outstanding citizens with stone or bronze statues. Though cold and motionless, they seemed to watch as I sauntered alone through the spooky, quiet high-domed hall.

Once in the rotunda, I reclined on a leather cushioned bench in the soft soothing glow of the dome lights. I glanced around at the historic images and the ceiling mosaics to see our founders represented as mythical figures representing our birth, our culture, and industry. I surveyed the circumferential gray and white fresco panorama of our country's historical progress.

When I dozed off, the figures, statues and paintings of the founding fathers surrounding me seemed to come alive in a hazy dream. Across the floor Thomas Jefferson seemed to speak to me. He spoke in a soft and slightly high-pitched tone as if to say, "Son, your country is quite safe, don't worry." Then it was quiet, oh, so quiet.

The Capitol Rotunda -- "... statues and paintings of the founding fathers... seemed to come alive..."
(Photo from Library of Congress)

Half an hour or so later a page rudely awoke me from my solace. He nudged me, "Get your butt up. It's time for you to go back." I again walked through the dim haze of the rotunda, the hall of statues, to the glaring, bright lights of the House chamber. I felt at ease, knowing I had been in the presence of the founding fathers.

It was not until forty years later when I crossed the "Lawn" of my son's College at Charlottesville, Virginia, that I again felt the mysterious presence of Mister Thomas Jefferson.

PAGING EXPERIENCE

There are many memorable experiences from my session as a Page in Congress. Perhaps the most significant ones involve seeing the government in action and how it really functions, both good and bad. There were congressmen who were just starting their political careers, those recently elected. There were the older, well-known political leaders of the nation. Working with these men and women was an exciting experience. We were only pages, yet we were treated as mature individuals by most of the members of Congress and even sometimes appreciated for doing our jobs as best we could.

I recall the times I would be on an errand to the Senate Office Building and without fanfare ride the electric subterranean tunnel rail car with members and Senators of national reputation or standing. For a teenager it was a remarkable experience to be in the presence of the nation's leaders in such a casual manner.

The most memorable rides were with Mr. Albin Barkley of Kentucky. Mr. Barkley was Vice President of the United States and President of the Senate. It was like riding with one's grandfather. "Climb aboard, son," he would say, when we were hesitant to board the little car with other Senators. Mr. Barkley was unpretentious, and he was always kind and talkative. He would ask our names and inquire about our home states and our congressmen. Surely, he didn't remember our names, we thought, but he was always pleasant and friendly to each of us.

Our job put us in contact with young congressmen who would later lead our country. Among those young congressmen were: second-term Massachusetts Congressman John F. Kennedy; second-term Congressman Richard M. Nixon of California; and first-term Congressman Gerald Ford of Michigan. Each of these men through varied circumstances became presidents of the United States.

Mr. Kennedy was a Democrat and frequently stopped by the Democratic Page bench and chatted with the pages. He really didn't seem too much older than us, even though he had served in the World War. We loved to visit his office to deliver messages or to run errands for him. His staff was young and bright, and always had some upbeat conversation for us. In "The Best and the Brightest," David Halberstam described the talent of the bright young Kennedy staff. Most of them seemed like college students or "neat adults." As teenagers we felt as if we were among our peers when we visited his office.

Mr. Kennedy often left his seat on the House floor and ventured to the back of the chamber and stood holding onto the brass rail surrounding the chamber. It was not until years later that I realized he was suffering back pain and he was relieving that pain by standing rather than sitting so long in the chamber.

Years later in 1962, while in the Air Force during the "Cuban Missile Crisis," I sat on the veranda of the Navy officer's club at Leeward Point, Guantanamo Naval Base, Cuba, and watched a special news program on a rabbit ears television set. Our President, Mr. Kennedy announced that he was evacuating the navy dependents and reinforcing the garrison at Guantanamo Naval Base as well as patrolling the waters around Cuba, I glanced at my fellow officers and whispered, "I used to work for him."

I had little to do with Mr. Nixon, since he was a Republican and only on occasion did I, as a Democratic page go to his office. Nixon was a controversial character, even in 1950. My best friend Dan McKinnon's father was a Democratic Congressman from California's 23rd District (Clinton D. McKinnon), next door to Nixon's district. To California Democrats, Nixon was already "Tricky Dick" because of his political shenanigans. When I went to Dan's home for the weekends, he admonished me not to mention Dick Nixon in front of his dad. "He would have a spell," Dan said. I didn't.

Congressman Gerald Ford was another story. He was a husky, tall, former Michigan University football player and former Naval officer whom we all respected. He was quiet though I heard his great laughter more than once. We rarely went to his office since he was also a Republican, but we never minded going there because of his friendly office staff. He was to prove his good image years later when he rescued the Presidency from the shame of the Watergate folly. Despite his presidential pardon for Richard Nixon, most feel he saved the country from further political turmoil.

There were many excellent speakers and debaters in the House. The debates ranged from passionate support for some legislation to hostility to the same bill or bills. There were at least two or three speakers who filled the Chamber. Of course, when Speaker Sam Rayburn took to the well for comments, the phones would ring off the hooks advising the members to be present for his comments. Speaker Rayburn was known for his ability to move legislation. His motto was, "To get along, go along."

It is said that while Mr. Truman was a Missouri senator, and perhaps briefly while vice-president, he would visit the Speaker's Office and Speaker Sam and Harry would share a couple of glasses of Kentucky Bourbon from the "fifth" the Speaker always kept tucked away in his desk.

My favorite congressional orator in the House was Mr. Dewey Short of Missouri. His eloquent and fiery speeches mesmerized those listening to his words by the sheer strength of his debating skills. His contemporaries dubbed him, "The silver-tongued orator of the Ozarks." Often as not, he debated a popular and articulate Representative from across the state line, Mr. Boyd Tackett of Arkansas.

On April 12, 1945, President Franklin D. Roosevelt died of a cerebral stroke while visiting the "Little White House" in Warm Springs, Georgia. Vice-President Harry S Truman became president. The new president's responsibilities were huge. Truman felt unprepared for the job. Many of the secrets of government had been kept from him by Roosevelt and his White House crowd. Truman was informed of The Manhattan Project (the secret Atomic Bomb program) only after he took office.

Truman made the difficult decision to use the bomb on the Japanese mainland after attempts to demand Japan's surrender had failed. The bombing of Japan resulted in Japan's unconditional surrender and the end of World War II. Truman never looked back, though he was criticized by many for the use of the bomb. It saved hundreds of thousands of military and civilian lives on both sides. It may seem easy to judge some seventy-plus years after the event, but at that time the world had suffered enough from the tragic World War.

President Truman's tenure saw the rise of the Soviet government's occupation of Eastern Europe and the beginning of the Cold War.

When invited by Truman, Great Britain's Prime Minister, Winston Churchill spoke at the small Westminster College in Fulton, Missouri, and coined the term "Iron Curtain." The term clearly defined the separation of East and West Germany and the division of all of Europe.

Mr. Truman defeated New York Republican Governor, Thomas E. Dewey in the 1948 presidential election. The success of the congressional elections that year resulted in the Democratic takeover of the U.S. Congress. Though low in national poll ratings at the end of his term in office, history has judged Harry S Truman among the great American Presidents.

On arrival in Washington, I possessed personal letters of introduction from my dad's boss (an Atlanta city alderman) to our two Georgia senators, Senator Richard Russell and Senator Walter F. George. Senator Russell headed the Senate Armed Services Committee while Senator Walter George chaired the Senate Finance Committee. In the House, Georgia's representative Carl Vinson headed the House Armed Service Committee. These were three of the most powerful committees in Congress.

I made my obligatory visits to our two senators and they were courteous, welcoming me to my job on Capitol Hill. Senator Russell was more animated in his conversations with me than the elderly Senator George. Each were generous in their kindness toward me while I served my appointment time in Washington.

While on duty, we were occasionally sent on errands to the Senate side of the Capitol or the adjacent Senate Office Building. Since we were House pages we were not often recognized by name, therefore it was foreign territory, yet most of the senate office staffs were receptive and courteous to the pages.

Of course, we were sent to all senate offices and there was never any problem. However, when I was required to go to the Texas Democratic Senator Lyndon Johnson's office, I always felt uncomfortable in his presence. He seemed initially pleasant with a hale and hearty loud Texas voice, yet I heard him more than once become ungentlemanly and verbally abusive to his male office staff members. It was embarrassing to see him chide his assistants unashamedly in the public hallways of the Capitol. I thought he was "vulgar and bad talking." Some of my friends said it was just "common Texas lingo." I preferred to keep a distance when I had to go to his office or have any contact with him on the Senate side of the Capitol.

Years later, after my active military service, in November 1963, I sat before the black and white television set mourning the death of President Kennedy, distressed that the man I had so little respected, Lyndon Johnson would be our president.

The inherited Vietnam War was his political downfall. Though he succeeded in completing some of President Kennedy's great civil rights legislation through his commanding arm twisting. He likely will be positively remembered.

I was greatly relieved in March 1968 as I watched on television when Johnson announced that he would not seek the Democratic nomination for the presidency and would not be a candidate for reelection. History will have to judge him.

CONGRESS AND THE KOREAN CONFLICT

The Congressional session had extended through the summer of 1950 because of the emergency in Korea. On June 25 or 26 (depending on how the date was determined by the international date line), the North Korean military forces, backed by Soviet influence and equipment crossed the 38th parallel and invaded South Korea. Our defenses (mostly advisors at that time), combined with the South Korean defenses, were inadequate to defend the southern territory. The North Koreans murderously pushed the South Koreans and American advisors to the southern tip of Korea, almost into the sea.

The one thing I couldn't get off my mind was the political arrogance I saw and heard from a minority of the members of Congress. In January of that year, a "Korean Aid Bill" had been presented on the House floor. I did not know then (nor did the public) that General Douglas McArthur, our commander in the Far East, and our ambassador, John Mucci, as well as Korean President Syngman Rhee, had begged the Pentagon and Congress for more military equipment and troops to protect against the communist threats from the North. We had supplied only light arms, inadequate for the defense of the South Koreans against the heavy mechanized equipment supplied to North Korea by Russia.

A husky Texas representative saddled up to the back of the House chamber in front of the Democratic page bench. He and his fellow member stood with their dusty Texas boots up on the ledge. They leaned on the brass rail surrounding the chamber. It looked like the younger member shifted his chew of tobacco from one side of his jaw to the other as he asked his friend, "How are you going vote on that Korean Aid Bill?"

The older Texan turned to him. I heard him say in a dismissive voice, "Hell, there ain't no Koreans in my district." He voted no.

The bill failed in the House of Representatives by a vote or 193 to 191. Six months later, the North Korean invasion began. I then wondered how many young men of his district were soon to be in Korea and how many would die there.

It was during those summer months, I discovered that our government failed to report the facts of a war. Part of my responsibility was to prepare the newspapers and update the (intelligence) teletype printouts on racks in the House reading room, directly behind the House chamber. It was obvious to me that the intelligence printouts did not correspond with the local or the national newspaper reports.

I suspected The New York Times and The Washington Post erred in their coverage of the situation in Korea. I was told that the "telex-printouts" were "classified" and I was not to discuss publicly anything that I read in these reports. These reports were for "Congressional eyes only."

I thought about this but said nothing to anyone. I assumed it was for national security that information was filtered. In the future, I would read my local papers and know that what I read was not necessarily true.

"VERY LITTLE TROUBLE WITH PAGES"

Pages were not the problem.

Most of the pages were well-behaved, even with such limited supervision of the page program. For many years, even in the 1800s, they were often described by the locals as a bunch of spoiled privileged kids. There were many boys selected off the streets by congressmen who felt sorry for these waifs and gave them jobs. Some were employed, especially to help their widowed mothers.

Records show that after the Civil War many sons of deceased veterans were employed to help their moms survive.

In the 1950s, there were no page dormitories. The pages who were from out of town lived in various places under various and not always good conditions. Over many years the congress studied the absence of adequate page accommodations and the bad conditions where so many lived in the Capitol city. Despite these studies, the congress did not respond to those needs they had recognized. Several congressmen championed bills that would provide housing for the pages, but those bills died in the committees and never came to fruition until after mid twentieth century.

During my appointment one location was an apartment over what we described as the "Greek Store." From all evidence, it had been a bookie office for gambling with numerous phone line outlets, said to be for communicating betting with bookies of horse racing and other gambling.

Several boys lived over the Greek grocery store and one day one of the pages disappeared. It turns out he was underage and was getting wine from the store below and getting drunk with a couple of buddies in the apartment. The rumor of his disappearance was that he was sent home by his congressman and the door keeper. The Washington police closed the apartment so that as far as I know, no pages ever lived in that apartment again.

During the past few years, a small number of pages have been dismissed because of drug problems and other unfortunate incidents. During the 1980s several congressmen were accused of inappropriate relationships with pages. One was censured for inappropriate email with a youth and a couple were found to have improper physical relationships with the pages, both male and female.

It appears the pages were less of a problem than the congressmen. In 2011, Speaker John Boehner and minority leader Congresswoman Nancy Pelosi elected to terminate the House program and replace the pages with college interns. They alleged the cost was too great and said modern communication technology has reduced the need for House pages. The Senate and Supreme Court continued the page program.

One of the congressional staff members noted privately that the office staffs were not as endeared with the intern program as with the young page boys and girls who had previously served the congress. They seemed to miss the bright-eyed youngsters that visited their offices.

Whether the page programs will be permanently ended, no one seems to know. Many former pages have organized an appeal to congress to reinstate this valuable tradition. This remains an effort in progress.

Sixty-six years after serving as a page, I returned to Washington for a reunion. The visit brought back happy recollections. Only a few from my decade returned. It was enjoyable to reacquaint with some and reminisce with new friends of all ages who shared similar experiences.

HOMEBOUND

The Southerner rolled on south

The "Southerner" was waiting in Washington's smoky National Terminal Station. With a booming sound and the screeching of its huge iron wheels it began to move. I rushed through the station, swung my suitcase up through the still open car door and climbed the steel steps into the passenger compartment as the conductor sang out "All Aboard." The Southern Railway was taking me back home to Georgia for the start of the fall semester of my high school. I would be replaced by one of my best friends, another Atlantan, Jimmy Jenkins, son of Atlanta's chief of police, Herbert T. Jenkins, for the next session.

The following school year was unexciting. I missed the page work and the tension and drama of being in the nation's Capitol. I thought about the great opportunity I had in Washington but realized that phase of my life was over. I would benefit from the insights I'd gained by the experience, but I needed to move on.

One day my school counselor called me into her office. She told me that she was in touch with several universities and asked if I would be interested in leaving high school a year early, that I had been offered a scholarship to the University of Chicago as well as Tufts University in Boston. "These are new early admission programs, admitting high school juniors to start college early," she said. I discussed it with my mother and dad, who felt I had been away in Washington the year before and that I should stay home and graduate with my friends.

"College will come soon enough. You should enjoy your senior year," my mom said. I agreed and through my counselor I thanked the universities for their generous offer.

The university offers sounded good, yet I intended to go to the Army Military Academy at West Point or the Naval Academy at Annapolis. I took all the pre-entrance exams, both physical and academic and passed. The Congressman who had appointed me as a page, advised me that I was accepted, but he was having to decide between another boy and me to determine which academy each would attend. I preferred West Point. It was decided, I would go to West Point. My representative assured me of the appointment. I did not apply to any other colleges.

A few months later I visited our congressman's office and told him that I intended to go to medical school after West Point. He called his administrative assistant, Mr. Bill Edens (the same assistant that had made arrangements for my living quarters in D. C.) to look into the matter. Mr. Edens learned that a West Point or Annapolis graduate would have to serve five years active military duty immediately after graduation before any graduate school would be allowed. (That is no longer the military policy.)

My family and I gave it great thought. Since a military draft was in effect, it didn't matter when I went into the service. Those of draft age were all going. To most draft eligible young men there was no question about serving our country. "Pay now or pay later," but to a seventeen-year-old youth, five years before graduate school seemed an eternity.

After I relinquished my appointment, it was so late, I applied only to southern colleges. I planned on four years of college and four years of medical school. My family could afford it all if I stayed near home. I accepted Emory's offer of admission.

I took a job at Rich's, Atlanta downtown department store. I planned to work there during school holidays to help pay my college expenses. During the summer of 1952 I worked in the young men's department and the Boy Scout department with another young man that became a pleasant friend. Our manager allowed us to take breaks together at the nearby snack bar and sit on the glass bridge that crossed the street between the main store and the store for home furnishings. There we sipped our Cokes and watched the attractive girls walk by.

We had a deal. My pal, Cecil Day, and I were "contingent" employees. We liked our manager and always asked him to check our big sales. We told the mothers of the young men we fitted that we wanted our manager to check all suits and large sales to be sure the mothers were satisfied. They liked that. We had almost no returns.

As temporary or contingent employees, we weren't entitled to sales commissions. Cecil and I wrote up our big sales on our manager's book so that he got a commission.

Late in the summer, I received a telephone call from Dean Gibson, the Director of University Development at Tulane University in New Orleans. He was coming to Atlanta on school business and wished to have lunch with my parents and me to discuss Tulane. My dad invited Dean Gibson to lunch with us at the Henry Grady Hotel.

After a pleasant conversation, Dean Gibson told us that he was able to offer a full four-year scholarship to Tulane. Since it was August and so late in the school year, all the usual academic scholarships had been given out. Mine would be a special scholarship and would require me to work one or two afternoons a week in one of the labs as an assistant to the instructor or professor.

After the first semester, if my grades remained high, the school would change the scholarship to a regular academic scholarship without the work requirement.

The lab job would be an additional opportunity to learn chemistry since I would work directly with the instructors who were also my teachers. The offer sounded good. I thought it would be exciting to attend school in New Orleans. My folks agreed and I accepted. Emory would wait. September arrived and I was on the train headed to New Orleans.

NEW ORLEANS

"The land of Dreams"

I was twelve years old when I first visited New Orleans. My dad took me on a whirlwind cross-country train trip. The war had limited train travel for civilians and since the war had ended everyone was anxious to return to traveling all over the country. A group of folks from Atlanta obtained a Pullman sleeper train car that was attached to regular scheduled trains and toured the South, the Southwest, the far West, and the Northwest through the Canadian Rockies and back home. My dad was determined to show me the country and expose me to adventures he'd never had.

I had traveled as far west as Arkansas and Oklahoma, but never beyond. Our train first took us to New Orleans where we visited the noisy French Quarter. I recall going into a restaurant for lunch and the maître d' met us at the entrance. "Sir, you'll have to have a coat to eat here." My dad eyed him curiously, then the maître d' said, "Oh but, we have one provided for the use of our guests," and he glanced at my dad and voiced a suggested size, turned away and quickly brought a light weight formal jacket and placed it on my dad. Now, we could enter and have our mid-day meal.

Our Pullman car remained in the station on a sidetrack while we visited. We spent the night in New Orleans; and returned a couple of evenings later. The car now attached to another train, we headed west for the night ride, stopping in San Antonio and El Paso for similar visits. While in El Paso we crossed the border into Juarez, Mexico. There, while shopping, my dad gave me a five-dollar bill to spend. Since I was a kid, a Mexican approached me and asked if he could make change into Mexican money. Naively, I gave him my bill and he returned a bunch of paper pesos. *Wow,* I thought, *real Mexican money.* My dad and I found a shop and as I proceeded to pay my bill, the shopkeeper handed me back my bunch of peso bills and said to my dad, "Señor, these bills went out during the last revolution, they are no good."

On to busy Los Angeles. There we had a few days to visit movie studios and the famous theaters and saw a few movie stars as they drove about the city, many in convertibles.

The best of the trip to that point would be the visit in San Francisco and Berkeley. We crossed the Golden Gate Bridge, toured San Francisco, and then Berkeley and the University of California, Berkeley campus. There we stayed in a small hotel on the edge of the campus. Years later, I would return to the Berkeley campus to see my daughter when she was a graduate student there, and I would stay in the same little hotel.

The trip got better as we visited the wonderful Yosemite Park, riding up the hills in open air Pierce Arrow extended automobiles, and seeing the giant sequoias or redwoods. Then, on through Portland to see the great Columbia River as it emptied into the Pacific, perhaps from where Lewis and Clark first saw the grand Pacific on their early 1800s pioneer journey.

Perhaps the most beautiful part of the journey was traveling by open railroad car through the Canadian Rockies where we stopped to stay a while in the Chateau Hotel on Lake Louise and the Banff Springs Hotel, overlooking the high Rockies.

Our trip carried us through mid-Canada, through North Dakota and finally to Chicago and home, ending a fantastic experience for a twelve-year-old. Half a century later I would again visit those areas and the Canadian Rockies.

This train trip would take me to New Orleans, to college. Alone, I left Atlanta with more baggage than a caravan would carry. I had no idea what to bring to college. I brought a steamer trunk. Why in the world I brought woolens to New Orleans I'll never know. The trunk remained closed and in storage until I returned to Atlanta the following spring.

The trip was an overnight ride in a Pullman car. In the early morning I awoke, looked out my train window and watched along the coast of Mississippi before we entered the state of Louisiana.

After a lush breakfast in the dining car, our train pulled into the New Orleans downtown train station.

I caught a cab. "To Tulane," I told the cab driver.

"You a new student?" he asked.

"Yes, I mumbled," curious, why he asked.

It was not long before I realized why he had asked. We drove along Magazine Street and he made several stops at several rundown-looking stores, with the meter still running. He said, "You don't mind if I stop a minute for some business, do you?" I had no idea where we were. I was at his mercy. What could I say? We eventually arrived by what I later realized was a dramatic detour of the route. The cab meter told it all. I was hooked and skinned my first day in town.

Upon arrival at my assigned dorm, I found my room, and found a note taped to my door addressed to me. It said, "To the guy from Georgia." It was signed Malcolm Wright, a Page School classmate from Hammond, LA. He invited me to his fraternity party. The note said, "Saw your name and hometown on the admission list and knew it must be my old classmate. We will pick you up at six."

We rode to Bourbon Street in a little English car, the name of which I don't remember. It was tight for four guys but easy to park on the narrow cobblestone streets of the Quarter. After what to me was a rowdy night in the Quarter, I had amazed my hard-drinking new friends by ordering only Cokes in Pat O'Brian's, the home of the famous Hurricanes.

Heading back to campus, we huddled into the little English car and drove out St. Charles Avenue, alternating between street and the parallel trolley tracks playing "chicken" with the big steel streetcars. We swerved along the tracks, on and off the street. We finally arrived back at my friends Pi Kappa Alpha house on Broadway, unscathed by the adventure. I returned to my dorm, never to visit the Pi Kappa Alpha house again. I joined a different fraternity.

Academically, Tulane was no harder than I expected. My Atlanta public high school had prepared me to do the work. My high school English had prepared me adequately to read and write and had introduced our class to a moderate amount of American literature. My math teacher was a "tough old lady" whom we dearly loved and respected. Her parents had been missionaries to China when she was a child.

At Brown High "Ma" Witcher preferred boys in her class and would tap us on our heads with a wooden yardstick when we were not paying attention. She prepared every boy for Georgia Tech engineering and most of us sailed through math with high grades in college. Our physics teacher, Mr. Floyd, was an associate professor at the Atlanta Division of the University of Georgia (later Georgia State) and taught in their night class program. Our chemistry instructor was retired Army Colonel Edgar Morris, who served in the Chemical Warfare section of the Army during WW II. The freshman year of college, however, was a year of adjustment in balancing academic pursuits and the unbelievable social schedule.

For a couple of friends, the social nightlife took its toll. However, most survived the temptation of New Orleans. The social life at Tulane was not only centered about the campus, but also entwined in the social life of New Orleans. The Mardi Gras season, before Lent, is the epitome of the society activities. Tucked within the gala parties, receptions, and balls is the high debutante season as the young New Orleans' families present their "eligible young girls to society." The festive balls were huge affairs held in the theaters and civic centers with bands, orchestras, and parading members in glittering costumes.

Receptions and parties could be rowdy affairs. Champagne, food, and music abounded, and no expense was denied the revelers. Invitations were reserved for the select few–mostly old New Orleans families. Unfortunately, many of these once-wealthy families had long since become the not-so-wealthy, yet they remained proud, conscious of their social standing, and continuously extravagant in their celebrations.

Tulane celebrated the season with a few days of vacation, yet the students were expected to be in class the morning after the balls during the season leading up to Fat Tuesday, followed by Ash Wednesday, the beginning of Lent, the time of religious repentance and reflection.

We were all settled in our freshman English class when a classmate quietly stumbled through the doorway into class, still in his tuxedo, his tie missing, and his shirttail hanging out below his coat. He staggered in, stumbled over a chair and cautiously took his seat in the rear of the class. He smelled like the gutter. Midway in the lecture we heard a thunderous bang and then a flutter of agitation; he had passed out, fell out of his chair, and hit the floor. The English professor looked up from his poetry and muttered, "Gentlemen, leave him be. At least he made it to class."

The professor then casually returned to his reading of Shelley.

Surprisingly, my name appeared on the New Orleans Social List. My other roommate from Mississippi knew a girl from Jackson who was making her debut to Society in New Orleans. Because of that, he and I became escorts to the debs. It was all new to me. I was certainly not on the social register at home. *"What the heck,"* I thought, *"try it and see."*

Our invitations began to appear in large formally decorated envelopes on the mail desk at our fraternity house. The other brothers began to raise their eyebrows at the notice taken of our new social status. "How did you guys rate those invitations to the Mardi Gras Balls?" they wondered aloud.

John, my roommate, and I decided to keep mum. "Let them guess," we said. "Yeah, let them wonder."

Our invitations read, "Rex Crew/wishes to invite to the Ball celebrating Mardi Gras this year of our Lord, 1953/as the escort of Miss Peggy Jane" followed by her last name, and then the actual date and time.

John and I casually picked up our invitations and opened them with great discretion and privacy in the living room, in close proximity to our jealous brothers. "Oh, my goodness, another invitation," we would nonchalantly remark, modestly slipping the invitations into our pockets, out of sight of our good brothers. They would then assault us and try to rend the invitation from us as we ran out the door.

I was delighted with my assigned date. The debs, by protocol, submitted the desired names of the escorts to a Deb Committee for approval and for invitations, so we were vaguely aware that we might be asked to the balls. Peggy was a slender attractive young girl from Jackson, Mississippi, with dark hair, a great smile, and striking brown eyes, truly a Southern Belle. She transferred to Newcomb College to make her debut in New Orleans. We had fun, though I teased her about the pseudo-glamour of the events.

The Mardi Gras Balls reminded me of the time, as a young kid, I had led my horse around the show ring in a few horse show events in Atlanta. Leading a young filly in a ring isn't much different from leading a lady at a ball, I mused.

One evening my date, Peggy, and I were discussing the cost of the whole debutante affair and I mentioned that the mere cost of one of her dresses, beautiful though it was, would pay an entire semester's tuition at Tulane. I asked why her family would pay that much for one dress.

Without hesitation she smiled and quietly answered, "'Cause my daddy loves me." What could I say!

Over thirty years later, I stood in the presenting debutant line at Atlanta's Phoenix Society Ball with my own lovely daughters in their beautiful dresses and understood what Peggy meant by her statement, "'Cause my daddy loves me."

Gibson Hall – College of Arts and Sciences,
Tulane University,
New Orleans, 1952-1955
(Photo by author)

I RECALLED

"Most respected doctor in town…"

Many years later, long after college, I was in Joseph A. Bank clothing store in Atlanta looking for a suit or coat for a special occasion. The tall young salesman, dressed in well pressed trousers, tailored shirt and fashionable tie, wearing wide striped braces, approached me, "Can I help you sir?" I nodded and we selected several jackets.

We tried on a couple of the jackets and were settling on one that would do for the special occasion. "Where are you from?" I asked. He told me the town in Alabama.

I thought for a moment, "I have an old college friend there who is a doctor." I named him.

"Oh, yes sir. His son was my best friend. Dr. – is the most respected doctor in town," he boasted.

"I bet he is," I answered. But my thoughts drifted back years to our fraternity house and a New Orleans Friday night house party.

Party for A Through K

TULANE ON BROADWAY
Saturday Night S. A. E. Fraternity Party, 1955

"Son, your mother thinks you have had enough of New Orleans."
(Photo from Tulane Jambalaya yearbook)

I vaguely remembered another fraternity brother and I carrying him up the stairs to the second floor, stripping him down to his shorts, and sitting him in a cold shower.

We returned to the party and forgot about him. An hour or so later we rushed back upstairs to find him still sitting in the shower happily singing a fraternity tune.

"Yes," I said to the young salesman, "I'll bet he is the most respected. He always was a good fellow."

A TIN ROOF BUSINESS

A blue-collar job

The summer after the first year of college presented few opportunities for employment. Since there seemed to be no job available, and to avoid boredom, I entered the Atlanta Division of the University of Georgia. I would take an elective psychology course that I couldn't squeeze in otherwise and I thought I might like to write one day, so I signed up for a basic journalism class.

Our professor, Mr. Rickenbacker taught us the first principle of journalism, accuracy. "We will start this class by reading the obituary pages then writing our own obituary, naming all relatives correctly and exactly. There is nothing worse than having an obituary screwed up. The family never forgets and never forgives any–mistakes–as it relates to their deceased loved one." It was a good lesson for life–or death–and I remembered its importance.

After the first week of class, I got a call from a friend's dad, "Hey, I think I've got a summer job for you if you are interested," Mr. Cofer said.

I drove over to East Atlanta to a small white, concrete block and wooden building with a tin shed in the back that had a peeling-paint sign, "Our Way Machine Shop." It didn't look like much, but it was a job.

The shop was owned by a chubby older fellow, I guessed about sixty, with thinning hair, wearing a wrinkled white dress shirt and a tacky multi-colored tie. He sat in his little office right off the main area where a huge vat with steaming oily slush bubbled on the surface. I was to learn when I asked about the steamy stuff, "Oh, that's our *Oakite* cleaning bin where we clean the motors." *Oakite* was a phosphoric acid and surfactant cleaning agent.

I entered his little office and he invited me to sit on a hard wooden chair. "So, you want a summer job?" he inquired.

"Yes, sir, Mr. Cofer called and said you could use someone for the summer."

"So, he sent you over, is that right?"

"Yes sir, he did," I answered.

"Well, I'm Mr. Orr. I own this place and our business increases in the summer, so we need a little more help. We work on and rebuild compressors of all sorts for the refrigeration companies in the Atlanta area; in fact, we contract with Refrigerated Express and maintain all the company's cooling units and the compressors that they use on their refrigerated trucks."

"Wow, that's a lot of work, isn't it?" I said. "Sounds important."

I could tell that he liked it that I was impressed with his little shop. To me, it did not seem such a little business.

He looked me over, "Can you drive a truck?" he asked.

"Depends on how big," I answered.

"We have a couple of delivery trucks, the largest is a ton-and-half and the other is an old pickup."

"Yes, sir, I probably could drive the pickup and maybe if someone showed me, I could handle the bigger truck, too."

He got up from his desk and directed me into the noisy machine room, where a couple of women in work overalls, and several more men, were sitting at what looked to be grinding machines. He raised his hand to get the attention of the work crew. They stopped the loud machines.

"This young man—now what's your name again?" he asked. "He will be working with you. You may have to help him get started but I think he'll be okay, if he takes the job."

"Yes, I'd like the job," I answered.

"Good," he said. "Come on back to my office and we can settle the details of what I'm willing to pay and what your hours will be and what will be your responsibilities."

I had paid my summer school tuition out of my own pocket. Since I now had a job, to keep from losing my tuition money, I did both. The classes were at night so I could leave work, go to school and fit the whole schedule in.

I agreed to his offer, seventy-five cents an hour, from eight to five with 30 minutes off for lunch. "You bring your own lunch, or sometimes we send out for lunch and you can eat in the back of the shop," he said. "We have a Coke machine out back."

The next day I reported to work at 8 a.m. on the hour. "Oh, yeah," said one of the ladies. "You have to come a little early then sign out before you clean up to go home. Mr. Orr doesn't allow cleaning up on company time, he's pretty firm about that. He watches every dime spent here."

I had noticed a big clock in his office above the little time clock and check in and out card rack. "If you're late he docks thirty minutes from your pay," she said.

He turned out to be a firm, but fair fellow to work for as I tried to give him more than his seventy-five cents per hour's-worth of labor.

The job of working on the air conditioning compressors involved picking them up from the companies and hauling them back to the machine shop. Some were brought over by other company trucks and their employees unloaded them for immediate repair.

My scruffy co-worker, Mr. Johnny, was a thin short fellow, always with a hand-rolled cigarette sticking out the corner of his mouth. He was about fifty, I guessed. "Mr. Orr don't allow no smoking in the shop, but he don't care if it ain't lit," he offered.

He seemed to enjoy his authority over the young college boy and always gave me the dirty work and the heaviest lifting. "Come on boy, let's lift," he gleefully ordered. That was okay, because I could do it. I was strong enough to lift the refrigerators that had to be disassembled before we could get the compressors out to repair or rebuild.

The reconditioning procedure involved first breaking the compressors down, removing the cylinder heads, the pistons, the rings, and saving all the bolts and screws separately for reassembly if they were to be used again. However, we generally used new bolts and screws since the old ones were mostly worn pretty badly or damaged.

The compressors were chain lifted over the boiling *Oakite* vat and dipped into the boiling solution for an hour or so. Then with heavy steel brushes we scrubbed the grease and paint down to bare metal. We then lifted the compressors by the chain lift and sprayed them with steaming water, then would swing them over to a long steel table to dry. The cylinder heads and the main body of the compressors were given to the machine operators where they were ground down on a moving side-to-side hand grinding machine. The heads and cylinders and pistons would be re-ground before reassembly and insertion of the rings and head gaskets.

Since I had never worked in any sort of machine shop, I found it interesting and though some might think boring, I was actually excited to see the compressors restored to functioning units. It was not too different, I thought, than that of a future surgery career where folks would be repaired and restored. My only concern was when one of the women commented, "Gee, you seem much better taking apart than putting back." Not good news for a future surgeon.

I did find that cleaning up before going to the night classes was an effort and I never felt clean enough to attend the classes. I always sat a seat away from the other classmates. We had a little dressing area where we could change from our work clothes to our street clothes but no place to shower our sweaty bodies.

I learned that women could do just as good a job as men and, in fact, I liked working with the women workers better than the men. I realized how important the World War "Rosie the Riveter" girls really were.

It was grimy work cleaning and rebuilding motors, but a learning experience. I became a blue-collar worker and was proud of what we accomplished. I would never forget those decent folks in the little machine shop.

Over fifty years later I read in the Atlanta paper of the death of one of the ladies that worked there. Bobbie Bailey, during the years of operation had taken over the ownership of the little business that had by this time become a multi-million-dollar corporation. I learned that she had become a huge benefactor of DeKalb Hospital and of education, especially at Kennesaw State University where an academic building now bears her name. Though only finishing high school she was awarded a justly deserved honorary doctorate degree. Bobbie had taken a tin shed operation to one of the largest businesses in the Atlanta area. I was proud to remember her and her kindness to me so long ago in that little building, known as *"Our Way Machine Shop."*

Note: Years later, while visiting the World War II shipyards at Richmond, California, I learned that the Kaiser Shipbuilding Company and Ford Motor Company (ship builders during the war) felt the women were more conscientious and much better than the men at welding seams of metal for the Liberty ships produced there.

COTTON BLOSSOMS

Pink in the field

During spring break of the second year of college I was invited to my roommate's home in Pickens, Mississippi. "W. B. is going to ride home with us and we're dropping him off at his mom's," volunteered John. W. B. was in his thirties — our friend, who had moved to and worked in New Orleans and promised John's mother that he would keep an eye on John.

Just below the Jackson outskirts, John's worn Buick began to have trouble. The lights dimmed and gradually stopped. It was barely dark, but we needed lights to get all the way to Pickens. We pulled up close to the back of an old flatbed truck. "If we keep close, we can make it by just his lights so long as no state police come by," said John.

We made it to the other side of Jackson and the truck turned off. We found a Texaco gas station and from the pay phone John called his brother Julian to come and get us.

Their house was a sprawling single-story antebellum farmhouse in the middle of huge farmlands. The century-old house had served several generations of Mississippi pioneers. The inside walls were plaster and painted tongue and groove boards.

I woke early the next morning and looked out in the yard where five Buicks were parked under a couple of shady oak trees. My folks had a recent model Buick, but I had never heard of anyone having five Buicks. "Oh yeah," said John. "We buy a new one 'bout every year and hand them down. Mother gets the new one and the rest just pass down till the last one is worn out and we trade that one in. My brother Julian, despite his youthful age has a special license to drive my daddy to Jackson 'cause daddy has heart trouble, so we each need a car."

John's dad invited me to ride through the farm since he had some business in town. "In town" was a crossroad village. We drove down dusty roads through flourishing green fields. "What kind of pink flowers are those?" I naively asked.

John's dad, a husky man laughed, "Why, son that's blossoming cotton. Haven't you seen cotton grow before?" He explained, "The cottonseeds are planted in long rows in late February or early March. They germinate in about a week or so and after two months, flower buds appear. Within three weeks the bolls develop flowers (mostly pink), and by fall the cotton bolls mature. Inside the bolls are fibers that surround the seeds. The staples are the long cotton fibers. The fibers inside continue to expand and split the boll apart. Before long the cotton turns brown with the fluffy white cotton bursting out, ready for picking."

That afternoon we drove a few miles north to Kosciusko where the cotton was "compressed" into big cotton bales for market. I had never seen so many folks in overalls working in such a business.

There were little kids, both black and white sitting on the fence watching the "Compress."

That night we went to the drive-in movie. "I've got us two dates for the picture show," John announced. "Your date is the sister of a girl I used to date in high school."

"Sounds good to me," I said.

We drove John's car, with a new battery and voltage regulator and good lights, to pick up our dates. "This is Sallie, and this is Julie," said John. My date, Sallie was fairly small in stature, somewhat thin but well-proportioned with what had been blonde hair now turning slightly darker. She had sparkling blue eyes and a friendly smile.

John's date, Julie, was a little older, a definite blonde. The girls were excited. "Which show are we going to?" one asked.

"We're going to the drive-in," John said.

We pulled into the drive-in, parked, got our popcorn and Coca Colas. John placed the tin sound box on the driver's side and the music began as the lights dimmed and the film projector flickered... "Republic Pictures features Roy Rogers, Dale Evans and their Horse Trigger."

Just as the movie started, Sallie smiled and shyly batting her lovely young eyes, slipped toward my side of the back seat. *These country girls are friendly*, I thought. I eased toward her. She began to snuggle up to me. John turned from the front seat and quietly announced, "You know Sallie's daddy is the deputy sheriff." I put a little space between us as Roy and Dale came singing down the dusty trail and we munched on our popcorn and sipped our ice-cold Coca Colas.

COTTON RUN

A big truck and three boys

It must have been after the second year of college. Many of us took a quantitative-qualitative chemistry during the summer to accumulate enough credits to apply for early medical school admission. The first day our professor entered the classroom, a huge auditorium we called the Sugar Bowl, and with a subtle grin announced, "Boys, don't worry. If you don't pass this course, you'll have another opportunity to take it in Wisconsin at their university next summer."

The course was held in the old red stone and brick chemistry building with no air conditioning and little breeze since we had to keep most windows closed to protect our chemical reagents in the lab. It was so hot and humid that we rushed to weigh our chemicals before each measured portion absorbed too much moisture and changed weight. It was often necessary to use the "finagle factor" to get our lab results close to correct. Most of us survived the heat and the chemistry course and avoided the trip to Wisconsin for a repeat performance. The course allowed us to cram in enough credits to skip the last year of college.

After the summer session, I was back home for a few weeks until the fall semester. I was out of school and with no job. It was August and it was hot in Atlanta. The phone rang and my mom answered, "Why yes, John, he's right here."

"How would you like to help us get to North Carolina?" The voice boomed on the line. After a pause John continued, "We're going to take one of dad's cotton trucks to Gastonia to deliver a load of cotton. Julian is off to his Army Reserve duty and there's no one else to drive."

"I've never driven a big truck," I answered.

"Hey, Joe and I'll show you and you can help us drive on the main highways. We're coming through Atlanta and we can pick you up out on the Bankhead highway."

"Sounds interesting," I mumbled.

"Okay we should be there about nine or ten o'clock tonight." We determined a good pick-up spot.

My folks and I drove out to the meeting spot and after a little while a huge dusty General Motors red tractor truck pulling a long flatbed trailer pulled up along the road's edge. It was stacked with bales of cotton, covered in chained down tarps. I climbed aboard and took a seat by the right door with John in the middle. "This is Joe Hand," said John. "Joe knows the way."

It was already getting dark and a heavy rain began falling. We could barely see the road as we began the gear-shifting going up the inclines into South Carolina. "We'll get some gas in Greenville and some late supper. Joe knows a big truck stop just before we get into town." John leaned over to my side and whispered, "Joe can't read but he knows the way by looking at the sign boards and some road signs he's memorized. He'll get us there."

The rain was coming down in torrents when we pulled into the truck stop. We bounced and shook as the truck rolled over the rough gravel in the parking lot. John and a station attendant filled up the gas tank and he went inside to pay and get some supper to bring out to the truck. We couldn't all three eat inside the grimy restaurant because Joe was colored. Blacks were not allowed to eat in the segregated restaurants nor were they allowed to use the "White Only" restrooms. Joe had to slip behind the truck to pee. Blacks had to go to the back door of the café to order and pick up their food.

"I'll get supper and we can eat in the truck," said John. He was not about to embarrass Joe by eating inside and then bringing a plate out to the truck to Joe.

After we finished our dinner in the truck and drank our Coca Colas Joe cranked up the huge truck. We had trouble moving so he had to rock the truck and trailer back and forth to get out of a gravel rut. We heard bumping and crunching but thought nothing about it.

About fifteen minutes down the road we stopped and pulled over to sleep. It was still pouring rain and was hard to see out.

"We can sleep here and get up to Gastonia in the morning before the mills close," said John. "They close at noon, but it should be no trouble." The three of us bundled in our blankets and rolled up coats for pillows and dozed off.

A tap on the window, then a banging woke us. Joe rolled the window down and there in the heavy rain stood a slight, scruffy, unshaven fellow in a yellow rain slicker, a home rolled cigarette hung on the side of his wrinkled mouth. He peered through thick glasses. He was not happy. Soon a second tall fellow in an old brownish army overcoat and a flappy wet hat appeared carrying a dim flashlight pointing it toward our direction. He had come from a dark Kaiser-Fraser automobile.

"Hey, boys, you all just ran over a car back at the truck stop," he shouted standing in the rain. Despite the thunder and lightning we could clearly make out his words. "Hell, you boys just backed over the side of a Ford."

John leaned over from the middle seat, "We what?"

"Just ran up on a Ford in the parking lot," the guy yelled.

"Who are you?" John sleepily asked.

"I'm a deputy sheriff in this county," he proffered.

He pulled out a worn wallet and flashed what he claimed was a sheriff's badge. The other fellow shined his flashlight down on the badge, but we couldn't see well enough to identify it. We knew we were in deep bad business.

"Are you white boys driving with this colored boy?" he snarled.

Joe sank slowly down in the seat as John climbed over and opened the driver's door. "Yes, sir, this is Joe Hand. He works for my daddy and he knows the way up to the mills."

"Well, we just don't see black boys driving with white boys in South Carolina."

"Any of you boys got any guns or knives in there?" the deputy gruffly inquired.

"No sir," John answered.

"Well, step on out of the truck. Yeah, all you boys," he ordered.

We stood beside the big truck fending off the rain with torn parts of an old tarp over our heads, not knowing what to expect next from these scary men.

After a couple of minutes John asked to go back to the truck stop and see the damaged car.

"You boys know this here's a hit and run case and with a colored boy along it don't look so good for you all."

John turned to Joe, "Joe, climb on top the cotton and use that tarp for cover. Watch it till I get back." John whispered to us, "If these red necks get mad, they'll set our cotton on fire and no mill will take it because of the danger of smoldering flash fires."

Joe slipped back to the flatbed and climbed the side toward the top of the bales of cotton and covered himself with part of the cover tarp. We knew that it was safer for Joe to be up on the cotton, out of sight with these mean-looking white men around.

John turned to me, "You stay in the truck and watch for anybody who might want to bother you all or the truck. Keep the windows closed."

The two men carried John to the Truck Stop in their old car and when he returned, he said, "I called my daddy and he's wiring money to take care of the damages. These men will follow us into town to the Western Union Telegraph office at the railroad station."

He got back into the truck and whispered, "These are some bad actors. I'm not even sure they are deputies. They just might be Klansmen, who knows! Every- body in the café just stared at us."

"I heard one guy snicker, 'Those white boys are driving with a colored fellow.'"

We got the money at the telegraph office; paid the seedy men what they demanded, then the tall fellow with shaggy whiskers sauntered up to John, "You boys know we kept you all out of jail, so I believe you owe us a little something extra."

I couldn't hear the conversation but noticed John unrolling a wad of bills and handing them to the grinning fellow as he stuffed them in his pants pocket.

"Lord, I was scared," mumbled Joe as he sat between us. John pulled the truck back on the highway, glanced warily toward the two fellows standing on the other side of the highway and we headed for Gastonia with our eighty bales of cotton.

"Joe, I was scared too," I whispered to him.

We made it to the mills, but it was past noon that Saturday morning. The mill had already closed. The husky watchman, in his faded overalls and worn straw hat stood on the loading platform and John sauntered up to him and asked about any help to unload the cotton. "Nope, not a soul here," he allowed, "not until Monday, boys."

He agreed to allow us to unload the bales ourselves and opened the big sliding doors on the loading platform, nodded to us, "You can go through here to the side of the building," and he pointed to where the cotton was to go. He handed John a clipboard with papers for him to sign to register the cotton. The watchman tore a copy from the several papers and handed it back to John as a receipt for the delivery. We unloaded the cotton bales ourselves. Some weighed 400 to 600 pounds.

Joe was an expert in moving the bales. I had never seen anything like it. He grabbed the bale using huge iron bale hooks and "walked it" down the floor to the brick wall.

John and I helped, and I did okay until suddenly I found myself flat with a 600-pound bale of cotton pinning me between the floor and the wall.

Both Joe and John burst out laughing as they lifted the bale off and yelled, "City boy, city boy."

We did not stop for gas in South Carolina on the way back.

COLLEGE AND MEDICAL SCHOOL INTERVIEWS

Competition and Hope

It all started the first day we wrote on our attendance card "Pre-Med." We were bright-eyed youngsters with no idea what lay ahead. When we filed into that first college chemistry class, the professor looked over the class of "would bees" and in his cynical voice pronounced the age-old cliché, "Look to the left and look to the right. One of you will not be here next semester." We looked, the other person looked, and each quietly said to him or herself, "I'll still be here." Yet, after the first exam we began to wonder.

It didn't get better unless we were truly those brilliant students our moms always thought we were. We went along, attended classes, took heaps of notes and tried to digest those notes until the wee hours of the mornings. It seemed that the science and math courses were designed to test our stamina as well as our brain power.

Many of the professors had little time for premeds. We were only interested in passing their courses as steps toward medical school. The professors could not understand our lack of passion for magic numbers, molecular mysteries, and the brilliant poetry of Shelley.

One of our college professors, "Jolting Joe" Boyer, taught chemistry for chemists. If we questioned him with a medical implication, he was quick to announce, as he leaned forward, both hands gripping his lecture table and shaking his head, that he had no interest in "that question."

Despite his negative attitude toward us, we still loved him. He was a brilliant chemist. He was young and he was one of us. Out of class, he could out drink most of our classmates. It was not uncommon to see Jolting Joe "under the influence" in the Quarter.

One of his students would usually bring him home safely. Our professor was not influenced by those good works. It didn't matter who the student was, the guy still earned the grade he made on his exams. "Jolting Joe" was tough.

The following day he would slowly enter the lecture hall, place both hands on the lecture table, glance up at the student-filled room, lick his dry lips, pull out of his pocket a little folded piece of paper that had the outline of his morning's lecture, place the scrap of paper on the table. He would then take a piece of chalk and begin writing chemical formulas on the blackboard as he began his lecture. If he had to erase more than one or two chalk errors that he made on the blackboard he would turn to the class, lift his head high, pick up the little piece of paper, turn, take a deep breath, and silently walk out of the great hall. He was done for that lecture. We always watched to see if he would trip off the podium.

The guys who kept the grades down were gone by the middle of the second year and the competition became a contest. I learned that most medical school admission boards look for bright candidates with enough humanity to be able to get along with coworkers and empathize with their future patients. They are not looking for Einsteins.

The board wants candidates who will fill the shoes of practicing physicians for thirty or more years. The committees look for integrity most of all. Integrity and stamina go a long way in the practice of medicine. No one can successfully practice without those two attributes.

SPRING OF 1955

I awake from the "land of dreams."

The spring of 1955 ended my sojourn in New Orleans. The school year ended, and I bade my friends "so long." I was headed back to Georgia. My decision to leave Tulane for Emory Medical School was settled when my dad took me aside and said, "Son, your mother thinks you have had enough of New Orleans."

It is a fact that after I was assured of an acceptance to medical school that my grades slipped to an embarrassing degree. It was true that my New Orleans social life was edging out my academic interests, so it was probably wise to get out of my current environment. It was time to "leave Dodge."

I wanted to stay with my classmates and attend medical school in New Orleans, but my costs would be lower at home living in the town where my parents lived. We weighed the options and with a little sadness I visited the office of my friend Dean Gibson who had enticed me to Tulane. I thanked him for the opportunity of attending the college and the acceptance to the medical school. It had been a wonderful experience, both the university and the city of New Orleans and it's exciting and unique society.

GRADY INTERVIEW

Just another summer job, or was it?

In June of 1955 I turned my attention to a new phase of life. Upon my return to Atlanta I looked for a summer job. I decided I wanted to work in a hospital to see what I was getting into.

I arrived at a red brick Romanesque, building, the original building of the Grady Memorial Hospital, completed in 1892. After an interview with the administrator, Mr. Frank Wilson, I got a job.

I was to drive the Grady Hospital ambulance. I was sent to the ambulance call room to meet the drivers. After answering a few questions from each, they shook their heads and looked at me with doubtful expressions. I wondered what they were thinking. I thought, *If they could put up with me, I could surely handle my relations with them.*

I would begin the following Monday and ride with one of the drivers to learn the streets and hospital procedures. There were no instruction or procedure books to guide a neophyte. It was learn by doing.

By driving the Grady Ambulance, I would see illness, poverty, and violence that I had never known before in the city I had grown up in and loved. I was to share the emotions and the challenges of young interns in early medical training.

I would spend the summer observing the fears, failures, and successes of young men and women that I would one day emulate. In the city, fraught with a combination of danger and delight, I would experience the ironies of medicine and human nature in life and death on the streets of Atlanta.

Original Grady Hospital Entrance
(now referred to as Georgia Hall)
Grady opened to serve the "underserved of
Atlanta" in 1892.
(Photo by author, 2010)

PART TWO

PROMISES

GRADY SICK CAR – WASHINGTON STREET

"As children, our world is wonderful, but one day we see reality."

I had no idea what a "shut in" was until I drove the Grady ambulance. At eight a.m. the ambulance, also known as the "sick car," left the hospital carrying an Emergency Room intern to visit the shut-ins and those unable to come to the hospital for their care. We visited private homes and nursing homes and provided follow-up care to the terminally ill, long before hospice was ever imagined.

The intern arrived at the ambulance office, reviewed the list of patients and noted the tentative diagnoses so he would have the right medications and supplies in his medical bag.

The Emergency Room interns worked a twelve-hour on/twelve-hour off schedule with no days off during the assigned month. All rotations in the hospital were monthly assignments. When on Emergency Room rotation, the interns vied for the "sick car" assignment, which got them out of the hectic Emergency Room for a few hours. While an ambulance driver, I learned to accommodate the young doctors who were barely three or four years older than me. It was good policy to be their friend as, one day, I would be under their supervision when I became a medical student and, finally, an intern.

Since I was a native of Atlanta, the city was easily learned. Most of our business, particularly the large indigent population, centered in an area south of the hospital, built about the same time, in the mid to late 1800s. Much of the city's blighted area extended into the back yards of downtown businesses. Many of the small older downtown hotels housed a disproportionately large number of the indigent elderly, as did the old homes south of the hospital, which were turned into multiple-family dwellings. Some of the old homes were called "flop houses."

The sick car was my introduction to heart-wrenching poverty. It was difficult for me to believe that people lived in such dreadful conditions.

"We ascended the worn winding stairs."
(Photo by author)

One of my first visits was to an address on Washington Street that had been a fashionable neighborhood at the turn of the twentieth century. The house was a two-story wooden Victorian mansion with porches decayed and collapsing. We stepped carefully upon the porch avoiding the missing and rotting floorboards to enter through the old front door.

The once-elegant hallway was tattered with multiple layers of faded, multi-colored, peeling wallpaper. A single bare light bulb hung from the ceiling on a long, frayed cord where a chandelier once lighted the hall.

We called out the name of the patient we intended to see. An elderly woman in a chenille bathrobe and pink slippers appeared from a side room.

"The old man you want is in the room at the top of the stairs," she quietly announced and nodded. Then she slipped back into her dark quarters.

We ascended the worn, winding stairs, holding onto an unsteady banister with spindles absent or splintered. The ceiling was falling with islands of brown decayed wood and water-damaged plaster hanging above our heads. The intern and I walked down the dusty hall, stepped over dried cat litter, dodged a discarded toilet and peered into what once had been a lovely bedroom. There, I imagined a tall canopy bed with porcelain bowls on nearby marble-top tables, candleholders and soft, high Victorian chairs.

What we saw, though, was a frail, elderly white man lying in a fetal position on a rusted iron bed. He lay on a tattered, gray mattress with newspapers spread out in place of sheets. He was covered with a worn patch quilt, shivering cold in a room with neither fan nor heater. The broken windowpanes were patched with cardboard fragments. The sink in the corner of the room had a worn iron knob on the cold-water faucet, which wouldn't turn on because there was no running water. A stench came from a portable commode that sat in the opposite corner of the room.

The man's elderly, toothless wife sat on an old rocking chair, holding his thin, bony hand as she stoically beheld him through smudged eyeglasses. She looked up with a wistful smile, touched her wrinkled face and brushed her long, gray hair from her forehead. She whispered, "Thanks for coming. I think I've done all I can for him." She placed a small handkerchief about her mouth, blotting a bit of snuff from the corner of her thin lips.

Without much ado, the intern looked at the emaciated form, wearing only an old T-shirt, and thin, soiled pajama bottoms, lying on the bed. He motioned for me to go out to the ambulance and get the stretcher. "Ma'am, we'll have to take your husband down to

Grady and see what we can do for him." His tone was gentle as he asked, "Is that all right?"

"Why, yes," she answered in a soft, shy voice. "Can I go, too?"

"Yes, ma'am, we'll let you ride with us, won't we?" He turned to me. I nodded as I turned to go get the stretcher.

We carefully lifted the slight old man from the bed.

He weighed no more than ninety pounds. He moaned softly and pulled his thin arms closer to his frail shivering body. The intern and I moved him to the stretcher, and I lifted the front and the intern lifted the foot of the stretcher. We carried the old man down the rickety stairs out to the ambulance.

The elderly neighbors looked on from the old porch in silence as we drove away. Would he ever return?

OTHER JOBS

Washing gloves and sharpening needles

In the old Grady, the ambulance on-call office was adjacent to the White Emergency clinic entrance. During the late night when we were not too busy, a new friend, a medical student from the Medical College of Georgia, and I helped out in the clinic. Paul Payne was a night nurse and between patients his job was to wash, dry, and powder the heavy reusable surgical gloves in the ER. We would then wrap them in soft cloth to be run through the steam sterilizer. A small paper marker was inserted inside the packing so that when the package was opened the marker would have changed colors to assure that the contents had been properly sterilized.

We sat together in the break room of the clinic and did our little job. We cleaned the glass medical syringes and placed them on small wooden racks to dry before putting them in the steam autoclave sterilizer. We also had to clean and sharpen the reusable hypodermic needles on a whetstone that was kept in the workroom.

Sometimes the needles would develop little barbs on the tips that would visually snag on the vein or soft tissues. These would have to be ground down. We had a magnifying glass so we could check the tips, not just feel the tips for sharpness. Another check was to use a wisp of cotton to see if the tip snagged on the cotton. Of course, this was during the 1950s before all the disposable stuff came into use.

The other larger instruments, tubes and bottle equipment were washed, then bundled and sent to central supply for further cleaning and sterilization. Only the small instruments, such as used stainless steel suture items, were sterilized in the clinic sterilizer.

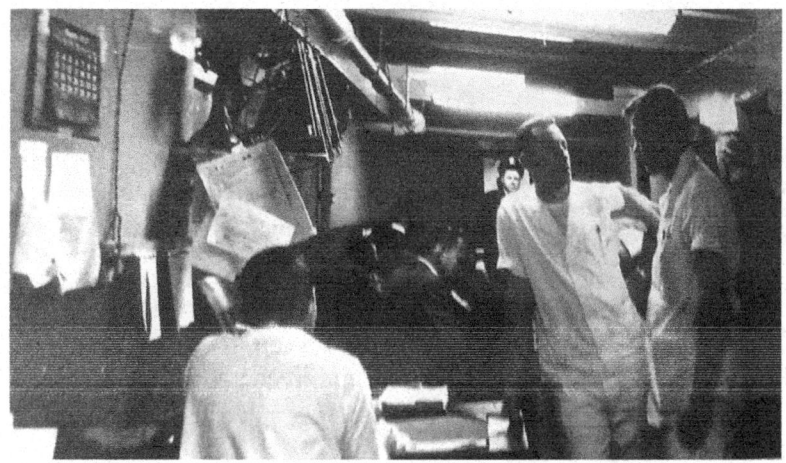

Grady "White Emergency Room" – 1955
Grady Interns and Emory Senior medical students
(Photo from Emory University Annual, courtesy
of the Woodruff Archives – Emory University Publications)

If an ambulance call came in, I was notified, and I left the clinic with an intern to answer the call. All the ambulance interns were taken only from the White Clinic since the ambulance office was nearby and the Colored Clinic was in another building. The other clinic with its huge volume of patients always needed more doctors.

The sanctuary, or break room was our place to rest, prop up our feet, have a cup of coffee and snacks, and occasionally place popping corn in brown paper bags and pop it in the wonderful new microwave ovens.

For Paul and for me the clinic was our introduction to our future and gave us a bit of insight not many medical or pre-medical students had. My friend, Paul Payne later became a prominent orthopaedic surgeon in Marietta, Georgia.

COKE IN THE OR

"It was the Real Thing."

We slammed the ambulance doors and walked into the hospital toward the call room. Just inside the ER stood my friend, Warren Brown, talking to one of the other interns. He reached out and grabbed me by the arm as I entered the room. "All through?"

"Yeah," I replied. "We're done."

"You want to go to the OR with me? We're taking the patient you brought in from the wreck out on Forrest Avenue. Lumpkin thinks the guy has a ruptured spleen and liver injury. We're going to explore him and probably take out his spleen. I'll be helping Dickinson and Lumpkin."

"Sure," I said. I had never been inside the OR. I followed my friend to the doctor's dressing room and changed into scrub clothes. The other doctors put on their scrubs and donned the OR shoes they had in their lockers. The operating room for Whites was on the fourth, the top floor of the White Grady hospital building. The orderly pushed the stretcher into the OR with attached steel IV poles holding two glass pint bottles of blood, running through long, faded, brownish rubber tubes into the patient's arms.

"He's been shocky, but he's better now with the blood," Doctor Lumpkin said to Sarah Brockman, the anesthetist,

They lifted the husky pale man, who was sweaty and confused, onto the operating table. The OR staff secured him on the table with a strap across his thighs and spread his arms out as if he was on a cross, tied down his wrists and adjusted the IVs to continue the blood and replacement fluids. The surgeon began to prep his abdomen with iodine, followed by an alcohol rinse.

"We've got more blood coming from the blood bank," Dr. Dickinson said to the anesthetist.

Sarah was older than the doctors who were in their late twenties or early thirties. She had been at Grady for over ten years. No neophyte to trauma surgery, she had seen and done it all. Very little bothered Sarah.

"Hey, you," she said to me as I ventured into the operating room, not sure where to stand. "Come sit with me behind the screen. It'll keep you out of the way, and you can still see the surgery."

"Yes, ma'am."

"Don't ma'am me. I'm not that old."

"Yes, ma'am," I repeated.

She laughed, glanced over at me with sparkling gray eyes and sized me up. "You're okay," she said as she carefully placed the breathing mask over the patient's face and began to squeeze the anesthesia bag, pumping in oxygen, hyperventilating him and pushing the IV curare to relax his muscles before inserting the endotracheal tube for direct control of the patient's airway.

"What's your name?" she asked.

I told her my name.

"Well, I'm just Sarah around here, not Miss or Missus!"

"Yes, ma'am," I again answered.

She shook her head as she pointed toward a stool for me. "Pull it up closer, out of those guys' way."

She then showed me how to insert an endotracheal tube. "Look here. See the epiglottis–see the vocal cords?" as she flashed the laryngoscope light of the silver throat and tongue depressor. "This is where the tube goes. Miss the vocal cords and the tube goes down the throat into the esophagus. That blocks the trachea and smothers the patient. We don't want that!"

"Yes, ma'am–I mean, no ma'am," I said.

She looked at me again and shook her head and laughed. "Just how far along are you in med. school, anyway?"

"I start in September," I said.

"Oh my, you're not even in Med. School, yet?"

"No ma'am, I'm just driving the ambulance this summer."

"Okay, then we'll show you what we do up here!"

I sat on the stool beside Sarah and looked about the room. The main White hospital was built in the early 1900s and it showed. The walls of the OR were clean and washed down with a strong disinfectant but badly needed paint. The OR equipment was old and run-down.

A thin orderly in a wrinkled long white coat rushed into the OR chasing a fly with his fly swatter. One of the surgeons yelled, "Get that damn fly before it gets in the wound." They had just opened the abdomen and were preparing to open the peritoneum.

The orderly skirmished about the operating room, swinging his swatter, here and there. "I got 'em," he proudly announced. He got 'em on the screen of the open window. It was so hot that summer that the OR windows had to be open, day and night, despite the holes in the screens. Rusty black rotating floor fans were set up in the corners of the room blowing over buckets of exposed ice to cool the room. There was no air conditioning at Grady.

"Damn, John, get the light down so I can see the spleen," Lumpkin said to Dickinson, the assistant surgeon. There was one overhead light and a portable lamp in use. Neither seemed adequate.

"Here's the tear in the liver and look how the spleen is swollen in its capsule," Lumpkin said. "There's a leak in the capsule and that's where all the damn blood is coming from. Keep that damn suction going or get another one," he impatiently muttered to my friend, Warren.

"How's his pressure, Sarah?" he asked.

"He's running 70 over 50. I think he's okay. His pulse is still about 110."

"We can get the spleen out if I can just see, damn it!" Lumpkin complained to his assistants.

Sarah continued to bag-breathe the patient, as she adjusted the nitrous oxide and oxygen mixture. She turned to me. "Honey, you know how you could help me?"

"No, ma'am," I said, thinking some big job was in store.

"You could go downstairs and get me a couple of *Cokes*." She looked at me as if she thought I didn't understand. "Coca Colas, cold Coca Colas, Honey, you know, caffeine!"

Doctor Lumpkin turned toward the head of the table and the anesthesia screen, lifted his bloody hands from the wound for a second, "Oh, Sarah can't work without her *Cokes*." He paused. "That's why she is being so kind to you, so you'll go get her a dope!" He laughed through the cloth surgical face mask then returned to the job at hand.

I left the operating room, bypassed the clanking elevator and ran down the old concrete stairs as fast as I could, to the Coke machine in the basement, got several bottles of Coke with all the money I had in my pocket, two for Sarah and two for whoever wanted one in that hot OR.

When I returned, I gave Sarah her Cokes to sip behind the anesthesia screen. She kept a stainless-steel bottle opener and paper straws amid all her anesthesia instruments.

"They've already got the spleen out and are putting in the sutures to the tear in the liver and they'll close soon," she said to me.

"Nurse," Dr. Lumpkin called out to the circulating nurse, "can you wipe my forehead again?"

"Yes, sir," she said, as the surgeon turned from the operative field to get his brow cleaned of dripping sweat.

I sat down on the stool beside Sarah, hidden behind the anesthesia screen, and we sipped our cold Cokes together. I had witnessed my first big surgical case and would spend many hours in the years to come on the other side of that screen with that wonderful anesthetist and her colleagues in the Grady OR.

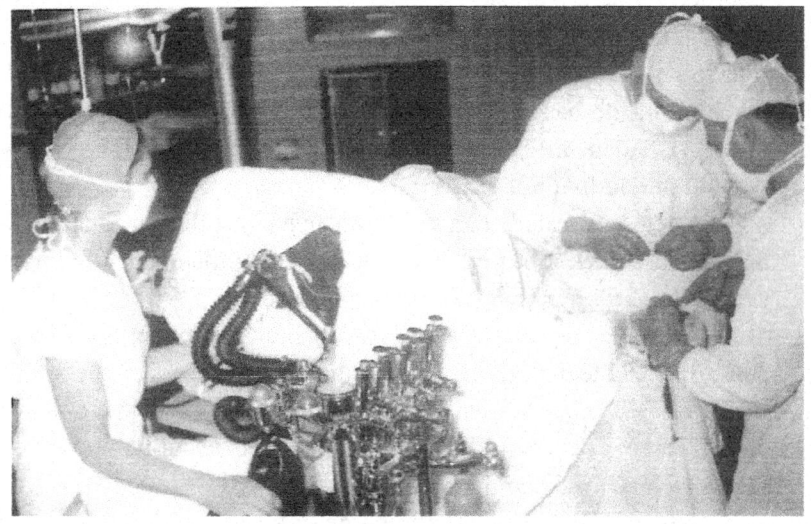

**"Well, I'm just Sarah around here... not Miss or Mrs.
We'll show you what we do up here."**
(Photo by author)

TERROR

"Some escape terror and others must submit to its presence."

At Emory, the freshman killer course had once been the terror of anatomy class. I was told that Dr. Blincoe was a formidable fellow. The late Dr. Ferrol Sams, in his book **Run With the Horsemen**, has a character resembling this professor that one pictures as the kind of guy that would be great on your side in a barroom brawl, but you would hate to come up against him as an angry opponent.

I was told his speech was soft and his words were selected with deliberation to have just the right intonation as he majestically described the body's integuments. To say he was precise and demanded precision in his questions and the responses he expected would be an understatement of the greatest magnitude. He was no slouch and was a match for any English professor. He was learned.

We heard stories of the medical students' paralyzing fear of this professor and his teaching methods. Students would awaken in the middle of the night in a cold sweat just with a dream or thought of Blincoe's anatomy class. "Pop exams" were his specialty. He would sneak into the anatomy lab late at night under the cover of dark, flashlight in hand, with his faithful African American lab assistant to set up the surprise Lab Exams. The students had spies volunteering to watch the lights in the anatomy building at night for the old scoundrel.

His presence haunted them day and night. They trembled when he approached their anatomy dissecting tables. The mere glance toward a student sent shudders down their stiff spines. Just the thought of his inquisition quizzes frightened each student. He was a terror, but he was fair, the upperclassmen said. Yet he would flunk you at the bat of an eye. Thank goodness Dr. Blincoe retired before our class arrived.

Our anatomy professor, Dr. Jim Miller, was a brilliant anatomist, yet a professor who instilled little fear in the students. With competent assistants our Anatomy class was straightforward. Of course, the memorization required was stressful, but tolerable.

Grey's Anatomy text was our bible and best friend. Dr. Blincoe had preferred another text, from which he would quote verbatim.

With the new electron microscope recently secured by Emory, our Anatomy Department seemed more interested in micro and cellular anatomy. The Biochemistry Department stressed cellular research rather than Gross Anatomy. New discoveries were on the horizon. RNA and DNA had just been described. Those of us who were surgically oriented suffered from the minimization of Gross Anatomy. That would not have been the case had we had Dr. Blincoe, but the clinical, medical and research crowd thrived with the new scientific discoveries and developments.

A BAPTIST

Earnestly Earnest – Pastor or Clown

My childhood friend and medical school roommate, Tom Scott and I had attended the Cascade Baptist church since we were little children. We had sung in the church choir since we were teenagers and we continued singing in the choir while we were in medical school.

One Sunday morning I was half asleep, yet quasi listening to the preacher who we called "Earnestly Earnest".

The good Reverend was preaching against sins of the flesh. He rambled on with a shout here – just enough to keep us awake – and a whisper there. He quoted the worn and frayed Bible that he held up in his left hand, slapping it occasionally with his right hand. He quoted ancient Old Testament prophets and other preachers. Finally, he approached the members of our congregation about all their own damning and sinful ways.

Holding his ragged Bible out toward the congregation he leaned from the pulpit and whispered, "Why, you know I visited one of our good sisters and her woman friend this week. You'll never guess what they were doing when I arrived. Up there on their porch," he began to crescendo, "right out in front of God and everybody!" he shouted.

I glanced toward my friend Tom and wondered, *what in the world?*

After a long and thoughtful pause the preacher whispered, "Why, they were smoking cigarettes," he paused, "and playing at cards."

Confounded by the preacher's comments, Tom and I both laughed out loud.

The congregation went deathly silent. Reverend Earnest turned toward the choir. His eyes glared like fire and his lips snarled. I could see him gritting his big, dull teeth. Not a word slipped from his curled lips. He turned back toward the congregation, raised his worn Bible toward us, shook it with a trembling hand then clutched it to his heart and slouched into his great cathedral chair, silent.

"Just as I Am Without One Plea," was the benediction hymn. Several "smoking sinners" were saved that day.

The next week Tom and I turned in our choir robes and became Methodists.

AFTER BAPTISTS

*"It ain't just the Baptists that fight sin,
but the Methodists too. But in a gentler way."*

Becoming a Methodist was not a big shift, except that the ministers were not so condemning. They preached more of a "Saving Grace" that dealt with the "Goodness of God," not the condemning God, that literal Old Testament "Yahweh," that vindictive awful God I had known. In political terms, perhaps they preached a "Gentler God."

My classmate and I contacted the Methodist minister in our neighborhood and had a conference with him. He was young, with a pragmatic view of the world. We were students at the Emory Medical School, a Methodist University and the Emory Theology faculty had taught Reverend Bevel Jones. We were on the same wavelength. We saw the healing Jesus, not the Jesus turning over tables in the synagogue. We saw Jesus telling Peter to sheath his sword. We saw Jesus weeping for mankind.

We felt more in tune listening to someone near our age and what we thought was a reasonable and practical Christian theology. Years later, our minister Bevel Jones, became Methodist Bishop of Western North Carolina and Eastern Tennessee.

DOCTOR FEARLESS FRANK

"He stood like Ichabod Crane in a long white lab coat, chalk in hand."

Dr. Bill Hardman, my late friend and classmate, remembered a story of our distinguished pharmacology or biochemistry professor that I had forgotten. We called him "Fearless Frank" and I should like to tell Bill's story.

"An excellent researcher, Fearless was allowed out of his basement lab in the medical school's Woodruff Building for his annual and perhaps his only lecture of the year, on some obscure chemical or pharmacological compound, none of us has ever heard of since."

Billy recalled, "His lecture was extremely boring, and half of the class was asleep." Perhaps that is why I don't recall the incident, as I was prone to doze off during those tedious pharmacology lectures.

"Dr. Fearless droned on and a little dog, apparently an escapee from the dog lab wandered into the lecture room of the Physiology

Building. Without fanfare the dog hopped up onto the podium where Fearless was lecturing, turned and faced the audience with his back toward Fearless, and pooped beside the desk. Dr. Fearless, without noticing, continued writing on the blackboard."

"The entire class applauded and with that one selfless act that little dog enamored himself to the whole class, portraying what each felt. Fearless thought we were clapping for him."

SECOND YEAR –
STREET PANTS DOCTORS

"White coats don't make the doctor, but it's a beginning."

Most of us survived the freshman year of medical school. Once beyond the first year we began our separate exploration of the fields of medicine. I made up my mind to be a surgeon early in medical school.

The second year was a transition from the pure basic sciences to pre-clinical work. We began the year by applying anatomy and biochemistry to the actual physiology of the living body. We conducted experimental work with live lab animals. For me, using live dogs and cats was traumatic. I was crushed every time we had to sacrifice an animal. I wanted to save them all and take them home.

At the end of the second year, we were allowed to wear short white coats, a transition from basic science to clinical medicine. The white coats, a sign of professionalism and gradual advancement in the field of medicine, allowed us to visit the wards. We would begin to work in clinics now as learning clinicians and not just rabble-rousing medical students hanging around classrooms or the basic science labs. We began our visits to the hospitals. We attended the ward medical teaching rounds, interviewed patients and observed the OR procedures.

ON THE WARD

"It was like going back in time."

We entered the huge Colored male medical ward. It was like going back in time. There were fifty white iron beds lined up against the front and back walls with a double row of beds head to head centered in the middle of the room. On our right was a single wooden desk with a green-shaded globe light and another in an opposite corner, the nurses' desks. Strewn about the surfaces were papers and medical charts. Each desk had a swivel chair. Two or three nurses and a single older male orderly attended the fifty patients.

The room was washed down with sharp-smelling Pine Sol and the worn wood floors cleaned and mopped daily with strong soap and water, then oiled weekly. The room reeked of disinfectant.

We had just visited the White wards across Butler Street, and they were no better. "Separate and equally bad," some said. These buildings needed a coat of paint. The wards were heated with steam radiators with peeling lead paint on each. Tin pans slipped under the radiators caught the sweaty drippings.

The cooling system consisted of open windows with dangling screens and antiquated electric fans humming loudly in the corners of the room. A new modern hospital was under construction just down Butler Street.

Built on the corner of Butler and Armstrong Streets, then called Jenkins Street in 1854 as the home of The Atlanta Medical College, Atlanta's first viable medical school, the original building had been used as a hospital for the Confederate sick and wounded during the War Between the States.

The Confederate Army had abandoned the city and evacuated the hospital, leaving only a few sick and wounded soldiers, but the town's civilian Doctor D'Alvigny rounded up the hospital staff, soused them with whiskey and put them in the beds under the sheets and claimed they were patients. He dared the Union army to burn the building with them in it.

I imagined the carnage that had passed through that old original building. I pictured the fictional Scarlet O'Hara bursting through the front doors to get a doctor for pregnant Melanie and dashing through the rows of wounded and bleeding, dodging the outstretched begging hands and grabbing old Doctor Meade by the sleeve.

The original structure was replaced in 1906. The Atlanta Medical College opened a portion of the building to serve the "colored" patients.

Not much has changed, I thought, as I looked over Atlanta's sick and dying. Since I had worked on the Grady ambulance, I had seen it before. But my classmates hadn't. Still it tightened my stomach and tugged at my heart.

In the far corner an elderly, emaciated, gray-haired fellow raised his hand and tapped a call bell on his bedside table. He mumbled something aloud to attract the nurse.

"What does he want?" asked one of the medical students.

"You see, he's got one finger up in the air," said the duty nurse as she guided our group into the room. "One finger means he wants a 'one spot,' a urinal. If the patient raises two fingers, he wants a 'two-spot,' that's a bedpan."

"How neat is that?" answered the baffled student.

"Yes, we have a hand system, so all the patients know how to get our attention," proudly answered the nurse in charge.

We visited several beds. The medical instructor picked up the charts from the foot of each bed and then recited the history. He then asked the students their opinions on possible diagnoses. Most hesitated to answer. We had just begun our physical diagnosis sessions. Only a couple of the street pants doctors made their observations known and the instructor went on with his diagnostic discussion. I noticed a female classmate staring at the bed of the patient under discussion. We moved on to the next bed.

"What were you looking at?" a classmate asked her.

"Oh my, didn't you see that huge cockroach come out from under the pillow and crawl across the top of that patient's hair?" she answered.

"Hell, no," the guy responded.

"I was afraid to mention it in front of the instructor," she whispered as she placed her hand to her lips in horror. The instructor noticed that she and the other student were having their own little private conversation.

With a sly grin, he asked, "Miss Chatty, would you tell us what this is around this patient's lips?"

The student looked carefully at the asthenic, grayish and dehydrated patient. "Looks like frost or salt."

"Exactly!" responded the instructor. "This patient is uremic. He is in kidney failure. This is called uremic frost."

"Wow!" mumbled one of the other students under his breath. "How did she know that?"

"Hell, Lee, you'd know it if you read the damn lesson on uremia, you dumb-ass," whispered a tall lanky classmate.

Our classmate Edith smiled as the instructor made a little mark in his grade book. The cockroach was soon forgotten. We moved on.

THE STENCH

"What's that crawling out...?"

We entered the Male Surgical Ward through the great double doors into a stench of disease and infection that was barely masked by the Pine-Sol used for cleaning.

Our eyes burned and our throats felt afire as we breathed the disinfectant vapors. Moans and groans filled the room as patients returned from the operating rooms. There were no intensive care units and barely enough recovery units so that the patients had to be watched, not only by the nursing staff, but by the patients' families, as well.

"He's done throwed up again," cried the thin woman standing by a patient's bed.

"Yes, ma'am," responded the tall nurse as she attempted to clean up the bed and the choking patient. "We just got to keep his throat clear," she shouted at the patient's wife. "Hold that pan closer, so he can spit up in it," she ordered the trembling woman.

"I'm doing the best I can!" The wife yelled back.

"Yes, ma'am, I know you are," responded the nurse in a gentler tone.

"Excuse me, while I help this other man," she blurted.

"Keep that pan close to him," she directed the other patient's companions as she quickly knelt down beside the adjacent bed.

"Hey, this is chaos!" whispered one of the medical students as we entered the surgical ward.

"It's the best we can do," advised the ward intern who appeared nearby taking off his white jacket and rolling up his sleeves to help the nurses and to explain the workings of the surgical ward to the young uninitiated medical students.

Within a few minutes the ward quieted as the nurses gave the needed injections of morphine for the pain.

In the bright northeast corner of the huge room, as the morning light beamed through the tall glass windows, students gathered to examine an amputee patient.

"This patient has uncontrolled diabetes mellitus," expounded the intern. "Who can guess why he has an amputation?" he asked the assembled group of seven naive young students. "You there," he pointed to a pale male student who stared at the bandaged stump.

"He hurt his leg," I guess.

"What makes you think that a man in his seventies would lose a leg just from a hurt?" he asked the student. The student blushed and dropped his head. He had no idea why this man had lost his leg.

"Diabetes with poor circulation is the most common cause of limb loss in this age group. He probably smokes, too, which might also suggest a cause for peripheral vascular disease," said the intern.

"Oh," mumbled the embarrassed student.

The intern unwrapped the bandaged stump. The sweet, sickening odor permeated the area and one of the male students began to sweat and looked woozy.

"What's that crawling out of his wound?" pointed out an astute student. Another student became flushed then ashen gray and ran from the room to the hall, holding his hands over his breathless mouth.

We all stared at the bloody necrotic stump. "Those are maggots," the intern calmly announced. "They are our little friends. They help clean up the infected necrotic wounds. They eat the dead nonviable flesh so that the wound can gradually close itself with fresh granulating scar tissue."

He pointed out the skin margins, "We couldn't close this wound because of the dead tissue." He paused. "Despite surgical debridement, until all the infection is cleared, it will not heal. This fellow is on intravenous penicillin and daily Tide soaks in that tin bucket by his bed."

"Sounds like ancient medicine," noted one of the apprehensive students.

"Some things have not changed since some of these buildings were used for the wounded soldiers in the Civil War," added the doctor.

We moved about the ward from bed to bed following our instructor. The patients ignored our youthful interest. They had seen many of us before, street pants doctors, now just different faces, passing through their world.

The old Grady Hospital on Butler and Armstrong Streets, 1959
"It was like going back in time."
(Photo by author)

BACK IN THE HALL

"Behind those curtains…"

Moving through the ward doors back into the dim hall, the students dodged folding curtain stands. Behind those curtains were more beds with silent dying patients lined up along the dingy walls. The ward was crammed full and overflowing.

"These patients have a fear of being put in the hall," the intern commented. "They are eased bit by bit toward the elevator at the end of the corridor. They know the elevator takes them to the basement, to the morgue. Sick and terminal – though most are – they know. They know."

He gently pulled one of the curtain stands aside. He picked up the patient's chart from the foot of the bed. The patient stirred, lifted his frail arm, slid his slender hand across his dry mouth and mumbled, "Put me back in 'de big room, doctor. I'm 'fraid of that elevator." He dropped his hand and glanced at the students. "You here to help me, aren't you?"

A female classmate, speaking softly to the intern, broke the dead silence. "What can be done for this man?"

The intern slipped the curtain stand back into place and eased away from the bed. "According to the chart, this man has terminal cirrhosis. Only a new liver would help him. We are keeping him comfortable before his elevator ride."

It would be many years before liver transplants were performed. On that day, there was little to do for these cirrhotic patients.

The intern lifted his hand and directed the student's attention to the end of the hall. An orderly and nurse were folding curtain stands and moving a sheet-covered gurney to the open elevator.

Note: The late Dr. Thomas Starzl, a Denver surgeon, later at the University of Pittsburg began significant experimental liver transplant research and surgery before 1963. By 1967 and 1969 he had surgeries that survived for over a year on the new immunosuppressive regime. He is credited as accomplishing the first successful liver transplants.

Emory's organ transplant program began in 1966 when Dr. Garland Perdue performed the first kidney transplant in Georgia. Now Emory has a well-established and recognized organ transplant department.

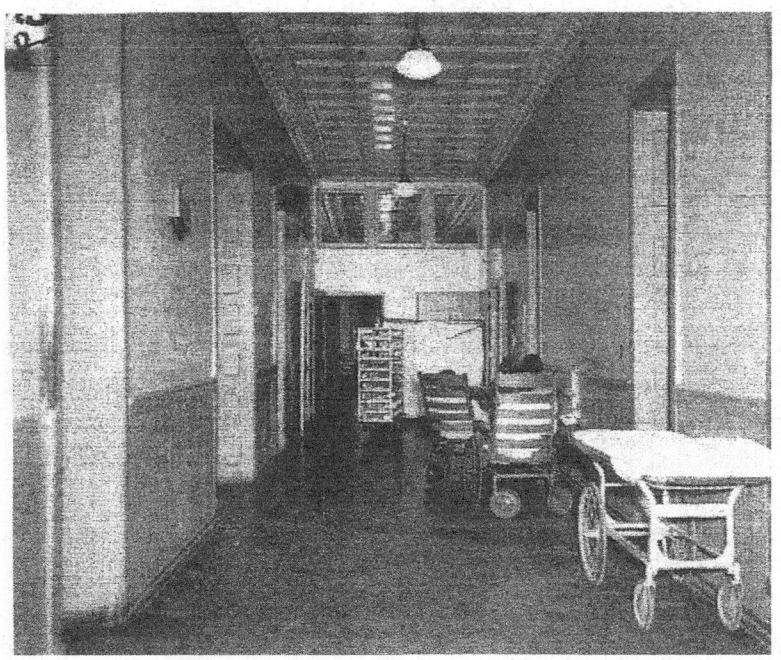

Grady Hall – Near the "elevator"
"Behind those curtains…"
(Photo courtesy of the Georgia State University Archives)

TEE HEE HEE – JESUS WAS THERE

"Shout Jesus, for He is your helper!"

Not one of us could have believed the volume of work that the OB staff performed without experiencing it ourselves. During the junior and senior years of medical school we reviewed the anatomy of gynecology and obstetrics and were thrown right into the delivery business. At Grady Hospital, residents and upper-level medical students with attending instructors present, performed most of the routine deliveries. The higher-level residents or the attending instructors delivered the complicated cases. These cases included women with high blood pressure, diabetes, or fetal problems and those requiring Caesarean-sections.

During my OB rotation, my attending physician was one of the finest on the staff. Dr. T. E. McCain was a slender fellow with a high forehead, thinning gray hair, round wire-rimmed glasses and a head that was flat on the sides yet pointed at the crown. The medical students decided he must have been a victim of a prolonged delivery that flattened his head, one of those babies that just didn't want to come out into the world. I learned later from my classmate, Felton Norwood, a pediatrician, that this condition was caused by an early closure of the cranial or skull fissures. Behind his back we called him "Tee Hee Hee" McCain because of his peculiar laugh.

He was noted for his long and precise lectures, stopping in the middle of his lecture if he spotted someone drifting off. He would reach into his coat pocket, pull out his little black grade book, call out the name of the offender and ask that student a question, drawn from the lecture or the reading assignment. If the student answered the question correctly, he'd say nothing, smile slightly, and continue his lecture. If the student missed the question, he took his pencil from his pocket, licked the point, made a black mark by that student's name and giggled, "Tee hee hee, missed that one didn't you." He then continued the lecture.

Old "White" Grady and the Integrated New Grady Hospital
The old Steiner Cancer Clinic is located
between the two structures.
"Down Butler Street"
(Photo from Emory University Annual, courtesy
of the Woodruff Archives – Emory University Publications)

One particular night, I was in the delivery room in the middle of an unusually difficult delivery. The mother was struggling but just couldn't push the baby out. We were using Trilene, a mild anesthetic breathing gas, which the mother could use for pain relief.

Suddenly, the head of the baby appeared. *Finally,* I thought. Yet the baby seemed stuck in the birth canal. I tried all the manipulations I could think of to get the baby out. With my fetal stethoscope I could hear the baby's heart rate increasing then drastically slowing. Trouble brewing, I knew. By this time, the mother had given up on the breathing mask and was shouting, "Help me, Jesus. Help me, Jesus." We were in trouble. Near panic, I frantically yelled to the delivery room nurse, "Get Dr. McCain, from the next delivery room!"

She gave him the message and he yelled back through the open door, "Tee hee hee, sorry, I've got my own troubles."

Tee hee hee, Hell, I thought, *Lord, what am I to do?*

The head protruded more. I could barely see the umbilical cord around the baby's neck. The baby was stuck and turning blue. The mother was still crying, "Help me, Jesus."

I looked over the delivery drapes and screen and mumbled to her in a fearful tone, "Better ask Him to help me, Mama!"

There was a moment of silence. All was still. Then I heard a low and prayerful voice, "Please, help that doctor, Jesus. Help that doctor!"

I could now clearly see the cord tight around the baby's neck. Without my asking, the calm and experienced circulating nurse intuitively handed me two large curved Kelly clamps. I double-clamped the cord then rapidly cut the cord between the clamps with heavy Mayo scissors. The head popped out, then the shoulder. I rotated the upper body and the baby was out!

I suctioned the baby's mouth and throat, lifted him and spanked him on the butt and whispered to myself, "Thank you, Jesus," as the baby let out the biggest damn cry I believe I ever heard. "Keep yelling, baby," I said. "Keep that airway clear!" We were all laughing and crying together.

A few minutes later, around the door a funny-headed guy peered into the delivery suite. I heard him say, "Tee hee hee, looks like you and Jesus did all right."

NEW PIEDMONT HOSPITAL

It was a hand-me-down job. A number of Emory medical students were employed at Piedmont Hospital. They were employed as externs, that is the senior students serving in the post of interns, supervised by the medical, surgical, and resident staff already employed at the hospital. We "worked up patients," that is performed history and physical examinations on patients that were newly admitted to the hospital and preoperative patients. Unlike interns we had limited authority. Externs could write orders, but the orders had to be countersigned by a full-fledged staff doctor. The medical externs worked mostly on the wards and the surgical externs also assisted in the operating rooms.

By spring the group of externs that were graduating medical school usually participated in the intern matching programs. A number of the Piedmont externs were "matched" at Piedmont and accepted as interns. Upon the departure of the graduating seniors a new group of externs (replacements) were selected often on the recommendations of those leaving. Therefore, the hospital often accepted those recommendations if the extern has done a good job and the staff felt their recommendations were warranted.

Throughout Atlanta several hospitals hired externs, some serving on medical or surgical staffs and some in specific specialties. Some worked as night nurses at Grady and one of my senior classmates worked at Georgia Baptist in the anesthesia department. A few others worked on obstetrics at Crawford Long Hospital, now known as Emory Mid-Town. A couple of students worked at the dispensary of Georgia Tech.

These were plum jobs that paid minimal, but fair wages, offered laundry and free meals. Some allowed the externs to live in the hospital with the other intern and resident staff. Many of us were local Atlantans who had "connections" with staff even before medical school. Our work was important to the hospital and for ourselves, important for gaining the experience of working with some of Atlanta's best doctors.

I was lucky enough to work in the surgery section at the brand-new Piedmont that had just moved the year before (1957) from its old buildings on Capital Avenue into its new modern buildings on Peachtree Road. We worked a full three-month summer (during vacation) and upon returning to medical school in the fall we worked "on call" every fifth night. Medical students often swapped school or outside schedules freely among themselves, so that these outside jobs benefited many, both in receiving a small stipend while gaining experience.

Working at Piedmont introduced me to many of Atlanta's finest doctors, some remained friends all my surgical career. If an extern did a good job and was respected by the staff, he or she had an inside tract into Atlanta medicine. Some returned to Piedmont as staff members after they completed their medical or surgical training elsewhere. Most of the staff doctors were good to us, most were patient, and encouraged us in many ways.

While scrubbing with so many of Atlanta's finest I learned a great deal of good surgical technique, different from the grind (learning from each other) that we pursued at Grady. Watching the surgeons taught each of us those little tricks and procedures that one can obtain only by working with the best.

There were numerous older doctors, some we had known as their former patients, so we were already endeared with these folks. I think they were pleased to see us coming along following in their footsteps and trying to emulate them.

Even in the best hospitals the OR can become a nightmare when things become complicated, but normally the private practice of medicine and surgery is routine and reasonably smooth, again unlike the stress and the confusion of an emergency hospital like Grady.

Of course, there were those doctors we considered as favorites. In the surgery department my favorites were the elder Dr. Edgar Fincher and Dr. John Aiken, each of whom had been my dad's doctor. Others were, the young Dr. Ed Rand and later Frank Wilson, both of whom I knew from Grady. One of our school volunteer instructors and associate professors was Dr. John Skandalakas, perhaps the best surgical anatomist in our training and who over the years became a dear friend.

The jolly Dr. Johnny Duncan was a long-term favorite. I suspect "Dr. Johnny" had delivered as many, if not more, babies than any Atlanta doctor in his long career. He was known for his kindness, humor, frankness, and his toughness as he seemed to practice forever.

One of my mom's dear friends, a young woman was his patient. She was pregnant with her first child. In great distress she phoned Dr. Duncan. She said with concern and emotion, "Dr. Johnny, I'm worried that I have a problem."

"What is that dear?" He answered.

"Oh my, my breast is dripping milk, I think."

Without hesitation, Dr. Johnny replied in his usual forthright manner, "Well, what the hell do you expect, Dear? Coca Cola?"

There was silence on the other end of the line.

Years later, upon Dr. Duncan's death, the hospital had a pair of his OR shoes gold-plated and hung them on the OR wall in remembrance of that wonderful man.

The dearest, I thought, was Dr. Floyd McRae Jr., whose father had been the first surgeon to join Piedmont's original physician, Dr. Amster at the Piedmont Sanatorium shortly after the turn of the twentieth century.

I recall vividly a special case when I was assisting Dr. McRae. The patient was a heavy lady and we were performing a gall bladder operation. A gallbladder case is perhaps the most grueling of the open surgical procedures. (Now with the new surgical "scope" techniques the job is much simpler.) It is torture for the first assistant who must hold a silver steel "Deaver" retractor, it seems for a lifetime, tugging so the surgeon can see the gall bladder, hidden way under the liver.

I had worked the prior summer as a scrub nurse at Grady and also at the segregated Spaulding Hospital with many of Atlanta's white as well as black surgeons. I was well aware of OR techniques and as a former scrub nurse and surgical assistant I mechanically and freely reached over on the instrument table or the Mayo instrument stand and picked up a couple of small instruments as needed.

Once a young scrub nurse gave me a killing look for entering her field of surgery. Perhaps I didn't notice her true ire and without restraint I again casually reached across the Mayo stand. Suddenly, she flashed a heavy silver "Kelly" clamp striking me across my knuckles. I let out a yell, "ouch!"

Dr. McRae looked up from the chasm of the surgery site and shook his head. He quietly whispered, "Boys and girls, what is going on here? Are we going to fight today or operate on Mrs. Zuber?" Mrs. Zuber was the nursing school housemother.

The offended nurse spoke right up with great indignation, "Dr. McRae, he reached over on my Mayo stand."

McRae laid his instruments down and inquisitively asked, "Son, did you reach over on her Mayo stand?"

"Yes sir, I did," I sheepishly answered.

McRae starred at me and with a wink, "Don't you remember, boys should always know where not to put their hands?"

"Yes sir," I answered. "I'll remember."

With a grin, that I imagined under her surgical mask, she responded, "Thank you Dr. McRae, maybe he will learn," and she then shuffled and rearranged her sterile instruments on her Mayo stand. With sparkling blue eyes, she nodded to me in absolute triumph.

At the end of my senior year I left Piedmont with what I thought was a positive medical experience. I moved on to a Grady surgery internship.

INTERNSHIP AT GRADY

"All of a sudden, from the skillet into the fire"

After graduation and a month or so of relative freedom, on July 1st we would feel like we had been hit in both knees with a baseball bat and knocked to the earth. A mountain of responsibility would fall upon each of us. We would be real doctors. When we signed our names to a medical order or document, it would have real authority. As interns we would descend from the peak of graduation to the trenches of the hospital hierarchy.

We would again become the bottom of the barrel. There is nothing much lower than an intern. Senior medical students could always go to the staff member who was responsible for the student's actions, but no more. We were it, and from July 1st, we would be responsible for our own success or failure and for the welfare and lives of our patients.

The so-called "straight surgery" internship rotated the individual through general surgery and all the surgical specialties, usually two months on each. Obstetrics was not included in my year's rotation. I had delivered almost 100 babies as a junior and senior medical student and I thought that was enough. Specialties included were chest, neurosurgery, urology, orthopaedics and a couple of ER rotations. Medical specialties could be elected but that would involve what was called a "rotating internship." The pathology portion would be covered while rotating on each specialty.

At 7:00 a.m. on July 1, 1959, I reported to the neurosurgery ward at Atlanta's new Grady Hospital. My first rotation as an intern began on the most difficult service and proved to be the most challenging of a long series of rotations.

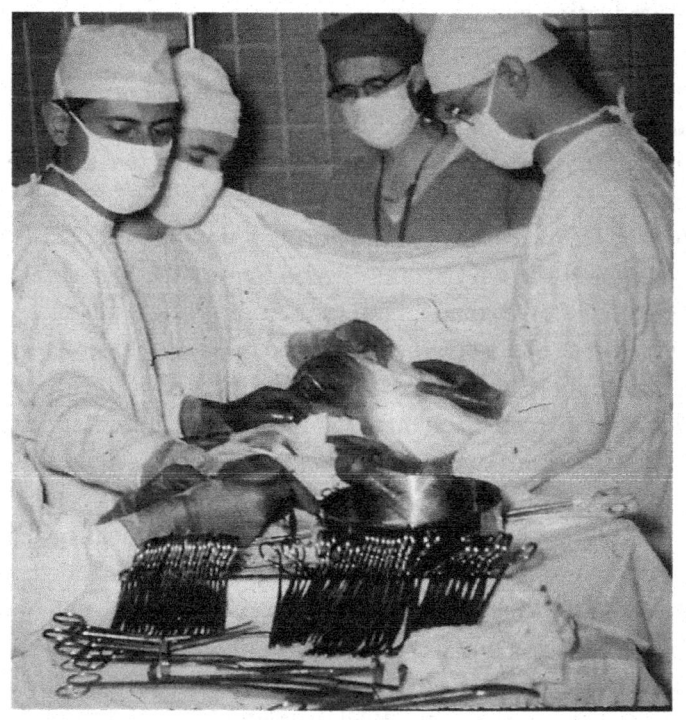

Grady O.R. 1960
"See one. Do one. Teach one."

Left to Right: Chest Surgery Chief Resident Poulos,
Surgery Intern Watts, Anesthesiology Resident Newberry,
and General Surgery Resident George
(Photo from author's collection)

COUPLE ON CREW STREET

I was maybe a little book smart,
but I was not at all street smart.

"Don't go down on Crew Street," an old woman said. "That's just poor white trash down there." I knew that was not true. In the 1930s, Crew Street was in a middle-class neighborhood with working-class people who went to church and reared their children to be honest citizens. They had ambitions that their children would finish school. In some parts of Atlanta that meant finish high school, as that was about as far as most of their parents thought they should go.

When the children grew up, most moved away from Crew Street for greater opportunities. Some of the people who lived on Crew Street still owned their own homes and were not itinerant renters, here today, gone tomorrow. Many of the elderly who lived in the area had simply lived beyond their ability to make a living. They had run out of money. Social Security provided enough for them to buy food and clothing but little else. Some received state welfare checks. Many were indigents of the city. Poor, but still proud.

There were furious debates in the late 1950s and early 1960s about the planned Government Medicare program that would offer medical coverage to those sixty-five years of age and older. Organized medicine clamored that it would be socialism, the end of medicine as we know it. Folks who had plenty of money and were able to afford high priced insurance claimed it would, "Ruin the economy, ruin the nation."

The best the indigent elderly had before 1965 was a Grady card, the key that unlocked access to medical care in Atlanta. There were problems with the Grady "charity care" as some called it: long lines, long waiting times, difficulty seeing the doctor one wanted because of the rotating schedules of the physicians. Yet, Grady offered the service of a dedicated staff with a desire to give good care to all. If the nurses and doctors had not been dedicated, they would never have elected to take the most difficult jobs and ones with the lowest pay of any hospital training program in the South.

Whites and Blacks coveted the Grady card. I saw patients arrive at the Gradys holding their wallets as if they contained gold. I saw patients open their wallets empty of everything except a ragged faded Grady card and present it for care.

While riding the sick car as an intern, it was my responsibility to treat the shut-in and indigent patients of the city and in surrounding Fulton and DeKalb counties. Each morning the sick car schedule offered a multitude of challenges.

One bright spring morning, we pulled out of the Grady lot and headed to Crew Street. As a former ambulance driver, I knew Crew Street. When we arrived, I alighted from the passenger side of the ambulance.

The driver volunteered, "I'll stay out here and listen out for the radio, if that's okay, Doc?"

"Sure," I answered. "If I need you, I'll let you know."

The house on Crew Street was a gray two-story, no more than two rooms wide and several rooms deep with a central hall. For an old house it was surprisingly well-maintained. A low wire fence along the sidewalk and yard, substituted for what once was likely a picket or iron fence. I stepped up on the worn, but swept, wooden porch and knocked at the door. There was a little hand-written note taped by the doorbell that read, "Out of order." Behind the door's frosty glass, I saw the thin shadow of a person. She peeped through the cracked door and politely said, "Oh, Doctor, do come in, we've been expecting you."

She was wearing a light-colored cotton dress. She had a white lace handkerchief in her left hand, which she gently placed in her dress pocket. [I could see she was a gentle lady.]

"Yes, Ma'am," I said, "I've come from Grady to see your husband. He's on our sick list for follow up."

"Oh, he's in here," she said. "Do you need to see his Grady card?" She led me into a bright little bedroom with flowered wallpaper and sheer white curtains, shimmering slightly as a cool breeze blew through the window. Propped up in the iron bed sat an elderly man with thinning white hair, a wisp of a mustache and silver-rimmed glasses. He was wearing a starched, but worn white shirt, buttoned at the top. He had just been shaved. They had likely prepared all morning for the doctor's visit.

I introduced myself, pulled out his medical chart and reviewed his medicines with him and his wife. She brought into the room several bottles of medicine, some empty, needing to be refilled. I helped him unbutton his shirt. He breathed deeply, a soft swoosh, as I listened to his chest. His heart sounds were clear, but I heard a few skipped beats, and a slight systolic murmur and noted a little congestion in the base of his lungs as he exhaled. I checked his blood pressure and counted his pulse.

Yes, he was missing an occasional heartbeat. Nothing, I thought, that a little change in his digitalis might not resolve. I looked at his bottle, wrote out another prescription and pulled a bottle of digitalis from my bag. "Take these instead of the old medicine," I said. I noted a bit of swelling in his feet as I removed the bed covers and altered his diuretic prescription to help remove some of his excess body fluid.

"He is in a little more heart failure than our last visit," I said to his wife, "but I think this change in medicines will help."

His wife left the room. She soon reappeared with an ancient silver tray and tea in a porcelain cup, decorated with little purple flowers and a home-baked biscuit, with homemade blackberry jam on the side. "I have brought you some tea, Doctor, I know your day is long. We want to thank you for coming," she said. "Do you take lemon or milk?"

The tea was tasty as was the little biscuit and my favorite jam. As I sipped the tea, I thought about this gentle couple. They were old and had problems that, at my age, I could not fathom. Yet, they accepted me as a competent physician. I knew book medicine, but I had no idea of what their lives were like. They needed someone older, more mature who understood them better.

I closed my medical bag and thanked the kind lady for the refreshing tea and biscuit and left their house. I walked by the budding rosebush at the edge of the cracked sidewalk, stopped for a moment to get a whiff of the lovely yellow roses, and glanced back at a blossoming pink dogwood in the yard and at the old house behind it.

I climbed into the waiting ambulance. The driver handed me the schedule clipboard. "How was it, Doc?"

I closed my eyes and leaned back in the ambulance seat, "Humbling," I whispered.

GRIM SENTENCE

"... handwriting on the wall..."

Doctor Glisson walked into my mom's hospital room and quietly said, "We're all finished." Glancing at his sad face, fear and darkness overcame me. It was as if I read the handwriting on the wall.

"How did she do?" I asked.

"I'm afraid I don't have very good news," he sighed. "The prognosis is not very good." After a few words with my dad, he said to me, "Why don't you come with me and listen to the dictation. That will explain what we did and what to expect."

I felt a cold chill when he spoke. I looked at my dad who remained silent. He had stood when the doctor came into the room, but now he slowly sat down in the visitor's hard chair. I could see tears well up in his dark brown eyes as he began to comprehend the doctor's blunt words. I had never seen him with tears before.

"You go with him," he said to me, clearing his throat. "You'll understand, then come back and explain it all to me."

"Yes, I'll do that," I answered.

The walk to the doctor's dictating desk, by the operating room seemed like an eternity. Dr. Glisson put his arm about my shoulder and said, "I'm sorry son, that we don't have better news. We did all we could."

"Yes, sir," I said, "I'm sure you did."

"I called in my associate Doctor--" I didn't hear the rest of his sentence. I was numb. We sat down by the dictating machine. He began to dictate. I didn't want to hear it but I knew I had to listen.

I listened as objectively as I could. The words were devastating as Dr. Glisson dictated the operative note on my mother. He detailed the area affected by the cancerous tumor. He described the cutting and the removal of tissue. He recorded the involvement of the lymph nodes, the palpable spread of the tumor cells.

He estimated the blood loss and recorded the amount of blood replaced. Finally, he described the closure of the skin and related the prognosis. "Survival rate is very minimal with this type of cancer. I estimate six to twelve months if the cancer is not completely removed. If the cancer is completely removed the five-year survival is likely ten to twenty percent. A series of chemotherapy or radiation will likely be required." He continued briefly with the technical details of ending the procedure.

I had heard enough. My mind began to block all that was being said. I didn't want to hear anymore but I waited until the dictation was finished. I stood up and thanked him for trying and doing his best.

He turned away, removed his scrub cap, looked back as he started down the hall and asked, "Would you like to come into the recovery room to see your mother?"

"Yes, thanks, I would," I responded.

I knew it would be bad, but I also knew I would have to face up to the horror of what my mother later stoically called "this business." I would have to explain it all to my dad. I would be as gentle as I could.

Her post op course was stormy. "We think she has an intestinal obstruction," announced Dr. Glisson as he returned his stethoscope to his coat pocket and replaced the sheets over my mom's abdomen. "She's still silent, no bowel sounds."

I stood at the foot of the bed and watched my mother, now confused, fade into unconsciousness then struggle to awaken as the nurse smoothed out the sheets covering her. She mumbled something, but I couldn't understand her.

"I've called Doctor Aiken who agrees. We plan to take her back to the OR when he comes over from Piedmont," said Glisson. "We think the obstruction and the resultant electrolyte disturbances are part of her confusion."

Saint Joseph's Infirmary – Atlanta, Georgia – 1960
The Catholic Sisters of Mercy opened the first charity hospital
in May 1880 to care for the destitute sick of the city.
(Photo by author)

The second operation was completed, and her surgeons entered her room. Dr. John Aiken spoke first, "She had adhesions from her initial surgery, and we've relieved those and hope she will improve."

Dr. Glisson spoke briefly to my dad and then the doctors quickly left the room.

A few days later she was sitting up in bed. She had recovered from the acute trauma of the second procedure and the correction of her electrolyte problem. The confusion from that imbalance abated. She was lucid as the surgeons once again gathered about her bed.

We stood and discussed her condition openly. They talked in plain language to her. She wanted to know exactly what her prognosis was. She was realistic about "this business". Her attending doctors left the room. I stood at the bedside mulling over the discussion.

My mom gazed at me, and with a sad smile whispered, "Come up closer." She reached out for my hand. "You know, I never realized you were a real doctor till now."

I was a real doctor, but I knew I couldn't help her. I gritted my teeth and turned away so she wouldn't see my tears.

THE GIRL IN BLUE AND WHITE

"That lovely girl…"

I heard her before I saw her. It was the rustle of her blue and white nurse's uniform that I heard. Then I saw that lovely girl tiptoeing down the Piedmont Hospital hall. She was slender, graceful and she smiled slightly as she passed. I was a Piedmont extern (a senior medical student) going to see a patient on 4-West that had had surgery and I had just passed that patient's nurse in the hall.

It would be over a year before I met her again. By this time, I was an intern at Grady. My classmate, Joe Stubbs, then an intern at Piedmont, had surgery and I was visiting him. "This is Ellen," his wife said as the lovely young nurse entered the room. She was the nurse I had briefly passed in the hall once before.

We spoke but she was obviously unimpressed with my Grady whites. Probably just another of those wise guys in white, she likely thought.

I saw her several times after that and asked her for a date. She was lovely, poised and gentle. I was already sure I loved her.

Within a short time after our first date, Ellen and I were dating whenever our schedules allowed. Sometimes our date would merely be dinner at Piedmont or late-night supper at Grady.

My time was divided between my intern work at Grady and helping my dad care for my ill mother. On my alternate nights I visited my mom at St. Joseph's Hospital and at our home after she left the hospital. She was terminally ill. Her blood count was so low that I often drew her blood. I took it to our hospital blood bank for a type and crossmatch. I would bring a unit home and hang the bottle on a bedpost to infuse the blood that she sorely needed.

Since I had externed at Piedmont, I easily entered the hospital after hours. The night watchman never really knew whether I still worked at Piedmont or not since I would often appear in my whites just slipping away from Grady for a little while. Ellen and I often met and sat on the hospital stairs late at night sipping cokes. Our work hours allowed so little time.

Toward the end of my mother's life, Ellen and I visited her frequently. When my mother needed to rest, she would encourage us to "go and have a little date."

My dad approached me one evening as I left our house. "Your mother doesn't want any more blood," he said. She had decided the end was near and she was prepared.

In December of 1960 she was invited by the Catholic nuns to come to Our Lady of Perpetual Help "to get stronger for Christmas." On December 15th she quietly died in the care of and surrounded by her Catholic Sisters and priests at the cancer home where she had spent so many hours and days as a volunteer.

Ellen and I continued dating and became engaged. In July, at the end of the first year of my surgical residency, I entered the military.

Ellen graduated from nursing school the following fall and our relationship, after a few months of being away on military duty, ended. She left for Europe to be with her family. She had not seen them for two years while she was in nursing training. Her dad was a military attorney in JAG (Judge Advocates Section) in Germany. I would see her again only briefly in Europe.

"The girl in the blue and white dress"
Ellen Anita Hunter
(Photo from Piedmont Hospital, 1960-1961)

In the military, I served as a low-level general surgeon and flight surgeon. I was often assigned temporarily in France and Germany, mostly while en route to other points on the globe.

During the last visit I had in Germany, Ellen and I met briefly in Frankfurt. On a scheduled date night our date was canceled as I was ordered to accompany a classified flight into Berlin. The East Germans and Soviets, in mid-winter were blocking the highways and the railroads into Berlin and interfering with our planes as they attempted to fly into the city.

On the last night I saw Ellen in Frankfurt, she drove me to the airfield and through the heavy fog I boarded a huge plane and (as in the movie *Casablanca*) flew into the dark night, not to see or hear from her again for nearly forty years.

SUMMER NIGHT 1960

Grady Hospital Emergency Room

The double doors burst open. "JESUS, what have you got?" I yelled across the clinic. A cop and an intern pulling a stretcher rushed in.

"Got a bad one," they shouted. "Run over!"

"Room One," I instinctively called out. "What happened?"

"Teenagers in Buckhead – out cruising."

Now frantic, I yelled, "Get her on the table."

She was slender with long blonde hair, delicate white skin, now gravel-scraped and crimson covered. "Strip her," I ordered the ER nurse standing nearby. We pulled out our scissors. I slit her white, now soiled blouse. The nurse cut her tight matador slacks.

"Is that a tire track across her chest?" the intern blurted out. "Oh, God, she's not breathing!"

The ambulance driver stepped back against the tile wall of Room One. "She fell out of a convertible and we think the back wheel of her car or the car behind them hit or ran over her."

I hesitated for a moment and took a deep breath. The nurse removed the pile of clothes. "How old is she?"

"Her license says sixteen."

Aghast, I muttered, "Just a teenager."

"Open the chest pack and the tracheotomy tray," I ordered the nurse and intern. "Get Dr. John from the other clinic. We need help!"

The intern wrapped her limp right arm with the pressure cuff to get an IV started. "She's got no pressure. I don't hear a pulse sound," he murmured. Her body was still warm. She gasped what might well have been a last agonal breath.

Though new in the clinic, I was the resident. I was in charge. I grabbed a bottle of iodine from the medicine cabinet and doused it over her left chest and soft breast, spread it with a clean towel, reached for the cardiac knife, opened its bright red holder and pulled out the knife, counted the left ribs and slashed through a midrib space, opened the chest cavity and felt the collapsed lung. "Chest retractor," I shouted.

I cranked the retractor open and with my gloved hand reached into the gaping cavity and grasped the girl's heart. It quivered as I squeezed the purple muscle. It was like a small football.

The other resident incised her throat just above the suprasternal notch, retracted the delicate muscles, opened the trachea with his sharp blade, spread the cartilage and inserted the silver metal tracheotomy tube. He suctioned dark, frothy liquid and began to bag-breathe her. "Got to get oxygen into her lungs."

I could feel the spongy lung inflating and softly touching my arm. "Epinephrine," I yelled. "Get me the long needle."

I backed my hand out of the chest long enough to stab the needle and syringe of "Epi" through the heart muscle. There was barely a quiver.

We continued squeezing her heart and bag breathing until my hand was numb. I could feel no more. I glanced at the nurse, "Get me more Epi." She leaned over and wiped the sweat and blood from my face.

"John, you pump for a minute." He began to compress the heart. I could see by his poignant expression, it was over.

I felt angry. This girl was mine. Her life belonged to me. How could he dare tell me it was all over? *I was the resident; it was my clinic. She can't die in my clinic.*

"Move over," I ordered. Feverishly, I squeezed the still heart. She was somebody's daughter. I couldn't give up.

"That's enough!" whispered John as he removed the breathing bag from the tracheotomy-tube and slowly pulled off his gloves. He placed his firm hand on my trembling arm and held it tightly. I attempted to pull away. He stared into my eyes, "You've tried. We can't save everybody."

My own heart cried out, "Don't stop." Reluctantly, I withdrew my hand from that girl's chest. I had done all I could.

The crimson-sprayed nurse, trying to hold back her tears, lifted a crisp white sheet and covered the beautiful girl.

My shift ended at 7 a.m., I shuffled out of the clinic and rode the elevator to the resident quarters where I shed my splattered whites, pulled off my sweaty socks, and showered in the steaming water. Then I threw myself across my bunk. Before I slept, I tried to remember when I had decided to be a surgeon. That morning I wondered why.

WHERE?

"The ambulance searched for the address given them by the police dispatcher."
This was the story told to them.

Drudgingly, he climbed the dark stairs to the apartment, turned the key and slowly opened the heavy door. Sprawled out lying on the sofa, agitated and sulking, a cigarette in her slender shaking hand, she looked up at him.

"No more drugs," he yelled.

"Please, please," she cried. "Just this time, I beg you!"

"No more," he whispered. "I'm leaving, I'm going home. It's over."

She struggled to rise from the sofa and trembling, she muttered, "What about me?" She wailed. "What'll I do... How can I live?"

She sank back onto the sofa, "Please, just one more!"

He eyed her sharply, grimaced, shook his head slowly, and stepped toward the door.

She sprang unsteadily from the sofa, still trembling, staggered across the room, knocking over a tall porcelain lamp, shattering it on the floor. He pushed her away. "Please, just this time," she screamed.

"No more and I mean it." He was angry, gritting his teeth, "Just look at you. You're shaking all over."

She stumbled over a small chair and, leaning over a small chest, she opened a dresser drawer. She reached in and pulled out a small black revolver. Brandishing the revolver with tears streaming down her cheek she begged, "I need it now. I promise I won't ask for more."

"Put that down," he yelled. She lifted her hand toward him. He moved to grasp her outstretched hand. Crack, the gun doomed!

He grabbed his chest, turned away from the woman and collapsed, falling to his knees at the threshold of the door. "Call Grady he mumbled. Call them now."

She shrilled into the phone, "He's been shot! Please hurry! He's a Grady doctor."

He coughed violently and blood-tinged sputum spit out onto the floor.

The woman hovered over him, sobbing, "Oh, God, I didn't mean to!"

Breathless, he cried, "Get my medical bag." Then, "There's a big syringe." He gasped, "Put the long needle on it." He pulled at his shirt and pressed his hand over the chest wound.

The woman scrambled to the desk near where the dark medical bag sat on the floor. She opened it feverishly, stirred her shaky hands inside yanking out sundry stuff and pulled out a large glass syringe and needles.

"Yeah, stab the needle here," he whispered, gasping for breath, moving his hand to the spot. "Start sucking out the blood."

Now more alert, she did as she was told, and the syringe filled with dark blood. She repeated the procedure emptying the blood, spraying it on the carpet and reinserting the huge needle.

"That's better," he whispered, breathing slowly, and coughing with less difficulty. Then he slumped back and closed his eyes.

The ambulance searched for the address… "We're on Lenox, but can't find the number," the driver hollered into the police radio. "Oh, I see her now, outside waving and screaming."

"Here, here," she cried out. "He's in here, upstairs."

The driver and intern glared at the man lying on the floor. "She said he once was a Grady doctor."

"Do something, please do something," the woman whimpered as she curled up near the still form.

The intern knelt down beside the man, feverishly felt for a carotid pulse, leaned close to the man's chest listening for any evidence of breathing. The intern felt his still warm skin, turned and spoke softly to the ambulance driver, "Better call the coroner."

PART THREE

MILITARY MEDICINE
AND COLD WAR

UNITED STATES MILITARY – 1960s

There's always been a minority of those willing to defend families and country.

Preface

In the 1960s universal military draft remained in effect. I was commissioned during internship and scheduled for induction after internship. However, I was given a year of compassionate delay until my mother passed away. During that time, I completed an additional year of general surgery residency that put me in good standing when I entered the military.

AFTER GRADY

A new challenge…

At 6 a.m. the red early morning rays of sunlight slipped through the windows of my quarters high up in the hospital overlooking the city I loved.

I got up, splashed cold water on my face. I shaved my scruffy whiskers and stared into the mirror. Holding my toothbrush tightly in my hand, I thought about the many sleepless nights and the draining days I had spent at Grady. I put on fresh, though frayed, starched whites, slipped on my blood-stained Hush Puppies and descended to the cafeteria. I picked up a cup of coffee and sauntered to the ward.

At 7 a.m. on 1 July 1961, I handed the surgery ward and its problems to the new resident. He would begin his first year of residency at Grady Hospital. A year before, after a year of surgery internship I had walked into the same surgical ward to begin my first year of real responsibility.

The new guy would no longer be the scut-boy intern but would be in charge of the surgical care of patients and direct the training of the new group of uninitiated interns. I led the new resident and his fresh interns to the nurses' desk. I introduced them, selected several battered aluminum charts with the sickest patients' history documented inside and walked the new guys down the hall to visit the critical and serious cases. Thus, ended two years of cloistered confinement in Atlanta's Grady Hospital.

MILITARY SERVICE

The early 1960s was a time of anxious international conflict. The post-World War II days pitted the two major Superpowers – the United States and the Soviet Union – against each other in Europe. China was a rising communist government and represented a threat to the stability of the Far East after the withdrawal of the French from Indochina in 1956 and the success of the revolutionary Viet Minh.

It was accepted by most Americans that the Soviet Union was ahead of the United States in the space program with the international coup in October 1957 of sending the satellite "Sputnik" into space. America was in catch-up mode. We felt the anxiety of falling behind in world leadership. I was to feel that anxiety when I entered the School of Aerospace Medicine, but it was balanced by the spirit of American resourcefulness.

SCHOOL OF AEROSPACE MEDICINE

...or just the flight surgeon's school...

San Antonio was scorching hot from July until October when the flight surgeon's class completed the intensive three months of Aerospace Medicine. We studied the medical implications of flight, including high altitude physical problems, flying stress, and the management of pilots, navigators, and aircrew members who met with such difficulties.

Our classes met daily but, on the weekends, we had both Saturdays and Sundays off. It was the first time in two years that I had two days off at a time. The young doctors were a rowdy bunch, not responding to military discipline, but tolerating the higher-grade officers and their instruction. We did however expand our knowledge of pulmonary, cardiology, and other areas of concern that the flying personnel might encounter.

We became acquainted with the plans for an early space program, useful for scientific endeavors and military protection or offense. We were fascinated when the space scientists and engineers taught us about the planned rocket programs mirroring President Kennedy's plan to land a man on the moon during the next decade. We learned that we were actually not behind the Soviets in rocket and potential space planning. We were essentially par with them and would likely land on the moon before the Soviets.

Upon graduation we received our "wings" and were assigned to our bases.

BASE ASSIGNMENT

"I wanted something different..."

When I opened the envelope with my orders and learned that my first assignment would be stateside, I asked my classmate, "Where in the hell is Dover, Delaware?"

I was disappointed. I had hoped for overseas orders. I tried unsuccessfully to get my orders changed. I wanted something different from the routine of hospital life that I had known for the last six years.

After a long drive from Texas I arrived at my base late at night in the pouring rain, barely before the midnight deadline to sign in. I had been lost on the dark roads of Maryland's Eastern shore and worried that if I didn't sign in on time, I would be considered AWOL (Absent Without Leave), a serious military offense. All I needed was to get started off on the wrong foot at my new base.

I settled into the BOQ (Bachelor Officers Quarters). I was the only bachelor flight surgeon. The married officers had special family housing and special living allowances.

I obtained permission to move off base and joined a group of fellow bachelor officers in a house known as the Ranch House. It was a two-story gray clapboard house just outside of town. A dusty road ran circuitously through the cornfields. A long driveway off the little road led to the front door and curved around the house into the rear gravel parking area.

A large porch extended from the front to the side. I imagined an old farmer and his wife once sitting on that porch watching the sunset. Young, vigorous pilots and navigators, ever ready for a party now inhabited it.

"You'll have Rafe's room upstairs," said the house chief, an older senior pilot. He managed the house and the bills. Each of us contributed a sum for rent and utilities and a special party fund that was often dried up. "It was that last party," the house manager said, "so we'll have to up the assessment."

"As long as two or more are gathered there can be a party," he was fond of saying.

UPSTAIRS

"Is there anywhere else to rest?"

Early that chilly fall evening the doorbell rang. "Get the door somebody," someone yelled from the rear of the Ranch House. I opened the heavy oak door and there stood two ravishing blondes.

"Is this where the party is tonight?" the taller of the two asked softly.

"Why yes," I answered, stunned at the appearance of the two strangers.

"She's Rafe Higgs' date," the other slender young girl said.

"Come in, yes, come in," I stuttered. Man, *where did these two come from*, I wondered.

"I don't have a date, I'm with her," the shorter girl volunteered.

"Hey, you're welcome, too," I mumbled, now embarrassed.

"Rafe's upstairs," I said. "Come in and I'll let him know you all are here."

We entered the living room. The girls looked around. "Who lives here?"

"Just military guys," I answered. "Where did you come from?" I inquired.

"Wilmington," the taller blonde replied. "Rafe and Will Brown invited us down for the party. Is Will here?"

"Nope, he's out on a flight and won't be back for a couple of weeks. I'm sure he'll be sorry he wasn't here."

The younger girl said, "Well, I'll just go into town and stay with my aunt."

"Oh, no, you stay," I said. "I don't have a date so would you be my date?"

She glanced at her friend. "He looks okay," the companion responded.

It was a great party, delicious Greek food, prepared by one of our housemates, sparkling drinks, and music blasting from a record player. We had many bottles of wine that we had brought back from France and the Azores. The guys always filled their allotment of duty-free alcohol when returning to the states. We had a full wine cellar.

About midnight, the party began to thin out. The records were replaying and had to be restarted. Johnny Mathis' voice faded into the dark night. My date left and drove to her aunt's shortly after midnight. I stretched out on the couch before the iron-grated coal-burning fireplace and covered myself with a blanket. I dozed off and was awakened by a tap on the shoulder. In the soft glow of the diminishing fire I saw the tall lovely blonde.

"Rafe passed out and the guys took him upstairs to bed. I don't have a ride to my friend's, and it is so late I don't have a way back to Wilmington."

I rubbed my eyes. "Rafe what?" I asked.

"He's upstairs," she repeated.

"Well, let's have another glass of wine and decide what to do," I said. I had consumed enough that I should not consider driving this girl to her friend's aunt and certainly not to Wilmington.

We talked for a long while. I realized this girl was really someone special, long blonde hair, lovely features, bright hazel eyes, tall and slender. She spoke with a soft New England accent and seemed remarkably intelligent. "You can just stay here, if that's okay?" I said. "We have an extra couch and I'll get you some blankets. You can stay by the fire. You know I really shouldn't drive."

"Yes," she agreed. "You really shouldn't."

I covered her with a sheet and a blanket. I fluffed a pillow and stoked the fire and wished her a good night. "You'll be fine here."

The fire died. In the dark, a soft voice whispered, "It's so cold in this house. Is there anywhere else we could sleep?"

"Upstairs," I answered.

We crept across the room in the haze of the flickering fire to the squeaky wooden stairs and climbed to the second floor. "This is where the bedrooms are. You can sleep in my bed and I'll find another." I opened my bedroom door and there was Rafe sprawled out snoring in my bed.

"Oops," I thought of the three bears and Goldilocks. "We'll have to check Rafe's room. I think they just put him in the wrong bed."

We opened the creaking door and, in the dark, found an empty bed. "Will this do?"

"For both of us?" she demurely replied.

"I don't mind if you don't," I said.

"Will I be safe?"

"Safe as you want to be," I answered.

292

We pulled down the covers and slipped in.

"Night, night," my Goldilocks whispered.

FIRST NIGHT FLIGHT

"Hey, Doc. we've got a night flight."

I had been on the base only a few weeks when my fighter squadron's operations officer called, "Hey, Doc, we've got a flight and wonder if you might be interested. We don't need an RO (radar observer) so there's a place for you."

"Great," I answered. "What time?"

"It's a night flight after dark. It's at nine tonight."

"I'll be there."

"We'll let the security folks know. Check in at the security gate," he answered.

I arrived at the squadron headquarters and the pilot met me in the briefing room. "Let's walk out to the plane after the equipment sergeant checks you for a chute and we'll be off," he said.

"I've not had the flight review for this plane," I said to the pilot.

We walked out to a T-33, a single engine jet, by the hanger. The ground crew pulled the ladder up to the plane and helped me into the cockpit. The ground crew sergeant fitted the shoulder straps and the parachute for me then commented, "All done, Doc. Have fun."

The pilot climbed aboard and checked me out and reviewed the instruments and especially the handle for possible ejection.

The canopy closed slowly as we rolled out to the runway. "Doc, we'll be up about two hours as a target plane over the New York Sector." He further explained that this was a practice exercise testing another squadron's intercept performance.

He reminded me, "Doc, since you've not had the orientation on this plane, if we have trouble and have to eject, I'll be sure you get out first. You got the ejection handle okay?" he asked.

"Yep, no problem," I answered.

Once we reached the practice target area, we established a specific altitude and soon were spotted on ground radar then by an interceptor plane.

We carried out our mission over the East coast and entered the New York sector. We were the intruder bandit and the plane from another base tracked us as we flew at the established altitude.

We were allowed limited avoidance procedures and during the flight dropped a couple loads of chaff (aluminum foil) to confuse the interceptor plane's radar. He performed a simulated attack using his radar to locate us. We were advised by ground control that the exercise had been completed and we were directed to our home base.

98th Fighter Interceptor Squadron Members
Dover AFB Delaware, c. 1961
(Photo from 98th Squadron photographer)

We returned and landed safely and rolled to our parking spot off the runway, thus completing my first night flight. I became addicted to those flights and my name remained posted up on the "air crew available" board.

SWEDEN TO CONGO

Air Force New Tape Operation...

From Stockholm we flew a circuitous route along the northern coast of East Germany, avoiding the danger of penetrating the forbidden Soviet–controlled territory. We flew to England then skirted France. At that time DeGaulle disallowed UN flights over France en route to the Congo. We flew along Spain's coast through the straits of Gibraltar to Libya and to Nigeria, where we crew rested and refueled, and on to the old Belgian Congo, now free of European control. In Leopoldville we settled at the N'Djili Aerodrome and shuttled throughout Congo.

I remained at the airfield until I was given a little white-washed villa with a young Congolese youth to be my attendant. It was located not far from the university on a hilltop along a dusty road. Some rebels and the local rioters and looters had knocked out all the windows so at night I could hear the distant and mysterious native drums communicating out in the bush.

While stationed in Leo my corpsman, an African American sergeant, opened many local doors. "Just come with me and I'll show you the town, Doc," he volunteered. By military regulations, officers were not allowed to fraternize with enlisted men, but he was "my man." In the medical corps we had a more casual relationship with our enlisted men. Most of the docs were barely military.

At night he and I slipped into town in one of the white UN Jeep trucks for entertainment. We favored the dance clubs and bars where we danced with the locals to the rhythmic drums of the Congo bands. I had never experienced such rhythm and I became a fan of African music.

My corpsman burst out laughing at me and remarked, "Sir, bet you can't dance like this back home." He was right. It would not fly in the segregated South. I was learning a new social order could exist.

The locals were receptive to the UN forces. I felt they realized that we were there to help quell the violence and assist in resisting the vicious rebel and mercenary forces of Katanga Province. The local merchants were eager to get our prohibited greenbacks since their local francs were essentially destroyed by the country's inflation. The official exchange rate was about ten francs to the dollar, but our black-market UN friends were able to exchange at forty or more francs per dollar.

Our duty hours were not at all routine. One evening we sat at dinner laughing and joking in a tin roofed and thatched hut near the airfield. A UN officer approached the table, excited. He was pale. He anxiously informed his fellow officers of recent news. "We just got a report of activity along the river." He meant the Congo. "It seems that a small Italian squad of about ten men was attacked last night after dark by the rebels and slaughtered." He took a breath and blurted, "And, by god, they ate them." A hush filled the room. We held our breath for a moment.

"Not so," grunted one officer, "I don't believe that could happen, not for a damn minute."

"That's the report we got. No survivors!" the other officer admonished.

It was bad enough to lose one's life, but it was beyond comprehension that cannibalism was involved. Just the thought terrorized us.

The next day I shuttled out to the bush and never learned if the rumor was true or not. I did however lock my doors and slept fitfully for days.

I found time to visit the UN Hospital in downtown Leopoldville and the Belgian Catholic Université Lovanium, a medical school, which was still turning out doctors for the Congolese despite the on-going civil war. We visited the wards and operating rooms in both hospitals. We were impressed with the services they were able to perform. *These guys are well-trained,* I thought.

One of the Belgian instructors commented, "When the young native doctors return to their villages, they have to make peace with the local medicine man." He added, "Without the approval of the witch doctor they cannot practice scientific medicine. If they have a serious illness to treat, the young doctor always calls in his friend, the local witch doctor and together they treat the patient." It was better than malpractice insurance.

After we delivered the heavy armored vehicles to Leopoldville, we delivered anti-aircraft guns and hundreds of barrels of jet aircraft fuel to Elisabethville and Albertville (our regular runs). The Congolese national troops (L'Armée nationale congolaise, or ANC), were deathly afraid of any aircraft attack and would not fight. "They run off into the bush unless the anti-aircraft guns are in place," said one of the airmen. "I'm not sure the guns ever hit anything. They just make a hell of a lot of noise."

Our shuttles included flights between Leopoldville, Elisabethville (now Lumumbashi) and Albertville (now Kalemie) bordering Lake Tanganyika. Temporary accommodations were provided at each location. In one location, I shared an abandoned villa with several UN troops. Most of the building's windows were broken out, presumably from the military conflicts, but at night the windows simply provided through-ventilation for the house. After dark, we listened to the native drums echoing from the bush and hills nearby while we dozed before a deeper sleep took hold. The UN forces, the Free Irish military, the Pakistanis and the Nigerians, all provided security as we, the Americans were acting as noncombatants to avoid international suspicions of American colonialism.

Our squadron completed its shuttles and we returned to Leopoldville. Because of the intense heat and humidity in Congo, we waited to take off until late night when the temperature dropped. I never quite understood. "It's the air density," a loadmaster claimed. We ended our mission and our planes returned north, bypassing de Gaulle's France.

N'Djili Aerodrome – Leopoldville, Congo 1962
UN Gate and guard station

UN Airplanes with jet-fuel cans nearby
The Swedish pilots in Congo flew the SAAB J-29s.

**UN Military Forces assembled at the N'Djili Aerodrome
for an airlift into the region of the heaviest military conflict,
deep in Congo.**
Note empty oil drums used to transport jet fuel.
(All Congo photos by author)

SECOND MISSION TO CONGO

Almost a year later I was called to the hospital commander's office after a staff meeting during which I had, in error, volunteered to return to the Congo. "I checked with the First Squadron and Major Jones has requested you accompany his mission to Congo," said my hospital commander.

We followed the same flight plan as on my first Congo mission except that this mission was with the 1st Air Transport Squadron in the C-133, a heavier plane than the C-124. It also had a longer-range capacity, thus avoiding a couple of the refueling stops and avoiding the stop in Nigeria. However, after we left Libya and during the night flight over the Sahara Desert the plane developed a propeller control problem and required us to return to Libya for repair. The mission was similar to the first Congo mission however, that one had been without significant problems with the airplane.

The "New Tape Operation" was the first successful major airlift mission to Congo using the C-133, a plane originally designed to carry the Atlas Missile. While in Congo, I repeated the shuttles to the UN-occupied areas and assisted with the care of the air crews and any medical problems related to the UN troops in the vicinity.

At the end of the airlift, base operations at N'Djili issued orders to go back to Rhein Main or Châteauroux where we had squadrons on TDY. The orders advised me to get the most expedient available transportation. I would in this case leave the squadron in Libya and catch a ride on a C-130 headed for Frankfurt or Rhein Main and ultimately home.

First successful C-133 Airlift to the Congo
1st Air Transport Squadron–1607 Military Air Transport Service
New Tape Operation with the UN in Congo Contingency, 1962-63
(Photo by author)

CUBAN MISSILE CRISIS
OCTOBER 20, 1962

It was simply a promotion party and then...

The 31st Air Transport Squadron was to celebrate the unit promotion party at the officer's club on October 20, 1962. The invitation invited all officers of the squadron and their ladies to the occasion. When I inquired about a certain young lady my hospital commander suggested it would be proper courtesy to invite her. She was the daughter of the late medical officer, Colonel Strong.

My hospital commander and I had previously visited the deceased Colonel's family to pay our respects and represent the medical section of the base. There I met his adult daughter, the "lovely Millie" as my friends called her. She sat quietly with her mother as we paid our respects. Millie was about 5 feet 4, slender, with soft blonde hair, tightly pulled back, and piercing blue eyes. She spoke softly. She and her mother disguised their grief with true and remarkable military stoicism.

Millie had dated a number of my fellow airmen before I came on base. I was hesitant to invite her to the promotion party for fear of stepping on one of my squadron members' toes. It was so soon after her father's death, I wondered if it was appropriate. I learned in no time, "Partying in the Air Force stood on little ceremony." She agreed, to go as my guest or, "my lady in this case."

We arrived at the Club before the party, my date in a light blue fall dress complimenting my military blues and her lovely blonde hair and blue eyes. We had cocktails and dinner with a number of the other young "officers and their ladies." Midway in the promotion celebration, the squadron commander stepped up on the bandstand and took the microphone.

"Attention, attention," he said. The music stopped. Dancers turned to the podium on which Colonel Cupko stood. Blurry eyes turned in his direction. "It's been a great party and I'm sorry to have to announce that our celebration will end at midnight for those on flying status. Each of you on flying status must report to Base Ops at 0500 with tropical gear for an extended mission. I can't give any details, but report first to Base Supply to receive helmets, flak jackets, and appropriate weapons. Bring all your North American flying charts, landing plates and necessary personal equipment. Remember, tropical gear. Oh yes," he said, "congratulations to the newly promoted officers. That is all. Dismissed."

Shortly before midnight, my date and I left the Officers Club and walked out into the dark and foggy parking lot. It was not unusual to have cold and fog in October so close to the Eastern shore.

We all wondered what the weather would have in store in just a few hours. Would the fog lift long enough to allow takeoffs or would we be delayed? We knew we were going out by 0800 or 0900. I remembered the rule, "No alcohol within eight hours of flight." Looking around I wondered if that meant only "No alcohol within eight feet of the airplane."

We bade our friends good night, drove slowly away from the Club into the fog, watching the center yellow line of the road. We could see only a few feet in front of the car.

"I'll stay at your house," volunteered Millie, "and drive you to the Base and bring your car home," said Millie. "You can't be late tomorrow."

In the living room we built a fire in the great stone fireplace. Soon the fire was blazing and crackling with flames from the dry hickory logs. The light danced on the walls like little Indians making their war chants, whooping it up about a bonfire. It was cozy and warm.

We decided to stay in the living room. Millie, dressed in a pair of my rolled-up pajamas, reclined on the sofa with an old army down cover and I found a place on a sleeping bag close to the fire. I had almost four hours to rest before starting a big day with my squadron. I wasn't thinking so much about tomorrow. I was just thinking about resting for a little while.

Despite the warm fire, the distant part of the room felt chilled. Millie slipped from the sofa and gently tiptoed across the room in the shimmering shadows of the fire, toward the warm hearth. She knelt down, then reclined beside me, placed the old Army comforter over us, placed her soft head on my shoulder and whispered, "Get some sleep soldier, tomorrow is a long day." We watched the glowing fire and dozed off.

OCTOBER 21, 1962

"From the kitchen I heard a soft voice..."

The clanging of the wind-up alarm clock startled me at 0400. Only the soft sparkling glow of ashes and occasional slender flames remained in the fireplace. The chill was again in the air. I peered out into the still dark morning. The fog was rolling in from the lake up the shallow frosty hill to our house. At the edge of our narrow dock, I could barely see the small light surrounded by a glowing halo.

It was peaceful outside our little world. I stoked the fire and added a log. I needed to get some warmth back in the room.

From the kitchen I heard a soft voice. "I've got the coffee perking and I'll have some eggs ready. Go ahead and shower. Remember, Colonel Cupko said tropical clothes and gear." I was glad I had invited this girl to the party.

Might as well take the Arctic gear from my travel bag and add some more appropriate tropical stuff, I thought. I kept an extra B-4 travel bag in the trunk of my car as I might be called any time to report for an unscheduled flight.

Millie dropped me off at Base Supply, blew a kiss over her fingertips and whispered, "Be careful. Come back safely." She would check with the flight surgeon's office or the squadron about our return.

Together, the airmen and officers moved through the supply line. Two bright-eyed airmen near me spoke about a possible adventure. "Man, do you really think all this means real war?" one whispered to his buddy. For the older sergeants and officers this was routine. It had, however, been a sudden Alert.

The line eased forward. We dragged our duffle and travel bags. "Move on," one sergeant growled at the airman in front of him, who appeared to be wavering in the line. The issuing airman asked each of us if we had certain items for tropical duty. Quinine tablets to prevent malaria were handed out in waterproof packages by a corpsman that was assisting the supply staff. We moved down the line. The supply sergeant handed me a helmet with the appropriate medical cover. The next sergeant wrote down a serial number and handed me a paper form, "Sign here, sir." He pointed to the crumpled yellow form. He then placed a khaki .45 Caliber Colt pistol and holster on the counter.

"Wait a minute," I said to him. "I'm a healer, not a fighter. I don't think a medic is supposed to have a weapon, according to the Geneva Convention." He looked at me with an odd frown. He did not think it was amusing. He glanced at my helmet then the flight surgeon's wings on my flight jacket.

"Hell, Doc, those bad guys think the cross on that helmet is a target." He smiled. "Take it, sir. Hope you don't need it." He moved to the next man.

The Operations Officer pointed to a large map at the rear of the briefing room. All I could see was the Southeastern United States and the Caribbean. "Gentlemen," he said, "you, and your aircrews, will be ferried by aircraft to this point – Charleston." He pointed his stick to a spot in South Carolina. "You'll remain here until your squadron's aircraft return from picking up marines from the West Coast. Those planes will be refueled, and you will replace those crews and fly the aircraft to our Naval base at Guantanamo Bay, Cuba."

"You will receive more information about the situation in Cuba before you take off." He paused, "Our commanders and our President consider this mission as urgent. No questions please and good luck."

OCTOBER 22, 1962

In Charleston, the "Alert Sergeant" awakened us at 0500 and announced that our planes had returned from the West Coast, were being refueled and would be prepared for us to replace the crews by 0800. We quickly showered. We gathered up our equipment including our side arms, picked up coffee and a quick walking meal at a portable kitchen. We assembled for our crew instructions and boarded our planes.

The aircraft commander turned from the left pilot's seat toward me and said, "Doc, come up here and sit. We have steel armor plates under this section of the crew compartment. It'll be safe if there is any ground fire."

"At least it will keep us from getting hit in the ass," blurted out the flight engineer from across the cockpit.

We approached Leeward Point. I could see airplanes on the ground unloading supplies for the detachment at Guantanamo. The planes were landing, unloading and taking off rapidly. Our plane was the first of our squadron. My orders were to stay on the ground until all our planes had completed their airlift shuttles. I was to go in with the first plane, stay as long as necessary and return with the last plane out.

My feet had hardly touched the ground after I descended the plane's crew ladder when a young Navy lieutenant approached me, "Hey, are you the doctor for this crew? We heard one was coming," he yelled over the roar of the groaning engines nearby.

"Yeah, I am," I responded.

"We need you at the Base Operations Terminal," he said. We briskly crossed the tarmac and walked into the building. "Over here," he said, and pointed to some white curtains hanging in the flight terminal, surrounding a group of women and children. "These are the dependents waiting for evacuation. These women are pregnant, and you will have to take care of them," he announced.

I looked over the throng of big tummies and the little kids scurrying around the piled-up luggage and duffle bags.

"Wait a minute, I'm the flight surgeon. I'm not an obstetrician. Where are your regular Navy doctors?" I asked.

"They're out in the field with the Marines and you're all we've got. In here are a couple of nurses and corpsmen," he said. "You're it, Doc." He grinned, "Our chief medical officer said to get one of the Air Force guys to take care of these folks till they get loaded to go. Oh yeah, we've got a delivery room set up behind these other curtains, if you need it."

"Hey, I haven't delivered a baby in three years, I'm a general surgeon."

"Doc, you are still 'it," he responded.

I thought I was going to war not the obstetric ward. I passed among the potential mamas and encouraged them, "Just keep your knees together ladies and we'll get you out of here safely. Let us know if you are having any contractions or anything that might suggest delivery time." A couple of corpsmen and nurses helped gather up the crowd and enlisted volunteers among the nearby sailors to help with the luggage and little kids. I couldn't believe I was ordering the Navy around.

Within a few of hours, we gathered up the last of the mothers, children and other civilian dependents to board the last evacuating Marine C-130. Two nurses and a corpsman with a couple obstetrical packs were loaded on the plane to be available should a delivery occur.

The crews revved up the engines. The plane began moving among the other transports, entered and sped down the runway, and within a few moments they were airborne. "Thank You, Lord," I said aloud.

The Navy officer slowly walked up to me, grinning, "Now, I can take you to your quarters."

**C-124 approaches the runway at Leeward Point,
Guantanamo Bay, Cuba, October 1962**
(Photos in Guantanamo by author)

Dependents waiting for evacuation from Guantanamo

The Military C-130 began to load the evacuating dependents.

SETTLING IN AT GUANTANAMO

The sun was setting as I glanced out from my quarters where shadows fell across piled up sandbags on tin roofing, covered by more sandbags. There were several young Marines, sleeves cut off, wearing flak jackets, with their helmets scattered nearby. They were digging more trenches about their bunker.

"Hey guys, what are you doing?" I yelled out my open window.

"Sir, we're just digging in," they said, as they leaned on their shovels in the still hot setting sun.

I looked out beyond the bunker. I saw a heavy barbed wire fence, fifty yards away, which I assumed was their defense perimeter. After a bit of bantering with the young Marines, I pointed in the distance, "What should I do if the bad guys come through that fence?"

"Hell, Doc, just get under your bunk and we'll take care of you!" the young lance corporal yelled back. He patted his rifle and pointed to the machine gun emplacement.

"Damn right," I responded, "I like that." I liked that Marine's attitude as much as I liked the crisp white sheets that were always available when we visited any Navy installation.

Later at the officer's club veranda, several men were gathered about a radio and others had a small black and white television that they were setting up, adjusting the aluminum foil attached to the rabbit ears antenna. They were trying to get a Miami station. "The President is making a speech to the country," one fellow said. Between the radio and the poor reception on the TV, we were able to hear his speech. The gathering was quiet as President Kennedy addressed the nation.

The newspapers recorded: "At 7 p.m. on Monday, October 22, 1962, President Kennedy appeared on television to inform Americans of the recently discovered Soviet military buildup in Cuba including the ongoing installation of offensive nuclear missiles."

President Kennedy ordered continued surveillance of Cuba and ordered a Naval quarantine to prevent further introduction of offensive missiles. He declared that any nuclear missile launched from Cuba against any nation in the Western Hemisphere would be regarded as an attack by the Soviet Union on the United States and would require a full retaliatory nuclear response upon the Soviet Union.

"He is talking about us," one fellow commented. We drank our beer, got up, and quietly returned to our quarters more determined by the President's strong speech.

"Hell Doc., just get under your bunk...."
October 23, 1962
U.S. Marine Detachment machinegun bunker Guantanamo, Cuba
(Photo by author)

BIG C-135s BEGAN BRINGING IN AMMUNITION

By daylight, the air traffic increased. The larger C-135 planes from McGuire Air Base began bringing in ammunition, grenades, mortar rockets, and other materiel. One of our pilots was fuming mad when he landed, complaining that he had brought only tents and tent stubs with his construction equipment when everyone else carried arms and ammunition. This day would be a long one.

A Navy lieutenant and I sat in the same gray jeep that had carried me to my quarters the afternoon before. "Like a cigarette, Doc?" he asked.

"Nope, don't smoke," I responded.

He began to puff on his cigarette, enjoying the calm as we both relaxed and observed the flight line activity, protected from the heat of the early afternoon sun by the jeep's canvas roof.

In the distance, I noticed one of the big C-135s as it began to make its downwind turn from our right to its left. The turn seemed awfully sharp, much closer than I had observed the other planes make. It looked like he was turning in slow motion. The silhouette of the plane appeared to be dipping the port wing too steeply. It seemed to stop, suspended in mid-air, and began to slide to the left, with the wing still dipping further toward the ground. I thought I heard a change, perhaps a higher pitch in the sound of the engines as if they were being throttled.

Then, the plane further dipped to its left, far from the end of the runway. It tumbled to the ground with a huge explosion followed by a gigantic ball of flame, dark black smoke billowing beyond the runway.

Without commenting, the navy lieutenant flipped his cigarette and started our Jeep and we headed down the runway, then off the end into a field just beyond the runway. We stopped the Jeep, jumped out and ran closer to the wreckage. The cockpit of the fuselage was lying on its left side. We approached the nose but could not see inside.

A young sailor who had been fishing beyond the runway on the water's edge was the first person to the plane and was at the nose of the cockpit. He was singed from the intense heat generated by the fire. He turned and ran to us yelling, "No survivors, nobody. I looked in before it blew up," he cried.

We were within twenty or thirty yards of the plane's nose as it was completely engulfed in flames. Then a huge explosion occurred in the midst of the fire.

The sailor joined us, and we ran back toward the Jeep.

The fire trucks arrived, and the firefighters scurried, barely ahead of us, to get their hoses set. The flames were so hot and the explosions so terrific that they abandoned the nearest fire truck and withdrew from the site.

The munitions were now exploding within the burning fuselage adding to the devastation of the already burning plane and the surrounding ground fire.

We fell to the ground, perhaps knocked down by the explosions, but I don't remember. We crawled away from the crash on our hands and knees. Shells and mortars were exploding. We looked up and saw one of the firetrucks hit by what must have been a mortar shell. It burst into flames. Black smoke enveloped the truck. Something was going over our heads. It must have been more mortar rounds. We raised ourselves up from the ground, "Run, Doc, run!" yelled the navy lieutenant. We ran to the abandoned Jeep, got it started, and evacuated the area.

At Base Ops, I reported to the Navy commander and the Air Force ground officer. I was the only Air Force flight surgeon at Guantanamo and the only flight surgeon EASTAF (Eastern Air Force) had on site and would have to begin to organize the party to inspect the wreckage for remains of the aircrew.

Air Force Headquarters was notified of the air crash and an investigating team was ordered immediately from Washington to Guantanamo. They would bring their own flight surgeon to investigate.

The air traffic was delayed only a few hours. Some planes circled or had to turn back because of low fuel or unsafe conditions. By late afternoon, air traffic resumed, but small fires continued into the night.

OCTOBER 24, 1962

The smoke had cleared...

The following morning a group of Navy and Air Force men and I hiked up a small hill north of the end of the runway at Leeward Point to observe the crash site. The smoke had cleared, and small pockets of the fire were smoldering. There were only bits of the aircraft left. We elected to go down the hill by vehicle to the crash site. As we got out of the jeeps, we could still feel the intense heat. It was so hot on the ground, that even in heavy flying boots we could barely stand in one spot without moving from foot to foot. We decided to await further investigation until the Washington team arrived.

Later in the afternoon, we returned to the crash site with the Washington investigating team. Body bags were brought to the site and the remains interred into the bags. A couple of dog tags were identified, which helped separate and identify the remains. "Over here," the other flight surgeon pointed. "Let's start looking for remains over here," he repeated. In a couple of cases the remains were sparse due to the intensity of the fire and resulting explosions. We did the best we could.

Our work was done. The squadrons from our base completed their airlifts without incident or significant delays. We successfully "evacuated the dependents and reinforced the American garrison." I thanked my Navy compatriots and climbed the well-worn crew ladder to board the last Globemaster as it prepared to taxi out to the active runway and depart Guantanamo for the United States. Subsequently, we picked up the members of the 101st Airborne from Ft. Campbell to await at air bases in Florida for the anticipated invasion of Cuba. After several stand downs the invasion was called off and we returned the 101st to their base and we returned to our home base.

In only a few days, since we touched down for our deployment in Cuba, our government and our president had settled the most critical incident of the Cold War and avoided a nuclear disaster.

ADDENDUM

Reference to the Guantanamo C-135 Stratolifter crash:
Found through Google on 7/18/13, posted on e-truth by Sharon Hernandez (shernandez@etruth.com).
On the 50th anniversary of the Cuban Missile Crisis Ms. Hernandez reflects on a victim of that incident, young 24-year-old lieutenant Jack Douberteen, a local "boy." We are reminded of the tragedies of the Cold War as well as the more momentous wars, yet one death of a hometown Elkhart, Indiana, man is itself a tragedy.

A list of the crew members of AF C-135, registration #62-41326 of October 23, 1962

Accident DCA93RA060
1, Capt. James Bailey – Lexington, Tenn.
2. Capt. John Baird – Fall Brook, Calif.
3. 1st Lieutenant Jack Douberteen – Elkhart, Ind.
4. Captain Edward Connard – Milton, Del.
5. 1st Lieutenant Hahl Hogge – Nampa, Idaho
6. T/Sgt. Lester Elliott – Duenweg, Mo.
7. S/Sgt. Booker Rigsby – Kingston, N.C.

According to the posting, Lt. Jack Douberteen was the co-pilot. We honor each of these young men for their sacrifice for our country's safety.

**"Then we saw it happen. It simply tumbled to the
ground with a huge explosion followed by
a gigantic ball of red and yellow flame,
then dark black smoke."**
(Photos in Guantanamo by author)

Crash site: Leeward Point, Guantanamo Bay, Cuba.
"We returned to the crash site. The ground remained hot twenty-four
hours after the crash."

Guantanamo Crash Site
Investigators search remnants of the airplane.

**A 101st Airborne Medic waits on the tarmac in Florida
anticipating a Cuban invasion, October 1962.**
(Photos in Florida by author)

Airborne troops and air crews on "stand down" awaiting invasion of Cuba.

After three "stand downs" the invasion was canceled.

BACK HOME

"I think it's over…"

Across the parking lot I could see my car. Beside it stood Millie in a light tan jacket with a scarf tied about her blonde hair. She had called Base Ops and the flight surgeon's office and gotten the schedule of our return. "Welcome back," she called out. I stepped out of the operations building into the chilly, fall air and hurried to the car.

"How was it down there?" Millie asked. "We were all so scared there would be a big war while you were gone." She shook her head and tossed her long lovely hair in the breeze of the open window. "Most of the dependents left the base for their families. The base has been on high alert. The news had us all afraid," she said.

"I think it's over," I said. "Let's go home." We headed for my lake house.

The fire in the big stone fireplace began to warm the cold house as Millie handed me a cup of steaming hot chocolate. We settled by the hearth as the flames began to slither up the chimney. Outside the sun was setting across the lake. The dying light reflected gently on the frosty water. "Now, where were we?" she sighed.

Weeks later our squadron flew to Adana, Turkey, to remove the nuclear warheads and missiles from Turkey that had been part of the secret agreement between President Kennedy and Premier Khruschev to end the Cuban Missile crisis.

Once the warheads were returned to the United States and placed in cold storage, I truly felt the conflict had ended.

A CASE OF WHAT?

"...wants to talk to you..."

The young corpsman strolled into my office and shook his head. I could see a shy smirk and I knew this was going to be comical, if not tragic. "Sir, Airman Jones [not his real name] says he wants to talk to you rather than the office corpsman."

"Sure, I'll see him. Put him in room four."

"Yes, sir," the corpsman answered.

I knocked on the door and without hesitation opened it. He looked to be about nineteen. He sat quietly, hands holding on to the edge of the exam table.

"You wanted to talk to me?" I asked.

"Yes, sir, it's kind of a personal matter."

"Okay. What's the problem?"

"Sir, I think I've picked up something."

I knew what he meant, and it wasn't lifting. "Where do you think you picked it up?" I asked.

"Think it was in Congo or Châteauroux."

"Did you go to Jimmie's in Châteauroux?"

"Yes, sir," he sheepishly answered.

"When did you get back?" I asked.

"A couple of days ago," he quietly responded.

"What are your symptoms?"

"Stinging and burning and a little yellow discharge," he confessed with a shaking of his head in disbelief.

"Have you been home yet?"

"Yes, sir, but I told my wife I was just too tired..."

I knew what he was saying.

"Sir, I tried to confess to my wife."

"What did you say?"

"Well, I told her I was sorry, but I had brought home a case of the clap."

"What did she say?"

"She didn't understand," he grinned. "She said, 'That's okay 'cause I'm tired of those cases of Madeira that you usually bring home."

I stepped out of the room. "Sergeant, get us a specimen from this man and wait for the lab report, then we'll start him on the usual penicillin regime. Advise him, no sex for at least a week to ten days."

FOGGY NIGHT TO BERLIN

"The fog was so thick... Nothing was flying."
February 1962

The fog was so thick that night in Germany that I knew nothing was flying. I wondered why I had been summoned. "You're to report in flight suit with cold weather clothes for a few days," the sergeant advised. He carried printed orders that read, "To observe stress on flight crews during flight exercise," whatever that meant. *Damn*, I thought, *who in their right mind would fly in this weather?*

"I don't know where you are going," said the sergeant. "All I know is that I'm to bring you to the airfield and to Base Ops."

The crew was on board. "We can't fly in all this fog, can we?" I asked the loadmaster as he helped me with my travel bag up the crew ladder into the cargo compartment.

"What in the world is all this equipment," I asked as I entered the cargo interior of the plane. All sorts of electronic stuff surrounded us.

For several weeks the East Germans and Russian military had blocked the railroads and highways from West Germany going through the East German Russian Zone of occupation into West Berlin. They were cutting off the food shipments, coal and fuel from West Germans in an attempt to starve and freeze the West Berliners in midwinter.

"They are also jamming our radar and harassing our flights into Berlin," said one of the navigators. (This was Russian Premier Khrushchev's European challenge to our new and untried President Kennedy on international politics.)

"We're going to fly into Berlin to test their radar jamming system," one of the navigators explained to me.

The engines slowly started whining and then sputtered to a roar. The blue exhaust flames lit up the fog and there was an eerie bright haze, shadows and glares of bouncing light about each engine. We taxied out and slowly moved toward the active runway following a ground control truck. We prepared to take off into the soupy fog that horrible night.

There were three landing corridors into West Berlin for each of the occupying western allies, French, British and the third for Americans planes. The Soviets occupied East Berlin. They had a separate airfield, Schönefeld, just outside of and south of Berlin in the Soviet Zone of occupation.

The weather remained terrible as we approached Berlin in a dense fog. At first, we could fly above the fog, but as we neared the city we descended to a lower altitude. Visibility was minimal to nil.

The East German and Russian radar jammers had begun sending jamming signals as we neared Berlin. Our radar was useless. We approached the field along the American corridor maintaining our altitude and direction. At the end of the runway we could barely see the haze of the landing lights. It was necessary for the huge Globemaster to drop suddenly, just short of the runway, then I felt the thud and skid of the landing. I was unable to see beyond the nose of the plane.

We taxied to the middle of the field, guided by a truck with flashing lights. We had overcome the radar jamming attempts by the Easterners with our new secret navigation system. The flight demonstrated to the East Germans and the Soviets that if they continued the railroad and highway obstructions, we would embarrass them with a second Berlin Airlift. The first Allied Berlin

Airlift had occurred in 1948 and lasted from 24 June until 12 March 1949 until the Soviets and East Germans opened their land blockade to Berlin.

We left the plane parked in the middle of the field so that all observers could see it. This demonstrated our Allied determination to keep Berlin open. We crew rested and took time to visit Berlin and see the recently constructed Berlin Wall that divided the city.

Berlin Wall February 1963
(Photo by author)

Two or three days later the fog lifted, and the weather improved. The East Germans opened the railroads and the highways into Berlin. We boarded our Globemaster and we took off for the West, completing our mission. I never understood the "secret navigation system" and inquired about it. But no one seemed to be willing to explain it to me. Since my clearance was "secret with need to know," I never pushed the inquiry

West Berlin, despite the Berlin Wall, remained free.

Lately released copy of a Presidential communication from
the early 1960s
[Now in the public domain]

In Part - Sanitized Copy
Approved for Release 2015/07/23 : CIA-RDP79T0093
///
///
TOP SECRET

THE PRESIDENT'S CHECK LIST—24 MARCH 1962
(This was before the USAF Berlin Night Flight in Jan. 1963)

3. BERLIN:
A.   TWO SOVIET FLIGHTS IN THE NORTHERN
     CORRIDOR THIS MORNING
TOOK PLACE WITHOUT INCIDENT.

B. THE EAST GERMANS SEEM TO BE BACKING DOWN
ON THE TRANSIT
VISA ISSUE IN THE FACE OF IMPLIED WEST GERMAN
THREATS TO
INTERRUPT INTERZONAL TRADE.

C. THE EAST GERMANS LAST NIGHT BEGAN SETTING
UP CONCRETE
OBSTACLES AT FOUR CROSSING POINTS IN BERLIN
SIMILAR TO THOSE
CONSTRUCTED AT FRIEDRICHSTRASSE EARLY THIS
MONTH

D. A REGULAR US ARMY SUPPLY CONVOY LEAVING
BERLIN WAS HELD UP

BY THE SOVIETS FOR TWO HOURS YESTERDAY.

[The president's Check List showing a continuation of
Soviet activity after construction of the 1961 Berlin Wall –
24 March 1962]

MADRID SHOPPING

"For a moment, she took my breath."

After crossing the Atlantic we landed at Torrejón Air Base and then headed into the city to the Balboa, a downtown hotel used by our transient air crews. An hour later, after changing into civilian clothes, I left the hotel and strolled a few blocks into an upscale leather shop along the Avenue in down-town Madrid. Entering the glitzy shop, I glanced around at the sophisticated counters arrayed with precious leather goods. I wandered over to where the gloves were displayed.

It was obvious to the young girl who offered to assist me that I was an American. She tilted her head ever so slightly, brushed the long wave of dark hair from her forehead, and in perfect English cheerfully asked if she could help me.

For a moment, she took my breath. It was like her big brown eyes peered right through me warming my soul. I stammered for a second then recovered and with my best manners asked to see some soft leather dress gloves. "For a lady," I said.

She moved gracefully behind the counter and lifted a couple of gloves from under the counter's glass top and carefully laid the pair over her delicate, slender wrist. She glanced at me with a friendly nod and reached carefully toward me displaying the gloves, "For your girlfriend or wife?" She inquired.

"Oh, no, it's a gift for my dad's lady friend," I cautiously replied.

She seemed surprised and repeated, "Not for your girlfriend?"

I likely blushed and then said, "Oh, I don't have a girlfriend right now."

After a fleeting moment of silence, we looked at each other and nodded, each with a slight grin. She, too, blushed and turned away, again brushing her lovely dark hair from her eyes, feigning not to notice me as I stood silent.

She turned back with another soft pair of fine leather gloves, and carefully but slowly placed one on her left hand, slipping her slender fingers into the snug glove. "How do you like this one?" She held out her hand toward me. I wanted to touch her. She ran her delicate fingers over the glove and closed her eyes, now softly caressing her gloved hand. She opened her eyes and for a fleeting second our eyes met and the room stood still.

Does she really believe the intended gift is for my dad's friend? I wondered.

"Does this person have a small hand? Does she have long fingers?"

"Oh, about medium," I muttered, not really knowing. "You do believe the gift would be for my dad's friend?"

She didn't answer for a moment. "These gloves are very fine for any lady," she added.

"I'll take two pair," I answered.

She placed several sizes and shades on the counter, and she helped me decide.

"Would you like them wrapped?"

"Yes, that will be fine."

She was meticulous as she placed the selected gloves in white tissue wrapping. I turned to leave with the gloves, wrapped in paper and small yellow ribbons about the package. "Will you be here tomorrow if I might like to shop again?" I asked.

"Yes," she said. "My uncle owns this shop and I sometimes help him. I will be here."

The following day I returned to the shop on the Avenue. I was determined to know more about her. I approached a counter where she was sorting merchandise. She glanced up with a smile. She hesitated before she quietly said, "You did come back." For a moment we stood gazing at each other.

"Yes, but not to shop today. I want to know if you would go out to dinner with an American stranger?"

She tilted her head slightly and placed her soft hand about her lips. "I'll have to ask my uncle. We don't often go out with

Americans." She further explained, "He is my guardian since my father died a few years ago. I have to have his permission."

"When shall I know?" I asked.

"Come back this afternoon."

In Spain, the shops close at midday and reopen about four in the afternoon. I puttered about the city walking the broad streets and briefly visited the Prado, the National Art Museum. A little after four in the afternoon I returned to the shop.

As I entered, a distinguished well-dressed little man eyed me over his gold- rimmed glasses. *I'll bet that's her uncle,* I thought. I sauntered up to the glass counter and approached the young lady.

She nodded and eased into the display aisle. "Hello," she whispered. "My uncle wants to know what you do and are you in the military."

"Yes," I replied. "I'm in the Air Force and will be here only for a few days with my flight crew."

With a strange look she asked, "Are you a sergeant?"

"A what?" I responded.

"A sergeant," she reaffirmed, now rather serious.

"Oh, I'm a captain, an officer," I answered. I wondered why she wanted to know, and it was only later that I learned.

"My uncle says you can take me to dinner, but I must be home early."

"I don't know where to go, but you can tell me the best place," I answered.

"My uncle says I can leave early, and you can meet me here."

"Will you thank him for me?" I asked.

We hailed a taxi and she gave the driver the directions in soft gentle Spanish, not the rapid style I had heard on the streets.

We entered the upscale restaurant and at the end of the long bar we descended a set of spiral stairs into an underground catacomb. "The tourists dine on the first floor and we eat here," she whispered.

It was, in fact, a catacomb with low stone ceilings, so low and all carved out that we had to duck our heads to get from one little room to another. The floor was sandy and gritty as we journeyed to our little table in the distant part of the dim room, lit with small electric lamps and candles.

She translated the menu for me, and we first selected the gazpacho, a cold vegetable soup. I had never tried this item and it was refreshing and I never forgot that first taste. I don't remember the remainder of food; I was so enchanted with her presence.

We chatted and she explained the sergeant reference. "My friend married a sergeant, stationed at Torrejón and they have two children," she related. "He transferred to Alaska and took the children. He promised she would come to America when he was settled. He has refused to bring her there and his mother is keeping their children. My friend has been to the base and to the American embassy and they do not help her."

Now I knew why she was down on sergeants. "I'm sure if she goes to his commander on the base and to the legal office, she can get this all straightened out," I volunteered.

Before the end of the meal she eased her soft hand across the table and patted my hand, "I'm sure you are not like that sergeant," she whispered.

In the taxi she moved closer to me. She felt soft and warm and with a small kiss she looked into my eyes and muttered, "Yes, you are not like the sergeants."

As we approached her home in an upscale section of Madrid, she leaned forward and tapped the driver on the shoulder, "Stop here," she said in Spanish. I didn't understand. She whispered, "I have to get out here, so my mother doesn't see us. She doesn't approve of American soldiers."

"Your uncle said it was okay for you to go out with me," I protested.

"My uncle is my father's brother and what he thinks is not what my mother always thinks." *Ah, a secret affair,* I thought.

We talked for a few moments and planned our tomorrow. "I will arrange for us to go to the bullfight tomorrow if you like," she volunteered. "All Americans want to see a bullfight. General Franco and his family will be there." She paused, "My uncle has connections. He will get us tickets."

The taxi followed slowly behind her as she walked the few yards to her locked gate, opened the iron door, waved and quietly said, "Tomorrow, call me, you have my number." She slowly closed the gate. I could see she was home. Having seen her safely home, I nodded to the driver and we drove on, "Balboa Hotel, por favor."

CHOOSE OUR OWN POISON

"Maybe, you should have gone into psychiatry... "

"You guys in the flight surgeons' office have all the fun," complained a disgruntled clinic doctor. "All we do all day is see dependents without much wrong with them. I don't mind the kids. At least they are sick. It's the colonel and master sergeant's spouses that piss me off. They are so demanding. They complain if they have to wait and insist that their problems are special. They drive me damn crazy."

"Maybe you should have gone into psychiatry," I suggested. "Then you could understand them." He didn't smile.

"You guys fly all over the world while we're stuck in this godforsaken clinic hole." He grumbled.

"We choose our own poison," I said.

His problem was he had gone into medicine for the wrong reasons. "My uncle in the Bronx makes ten times as much as we do," he complained. The guy resented being in the service rather than in the big money practice.

It was true we had more fun treating the flying personnel. When our clinic became tiresome, we could check the schedule. When our time came, we could call our squadrons and check to see what was going out. The guys assigned to the Airlift Squadrons could fly all over the globe. Those with a fighter squadron could fly in supersonic planes just for fun. We were delighted when the ops officer called, "Hey Doc, we've got a parts pick-up. Would you like to fly today?"

"You bet, sir," I always answered.

The men of the squadrons loved to have the flight surgeon flying with them. It was part of working together and acquiring the squadron's confidence. It was essential that the flying personnel have assurance in their flight surgeon's personal interest and that they felt free to honestly discuss any problems with their docs. We were their priests in white coats.

On occasion we flew high altitude flights to check some element of the altitude partial pressure suits or potential decompression problems. These classified flights were over fifty-thousand feet. [Any altitude above this was classified.] Sometimes we invited select members of the hospital staff physicians to go through the altitude chamber and fly with the fighter squadron. These guys were the ones who helped us in the flight surgeons' office with diagnostic evaluations of various problems, such as the cardiologists whose determination affected the ability of the men on flying status to perform their flight duties.

The medical physicians who worked mostly in the general and family clinics never understood the potential dangers of flying. They never had to investigate crash sites in which our flying friends might be involved. They never had to collect those remains, some merely ashes, and visit the families. As I said to the other docs, "We choose our own poison."

TDY IN PARIS, C'EST LA VIE

"Going to Paris, 'eh, soldier?"

I was not TDY in Paris, but was with one of my squadrons in Châteauroux, France. Fortunately, on weekends I was able to sign out to the regular assigned medical officers and staff at the base hospital. As a flight surgeon, I could cut my own orders so I decided that an R and R (Rest and Relaxation) would be a good thing, especially with Paris so near. All I had to do was hop on the train in civilian clothes, passport in my pocket with a few francs and head up through Orleans to Paris.

"Doc," one of the bright young lieutenants from our squadron said, "if you wear those plain black Air Force shoes, they can spot you in a second as an American tourist."

"What should I wear?" I asked.

"Italian shoes," he volunteered. "Yeah, Italian shoes."

"Aren't they expensive? Where can I get them?" I asked. "Certainly not at the BX."

"Nope, you have to get them in Paris. I don't think any of the shops in Châteauroux have any. Besides, the locals would price them too high 'cause they know you are an officer and they think you can pay the price."

He added. "You may not know it, but these French like us for our money. If the base didn't have such a big French payroll, de Gaulle would have run us all out years ago. They have already forgotten we chased the Germans out of France. It's all business to them."

He paused, "Did you notice the F-104s on the runway with Iron Crosses on them? A German squadron just arrived with the NATO exercise. Now the French and Germans are big friends."

"Well, I'm not buying Italian shoes just to go to Paris for a few days. Anyway, those Italians make their fancy shoes too narrow for my foot." I said.

"You'll do a lot better in Paris picking up girls with Italian shoes," he further commented.

"I'm going to see the sights," I answered with a grin. "Besides that, I've already treated too many of you guys who went to Paris and saw the *wrong* sights."

"Okay, Doc, have it your way."

The train slowly left the Châteauroux station at 0800 on a cold March Friday. I boarded the train dressed in the most cosmopolitan outfit I could think of, a white shirt with a heavy black wool typical high neck French sweater, gray wool pants, and a tweed gray jacket. All I thought I needed was a black beret. The first thing the train conductor looked at as he punched my ticket was my pair of black Air Force plain-toed shiny shoes then calmly asked in broken English,"Going to Paris, 'eh, soldier?"

"*Mais, oui!*" I answered in my best French. He just laughed. He handed me my punched ticket and turned back into the train's passageway.

I was alone in the second-class compartment when the train began to move out of the station. A few miles toward Paris the conductor opened the compartment door and seated a family of four, two adults, and two little kids. "*Bonjour,*" the father said as his wife handed him a wicker basket. It was soon apparent that my two years of high school and one advanced year of college French would not do, so we spoke in fractured French and broken English.

We were barely settled when the father opened the basket, popped the cork on a lovely bottle of red wine, and broke bread as his wife sliced the cheese. He offered me a big piece of bread and cheese and a glass of the red wine just produced from the basket. "For you," he said, and we toasted "Viva la France, Viva l' America!" I then toasted, "Viva Mes. Lafayette." He grinned, "Oui, Mes. Lafayette."

My lieutenant was wrong. There were some French who still loved us.

"*J'ai faite l'armee quand j'etais jeune!*" he boasted. (I was in the army when I was young.)

"*Je vois,*" I answered. We were all smiles.

The ride was pleasant. The family got off in Orleans and I thanked them for their hospitality. "*Merci, le pain et vin,*" I said.

"*De rien,*" the father answered as he packed his family off the train and waved from the platform.

In the railway station in Paris I stepped off the train with my brown paper shopping bag stuffed with two pairs of shorts, socks and one shirt folded about my camera. I refused to carry a suitcase. I wanted to fit in as best I could.

I walked from the station glancing furtively at my Paris map looking for directions and a cheap hotel. Finally, near a small statue of Voltaire at a narrow intersection, I spotted what appeared to be a little hotel. I entered the tiny foyer, walked into the small lobby, and rang a bell that sat on what I thought was the registration desk.

A few words of mixed French and English got me an attic room, up two flights. I laid a handful of francs on the desk. She counted out the amount for a few days, gave me a slip of paper, "*La note*," and pushed the remainder of the francs back toward me. "*Merci,*" she said. She handed me a key on a brass pendant, embossed with the hotel's emblem. The young woman pointed toward the stairs, nodded and smiled.

"Do you have bags?" she asked.

"*Non, seulement ce sac en papier,*" I answered.

"Oh, I see!" she responded in perfect English.

The room had one single bed, one straight back chair, a wash basin and pitcher, towels and a small window that swung open and looked out over the narrow cobblestone street. I was delighted with my find. Down the hall was the "salle de bain, les toilettes." I never found a shower and assumed after inquiring without success that the basin and pitcher would have to be my spot bath site.

I ventured out to the street and began walking toward what I thought was the Champs-Elysées, only to finally give up and hail a taxi. I had written down the address of my hotel so that if I got lost at least I would have the address and could get a taxi back. I kept the brass key holder in my pocket in case I lost the paper.

As I got into the taxi the driver started without my telling him where I wanted to go. I was confused. I wanted to go to the Eiffel Tower and then the Arch of Triumph but for some reason in my best-attempted French I leaned toward the front seat and announced, "l'Arch de Triomphe, s'il vous plait."

The driver turned and with a disgusted look responded, "Dis ess l'Arc de Triomphe!" and he pointed his finger out the window.

I forgot my French and I answered in English, "I mean Eiffel Tower, if you please!"

He shook his head and darted into the circle traffic and turned the car about and headed for the Tower. I was glad to get out of his cab when we arrived. I paid him in new francs as best I could count, and he skirted away. He did not smile!

On the top of the Tower, I met two cute American girls from Texas who were spending their "college year abroad" in Paris. I took them to lunch on one of the Tower landings and they invited me back to their apartment. We met several times during my visit. One of the girls had a car so we enjoyed the terrifying Parisian traffic. I did not drive, as my license was an international one solely for use with American military or UN vehicles.

"Dis ess de Arc de Triomphe"
Place Charles de Galle

One late afternoon we went to the Cafe de la Paix, a short distance from the Palais Garnier. It was so expensive that we only had soup, bread and wine, but enjoyed the wonderful atmosphere.

They were both delightful girls and we wrote for a while, but my distant assignments ended any possible long-term relationship. By letter the cutest one, Jane, invited me to go with her to Minorca, one of the Spanish Islands, to meet her family who would be vacationing there.

When I got back to the base in Châteauroux, one of our squadron's navigators came up to me and said. "Hey, I wish I had known you were going to Paris. I have a cousin who is there for a year. She's at the Sorbonne."

"Oh," I said, "I'm already seeing someone in Paris."

"She's cute, and I think you would like her," he insisted. "Let me write down her name, address and telephone number. When you get back to Paris look her up."

Roger wrote out her name, address, and phone number in Paris, folded it, and then handed it to me. I started to put the slip of paper in my wallet then I unfolded it. I looked at the name Jane— and address and exclaimed, "I can't believe it! This is Jane, the girl I met in Paris. C'est la vie!"

Note: Over sixty years later I visited Normandy with some other veterans for "D-Day Celebrations" and learned the French, at least in Normandy, still loved us.

A FRENCH TOWN AND LINEN TABLECLOTHS

... a fine little restaurant...

There's nothing like a fine little French restaurant with linen tablecloths and napkins, polished silver, sparkling crystal, and porcelain dinnerware. That's just the kind of a fine little restaurant I enjoyed on my visits to the town of Châteauroux – a few kilometers down the rural road, through farmlands and hedgerows – near our Air Force base in France.

Amidst the snug little buildings in the old town was the stone Cathedral Saint André. Though destroyed during the French Revolution, it was rebuilt in the late nineteenth century and has served generations of worshipers. *How many baptisms and weddings and funerals has this edifice served?* I wondered. With respectful awe I often visited the church. In the1960s the services were still performed in Latin, a universal tongue. Even though I was not a Catholic, I could follow the liturgy. The cathedral's ambiance always satisfied my worshiping needs.

Happily, our squadron kept an old, black four-door Citroen, at the base for those transiting the base. We never knew who owned the car. It was simply there, keys available for anyone's use. Many days and nights it transported us about the countryside and into the town.

One of the stops in the town was the famous "Jimmie's" that enticed our men for the night's entertainment. "If you haven't been to Jimmie's, you haven't been to France," I was told. There we drank the local beer and wines, listened to small musical groups and had a darn good time. Jimmie's also provided available companions for the night, not to be missed by our troops.

Yet, my favorite spot was the little French café on a busy corner of a narrow intersection, not too far from Jimmie's. The checkered white and black tile floor, the lovely oak panels and the small pastoral oil paintings hung on the walls were typical of the mid-century European dining establishments. The highlight of the evening was to slip into the bright restaurant, to be met at the door by the diminutive maitré d' in black trousers, crumpled white shirt, a slightly tilted bow tie, and the typical, warm, welcoming French smile, "*Bonjour, Monsieur.*" He would greet us and lead us to our favorite table by a tall window overlooking the busy, narrow, cobblestone street. "*C'est, okay?*" he would inquire.

"*Mais, oui,*" I answered in my marginal French. How delightful it was to sit at the table with all the amenities of the French cuisine, the white tablecloths arranged with lovely settings and a small crystal vase of freshly picked white and yellow flowers (the colors depending on the season) and the busy *garçon*, his white apron flying in the breeze as he delivered the first bottle of the house *vin blanc ou rouge.*

He stood erect, twisted the cork and the slight pop enticed us as he opened the slender clear bottle and poured the first sip. He smiled slightly, nodded approvingly, as we properly and briskly swirled the wine, sniffing as if we knew what we were doing, then sipped and toasted the group. *"Bon appétit."*

The fine French bread and the delicious *potage* devoured, the main course of *poisson grille spécialité* presented, and then a *mousse* dessert ended our wondrously simple dinner.

Our bill, *le note*–in those days a modest sum–was presented. We paid and left the café satisfied, a group of happy young airmen.

LIBERIA AND BACK TO RECIFE

... Down a dim hall...

Our flight took us through the Caribbean to Surinam then to Recife, Brazil, and across the Atlantic to Monrovia, Liberia. The air at Roberts Field was hot and stifling as we taxied to a huge rusty tin hanger. We rolled down the runway to a stop. Several dusty trucks appeared with a consortium of men as our giant clam doors opened to deliver the radio electronic sending devices. Our pilot descended from the plane and was met by a tall English-speaking Liberian and an American diplomat in short sleeves and walking shorts. Our loadmaster spoke to the civilians.

A local man from the Voice of America directed the off-loading crew, "Unload here and we will carry the equipment into town for assembly,"

We were driven to a small hotel on the edge of Monrovia. We passed local markets and I was struck with the beautiful indigo clothing. I am told that for ages the purple and blue fabrics of Liberia were among the most desired in Equatorial Africa. Once in our hotel, we changed into civilian clothes and dined in an African American café. We crew rested and spent very little time in the city. A day or so later we returned to the aerodrome, taxied out to the runway and headed west across the Atlantic.

It was a smooth flight across the water. We met only slight western head winds. We passed over Ascension and later asked for landing instructions in Recife. We taxied by lovely silver ladies, the World War II Boeing B-17s of the Brazilian Air Force, all lined up and shiny off to our right.

Our trip carried us to a small hotel, Cora's Place, and by evening we headed to the House of Blue Lights lounge where we had visited on our flight earlier en route to Liberia.

Her mother's brother or some relative owned or at least managed the "House." I never really knew, and she approached me as my crew and I sipped the mysterious drinks provided by the House. I had talked to her during our previous visit. "I'm not one of the girls," she boasted. "I'm a manager."

We sipped our drinks and she sat closer to me on the plush velvet sofa. "You are different," she whispered. "You are not like the others. Why didn't you go up-stairs with the girls?"

I mumbled something like, "I'm just here to relax, not that."

We talked for a while. She said she had relatives in the States and had visited in California. "My uncle owns a winery in California," she volunteered. After a few more intoxicating drinks she took my hand and whispered, "Come with me. You're nice."

I had no intentions of any liaison, but after the several drinks of unknown but strong and tasteful ingredients, I took her hand and we climbed the stone stairs to the second floor.

Down a dim hall we entered a small room, showered, and she directed me to a tall worn Portuguese mahogany door and into a dark room. The balcony doors were open, and a warm wisp of air filled the room. The moon was barely up in the sky, yet lighted the room with a shimmering hazy glow. She stood in a sheer white gown as the light from the balcony outlined her slender form. She moved closer to me, touched my lips, turned, slipped to the side of the room, lifted the cool crisp sheets and invited me in.

It was barely sunrise when she nudged me. The shimmering moonlight that had sifted through the veiled window had now become gleamy pink and yellow slivers of light. "All your men have gone," she whispered. I slipped out from the sheets, quickly dressed and she led me to the latched door downstairs. She scribbled her address and drew a map on a sheet of bright stationary directing me the few blocks back to Cora's Place.

With moist brown eyes she looked up at me and with lovely English she murmured, "You will come back?"

I nodded, "Hope so."

She touched my lips and whispered, "Be safe until you return."

The street was empty. The street washer had just passed as I stepped onto the wet, shiny bricks, and walked briskly, following the little map she had made for me.

They were getting breakfast at Cora's as I knocked on the locked front door.

A dark-skinned woman opened the door. She smiled but didn't speak. I showered, dressed in my flying togs, sat down to Cora's eggs, potatoes, and coffee and soon we left in the extended blue Chevrolet for the airfield. We taxied by the now glistening B-17s in the bright sunlight and were airborne to the North, headed home. The crew members were quiet as we thought about Recife. I never returned.

SUSPECT

"Yeah, I just thought you ought to know…"

Major Perry stood outside the office door talking to the NCO in charge. It was unusual to see the administrative officer in the flight surgeon's office. My first sergeant eased in my door and quietly announced, "Major Perry would like to talk to you in private."

"Sure, send him in," I responded.

"Hi Major, what can we do for you, Sir?"

The husky, mild mannered, but serious officer carefully shut the door and took a seat across from my desk. He leaned forward as if to whisper a secret. "Doc, did you know that the Air Police have been following you around when you were off duty?"

"They what?" I asked.

"Yeah, it is kind of a long story. You've been a suspect in a pornographic investigation."

"In a what?" I responded incredulously.

He stammered and said, "Don't worry, it's okay. You've been ruled out."

I sat quietly for a moment and wondered what he was talking about.

"You mean the APs have been following me around when I'm off duty?"

"Has anyone been using your car or have you lent it out to anyone?"

"Not that I recall, except that Sgt. Brewer took my car to his dad's shop for a set of new tires a few weeks ago. You know he owns a tire and repair shop. Even when I've been out on a trip the car has been in the base parking lot or at my house. I do leave an extra set of keys at my house. If anyone used it, it was without my knowledge."

"Well, the police in town have reported a man in a white Chevrolet coupe with Georgia plates trying to pick up young girls to be photographed naked."

"Damn, I've got a car fitting that description. No wonder I've been followed."

"Doc, a couple of the girls reviewed several photographs, one of which was yours mixed in with several other photos and they did not identify you as the suspect. They said he was a younger fellow. Are you sure someone else hasn't been driving your car?" the major again asked.

"Nope, no one," I answered. "How many times has this happened that someone's been trying to pick up girls?"

"Several," he said.

"We can check to see if any incidents have occurred while I've been away from the base. I'll get my flight records." I started to rise from my desk.

"We've already checked, and you were not on TDY when these occurred."

I sat back down and leaned back in my chair. "Major, I don't know what to say. The only cameras I have are a small 16-mm Minox that I keep in my flying togs and a 35 mm Argus C3. Those cameras wouldn't likely be useful for such purposes. Whoever it is must have some sophisticated camera equipment, maybe a studio with lights and stuff."

"Well, Doc, I wouldn't worry about it, but I thought you needed to know," the major said. He rose from his chair. "Yeah Doc, just thought you ought to know."

"Major, I'll keep a sharp lookout for any car similar to mine."

COAST GUARD AND A SURPRISE

"...similar to mine in the parking lot..."

"Doc, as you know, the 98th Squadron lost a plane over the cold Atlantic waters a few months before you arrived on base. There was no recovery of the aircraft or crew. It just disappeared off the radar," said the commander, shaking his head. "It is imperative we have a successful water survival exercise."

You need to go down to the Coast Guard station and coordinate our schedule with the Ops officer for the exercise. We'll be using our choppers for the actual water pick up and their boats for our crews to enter the water," said Col. Crain. "When you schedule the visit let us know and Capt. Madrey will go down to the station with you."

The survival exercise would be in the icy water at Lakehurst, New Jersey, that simulated the Atlantic waters of winter. "We've got to be prepared for cold water with the new rubber survival suits," said the commander.

Capt. Madrey and I drove my car the few miles to the Coast Guard Station, to coordinate the exercises. We pulled into the gravel parking lot leading up to the white wooden building with a small light tower alongside and I noticed a white Chevrolet coupe. On further inspection I recognized a Georgia license plate.

Upon entering the station, I commented to the Coast Guard lieutenant, "There's a white Chevrolet similar to mine in the parking lot. Whose is it?"

"Oh, that car belongs to one of the sailors," he said. "He's sitting over there by the radar set." He was a young fellow who looked to be no more than eighteen or nineteen years old. He barely noticed my presence. I didn't speak to him.

"Has he any hobbies?" I inquired of the lieutenant.

"Yeah, I think he scuba dives and does a bit of underwater photography," he said. "The other guys say he is quite good. Why do you want to know?"

"I just thought it interesting that we should both have similar cars, each with Georgia license plates."

We sat down with the lieutenant and worked out the plans for the survival exercise, then Capt. Madrey and I returned to our base.

The following day I walked into Major Perry's office and he gestured for me to take a seat. "Major, I think we've found your mystery Chevy."

RELIGION IN THE MILITARY

"... Yes, I believe all that stuff..."

My metal dog tags listed my serial number, blood type (A positive), and religion (Methodist). After assignment to my base, I looked around for a church. I visited a local Baptist church and they gave me, first, a tithing card, and then, introduced themselves. The local Methodists gave me a list of committees I could be on if I became a member. I went to the Episcopal Church and no one spoke to me. *Hey*, I thought, *here I can worship in peace.*

The base Episcopal chaplain and I served on the military Court Martial Board and during those rather stressful sessions we became acquainted. We were the "gentle members" of the Board, each trying to find some compassionate solutions to the airmen's problems as they appeared before that tough military board. Besides that, we in the Flight Surgeon's office, frequently after wringing our hands over some of our airmen's difficult problems, simply said, "Let's refer this to the Chaplain's Office." He was our "go to" guy.

The Chaplain and I frequently met at the Officer's Club bar where, over a pail of beer, we solved many of the difficult social problems of our base. We became crusaders for the welfare of our men.

One day I expressed my interest in the Episcopal Church. He talked to me about the faith and doctrines of the Church and its ramifications. I said to him, "Yes, I believe all that stuff. I think I should like to join your church, but don't I have to have instruction and pass a test?"

The Chaplain looked at me, and with a grin, raised his frosty glass of beer and announced, "You just passed, Doc. Come to Christ Church Sunday and I will speak to the bishop. He will lay hands on you and he will confirm you."

"It's that easy?" I asked.

"Yes, exactly that easy," he responded. "Welcome to the Episcopal Church!" Since that day the Episcopal Church has become an important part of my life.

A SAILOR IS BORN?

"... a little 14-foot open sailboat..."

Before leaving Dover, Ed Levine, one of my pilot friends, and I bought a little fourteen-foot open sailboat. The only problem was that neither of us could sail. I had sailed with an older fellow I met at a Dewey Beach bar. "Come go with me and I'll teach you to sail," he had volunteered. After a few trials in the water I felt I somewhat understood wind and the theory of sail. Unfortunately, I didn't continue with his tutoring and I learned later that he was a "national champion sailor."

Nevertheless, Ed Levine and I thought we would become real sailors. Try as we might, we had trouble simply leaving the shore on the inland Rehoboth Bay. That did not, however, deter us "would-be-sailors" and we eventually managed to sail the craft well, enjoying the breezy Bay.

"Yes, I'll go out with you guys," my Goldilocks boldly said. *What a brave girl!* I thought. She was special. I met her at one of our Ranch House parties and saw her when I could on weekends at the beach and with friends. For a while we had a little romance going. She moved to Philadelphia before I left the service and we gradually lost touch.

Much to our relief, in our little boat, we managed to leave the shore and got under sail without capsizing. She appeared relaxed and as we headed offshore, I noticed how lovely her blonde hair was, blowing and glittering in the warm sun and gentle breeze. Recalling our adventures, I must say that "Goldilocks" was a good sport to trust such incompetents.

It was a delightful summer of sailing and a surprise to our friends that we didn't drown. Ed and I kept the boat at the local dock or sheltered it at the beach house a group of my friends and I rented for the season.

Eventually, I gave my share of the boat to Ed when I completed my assigned military duty. I assume he survived his future trials and errors.

FORT HOOD:
THE ARMY'S HELL HOLE

The hottest, driest, worst place I had ever been

I was at Ft. Hood, Texas, for combined Army and Air Force maneuvers when I received a call from my hospital commander, "We have a mission going through Dallas. They need a flight surgeon and you need to join the flight."

"I'll check with the Army and see if they have anything special going to Dallas," I responded.

There was one lonely bus stop at Fort Hood after sundown. The night was dark. We stood under the flickering bare light bulb, listening to the squeaking of the swinging Greyhound Bus Stop sign outside an old wooden Army building. Soldiers and civilians of all description waited around, puffing cigarettes, sitting on boxes or suitcases, leaning against the peeling, gray splintered wall of the building. I was the lone officer in this dusty crowd waiting on the lone bus to Dallas.

"It ain't a direct ride," one civilian fellow said. He wore overalls and a crumpled western hat was pulled down over his eyes.

"You mean it isn't an express," said another fellow.

"Yep, sometimes there ain't enough seats and you get left behind," chimed in the first guy.

Rank and orders meant nothing that night. It was dark with only an early waxing crescent new moon hiding behind high clouds. Under that single 60-watt dirt-covered bulb we all looked alike, just gray shadows with our boxes and duffel bags, some going home on leave and some just leaving.

"Where do we get tickets?" I asked one of the soldiers.

"Heck, you just pay the driver, no tickets," a corporal answered.

Two headlights peered through the night's haze as the motor coach rolled to a squeaking halt, crunching the gravel beneath its wheels. The coach seemed to settle to the ground as the front door slowly opened.

"All aboard," the driver shouted as he peered through his steel rimmed glasses at the waiting bunch. His bus driver cap perched on the back of his thinning gray head; a toothpick balanced between his teeth.

We passed under the glow of the dim light and squeezed through the door of the big Greyhound.

"Only a couple of seats left," he muttered, now eager to pack us all in. "All the way to the back, boys," he yelled. "Ready fares. Don't have much change tonight."

The fellow in the dusty overalls moved onto the bus steps, eased up to the driver's spot, fumbling in his pockets until he found a couple of bills and dropped a hand full of change on the floor. The driver leaned out of his seat and frowned at the guy. "Hell, boy, don't worry about it. I'll get it later. C'mon in and find a seat, that is iffin you can."

With payment accomplished, our band of strangers moved down the dark, narrow aisle, dodging bags, suitcases, vegetable sacks, and Army duffels protruding from the overhead racks. *This must really be the local milk run,* I thought.

There seemed to be no more seats. Out of the darkness a GI yelled, "Come on back here, buddy. We can fit one more."

Seven of us filled the five spaces at the very back of the bus, our heads pressed against the back window. The interior lights glowed dimly then went out as the bus began to move forward and the confusion of jostling for space diminished.

Streaks of light in the dark sky shown outside the hazy windows of the bus as we pulled into the Dallas bus station; a neon sign with the letters "D LL S" added little light.

I stumbled along with my big khaki travel bag as I clamored down the Greyhound steps, relieved to be in the fresh, cool night air, out of the stuffy interior of the crowded bus. At least I was out of the frying pan at Fort Hood, which I thought must be the Hell Hole of the Army.

Now, to get a taxi to Love Field. I worried there were not many taxis at four a.m. Most of my traveling companions were in the terminal, changing buses or stretching out on the hard-oak benches in the bland, fluorescent-lighted waiting room of the station. I was alone on the platform.

In the quiet, I heard a hoarse, gravelly voice behind me, "Want a taxi, soldier?"

"Right," I said, "I need to go to Love Field."

The driver emerged from the shadows, dropped his cigarette on the concrete platform, stamped it out with his boot, and mumbled, "Yeah, son, I'll get you there."

Inside the cab I stretched out on the cheap fake leather backseat. I couldn't straighten my legs. They felt numb and stiff. I had been cramped on that bus seat for nearly five hours without moving.

There was a special loading area at civilian Love Field for military planes. I had what we called "TELE" or "TWIX," brownish copies of rather vague military orders, which simply named me and listed my serial number among several other airmen and informally described our destination by saying, "squadron so forth would continue to such and such destination as directed," with no real destination listed.

I had no idea where I was going, but the paper convinced the civilian security officer that I was for real, perhaps lost, but obviously no threat to the nation. He allowed me onto the tarmac where a huge silver plane stood in the dim glow of a red sun rising over Texas.

I wiped my dry eyes, licked my parched lips, rubbed my hand along my scruffy beard and approached the giant bird dragging my bag behind.

"Hi, Doc," yelled the husky loadmaster from the open jaws of the great silver monster. "We're all loaded but couldn't take off. The commander said we had to have a flight surgeon with us on this mission. We're waiting for you."

"Why me?" I yelled back.

"Your colonel said you were on duty at Fort Hood," he answered. "You were the closest flight surgeon available."

"Where are we going?" I yelled.

"Can't tell you. You've got to get closer," he quipped.

I threw my bag up through the narrow hatch doorway into the belly of the plane, climbed the well-worn metal crew ladder into the immense cargo compartment and asked, "Now, where in hell are we going, Sergeant?"

He squinted behind his tinted glasses, pushed his cap back, wiped his hand across his forehead and quietly answered, "Captain says Vietnam!"

From the frying pan into the fire, I thought. Perhaps the only place worse than Fort Hood.

FAR EAST – PACIFIC SHUTTLE

Go west young man, all the way to the Far East.

We left Dallas en-route to the Pacific by way of the West Coast to Hickham Air Base in Hawaii. It was eerie to sleep in the old wooden barracks where our men of the Army Air Corps had been during the Japanese sneak attack on Pearl Harbor in 1941. I felt the subtle presence of those who had been at Hickham and experienced the horror of that day.

We ventured into the city, caroused the bars and the night spots and had to assist one of our young lieutenants out of a club when, uninvited, he had joined the band and tried to teach the drummer how to play his drums. "I've been thrown out of better places," he yelled as we shoved him into the taxi and headed back to Hickham.

On leaving Hickham airfield, our pilot flew over the coast so we could see Pearl Harbor from the air. It was chilling to see the Navy base just as the Japanese attackers had seen it during the infamous air raid on Sunday, December 7, 1941.

Our next stop was Wake Island, in the middle of the Pacific for a crew rest and refueling. I was amazed that the navigators could find such a speck of land in the middle of the huge ocean.

On landing, we were met by the ground safety officer, whom I had known back in the States. His job was to be available on the island should any nuclear-carrying plane crash or have a nuclear "incident." Together we explored the island and snorkeled offshore investigating an old sunken rusty Japanese ship. It had been sent to the island to bring food to the starving Japanese garrison occupying the captured island during the war. Wake was one of the islands captured early in World War II after a fierce defense by the American garrison on the island. Our navy failed to attempt to rescue the men because of the already shattered naval forces at Pearl Harbor and the fear of losing more of our navy, especially our aircraft carriers.

Our stay on Wake Island was followed by Guam, then by a landing in the tail of a Pacific typhoon at Clark Air Force Base in the Philippines. I thought I had been in bad weather before, but nothing to match the end of our flight into the Philippines. Old Shaky, our plane, earned its reputation for toughness and durability on that leg of our mission. I don't believe many other planes could have withstood the battering we received that day.

Ultimately, we arrived at an airfield outside Saigon, Viet Nam. We taxied down the runway; I opened the top hatch and climbed the ladder to peer out the top of the airplane into the humid sweltering heat to look around. A minute or so later the flight engineer grabbed me by the legs and jerked me back into the plane. "Damn, Doc," he said. "Don't you know there are Viet Cong snipers out there off the runway just looking for someone stupid enough to pop their head out of the plane?" I was stunned and hadn't really given it a thought. At that young age we all felt invincible.

Later, we flew to Bangkok and our squadron shuttled between Saigon and Bangkok. What I didn't realize till later was that along with CIA ventures, our planes were also running shuttles into Cambodia while we helped set up the radar stations that controlled the air war over Indochina. I couldn't read the signs. I didn't know the difference.

After our shuttle was completed, the task force of airlift planes returned to the United States. We flew by the Golden Gate Bridge, glowing in the dark night, a welcome sight. How many American military men and women in past wars sailed under or flew over this welcoming bridge? I thought about their feelings of finally arriving home safely.

PART FOUR

MILITARY/
HOME TO GRADY

GRADY SURGEON AGAIN

...war hell, this is the war...

Earlier that warm July morning, after signing out, I walked out of the 1607th Military Hospital and took a deep breath of warm fresh air, anticipating the long drive home. I decided I would try to drive to Atlanta in one day getting there before midnight. Shortly, I met one of my corpsmen in the drive. I had served with him for nearly two years. I stopped, spoke to him briefly and thanked him for his good work. "Where are you going now, Doc?" he asked.

"Home," I answered. "Just home."

After fourteen hours on the road, I arrived at Grady Hospital in the dark of night. While unloading my car, I was trying to figure out where my quarters in the hospital would be when a friend, Will Hansom, appeared on the loading dock.

He yelled down from the landing, "Where have you been? The professor has been trying to find you. Your contract started over a week ago. He is mad as Hell!"

I looked up at him standing on the dock and answered, "Hey, I've been to War!"

"War hell, this is the war. Don't you remember?" he answered. "You're back at the Gradys."

Will was right. I had forgotten. Grady was its own combat zone.

HOME TO GRADY

Back to reality

Though I had called the hospital administrator before going to the Far East, he had failed to notify the head of surgery that I would be late. The professor was angry. He had a right to be. There was always friction among the University and the hospital administrators, and the hospital staffs. I had signed two contracts, one with Emory Orthopaedic Department and one with the Surgery Department of Grady Hospital. I should have called the orthopaedic chief, Dr. Kelly, instead of depending on the hospital Administrator to do my bidding or as my dad would say, "Son, never depend on someone else to carry your water."

My failure to notify my surgery chief was inexcusable.

While on the loading dock, I thought of repacking my bags and heading back to the Air Force to a military residency. Before I left the service, my commander had invited me to continue in the military and offered me a residency at one of the Air Force's major teaching military facilities.

It was hard to have served in the military as an officer with considerable income and responsibility and return as a lowly impoverished resident and take the usual "guff" from the upper staff.

Several of those, now ahead of me in the program, had been on the same level or had been below me in the pecking order. Several of them would dodge the draft and military duty altogether, which did not enhance my respect for them.

I learned as a child in military school not to be a quitter. I had signed the surgery contracts and I had to make my word good. It became an honor and gut thing. I bit my tongue, gritted my teeth, said nothing to anyone and decided by damn, to tough it out, at least to the end of my first year's contract. It would be foolish to let my ego stand in the way of an excellent surgery residency. Beside all that, working at Grady gets in your blood. It was in mine and I was back.

BACK IN THE TRENCHES

It doesn't get any worse than the Grady trenches...

I was back in the Grady trenches. I resumed my surgery training. As residents, we understood each other's individual strengths and weaknesses. It was us against the world as we attempted to simply survive and serve our patients.

The shortage of surgeons at the levels above and below us did two things; it made more work for us and it provided greater experience as we were plunged into advanced surgery positions by necessity. During the whole residency, our shifts were longer, our responsibilities greater, and our sleep less. We calculated that we had experienced one and a half residencies in our few years in the program. Yes, as my friend had implied, "Grady is where the war is."

The hours were long. The work was hard, but the exhilaration of being a part of Grady, the ultimate feeling of even a little progress or accomplishment as we ended each day yet resonates in my memory. We were simply participants in the long line of scruffy Grady doctors, as in many other large city hospitals, in the march of time, doing what Grady was designed to do since 1892. That was to care for the "underserved of our city," those who had no place else to go. We worked in the trenches, but by damn, it was important, and it was necessary.

MILITARY DRAFT

Several of us served in the military and the Viet Nam War was escalating by 1966. I had pangs of guilt that I had done my time and had left. I thought of those still on active duty, now in more dangerous situations than I had experienced. (I was still serving on weekends in the Air Force Reserve at Dobbins AFB as the flight surgeon, despite the tight hospital schedule.)

At Dobbins, I served with a fellow Emory graduate, Alexis Davison, a cardiology resident. He was responsible for all the cardiac questions and concerns in our section as it related to the flying personnel. I don't think I could have done the job without Alexis' help.

An interesting fellow, Alexis, an Atlantan, had served as a physician in the American Embassy in Moscow. His mother had been a nurse in Russia during and after the Russian Revolution and had married Alexis' dad who was an American volunteer in the Red Cross in Russia. Since Alexis spoke Russian at home, he was the perfect one to serve in the embassy. Unfortunately, because of a Russian spy incident in our country, Alexis was cited by the Soviets as a spy and sent home to the U. S., *persona non grata,* in retaliation for the expulsion of the Soviet diplomats.

The military draft was still in effect, yet some of our contemporaries were not going. We wondered why and how they were going to avoid the draft. Some had children and perhaps would be deferred. Some had complicated family situations, but we were not sure why they or others without children could manage to dodge the draft.

All wars produce some degree of bitterness or recrimination between those who serve their country in the military and those who don't.

One of the married guys was very quiet about his deferment. We didn't know why. We never asked and he never volunteered a reason. He had a couple of young children. Yet, others with children were called to serve. *Hmmm,* we wondered.

One of my younger contemporaries had been an enlisted man before medical school during the Korean conflict and he was adamant about everyone doing his part.

Another fellow resident announced that he had been refused a military scholarship because of childhood asthma. He boasted that he wouldn't have to serve in the military.

Our former enlisted man once informed the deferred asthmatic, "Your draft board called and asked about you. I told them that I had never even heard you, sneeze."

We questioned whether the military might be too tough for some, yet we wondered, what was physically tougher than Grady? Certainly, there was not a much more stressful job anywhere.

CLINIC ROTATIONS

Willing to do their share

Most of the interns and residents were willing to do their share, no matter how difficult it became. It was a thing of pride, working fairly with the other intern or resident. My friend Elliot Ackerman was not an exception. Perhaps he was one of the best. As residents or interns we never wanted to leave a ward in disarray or an Emergency Clinic full of patients for the next shift. There was usually the push to settle the ward or to clean the clinic before the next shift came on duty. There was often an apology when an intern or resident left medical problems unresolved or at least not "in the works" in the clinic or on the wards. Not uncommonly, the staff members stayed over, even though they had already worked twelve or even thirty-six-hour shifts.

I understand that current labor laws in some states limit medical training shifts to 30 hours straight or 80 hours per week, maximum. I am told that even now, many interns and residents have to be made to leave at the end of their shifts to comply with these regulations. Currently, at Grady Hospital the staff members rarely stay overnight in the hospital. I always felt living in the hospital kept me closer to the patients and their problems. The current schedules seem unusual, but it may no longer be the grind it once was.

One of my medical school friends, a Veterans Administration Hospital general surgery resident rotated through Grady for acute Orthopaedic Ward and ER experience. We thought the Veterans Administration practiced good medicine, but the rotations were soft government duty. As medical students many of us had rotated through what we then called the "nine to five" Veterans Hospital.

After his second or third thirty-six-hour Grady shift, I met the visiting resident in the hall on evening rounds. He had operated all day the day before and was up all night with problems on the ward. He met a day clinic intermixed with emergencies in the afternoon. He completed more than his usual thirty-six-hour haul. He looked like hell. As we finished rounds and stacked the patient charts on the nurses' desk, I casually said to him, "Jack, why don't you just take the rest of the day off." He stood in the dim glow of the hall lights, a mute zombie. He turned, shook his head, thrust his hands into his pockets, shuffled slowly down the hall and headed home.

The person that habitually left work undone gained a reputation of being a "sluffer" and they might not have their future contracts renewed at Grady. The resident above them would judge them harshly on reports and when next year's list of staff members was published, they might be out of luck for the next level of medical or surgical training. "Oh, they decided to go to some other lighter program," would be the comment on their absence. "Good riddance," would be the overwhelming unspoken response.

We were better off without the "sluffers." At least we knew what had to be done and each individual intern or resident somehow would rise to the occasion of getting the patients properly treated.

In an internship or resident training program such as Grady's, each hour was precious. There were so few hours to rest. Each off-duty hour was coveted, if for no other reason but for physical survival.

Sometimes, we slept on stretchers outside the operating room prior to surgery until the anesthetist had the patient almost asleep then we would get up and scrub. Some fell asleep while sitting and talking to patients in the clinics. Some fell asleep in surgery holding the steel surgical retractors. A rare overtired doctor would topple over into the wound. In the ER we might doze in the treatment room on the surgical table until a patient required that table. Those little power naps kept us going for many hours. I calculated that a quick ten-minute nap could produce four more hours of labor.

The high-water mark of a thirty-six-hour shift, at two or three a.m. was to go to the intern or resident's quarters and simply shower or change socks. No one knows how wonderful a simple change to fresh socks can be, dry white cotton socks! It's as if to say, "This is the first time I've been able to do anything for myself for hours – or maybe days."

CHANGES IN PROTOCOL

"Tell him Ol' Ben has been here…"

Ben Rutledge appeared in the chart room of the male orthopaedic ward early that dark winter morning. Ben was a husky, tall fellow, big round face, ruddy cheeks, bright eyes, and a scruffy head of hair. He comported himself upright like the tough soldier that he had been. He was a retired Army colonel, now on the staff at Emory and Grady. "I am your new rounding man," he announced.

"Yes, sir," I responded. I was new on the ward, yet I knew Dr. Rutledge from Emory. "We're waiting for the chief resident for rounds," I answered.

"Hell," said Rutledge, "we can make rounds without him. Let's get started."

We headed down the hall and entered the first double room. "Tell me about these guys," he gestured pointing to the first bed with the patient in a long leg cast. The blood-stained cast went from his groin to his toes. An odor of infection – a sickly sweet aroma – assailed our senses.

With the usual monotone used when presenting a patient, I began, "This thirty-five-year-old man sustained an open comminuted fracture of his right tibia and fibula in a motorcycle accident three weeks ago. We took him to the OR and debrided the dirty fracture site, washed it with saline, Betadine, and irrigated it with a Bacitracin solution. We've since windowed the cast and cleaned the wound. It looks fair, though with still an odor of infection. We're altering his antibiotics."

Dr. Rutledge interrupted my presentation with a sharp question. "Yeah, I understand all that, so how long has this fellow been up in this traction?"

"Since surgery," I answered.

"You mean this patient has been in this traction three weeks?"

"Yes, sir," I responded, wondering what Rutledge had in mind.

"Has he walked yet?"

"No, sir, he's just been in the bed."

Rutledge stepped over to the bed. The patient watched him intensely. "Hasn't put weight on this fracture yet, huh?"

"Nope, not yet," I answered.

"Show me the X-rays," he grumbled. I had the file folder in hand and tilted the bedside light to show Dr. Rutledge the series of films. He held the films up to the light. "Alignment looks reasonably good so why isn't he up and weight bearing on this leg?"

"This is our protocol," I answered.

He reached into his coat pocket and pulled out a three-inch knife, carefully opened it, reached over into the traction ropes, grasped each rope, and began cutting. "Hold the weights till we get all this damn traction down," he said.

"Sir, this is our department protocol, traction for three to four weeks then ambulation," I repeated.

"Hell," he said, "look at those X-rays. There's still space between the main fracture components. All you are doing is distracting the fracture, lucky if it heals at all."

"Stand up!" he gruffly said to the young fellow as he placed his arm under the patient's shoulder. "Touch it down." The patient looked scared.

"After twenty years treating paratroopers, I've learned that weight-bearing and compression is the best way to heal these folks."

"Sir, what will I tell Dr. Kelly about all this traction being down when he rounds this afternoon?"

"Hell, leave Bob to me," he said with a big grin. "Just ask Ritchey, he knows." (Dr. Sterling Ritchey was another retired military officer on the Emory staff.) "He's treated the same population that I have."

We then moved into the open ward where he continued with his cutting-down spree.

The chief resident appeared on the ward, "Sorry I'm late, just finished in the OR." He still had on his surgical scrubs with a white coat covering them.

Rutledge took him by the arm and led him around the open ward of twelve or more patients. "Look around, I've cut all the traction ropes down and you can have these guys in balanced traction only at night and between walks in the daytime while *I'm* attending."

The chief resident looked stunned when he saw that our new attending surgeon had cut down every bit of traction. The ropes were dangling like dismasted ships. The traction weights remained on the floor at the foot of each bed.

"Good Lord," he stuttered, "what are we going to tell Dr. Kelly?"

"Hell," said Rutledge. "Tell him, Old Ben Rutledge has been here, and we've got a new protocol."

"Yes, I'll do that," the chief resident answered cautiously. With the new Rutledge protocol, the healing rate of lower extremity fractures at Grady improved precipitously.

NOVEMBER 1963

Everyone remembers where they were that day.

It was in the fifth month of my residency after military service when a pallor descended upon the hospital. As I walked out of the mid-day surgery clinic an ashen gray fellow resident, rushed up to me, "Have you heard the news?"

"What news?" I answered.

"The president, the president has been shot," he stuttered.

"You mean *Kennedy*, our president?" I asked, astonished.

"Yeah, in Dallas, I think," he said. "It's on the TV."

We hurried to the elevators and ascended to the fourteenth floor. In an open break room in the intern quarters was a large TV set. Interns and residents stood around dumbfounded as they watched the screen. The news flashed and a reporter confirmed the wounding of the president. "The president has been shot in Dallas, Texas," the reporter announced. "Texas Governor Connally has also been shot. We don't know the extent of the injuries."

It was not long until the news commentator Walter Cronkite, with tears in his eyes appeared, removed his glasses and solemnly announced, "It is official," he glanced up at a clock on the wall in the studio, "that at one o'clock President John F. Kennedy died at Parkland Hospital in Dallas, Texas." We all stood silent or sat numb in the little room. A few sniffles were heard as we gradually moved about and eased out of the room, wandering back to our wards or clinics.

That night I returned to the bachelor apartment in Atlanta's Colonial Homes that I shared with three other Grady residents – Jim Hoffman, John Whitehurst, and Charlie Clayton – all of whom had just returned from military duty. I pulled up a chair in front of our small black and white television as the dark night descended, sipped on a couple of beers and cried openly.

I remembered the young lean man, the smiling face of Congressman John Kennedy, as he often stopped by the Democratic page bench at the back of the House chamber and chatted with us in a casual, friendly manner. I remembered sitting in freezing Philadelphia cold at an Army-Navy football game and watched him cross the football field and switch sides during intermission. I remembered the bright staff in his congressional office. I remembered the good man.

I remembered his speech about "sending a man to the moon within the next decade." I remembered listening to him by radio and watching a black and white television set with poor reception on the veranda of the Guantanamo officers club as he announced the military buildup on our base at Guantanamo, Cuba. I remembered his strong speech resisting Soviet intrusion into the Western Hemisphere on the island of Cuba and the dangers it posed to world peace.

I remembered the young folks in the Far East and their enthusiasm and questions about our president and his beautiful wife Jackie. Most of all, I remembered his inspiring inauguration speech, "Ask not what your country can do for you, but what you can do for your country."

I mourned the loss of our president. I also wondered about the man who was sworn into office. I remembered Lyndon Johnson's reputation as a "powerful arm-twisting politician." I recalled his abusive verbal treatment of his office staff. I recalled his bullying ways that I had witnessed in the Senate wing of the Capitol when years before I served as a page. I wondered what sort of a president he would be.

I feared for the future of our country under the leadership of this former Texas senator. As a young man, I respected him so little while I worked in Washington. I was soon to find out what sort of a president he would be.

Despite his continuing Kennedy's social and racial policies and reforms, I experienced, as did the nation, the disastrous continuation and escalation of the Viet Nam War. I recalled the rumor that he had told the army generals and navy admirals, "Gentlemen, you will have your war."

Many thought President Kennedy would have seen the handwriting on the wall and would have "drawn the war down" to some negotiated peaceful resolution, not unlike the previous Korean Conflict that former President Eisenhower had resolved.

Our nation never got to witness how Kennedy would have handled the situation.

That November day still lives tragically and vividly in our national memory and in the hearts of those who lived during that dark history.

SAILING

Try my hand at sailing.

Upon returning to Atlanta I was determined to try my hand at sailing again. Stuart Shippey, a surgery resident, and I joined the Lake Lanier Sailing Club. Stuart bought a fiberglass Flying Dutchman and began to teach me to sail the racer.

While hanging around the sailing club I was invited to sail with a fellow on his beautiful classic wooden Flying Dutchman FD-300, which was manufactured in the Netherlands.

The sound of the race gun boomed, and we left the starting line on a smooth port tack leading the fleet. It was not long before a gust of wind lifted us out of the water. My inexperience on the "trapeze" was on display when I tried to balance the boat on a sharp steep plane to no avail and over we went. "Don't worry," my new sailing friend yelled, emerging from under the water, hanging on to the hull and spewing cool lake water. I twisted in the water to get loose of the trapeze sling and slipped from under the main sail. "We'll push and swim it to shore and drain the boat," he said calmly.

In knee-deep water along the shore we successfully tilted the boat and bailed out the water. The boat was protected from sinking by two inflatable canvas and plastic air bags, one under the bow and the other under the deck of the stern.

We didn't win, but after such an exciting day, I offered to buy the boat. We agreed on a fair price and a few days later we met at the clubhouse. At the bar we settled the deal and I was the owner of an Olympic class Dutchman. The sleek red boat would give me many hours of pleasure at the Lake Lanier Sailing Club when I could escape Grady and later on the same lake when I went out into practice.

JANUARY 1964

... a girlfriend she thinks you might like...

After an easy pathology rotation, five eight-hour days and half day on Saturday, I returned to the ward. My schedule was now thirty-six hours on call in the hospital and twelve hours off. I had little time of my own.

While on pathology I dated a cute girl from New England. She was lovely and reminded me of Ellen, to whom I was engaged before the military. When I rotated to the ward, my spare time was spent trying to rest and there was little time for romance, though I was really fond of the young lady in question.

In the Grady cafeteria I ran into Richard Naiman, a classmate one year behind me, and now a medical resident. He had married my grammar and high school pal, June. "Hey, June wants to invite you over to our house for dinner. She has a girlfriend she thinks you might like."

Gee, I thought, *my rare night off and she wants me to meet someone new.* I was not enthusiastic. "Well, okay," I said. "but don't expect any big romance. I'm already seeing someone from pathology and she's mighty cute."

"If you're off Friday or Saturday night, June can plan dinner. It'll be a little pre-Christmas meal," Richard mumbled.

"Okay, Friday. But I may run late. The ward is hectic."

Friday was a horrible day and I went up to my room, showered and lay down to rest for a couple of minutes. Near midnight I awoke, looked at the clock, picked up the phone and dialed June and Richard's number.

In a flat voice he muttered, "Why don't you answer your phone? We called and paged you. Supper was at seven and we waited till ten to eat." He sounded pissed. "Your date wondered what kind of a guy you were that you didn't even call."

"Sorry," I said. "Can I have another chance?"

"Don't call us. We'll call you," he replied.

The sleep's better than the food and probably the date, I thought. It didn't sound like a second invite was going to be forthcoming

When a second invitation did come – same story – I slept through it, too.

While in the recovery room checking a post-surgical patient and bent down on my knees fixing a chest surgery thoracotomy tube into a large suction bottle, I heard a voice. It was Richard. He had been called to see someone about an EKG that the orthopod couldn't read. He leaned down and whispered, "This damn EKG is normal. Who called me anyway?" I was not about to tell him I had called the medical resident for a consultation.

"Must have been Burkhardt, he's the chief," I lied.

"You Orthopods can barely read and write," he said. "No wonder you all can't interpret an EKG." He was probably right.

"Hey, we're hell with a hammer and chisel," I proffered.

Richard smugly answered, "Yeah, you're probably right. Oh, by the way, June wants to give you one last chance to meet her friend and have supper with us. What do you say?"

At that moment I reflected on something my mother said to me when I was a teenager and she wanted me to meet her friend's daughter. It was always "some friend's daughter with a wonderful personality."

368

"You don't have to marry every girl you date," she said.

"Okay, I'll try to come over. Thank June for her forgiveness."

January can be chilly or warm in Atlanta but this night it was brisk and pleasant. I arrived on time and even brought a bunch of flowers I got at the hospital gift shop. I had no idea what they were, but they looked pretty and smelled good.

The table was set, and the lights were dim. Candles reflected glimmering light on the fancy crystal, probably a wedding gift, June had set for the occasion. "This is Barbara," June said. "We work together. She's Harry's and my research assistant."

Harry Williams was a professor in the pharmacology department, a favorite of the students. He had a PhD and an MD. That made him special. *If she works for Harry, she must be smart. She must be okay,* I thought.

It was dim, but I knew I liked this girl already. She was slender with brown hair and big brown eyes. She had on a simple white blouse and a dark skirt that showed her figure to its best. I was glad I had finally made it to dinner.

Richard had started a glowing fire in the fireplace. It created quite a pleasant atmosphere. The dinner was great and called for seconds.

Barbara helped June clear the table and Richard and I eased over to the fire. He poured me a glass of sherry and I sipped, thinking, *This married life isn't all bad.*

We visited in the warm, inviting living room while June and Barbara tended to June's two little daughters. June was in the process of carrying her third baby while also finishing her PhD in pharmacology.

Outside in the dark, I walked Barbara to her car. "Do you think I might see you again?" I asked.

"Why, yes, I would like that," she answered.

"I've got a sailboat up on the lake that I need to bring back before it gets too cold. Would you like to ride up there? And if the weather is okay, we can sail on the lake then haul it back to Atlanta.

I get off before noon Saturday and am off until Sunday morning," I said.

"Yes, that will be fun," she said. "Call me."

"Stuart, I've got a date with this really cute girl Saturday to go up to the lake and sail then bring the boat back," I said to my sailing buddy. "I don't think she can sail so if you'd come with us that should work out okay."

"Yeah, I'm in the dog lab this month and got plenty of time. Sounds good," he said.

I picked her up at her apartment and then we picked up Stuart. "Stuart, this is Barbara, she works in pharmacology research with Harry Williams at Emory."

"Hello," he answered politely with a slight smile. He slammed the door. We all three sat in the front seat of my '59 Chevy.

Getting the boat into the water was no trouble. We raised the sail and the main blossomed in the breeze. We took off. The boat was a two-man racer, so we were crowded. Of course, neither Stuart nor I were much more than amateurs. The boat had a trapeze where one crew member would swing out to balance the boat on a tight planing course.

After demonstrating the procedure, we put my date in the harness and we swung her out over the water. Down in the cold water she went dipping her behind. "Sorry about that," we proffered.

She was a good sport, but I wondered what was really going through her mind. She probably thought we were a couple of hotdogs, and with a big sailboat, we were a bad combination.

We'd done some night sailing and it was near midnight when we left the lake. We stopped by a truck stop that looked so rough that I suggested that I get the coffee and leave my date and Stuart in the car. Some days later I learned that she was not too happy with us because she had needed a potty break and as thoughtless guys, we hadn't thought to ask.

We hauled the boat back, stashed it in my carport at the old Colonial Homes Apartments and I took her home. Stuart had been unusually formal, and it was not until later I learned she had been dating him before I came along as a blind date.

In February, I was confused about my two girlfriends, the girl from New England or Barbara. I didn't know what to do with either of them. "I thought I'd take some time off and think and try to decide what direction I should take. I went skiing in Vermont with a couple of friends. Even for a short week I missed them, but I made a final decision.

Barbara met me at the airport. We dated through the spring, became engaged, and decided to marry in May.

"No, you can't have time off during your Emory rotation, not even to get married," said my professor's secretary. "Dr. Kelly doesn't allow time off on this rotation," she stated.

I had rotated to Emory, an easy rotation, for the academic part of the residency and we took calls for both Emory and Egleston Hospitals and Aidmore Children's Rehabilitation Hospital. We also were supposed to be doing research for an academic publication. In the hospital our job was to watch, listen, and assist in surgery. We were to run the ward for the professor, doing the nitty-gritty tasks of keeping the private patients safe and happy. It was a comedown from the Grady rotation where we had to do it all. We were mere servants doing the professor's scut work. No wonder they didn't allow time off.

By August, I was back on Grady rotation. Barbara and I married in Athens, Tennessee, an Episcopal service in the First Baptist Church. Barbara was a lovely bride. My dad was my best man. My pals were among the groomsmen: Warren Brown, a practicing plastic surgeon I had worked with when I first began driving the Grady ambulance; Jay Williams a former medical school roommate, now an internist; John Whitehurst, a chest and head and neck surgery resident from Grady, and one internist, Joe Stubbs from Piedmont Hospital. June, who had introduced us, was the bride's maid.

Since my future in-laws were strict Baptists there was to be no alcohol at the reception with the exception of champagne for those who drank. My classmate Joe Stubbs, however, spiked one bowl of punch with vodka and when the punch was about to be discarded, he, after having a few himself, yelled at the attendant, "Hey, don't pour out that good liquor."

Barbara Joy Vincent
1964 wedding photograph

Years later, my mother-in-law coolly asked, "Whatever happened to your good friend, that red-headed doctor who saved that punch?"

That red-headed classmate, Joe Stubbs, practiced medicine longer than any of our classmates and I considered him the most conscientious and best physician in our class. It was said that his patients simply wouldn't let him retire. How great can that be, that patients are so devoted to their doctor?

Barbara and Jerald L. Watts
Attending the Georgia Orthopaedic Society Meeting
(Photo from The Cloister, Sea Island, Ga.)

FLYING DUTCHMAN

"I'll take your boys sailing"

Our surgery professor, Dr. Ritchey, lived on Lake Lanier across from our dock and invited us up for a cookout.

"Sure, we'd like that," I responded.

"Why don't you all sail over to our cabin and spend the afternoon?" Ritchey asked.

"I'll take your boys sailing," I volunteered.

Our sail over was easy and took only a couple of hours. We tied up at Dr. Ritchey's dock and climbed the steep hill to his rustic lake house. After the cookout, I noticed his boys—one ten, the other twelve—hanging around the dock looking at my boat. "Want a sail, boys?" I inquired.

They were delighted and we gathered at the dock, fitted on life preservers, and prepared to launch the boat when the chubby twelve-year-old jumped from the dock into the cockpit of the boat crashing his tennis-shoed foot through the thin 3/8-inch hull. Swoosh, the water rushed into the boat.

"Oh, Hell," I mumbled silently, trying not to upset the little group of watchers. "Let's pull the boat over here to the shore," I ordered my friends.

"Tip it and drag it before it sinks," I said frantically. We succeeded in getting the boat to the shore, tilted it on its side and inspected the hole and splintered shiny red hull.

The kid was quiet. He didn't know what to say. He had just smashed my boat. "It's okay," I said trying to comfort him as he began to cry, tears streaming down his pink, chubby cheeks.

"It's okay, we can fix it," I reassured the kid.

"We're surgeons, we fix things," I echoed as his father arrived down the hilly path to the boat.

Dr. Ritchey stared at the fractured hull, frowned at his son, and turned to me, "I'll get someone out tomorrow to fix it. You can take one of my cars back."

"We can patch here," I suggested. "Yep, can patch it here and I can sail it across the lake."

At the house we found several ¼-inch pieces of plywood, cut them big enough to cover the inside and outside of the hull and smeared spackling paste to seal the space between the two boards, filling the defect. We then drilled small holes and secured the boards with multiple screws, inside and outside.

I took the boy aside and said to him, "That's how orthopaedic surgeons fix things."

His tears were gone, and his eyes sparkled as he realized he was off the guilt trip. "We'll sail next time," I assured him.

Barbara and I set sail, just before dark to cross the lake. We took several good-sized buckets to bail out the water that we knew would seep into the boat despite the "expert repair."

We sailed toward home with the damaged hull down in the water and bailed as water continued to seep in and invade the hull. We then tacked with the good side of the hull down and feverishly bailed till nearly dry. We repeated the exercise till dark and a small island at mid-lake appeared. Unable to navigate in the dark we pulled up the center board and beached the boat. We found a dry spot just above the beach edge, spread a canvas, built a fire and covered ourselves with a couple of blankets borrowed from our host.

Bright sun filtered slivers of light through the pines and woke us. We stoked the fire, broke some tree branches, stabbed them into some marshmallows and a few wieners saved from the picnic, and sipped a couple of Cokes. Then we pushed the "Dutchman" back into the water and sailed to our dock. After we loaded the boat on its trailer, we towed it back to the city, for real repairs.

More sailing

Has it been over half a century? It seems only yesterday we sailed off St. Simons and Sea Island. We sailed often during our courtship and early marriage and Barbara should have been forewarned of the dangers of sailing with me, an inept but foolishly daring sailor. Yet we challenged fate with our continued sailing adventures.

September was still a hot early fall month when we latched my boat trailer and my "Flying Dutchman" to my big, white Chevy and headed for the Georgia coast. As a surgery resident, my income was on or below the poverty level. Why buy new tires for a boat trailer when the Shell Tire store had retreads on sale at half the price? Yep, retreads would be okay because I didn't really use the trailer that often. I had not thought about those hot Georgia asphalt highways and the dangers of traveling with second-rate tires.

We had a few days off, so we headed for the Georgia shore. We were newly married with no kids. Other than our jobs, we were free mortals, free to do as we pleased.

This day it was unusually hot when we left Atlanta and about two hundred miles down the road, lumpity, bumpity was all I felt as I looked out my rear-view mirror and could see my boat and trailer swerving and bouncing. "Oh, no," I said, "bad tire, I bet."

"It's flat as a flitter," I said to my recent bride after pulling off the road and inspecting the tire. An hour later, after hoisting the trailer and changing the retread tire, we pulled back on the road and headed for the shore. That flat tire should have warned me, bad omen. However, when you're young, bad omens never really sink in. We were indestructible.

Down by the Coast Guard Station on St. Simons Island we launched our nineteen-foot Olympic class boat. It had a shallow hull, aluminum drop keel and outboard rudder and tall mast for a large main sail and sailing jib. It had a wonderful and colorful red and white spinnaker with big letters, "FD-300."

At the Coast Guard station there were small signal flags blowing in the mild breeze, but they meant little to me, the daring sailor. After all I had sailed on this little craft for months and should have no problems.

My bride and I sailed across the bay toward Jekyll Island and back through modest waves. What I didn't pick up was the change in the breeze, a gathering intensity. "That was fun," Barbara volunteered.

"Yeah, but I want to make one more run to Jekyll," I answered.

"Seems windy," she complained. "Don't you think?"

"Oh, we'll be back before it gets much more," I claimed.

We set off again. Midway in the bay, an unexpected gust of wind lifted the jib, swirled us leeward and over we went into the water. "Over we go," I yelled. "Hang on to the boat."

I surfaced and she seemed caught under the swell. I swam to her side and grabbed her as she jerked away, pulling at her life vest. Down we both submerged again as a swell poured over us and the boat. "Don't pull off your vest," I yelled.

Bubble, bubble, we again sank under the water. Half out of her vest she cried, "It's holding me under."

Sure enough, the snap on the life vest had snagged on the side stay rigging and was pulling her under on every swell. We managed to disentangle the vest and pulled each other into the water-filled cockpit. We both coughed and spit up salty, frothy water.

I released the mainsail and it plummeted into the cockpit. "Keep bailing," I yelled as we scooped canvas buckets of water from the cockpit. We breathed deeply and managed to hold the jib loosely, flapping in the wind. "I can control the jib and we can drift to shore," I whispered, now relieved that the boat was under some control. The heavy aluminum rudder had disappeared when we capsized so we had only the jib and center board down to control the boat.

In the 1960s many boats had plastic air-type flotation tanks or air bags under the bow and stern deck to keep from sinking. As we felt the danger ebb, we heard an ominous buzz or low swishing sound. "Oh, damn the air bag has torn," I said grimly, as the stern sank below the water line now allowing the cockpit to refill with water.

She looked at me with fearful eyes and I put on my bravest smile, "It's okay, we'll get help, don't worry." We continued to bail water and hold the jib lines, trying to reach the shore some long distance away. The waves calmed but we capsized a couple of more times as a gust of wind filled the jib, lifting us up then smashing us back over in the water.

We yelled and waved our paddles to passing boats, but no one seemed to notice us. A couple of small planes flew over, but they must not have seen us either. Now really worried, we could see the St. Simons lighthouse further and further away. We waved and we waved, but no one came. We were drifting beyond the shores of Jekyll. We were drifting out to sea with the tide.

The sun was setting over the land with a beautiful glow but for us a fearful sunset. We were in the water four hours or so, we estimated, when we saw a speck in the distance, a boat turning in our direction. "Oh, Jesus, thanks," I murmured. Maybe help was on its way. Maybe he saw us. We both held our breath as the boat appeared closer and closer–beautiful, probably the most beautiful boat I ever saw. As she eased up to us, a middle-aged, well-tanned husky fellow leaned over the rail, waved his hat. "Hey, can we help you?"

The fellow threw us a line and we pulled alongside the stern of his big boat. "Do you need help up the ladder?" he shouted. "Tie up to the ladder and I'll help you. We'll take care of your boat later."

We boarded his boat. He gently pulled Barbara onto the boat's deck and his lovely gray-haired wife threw blankets over us. "You must be cold, dear," she said. "Sit here and we'll get you some hot tea or hot cider, if you wish."

With sighs of relief, we clutched the blankets and they took us below. Within a few minutes we were dry, and our hosts wrapped us in heavy cotton robes. Our new friend and ship's captain started the engines only to have the engines falter, sputter and die. He shifted the gears to neutral and stood silently. Then he quietly said,

"I think the line from our boat has snarled the propeller." He did not try to start the engine and we began to drift seaward.

Oh no, I thought, *not again.*

I stood over the rail looking down into the now rough waves. "Yep, I think it's the tow line," I said to our captain.

Minutes later, I was back in the water. Like in a Tarzan movie, I dived under the stern, big sharp fishing knife clutched between my teeth. I fumbled under the hull near the stern to the propeller shaft. I could barely see in the dark water but felt until the shaft was identified. I whittled, as best I could, the line about the shaft and propeller as the swells lifted the stern, banging my head, which was protected solely by my free arm as I tried to hold the boat away. After coming up for air a couple of times, I felt I had cut enough rope to free the propeller. We were still drifting. I struggled back onto the big boat.

I stood by our host, with a blanket over my shoulders getting my breath. He put the gears in reverse to see if he could unwind any line that might be still on the shaft.

The engine rumbled. Blue foamy water spewed from the boat's exhaust openings. He shifted the gears from neutral to reverse and frayed fragments of rope floated up around the stern. The prop was free. We retied the tow line to my boat and went below.

"Put these on," his lovely wife said, handing us some khaki shorts and cotton sweatshirts. We slipped on the new warm clothes.

She stepped over to the galley and returned with sparkling cocktail glasses filled with fresh frozen daiquiris. We sipped our wonderful daiquiris, the best we ever had, as she brought out broiled fish and served us dinner.

They invited us to stay the night, but we demurred. "Thank you, ma'am. You've already done more than enough for us," we said.

They dropped us off at the Coast Guard dock. We pulled our "Dutchman" alongside the dock, crammed the sails into the sail bags and secured the boat for the night.

Back at our hotel, The King and Prince, we dozed and listened to the roar of the treacherous breaking surf out our open window and said our prayers, "Thank You, Lord, for the end of this day."

The following day we attended Christ Church on St. Simons Island, the church where John Wesley had preached under the great coastal oaks early in our country's history. We were two grateful sailors, "Saved from the sea."

When we collected my boat, we visited the Coast Guard station. I spoke to the young two-striped lieutenant. "We were adrift for four hours and we never saw any patrol boats out."

He frowned, shook his head slowly, glaring at me, "Didn't you see the signal flags – those red flags with black squares – up yesterday?"

"Yeah, I guess I did, why?"

"Those were storm warnings. We never go out under those conditions."

HER NAME IS LAURA

"A call for you, Doctor…"

"I've got a call for you, Doctor. I think it's your wife," whispered the nurse as we stood at a bedside discussing a patient's case. I was a Senior Resident on my last spring rotation at Emory and Egleston Hospitals.

"Yes, I'll take it at the desk," I answered.

"They're getting regular," my wife said.

"How regular?" I responded.

"They are *regular,*" she moaned.

"I'll be home in a few minutes, just hold on," I said to her.

"Guys, I have to go home," I yelled across the hall to my fellow residents. "It sounds like it's delivery time."

"Don't worry, we'll take care of this damn place," the other resident answered.

I pulled my car into our drive. She was sitting in the kitchen in a hardback chair holding on to the stove. "It really hurts," she held her tummy.

"Right," I said. "Let's get in the car and head for the hospital."

We rushed through the Emory ER and the orderly pushed Barbara to an elevator in a rickety rolling chair. "OB's on three," the orderly announced.

Dr. McKinsey met us as we rolled into the operative area. Bill McKinsey had been my OB chief resident when I rotated through Grady Obstetrics as a junior and senior student. "He's darn good," I whispered to Barbara.

"Yes, I know," she groaned.

I waited outside the exam room and Bill came out. "Nearly ready, but not quite," he said. "We're going to sedate her, and in the morning, we will give her Pitocin and deliver her. She should be ready then. You can sleep in the OB resident quarters, if you like," he volunteered.

"Sounds good to me. I'll check with the other guys on my service. They can handle the ward."

I couldn't sleep for the anxiety I felt. *Everything's going to be okay,* I kept saying to myself, but I worried about all the other possible complications, cords about the infant's neck, the placenta blocking the birth canal, prolonged labor, anoxia to the baby, and bleeding. I got up and headed down to the OB floor. "About ready," the nurse said. I chatted with my sleepy mama-to-be.

I couldn't hear the baby, but Bill McKinsey appeared through the double doors with a big grin. "All done," he said. "Eight-pound healthy little girl. Pink and APGAR * is good. Mama is fine."

I remembered the Grady OB rotation and I whispered, "Thank You, Jesus," as I had heard so often. I had delivered nearly a hundred babies at Grady. The nurse brought the baby into the room and a groggy Barbara mumbled. "Is she okay?" She looked at the baby and dozed off.

I leaned over her bed and whispered, "Baby Laura's fine."

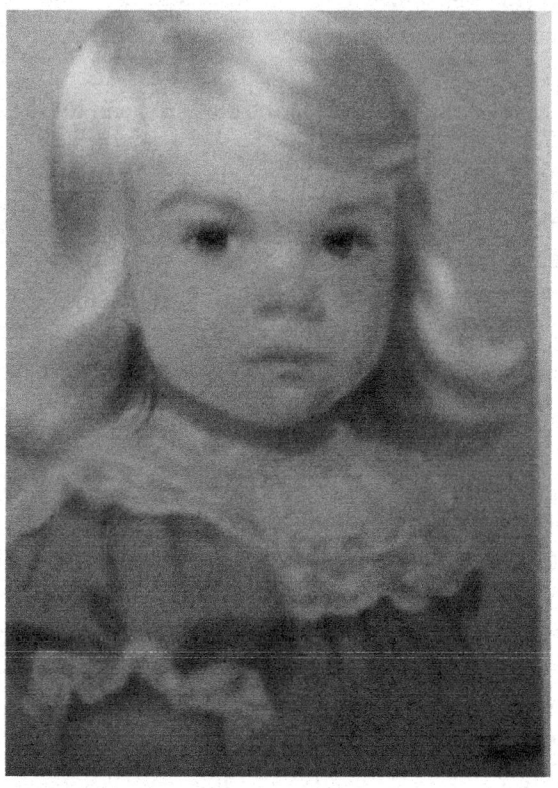

Laura Elizabeth
From pastel portrait by Mid-Twentieth Century American Artist
Robert Templeton (1929 – 1991)

I walked out of Emory's front door into the bright Georgia sunshine, sat on a stone bench along the walk, glanced at the newly blossoming leaves and full flowers of this wonderful May morning. I thought about our beautiful baby, and hummed, "Sweet Georgia Girl."

Note: APGAR – A rapid clinical evaluation of a newborn, named after the anesthesiologist, Virginia Apgar who designed the system, hence the name APGAR. The system involves an observation grading of the infant at 5 then 10 minutes after birth. A = Appearance - skin color, P = Pulse - heart rate, G = Grimace - reflexes, A = Activity - muscle movement, and R= Respirations - breathing activity. Grading from 0 to 2, added for each letter determines *the* score. Total *8 to 10 is a very good score. Lower values suggest further investigation of the infant.*

PART FIVE

AFTER THE GRADYS

AFTER THE GRADYS – HOW DO YOU GO OUT INTO PRACTICE

More to come; the brood was growing.

Before going into practice, we wanted to visit some relatives and let them meet our new daughter. Laura was six weeks old when we drove to Arkansas to visit my great-aunt, Alice Perdue. Alice was the only living relative of her Perdue generation. She was ninety. I wanted her to meet our new baby before she passed away.

I bought a new car and planned to drive it to Arkansas. The only problem was that it didn't have air conditioning. (I was so impoverished with a Grady salary that I probably thought I couldn't afford air conditioning.) We drove through Athens, Tennessee, and borrowed my father-in-law's new air-conditioned automobile.

We drove to Memphis. Since it was getting dark, Barbara wanted to stop but I was eager to get as far as we could. "Just across the bridge, we'll stop," I said. Bad idea.

We crossed the "Mighty Mississippi River" and could not find a room at any inn. I knew at that moment how Joseph must have felt when he couldn't find a "room at the inn" for Mary and the unborn Christ child. In desperation, we located an old motel at a truck stop with rooms that had not been used for weeks, maybe months. The proprietor felt sorry for us and let us a room. The beds were old and sagging and the sheets were dusty. *Not much better than a stable,* I thought, *but at least a bed.*

The next morning, we headed for Pine Bluff and Aunt Alice's home. She, a long-time widow, and her housekeeper Bertha, rented rooms to the transient railroad workers who were staying in the town.

We stayed with her in her old gray two-story house for a day or so then moved to a nearby air-conditioned motel.

Our return to Atlanta was uneventful. I sold our house to a Grady intern and made a small profit, just enough to make a down payment on another house in a new town.

We moved to Gainesville, Georgia, after the first week of July. We had looked at several surgery practices and put names of places and practices in a hat and kept drawing from the hat. We went to the one that kept coming up last. It was on one of Georgia's finest lakes and as a new sailor, I thought it would be the best. I soon was so busy that I had little time for sailing.

I joined a surgeon who had gone into practice only one year before I completed my training. The town had no orthopaedic surgeons. The general surgeons had told him that they did their own orthopaedics and didn't need an orthopaedic surgeon.

The surgeon I joined was a few years older and had practiced for several years as a general practitioner in Blairsville, Georgia, before returning to a surgical residency at Grady. He was fair in his offer. The association with Dr. Little taught me a lot about general family medicine as I attempted to care for our patients.

A year later, we would have our second child. It was late at night when Barbara complained that the labor pains were regular and severe. We got a neighbor's daughter to stay with Laura and we headed for the Hall County Hospital where I practiced.

Dr. Bill White was on call and admitted her directly into the hospital. A few hours later we had our second little girl. "She's just beautiful," said Bill White as he came out of the delivery room and announced a safe and uncomplicated birth.

"Her APGAR is the highest I've seen in a long time," he said. "I think she's going to be very bright."

We took Allyson home and put another bed in what was now a real nursery, with Laura and Allyson sharing the room.

D. Allyson
From pastel portrait by Mid-Twentieth Century American Artist
Robert Templeton (1929 – 1991)

Eighteen months later we had our third child. The experience was similar to the last delivery. Bill White again greeted us with the good news, "He's mighty good looking, just like the girls and his APGAR is great."

Convinced that another girl was on the way, we had no name for him when we left the hospital. We couldn't name our newborn Patricia as we had planned, so days after bringing him home we named him Jerry II. It was December 1968 and his sisters thought he was a Christmas present, a Christmas doll. With this beautiful son, our family was complete.

Laura, now two and a half, moved into a youth bed in another bedroom and Allyson and Jerry stayed in the nursery.

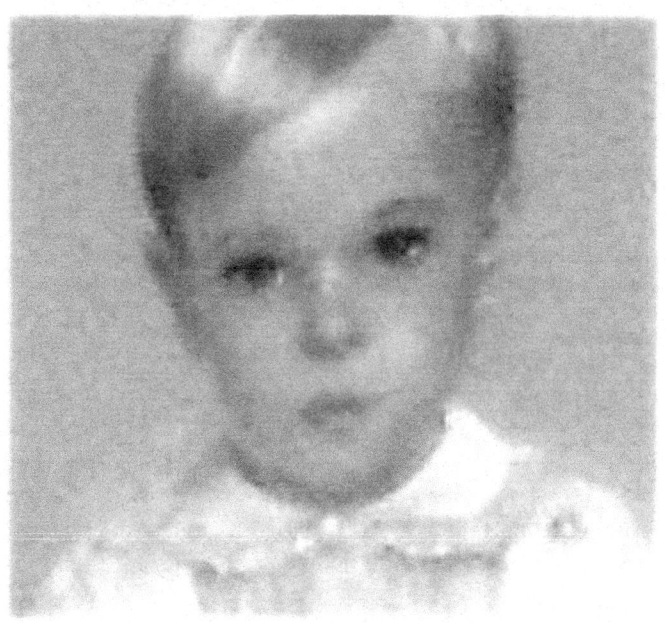

Jerald (Jerry) Lee II
From pastel portrait by Mid-Twentieth Century American Artist
Robert Templeton (1929 – 1991)

PRACTICE

"Practice in North East Georgia wasn't much different from Grady."

My partner, Charles Little, and I were the first specialty trained and first board-certified orthopaedic surgeons in Northeast Georgia, consequently we had a large referral practice which received much of the trauma surgery from north Georgia into western North Carolina and east Tennessee along the Georgia State line.

As I have said to my friends, "Our practice was not a silk purse practice." There was a great deal of charity work, as the rural family doctors had nowhere else to send their patients north of Atlanta. It was almost like Grady. Yet, Medicare had just become available for the elderly, so a small portion of the elderly obtained insurance coverage despite the resistance of many medical organizations.

A few years later there were other orthopaedic surgeons in town with more selective "financial" practices, but we in our practice treated them all without regard to ability to pay. A few limited their Medicaid practice to only emergency cases then discharged them from their practices. I was disappointed in a couple of my fellow surgeons. I thought that was what doctors did, treat everyone. Needless to say, I repeat: Ours was not a "silk stocking practice."

After the abject poverty of Grady, I couldn't believe that they paid me a living wage for what I loved to do. I confess I was a poor financial manager and did not accumulate as much of the world's treasures as some of my more business-oriented friends and contemporaries, but I'll bet I had more fun, doing things my way.

One of my first encounters with the economics of medicine was in connection to the office charges for doing a hip fracture operation. I operated on an elderly woman from up in the North Georgia Mountains. On her first post op office visit her husband drove her down in his old beat up Ford pickup truck. After the office visit he wanted to settle up on the medical bill. He had not subscribed to the Medicare program, as he said, "I don't want that federal government in my business."

My secretary called me from the examining rooms to talk to this old fellow. He met me in the little business office, or at least that's what we called the tiny closet sized space. There he stood in his blue overalls and his dusty and worn work boots with a hand-rolled cigarette twittering between his tobacco stained thumb and index fingers. He put his cigarette in the ashtray twisted it until it was extinguished and said, "Doc. I thank you for taking good care of my wife, but I want to talk to you about the bill."

I really didn't know how much the office charged as my partner had set all the charges before I arrived.

I looked at the bill and noted the charges. It was more than I had made in nearly a month as a Senior Resident at Grady. "Yes, I do think that is a lot."

"Do you think we could take about a hundred dollars off the bill?" he asked.

I glanced at the bill again, looked at him in his work overalls, thought for a minute and said, "Why, yes, I think that would be fair."

He reached into his scruffy overalls pocket and pulled out the largest roll of hundred dollar bills I had ever seen and peeled out a few and laid them on the secretary's desk. "Hope that will do it!" He shook my hand firmly and he was out the door. "I don't need no receipt," he said as he headed toward his truck and back to the mountains.

My partner heard the conversation and approached me in the narrow hallway. "I heard you cut his bill," he said.

"Yes," I answered. "Did you see his poor old truck outside?"

"I did," said my partner. "I know that fellow. I treated his family when I was in general practice. He's from up around Blairsville and he is the richest darn bootlegger in North Georgia and he just took you for a ride, Sucker!" He smiled, turned and walked back down the hall shaking his head.

Our concerned secretary stopped him in the hall and whispered, "I don't think your new doctor understands office overhead."

There were other interesting cases. One was a case of a "chicken catcher." He was a tall lanky black guy who came into our office holding his right hand in a large bulky bandage. I unwrapped the bandage and examined his injured hand. I asked what kind of work he did, and he answered, "I'm a chicken catcher."

"A what?" I asked.

He repeated, "I'm a chicken catcher."

I asked, "What is that?"

He explained that in North Georgia, a center for chicken production, a "chicken catcher" caught chickens, as the name implied. At the poultry barns he could hold two to four chickens between his fingers on each hand and place them into open wooden chicken crates, then drive them in the huge chicken trucks, mostly during cool nights to deliver them to the poultry plants. There, they were processed, frozen, then shipped out for consumer consumption. His problem was that he had cut major tendons to his dominant thumb and could no longer hold chickens in one of his hands.

"Who bandaged your hand?" I asked him.

"That other doctor," he said, and he gave me the doctor's name. He told me that other doctor, the plastic surgeon, referred him to our office.

"Go see those doctors down the street," the surgeon told him.

The patient was then told that he could not afford the plastic surgeon's price since his injury was not a worker's compensation injury. He was referred to us, because our "prices were lower."

"Lower?" I said.

"Yes," he responded. He looked puzzled, scrunched up his nose, and rubbed his face with his good hand.

"Well," I said, "that's the way plastic surgeons are." I took this as a challenge and told him, "I will give you the best darn repair job in town."

We did repair his lacerated tendons and sent him back to the plastic surgeon for follow up after he had returned to "chicken catching" with a near perfect surgical result. Weeks later, I told this story to several surgeons in the doctors' lounge at the hospital. Of course, the plastic surgeon, present and red-faced, denied the whole embarrassing story as a made up orthopaedic surgeon's fable.

IT'S ABOUT MY BILL

It was always about some bill it seemed. She was a gentle little lady whose chief complaint was, "I've got this arthritis in my hip. Can you do anything about it, Doctor?"

After a bit of conversation, a history review and a cautious muscle and neurological exam, carefully moving her hip and back in various positions I suggested a series of X-rays to see if there was any radiographic evidence of arthritis or other significant pathology.

After reviewing the X-rays and sharing my findings with her, I counseled her about her activities, prescribed some anti-inflammatory and mild analgesic medications and scheduled her for physical therapy.

"Yes, ma'am, there's a bit of arthritis in that hip. I think this will help. I'll see you back in two weeks. You don't need any surgery on that hip."

A few moments later my secretary called me and asked me to speak to this lady about her bill. Same old story.

"Yes, ma'am," I responded, and I eased down the hall to the reception desk.

She stood holding her bill. "Doctor, I appreciate you seeing me today, but I want to talk to you about this bill. Don't you think it's a bit high?"

I glanced over the bill and it seemed about right for the services rendered.

"I mean the X-ray bill," she quietly gestured, pointing her slender, shaky, arthritic finger to the paper and the figures.

After some conversation I explained that young though I was and new at practice, I had learned about cost overhead, the thousands of dollars for the big expensive X-ray machine, the x-ray films and the cost of the developer solutions and the cost to the office of the salary of the x-ray technician. "Ma'am, we have to cover our costs for all that."

"Well," she indignantly said, and looking me straight in the eyes, she continued "I understand the costs, but I didn't know I was going to have to pay for the whole thing today!"

I could not help but laugh and responded, "Yes, ma'am, I see what you mean. We'll just cut the bill in half. How does that sound?"

She nodded approvingly and added, "I guess Medicare will be all right with that."

BOARDS

"They had my future in their hands…"

I loaded a suitcase into my car with a change of clothes on one side and with study material on the other – Campbell's Two Volume Orthopaedic text and a single pathology book with micro slide photographs.

I hadn't slept much the night before and had just finished a hip nailing on an old debilitated lady. I was worried about leaving the patient but thought my partner could look after her.

My wife was expecting our second child, so I drove her and our daughter to her sister's home in Knoxville and there they would not be alone. Then I headed for the airport.

My plane left for Chicago at four and I arrived at the Palmer House that evening. "Room 1213," the desk clerk said as he handed me my room key. Bag in hand, I rode the elevator to my room. It was small with a single bed. Just as long as it had a decent reading light so I could cram for the exam, I didn't care. I laid my texts out and began thumbing through. *Oh, hell,* I thought, *I hope they don't ask me about bone sarcomas.*

Supper was a quick trip to the hotel's café and then back to my room. At two a. m. I closed my books. At three a. m. I sat up in the bed, startled and sweating, rushed to the desk grabbed my pathology book and looked for sarcomas of the spine. Jesus, I thought, surely, they wouldn't ask about those.

At Grady prior to the exam, Tom Whitesides, one of my young professors, had reviewed pathology lantern slides with a group of former and current residents to prep us for our boards. "There will be no micro-slides," he assured us, "only projected slides." Projected slides magnify the cellular structure and are easier to evaluate and they're usually selected for identification of specific pathology.

I felt too anxious for a real breakfast when my two alarm clocks rang at 6 a.m. *Must get some coffee and maybe toast, at the most,* I thought. I descended the twelfth floor from room number thirteen. I was not superstitious but, why that number room? I grumbled.

Two years before, I had taken and passed "Part One" of the Boards, but the National Board Committee decided to change the testing rules to give part one and part two together, which meant I'd have to take the basic science portion again. Our program in Atlanta took the first part of the board exam, but the other program in the city didn't. Wow, we wondered, did they know something we didn't? Our professor, Dr. Kelly and the other program's chief, Dr. Lovell had never been friendly, and we wondered if that had anything to do with the other program having some heads-up information.

The written part was easy. One had to mark in the right answers with little or no written discussion. Either you knew it or you didn't. It was that simple.

Next came the Oral Exams with the Board faculty to determine the candidate's knowledge and determine whether the candidate was competent enough to become Board Certified to practice surgery.

My dad once – or perhaps more than once – said, "Son, never be in a position where someone can walk in and fire you." My goal was to be independent, enjoy my work, give good care, and educate my children. In private practice I answered to no one but my patients. But this day I was dependent on these examiners to practice surgery, my chosen profession.

It dawned on me that these old guys had my professional future in their hands. Suppose I get some jerk as an examiner, or some guy who doesn't like Southerners, or someone who has just had an argument with his wife? I was disturbed at their power over me.

How could they say whether I could practice or not? I had trained at Grady. I had seen it all and probably done it all. I closed my eyes for a moment and said to myself, don't think about all that right now. Just do your best. Respond with what you know is correct; don't try to impress these guys. Just be yourself.

My 3 x 5 schedule card directed me to a room down a dark hall. On the door was taped a paper that read, "TRAUMA," my seven-fifteen a.m. first exam. Across the hall was a table with a coffee pot and some cookies. A white-haired lady volunteered, "Is this your first exam, young man?"

"Yes, ma'am," I answered.

"Coffee, before you go in?" she asked. Her name tag read, "Mrs. Stinchcomb." Her husband was President of the Academy and Examiners.

"Thank you, ma'am, I do need a cup."

The door squeaked open and a pale fellow about my age ventured out of the room. He looked like he had just seen the Devil. He shook his head. *Oh, Hell,* I thought, *Bad sign.*

"We'll call you in just a minute," an elderly fellow said. He slammed the door.

"They're going to talk about me!" the examinee volunteered.

"Oh, you probably did okay," I answered. He walked away.

"Next," the same old fellow said as he opened the door for me to enter.

The questions were straight-forward with no tricky ones. How would you treat this, or how would you treat that? We looked at X-rays on a view box and I was out in just a few minutes.

The same person who had offered me coffee smiled and said, "That is the quickest anyone has been in and out so far."

"Is that good or bad?" I mumbled.

She shook her head, "Probably good," she said. I needed a friend and she filled the bill.

Down the hall taped to a door was the dreaded sign, "PATHOLOGY." The door opened and tall dark-haired man leaned out. "I think you are next."

I entered the room and there in the dim light were two microscopes. "Oh," Tom had said, "No micro-slides." And there they are. The examiner invited me to sit by the scopes. I noticed that on his watch-chain hung every academic key I had ever seen. A professor, I surmised.

"Son, I don't expect you will get every diagnosis right, so we'll just look at the mystery slides and I'll ask you to describe what you see." We looked at bone slides with all kinds of activity going on in each, osteoblasts and osteoclasts forming, destroying or recreating bone as the case might be. There were different cells replacing bone, cancer cells of questionable origin. "Just tell me what you see," he said.

I described the tissue as best I could. "Now, tell me what kind of conditions are compatible with the microscopic activity that you see." After a few minutes he stood up and said, "I think you have done okay. Good luck with the rest of your interviews."

"Thank you, sir," I said gratefully, and I was out in the hall sooner than I expected.

"Next," the examiner said to the waiting candidate. I had sweated the pathology and I was glad it was over.

The door to the exam room opened. A husky young man walked out past me. He didn't speak. He was shaking his head. *Oh my*, I thought, *it's going to be a bad one*. I stepped to the door and the examiner held his hand up. "Not yet," he admonished.

I stepped back. My time was already about ten minutes past the time on my schedule card. He had kept that other guy for far too long. He must be a tough examiner, I thought. He closed the door and I backed into the hallway. The sign on the door read X-RAY INTERPRETATIONS.

My scheduled exam time was thirty minutes with ten minutes between oral exams. Five minutes later the examiner opened the door. "Okay, come in," he mumbled. It took a while to get used to the dark room. Without a word he held up an X-ray and flipped it up on the view box. It was upside down. He seemed flustered. This was not the film he wanted. I was told that the examiners switched films so the examinees couldn't tell each other about the selected films. After rumbling through his large brown envelope, he selected a film, a skull X–ray with patchy, hazy defects in the parietal and frontal regions. "What about this one?" he asked.

"Do you want the diagnosis or a description?" I asked, thinking about the pathology exam and wondering just what was expected by this examiner.

"Either," he answered and nodded toward the offered film. I gave him a description and what I thought was a differential diagnosis. He said nothing, pulled the film off the view-box and selected another. Without much conversation I answered the questions as best I could.

He glanced at his watch. He had spent fifteen minutes with me. My time was up. He got up and moved toward the door. The bright light from the hall was almost blinding. He mumbled, "That's all, Doctor." I had no idea how I had done. Even in the cool room I had felt sweaty. He ushered the next examinee into the room with the same flat attitude as I had observed. The door slammed. I was glad to be out.

The next exam was GENERAL PRACTICE ORTHOPAEDICS. "Have a seat," the obvious head of the panel said, without introducing anyone on the examining panel. I was identified by a number on my card. Several questions into the interview one of the examiners, with X-rays in his hand, asked about a severe shoulder fracture case. "How would you handle this?" he asked.

We went through the usual conservative management, the use of a sling to immobilize the arm and on to the surgical care. Each step was met with "That didn't work, so what's next?" Eventually, we got down to the point of suggesting removal of all hardware and replacement with shoulder prosthesis.

"What prosthesis would you use?" the examiner at the end of the table asked as he crossed his arms and leaned back in his chair.

I thought for a minute. "I think I'd use a Neer prosthesis," I answered.

The examiner sneered, "A what?"

"A Neer prosthesis," I sheepishly answered.

"Son, you know there several other prosthesis products out there, why a NEER prosthesis?"

I said to myself, "*Oh, damn, they're on my case.*"

"I've been happy with that prosthesis in residency and a few in practice." *I've said it and now I've got to defend my choice,* I thought.

"Doctor, I just can't believe you'd use a NEER when there are so many other choices," a second examiner exclaimed. One fellow never asked me anything and I wondered why. Was he the hold-out guy, just watching for any mistakes? Was he the guy that held the swing vote on my exam performance? Those guys did not look friendly.

"Sir, I have to say I've had good luck with that prosthesis." I began to squirm uncomfortably and a dry feeling in my throat almost choked me.

The examiners were silent, sizing me up, I thought.

They leaned over, huddled about the examiners table, and I could hear whispers, but couldn't understand anything they said.

The fellow I assumed was the chief examiner got up from the table, glanced at his fellow examiners, then looked sternly at me and mumbled, "Son, we on this panel, *mostly* think you are unusual to use that item." He shook his head. I felt my heart in my throat.

He paused for a second; "By the way, we'd like to introduce you to Dr. Charles Neer, down at the end of the table!"

A middle-aged guy, the quiet one, stood up from the table, leaned over and grinned, and reached out to shake my hand, "Thanks, son for your good judgment. Good luck on your next exam."

I quickly packed my bag, got on the phone and called the airport. "When's the next Delta flight to Knoxville?" I asked.

"The best flight for you is in three hours. We have one in an hour, but you couldn't make that."

"I believe I can," I answered. I grabbed my bag. I wanted to get out of the Palmer House and Chicago as fast as I could.

"Where to?" the scruffy taxi driver mumbled as he reached over and pulled the taxi meter flag into an up position.

"O'Hare Airport," I answered cautiously.

I sank into the worn, plastic back seat, glad to be through. I didn't know whether to be relieved or what.

I noticed the cab driver kept glancing curiously back in the mirror as he adjusted his leather cap. "Are you one of those boys taking that big test? I've had several in my cab today."

"Yeah, how'd you know?"

He stared back into the mirror and after a moment of reflection, nodded slightly. "I believe you passed," he retorted.

Again, I despondently asked, "How can you tell? How can you possibly know?"

He turned his attention to his driving for a moment, then with a serious expression visible in his mirror said, "Because you look just like my son when he took his big test. He's a psychiatrist."

I rushed into the airport carrying my bag and worn textbooks, sailed by the ticket counter toward the passenger gate and headed home where they all loved me.

TRAPPED

Listen to your patient but think beyond.

"Listen to your patient, they will always tell you what is wrong," our professor, Dr. Willis Hurst taught. He was correct. What I failed to understand was that on occasion we must look beyond what the patient tells us.

"It's been hurting since that forklift hit me in the back," he said. His history was a common one of injury and failure to improve despite proper treatment. Before he came to our office, he had already seen several doctors, physical therapists, chiropractors and last but not least, his lawyer. (In what order, I was not sure.) All practitioners had given up and, ultimately, he was referred for orthopaedic care and further diagnostic studies.

His complaints were compatible with a midline disc protrusion or rupture. He was first admitted to the hospital for traction, strong medications and a myelogram. He still complained bitterly of unrelenting pain. He was not better at discharge. My associate and I could find no localizing signs to account for his severe complaints. The myelogram was questionable at best for a disc rupture or what was then termed instability of the spine.

Another independent consultation was obtained without significant suggestions or help. Nevertheless, his pain persisted, and he begged for some sort of surgery that might relieve his pain. I was taught one rarely operates just for pain relief.

Eventually, on the second hospitalization, my partner and I agreed to carry out "exploratory surgery" of the spine. We would examine and remove the disc if indicated and perform a spinal fusion to stabilize the spine in the hopes of obtaining pain relief.

With current diagnostic studies, including CAT Scans and MRIs that give more definite information than was then available, it is rarely considered appropriate to simply perform an "exploratory" procedure.

We explained the possible complications and hopeful results without promising him anything. We didn't know what else to do, since even the other independent consults resulted in no help except to agree on surgery. We operated with reluctance and removed the bulging disc and stabilized the spine with bone graft. It was a big operation.

Shortly after surgery, he began to have "delirium tremens," commonly called the D.T.'s. We learned that he was an alcoholic, though in his history, he had denied the use of alcohol. Since he was in the intensive post-surgical care section he was away from his source of alcohol. He had withdrawal symptoms. We learned that on his first admission, his family and the ward orderly had smuggled him a quart or more of vodka each day and he had hidden it in his bedside table. After nearly dying from withdrawal, the medical doctors supplemented his intravenous solutions with alcohol and mixed vitamin injections and weaned him off slowly. He was finally discharged. His wounds healed and he was followed in the office.

Months later, he confessed that his pain was never as severe as he had claimed and he had "begged for the operation" because his lawyer in his suit for injuries told him, "If you get surgery you will get a bigger money award." We wondered if this was true or not.

We felt damned foolish for having fallen for such subjective complaints. We felt trapped by our own ill-conceived sympathy. How dumb, we thought. We had been fooled into questionable surgery.

Unfortunately, for the patient, the lawyer lost the case and the patient received little or nothing financially because of the alleged fraudulent litigation and "false claim of injury" determined by the court.

The said lawyer was later disbarred on other charges.

DRIVING HOME

There has always been the contention that lawyers and bankers and doctors seem to act too rich for the average folks. It was in the late sixties and I was driving home from Hall County Hospital, listening to one of those radio call-in shows on WDUN.

The folks were mostly complaining about the cost of living, insurance and a couple expounded about those "rich doctors and lawyers who lived in those big houses and drove fancy cars."

"Yes, Ma'am," said the announcer as he recognized another caller.

She was furious and began to light into the last complaining caller. "Am I on the air," she asked?

"Yes, Ma'am," responded the announcer. "You sure are."

"Well, I want to correct that last caller," she blurted out. "I been living in Hall County all my life and I always got good care at the Hall County Hospital and all them doctors don't drive big cars and most of them cares a lot for their patients."

There was a pause, "Yes ma'am, I hear you," the radio guy responded.

"And besides that," the call-in lady continued, "I know for sure my doctor, Doctor Dixon, is a good doctor and he don't drive no big car. I seen him in his old green truck out by the emergency clinic going to work and know that's true, so I don't like hearing those bad stories on this radio program. Yes, we have good doctors and they mostly takes good care of us old folks."

"Thank you, ma'am. We appreciate you calling in." said the announcer, "and now we have another caller on the line, just on that same subject."

It seems that society is eager to criticize certain professionals until it comes down to their own lawyer or doctor. I've heard folks exclaim, "They can talk about all those crooked lawyers and rich doctors, but don't talk about mine."

WHEN MY DAUGHTER COMES OVER

It was the instruction sheet.

She was a pleasant middle-aged woman, slightly chubby, neatly dressed, with a delightful smile as she listened attentively to my instructions. She had a problem with her knee swelling. After reviewing her X-rays, we diagnosed mild degenerative arthritis and placed her on an anti-inflammatory drug and scheduled physical therapy.

"No surgery is necessary, at least not now," I said to her.

After several visits to the office, I saw little improvement. "How did physical therapy go?" I asked her. I reviewed the report and the therapist had mentioned that she thought this little lady was not doing her home exercise.

"Did the therapist give you written instructions for your home program?" I asked.

"Why yes," she answered and glanced toward the floor.

"Did you read those instructions?" I inquired.

She glanced across the room and quietly said, "I have to wait for my daughter."

There was a long pause and I suddenly realized this lovely lady, though in her fifties, could not read.

With tears welling in her eyes she slowly, whispered, "I have to wait 'til my daughter reads them to me."

"Yes, ma'am, how about me going over them with you now?"

She glanced up at me and said, "That would be fine."

When she left, she gave me a big hug, clutched her new instruction papers, and with a curious smile commented, "My friends laugh at me 'cause I can't read. But you don't." Thinking of her comment nearly broke my heart as I felt for her and her embarrassment.

AGITATED

The door squeaked open, then quickly closed.

From the hall, I noticed one of the examination room doors slowly squeak open, then quickly slam closed. After visiting another patient, I entered the room with the peeping door. Inside was a short husky guy with a scruffy beard. He wore worn, faded overalls. He twitched as he stood, turned and nervously sat on the exam table and moved his hands hesitantly in and out of his pockets.

Before I took his history, I noted his agitated demeanor. He nodded, and commented hesitantly, "It took you long enough." He then had a coughing spell, pulled out a wrinkled handkerchief and wiped his mouth and grizzly beard.

For a few moments I watched him without saying a word. "Sorry, I'm running behind. I had to help solve another patient's problem. Hope you understand."

He mumbled something inaudible. I flipped open his chart with his chief complaint and a bit of history, glanced up at him and quietly asked, "Are you upset about something?"

He glared at me, nodded and in a sour tone commented, "Nobody seems to be concerned about my troubles. I've been to other doctors and to the VA and they don't care. Darn, they just don't care."

Oh, that's it, I thought, *a frustrated veteran who thinks no one cares.*

"Were you in Vietnam?" I inquired.

The war had recently ceased. Many GIs had suffered after long traumatic experiences in combat to return home with Americans yelling at them, "Baby killers," waving anti-war signs, and spitting on them at airport terminals. I was told that on arrival the men had to exit the Atlanta terminal by a side door, out of public view to avoid the hostile crowds. Many repressed problems were now noticeable among the returned veterans.

"Damn right," he answered, then asked angrily, "Were you in the service?"

"Yep," I answered cautiously.

"In Nam?" he inquired.

"Yes, but only once for a short time," I responded. "I bet it wasn't as long as you. We just hauled in stuff, not long on the ground." I knew that my service had not compared to his.

The comment, however, seemed to soothe his anger and he relaxed. I guessed he thought he had found someone who might understand him. "I'm sure you went through much more than me and most of us," I added.

He nodded and relaxed and breathed what seemed like a sigh of relief.

After a short silence he commented, "Maybe you can listen to me."

"Yes, that's why I'm here," I responded. "I'm listening." Perhaps this was my first encounter with PTSD – Post traumatic stress disorder.

A FAMILY AFFAIR

"The best rewards…"

Most of the best rewards in a medical or surgical practice are not at all financial; they come from treating multiple family members successfully. There was a family in North Georgia of considerable renown because of the sports ability of one of its youngest members. I became acquainted with this young man when I treated him for a leg injury while he was in high school. It was not miracle management, but usual and customary treatment. Fortunately, he did well and went on to a successful national professional career.

Some years later, his grandfather appeared in my office with his wife. The grandfather was a husky, pleasant old guy. He was a prosperous, upstanding North Georgia farmer, an outdoorsman. His problem was a developing arthritic and painful hip. I treated him conservatively without surgery, with only anti-inflammatory medications and advised him that he might require a total hip replacement in the future. He was adamantly resistant to any surgery and I agreed.

Not more than a year or so later this elderly gent was brought into the emergency room by ambulance. He had been out in the woods on his farm cutting trees with his chain saw. One of the trees fell on him and knocked him to the ground.

"Sir, you've broken your hip and your opposite leg," I told him. I showed him the X-rays, adding, "That's the bad news."

"What's the good news?" he asked.

"The good news is that you broke the already painful and arthritic hip."

"Is that so?" he groaned. "What are we going to do about it?"

"Well, the good news is we can fix it. We'll do that total hip replacement we talked about last year. We'll put a plate on the broken tibia on the other side too."

"Well, Darn!" the old fellow said. "Am I in bad shape?"

He looked over at his wife by his bedside. She volunteered, "I've told him to stay out of the woods with that chain saw."

"Well, honey, you know I love to work in the woods. This isn't gonna stop me."

"Maybe if the doctor tells you to stay out of the woods, you might." She looked over at me, listening quietly.

"Ma'am, you know boys do like the woods," I answered.

We operated after all the blood work, cardiac and medical work-up showed him to be in unusually good health for a man of 80 years. We performed a total hip replacement with a metal ball and plastic cup and additional surgery with a metal plate on his opposite tibia. He did well.

Six months later, I received a telephone call. "Doc, he's out in the woods with his chain saw again," his wife said. "Can you help me stop him?"

"Ma'am, you've been married to him sixty years and I've known him about three years. I think we've got a lost cause. If he's happy, let him go and if another tree falls on him, just call me," I responded.

"Lord, you're not much help!"

"No, ma'am," I said, "not much."

A year later their daughter, now our family friend, called on the phone, "It's mama this time. Yep, broke her hip and she says to call you."

I met them in the ER and after a medical consultation took her to the OR. She had a femoral neck hip fracture and we inserted a simple metal hip prosthesis to replace the fractured bone. She did well after surgery.

Months later, while visiting her other daughter in Atlanta she had a fall, broke her other hip, and was taken to a north Atlanta hospital. When the surgeon admitted her, he said to her, quote her daughter, "You are so lucky to have gotten to me."

According to the daughter, he was abrasive and arrogant. He performed a hip prosthesis operation, replacing her fractured hip (a standard procedure). After surgery she wasn't able to walk without pain and complained of shortening of her involved leg.

Her daughter brought her to our office. "I thought he knew what he was doing. He said he trained in New York and was better than anybody in North Georgia," she volunteered. "I've not had a day without pain."

We X-rayed her and realized that the shaft of the prosthesis had collapsed, shortened, and probably rotated, and was painfully loose. I couldn't believe the former doctor's conversation with this sweet lady.

I tried to make excuses for the Atlanta doctor but felt that he had perhaps cracked the base of the neck in the femoral shaft while inserting the prosthesis and had failed to realize his mistake. I thought he should have at least cemented or wired the neck of the femur to shore up the femoral shaft.

I "revised" the prior operation with a longer stem prosthesis and bone cement. This procedure relieved the shortening, the rotation, and most of the pain.

She was satisfied and wanted to sue the Atlanta doctor. I explained that it was a technical error and probably could have happened to any surgeon and probably, she couldn't sue him for having such a big mouth.

I did not however, miss the opportunity of dictating a letter to him about her management and mentioning how "lucky she had been to have him as her earlier doctor instead of those other North Georgia doctors." He never responded. At future Atlanta Surgical Society medical meetings, he avoided me.

She did reasonably well after her revision.

"EVERYONE HAS A BAD DAY"

"I still felt bad."

Every operation is not a success, no matter how much we hope for wonderful and miraculous results. Every surgeon's feet are made of clay. Do not trust those who pretend they are not. Life gives no particular benefits to surgeons, though many of them (we're all guilty on occasion) think they live on a different plane from the rest of the world. Most surgeons have strong egos, but as my dad once said, "Don't stumble over your own ego, son."

This ego business cannot be more exemplified than in a surgical practice where all the elements of success may act against the individuals involved. Take, for example, a case I was involved in during my early surgical practice as a young practitioner of the "noble art of medicine and surgery."

A young, white, male truck driver came into my office with a history of injury to his back some months before in an industrial accident. His complaints were consistent with a severe back sprain or possibly a ruptured disc.

I listened to his history, examined him, ordered and reviewed lumbar sacral routine X-rays. I told him that I could not see a ruptured disc on routine films as the disc is really translucent to X-rays.

There was no obvious fracture of the spine or of any of its components, yet I was worried about a small to moderate separation at the "pars" portion of the spine, an area, which may have a developmental bone deficit. In this case possibly a congenital failure of growth, easily injured.

We elected conservative treatment: no work involving heavy lifting or truck driving, a physical therapy program and appropriate analgesics and anti- inflammatory medications.

We continued conservative treatment for a couple of months. We performed additional myelogram studies, which suggested a mildly protruding disc along with the "unstable pars [bony] defect."

Our patient was doing everything he could do to get better, but his home and financial situations were deteriorating since he had to live on Workman's Compensation alone. He and his wife were counseled by their church pastor for marital problems. In other words, his life was a mess.

We discussed the likelihood of surgery, but he wanted to wait, and I agreed on a conservative approach until all avenues of reasonable care were exhausted. I explained that a disc operation and spinal fusion were not to be taken lightly.

Surgery was finally elected. I explained the surgery would require exploration of the spine, nerves and a fusion, requiring a bone graft from his pelvic bone. It was a big operation and not without possible complications. He understood and wanted the operation and a chance to recover, if possible. I could give him no absolute promises.

His wife was still seeing the preacher for support. But he no longer participated in these pastoral visits.

Surgery was performed early one morning without any obvious complications. He lost a moderate amount of blood but did not require any transfusions. I removed the partly ruptured lumbar disc and fused the lower spine. I used his pelvis (iliac) bone as the donor bone graft. At the end of the operation, the OR nurse reported the sponge and instrument count as "correct," i.e. no missing sponges, and no missing instruments. The anesthesiologist reported satisfactory response to the anesthesia. All seemed to go well. After a few days post-op, he was discharged.

On his first office visit he had a little redness about the surgical bone donor graft site. I opened the wound slightly and put in a small rubber drain tube to drain any infection that might be present. He informed me that his wife had "run off with the preacher," the one that had counseled them for their marriage problems.

"Damn," I said. "How did that happen?"

"She just ran off with him," he answered, as he shrugged his shoulders.

I felt sorry for him. How much more trouble could this guy have, I wondered! He was such a good fellow. He didn't deserve this.

When he returned for follow-up he was in better spirits. "I'm getting use to bad news," he said. "They're about to foreclose on my house. My workman's insurance checks are behind. They're trying to cut me off."

"That is not fair. I'll get my secretary, or I'll clear this up with the insurance company and compensation board. We'll call for you," I said. His wounds looked good. We had pulled his drains from the donor wound site on the last visit. "We need to get an X-ray today to check the spinal fusion site," I told him. When the films came out of the developer, I flipped them up on the view box to show him. "Oh, damn," I said as I saw a thin line (radio opaque) object at the donor site.

"What's the matter," he asked?

"I think we've left something inside the donor surgical site, maybe part of the drain or even a sponge." I choked as I told him. "Damn, I feel embarrassed. We'll have to get it out." I apologized. I couldn't believe there was a "retained object" left inside the wound. I looked at the chart. Yes, the head nurse reported the sponge count as "correct," no less. "Damn," I repeated.

"I'm not having any pain; it's not bothering me. Leave it in," he said. "Leave it in."

"No, we need to remove it. It might cause trouble later," I told him.

He looked at the films, "Hell, Doc, everybody has a bad day sometimes, so let's just take it out, then. Don't feel bad," he said.

I called the hospital and the Operating Room and scheduled the removal of the foreign object. He received a letter from the hospital explaining the error and that the "foreign object" would be removed at no cost to him or his insurance carrier. We took him back to the OR and gave him a light anesthesia, cleaned the wound, made a tiny incision and with a large stainless-steel hemostat pulled out a long radio opaque marked surgical sponge. I held it up to the anesthesiologist and the OR staff.

"How did this get left inside with a correct count?" I asked. No one knew. They all shook their heads.

My patient, now my friend, ultimately did well after his surgery and returned to work. He had every right to sue us, yet he was willing to say, "Hell, Doc, everybody has a bad day sometimes. Don't feel bad."

I still felt bad.

Postscript:

Two years later the statute of limitations elapsed. The nurse supervisor called me into her office. I learned from the operating room supervisor what had really happened. The anesthesiologist had thrown a "non-surgical sponge" he had used to clean the patient's breathing tubes (one not marked for the X-ray to read) into the wrong operating room count sponge bucket, instead of his own receptacle or trash bucket, by mistake. They are never mixed in the operating room. The Head nurse had replaced the original circulating nurse in the OR. She counted the non-surgical sponge with the rest of the marked sponges; thus, we received the report of a "correct count."

If the non-surgical sponge had not been in the count bucket, the count would have been incorrect and would have led to the discovery of the error. The missing surgical sponge would have been located in the wound and the problem immediately corrected. Then again, "Everybody has a bad day!"

FRACTURE AND SURGERY

The patient was far smarter than the doc…

He was a husky African American sitting in the exam room with a swollen right arm. He was patched up and referred from another doctor. With his uninjured hand he held out a large manila envelope with X-rays inside.

"The X-rays show bad fractures of both bones," I said to him. "What happened?"

"I'm a steel worker. A big metal rod fell across my arm."

I gazed at the films he had brought from his referring doctor, "Gee, this fracture will require surgery because it's so bad."

"What do you mean, Doc?"

I explained that in his line of work he would need a strong healed arm if he were to continue his heavy job. "We could try to fix it without surgery but I'm afraid that with the displaced pieces of bone, it may not heal right."

He looked dismayed, "How much work will I miss?"

"About eight weeks before full duty, maybe more," I answered. I further explained the surgery. "We'll operate on the fractures and will put metal plates and screws on the bones. If that doesn't heal then we'll have to go back and re-operate and take some bone chips from your pelvic bone to add a bone graft."

He frowned and thought about what I had said. Without a moment of hesitation, he glanced at me with a serious smile, "Why don't we do the second operation first, Doc?"

Damn, I thought, *this guy is far smarter and more practical than me.* It was good to have a thinker for a patient.

This good man contributed to my Principles of Surgery, "Always do the second operation first."

TREATMENT IN A SPICA

In the emergency room I found the typical motorcycle victim. "He's in bay four. Dr. Nicholson sent him down from Hiawassee," the ER nurse yelled out as I entered through the double doors from the emergency entrance. I pulled the curtains back in bay four and observed an ambulance attendant still standing beside the stretcher, holding a bottle of IV fluid. "They have already drawn blood on this man," he whispered. Then he left to join his ambulance partner for his next call.

The ER nurse followed behind me and we began to evaluate the patient's injuries. He was awake and fairly alert, writhing in pain despite the injection for pain the ER doctor had ordered. "I never saw him, he hit me in the middle of the intersection," moaned the victim. "Oh, my leg hurts," he cried out.

Yep, the usual "chief complaint" that we heard over and over from the motorcycle victims. To make a story short, he had a bleeding compound fracture of his left thigh and after chest X-rays, we determined several rib fractures and an early left pneumothorax. After a further cursory exam, I said, "Get the OR on the line and tell them what we've got and get me the chest tube stuff and we'll go ahead and put in a chest tube here. Oh, yeah, check the Blood Bank to see if his blood is ready and we'll head to the OR."

After inserting the chest tube and after checking the portable chest X-rays, we rolled the guy to the OR. There we cleaned and debrided his femoral wound, inserted traction pins through the femur, and strung him up in overhead skeletal traction, rolled him to the recovery room and later to the ward where he would remain in traction for several weeks. Since the wound had been so dirty, we elected not to do an open fixation, but to continue to treat the wound with antibiotics, and traction, maintaining the alignment of the fractured femur. A few weeks later the soft tissue wound healed adequately and the bone remained in satisfactory alignment to place him in a long leg plaster of Paris body spica cast. He could now be handled at home with out-patient follow-up.

We planned to send him home by ambulance, but I was told the family had no money to afford an ambulance. I wondered about their plans, so I followed them out the hospital exit and there his two husky, scruffy brothers lifted him into the back of their dusty Ford pickup on to an old cotton mattress. *Wow,* I thought, *some transportation!*

Four hours later I was called back to the emergency room. "Your man in the spica cast is back," the nurse said.

"What do you mean?" I mumbled.

"He's back," she said. "His brothers must have gotten drunk after they picked him up and they ran off a mountain road and he was thrown out of the truck."

I could only imagine a disaster. When I arrived in the ER, he was laughing at being back in the ER. His brothers had stopped by a local joint before they took him home and had brought several six-packs and some moonshine out to the truck where they celebrated his home coming. He like his brothers reeked of alcohol.

"Damn," I mumbled to the ER nurse, "the cast is banged up, but he is just fine, saved by the cast."

His brothers checked out okay, only bruises and scrapes. They were discharged to the county sheriff's care and our victim was readmitted for observation. *Damn good cast,* I thought to myself.

CREUTZFELD - JAKOB DISEASE

"What's that?"

"Dr. Neal is on the phone about a patient in the ER," said my nurse.

"Okay, I'll take it in my office."

"You there?" came a stout voice over the phone.

"Yeah, I'm here."

"Thought I was talking to your nurse," said the voice on the other end of the line. "I don't think she got the message I was trying to tell her."

"What was the message?" I asked.

"Ever heard of Creutzfeld-Jakob Disease?"

"Hell, what's that?"

"It's a degenerative brain disease, you dumb ass. Then again, orthopods can barely read," laughed Neal over the phone.

"Yep, never heard of it. Thought it might be some rock band."

"Well, I've got a patient in the ER with a broken hip and he's got that disease. Don't know much about it, but my associates tell me it's contagious. It is slow in presenting and is a fatal brain and nerve disorder."

"So, what's that got to do with the broken hip?"

"Well, I guess you'll have to be very careful operating on this fellow, because we don't know how infectious it really is. But my partner says it is infectious and if you cut yourself in the OR you might get it. It may have a long incubation period. I just don't know."

"Damn, you've got the best patients for me. As usual."

"The guy's on Medicaid and I thought you might take him, talked to another orthopod and he said call you."

"Yeah, that jerk tries to avoid anyone who's on Medicaid or can't pay."

"Well, I've got this fellow in the ER and his wife is with him. She's done a hell of a job taking care of this poor guy."

"Tell the ER I'm coming and tell the nurses to wear double gloves and be careful handling any blood or body fluids."

He was a frail white male, lying on the ER stretcher. His speech was slurred, and he exhibited a slight tremor as he reached his hand out to me. He tried to thank me for coming but couldn't get the words right. His wife hovered over him stroking his sweaty forehead and hair. She was his caretaker and seemed devoted and without fear of his disease. His left leg was rotated outward, suggesting a complete fracture, a broken femoral neck or shaft fracture with the femoral shaft turned away from the hip socket.

X-rays confirmed a femoral neck fracture that would require a metal hip prosthetic replacement. I was pleased knowing this fracture would involve less blood loss and would not require as much dissection and muscle involvement as a comminuted (shattered) shaft fracture. Those could be bloody.

The problem was getting a volunteer nurse to help me. I didn't feel right asking for help from someone who might fear the possibility of contamination and the likelihood of being exposed to any contagious blood or tissue.

"I'll help you," a young nurse volunteered. Her husband was a Baptist preacher and she felt it was her Christian duty to help in this case.

"Ms. Strickland, you sure you want to help on this case?" I asked.

"If you're willing to do this operation, I shall be pleased to help."

How brave, I thought and again asked, "You sure?"

"Yes, I'm sure my husband will want me to help."

I don't know enough about this condition to know what precautions are necessary, I pondered. "Call the OR and tell them we need absolute sterile conditions with the minimal help, only one other nurse to go in and out of the room," I muttered. "I'll pick out the fewest required and oldest instruments and we'll throw them away after the procedure. I don't know what methods are required to sterilize these instruments." I called Emory and asked if anyone knew. They had few suggestions except that we should increase our precautions and let them know how the surgery progressed. They were little help.

Wearing double gloves, we prepped the patient's skin with iodine solution, followed by an alcohol wash, draped the hip and leg carefully. "Don't hand me any sharp instruments and I won't hand you any. Fix the needles but put them on the edge of the Mayo stand and I'll pick up the needle holders. We must have no breaks in sterile technique and no cuts or needle punctures, since I still don't know the ramifications and dangers of this procedure with this disease," I firmly advised my nurse assistant.

(This incident preceded the scare about the possible contamination from operating on future AIDS patients. We were so uninformed about these diseases. Ignorance about a disease can be frightening.)

We carefully performed the operation, cutting through skin, dissecting and separating the hip muscles, removing the femoral head from the acetabulum (socket) and inserting the steel hip prosthesis. "Not much blood loss and thank goodness no breaks in technique," I said to the young nurse, grateful for her bravery in assisting.

After the procedure, we collected the drapes, old instruments, suction tubes and bottles, our gowns, and any other possibly contaminated objects involved and sent them down for incineration. The room was sprayed and closed for twenty-four hours. We were taking no chances. We had selected the fewest required instruments, kept the room sealed, probably more precautions than necessary, but we didn't know any better.

"I'm sure you'll get a good mark in heaven for daring to help on this case," I told the sweet nurse.

"Well, how about you, doctor?" she asked.

"Hey, this is my job," I answered. "It's what I do." Secretly, I was still scared.

The patient did well. His wife took him home. Two years later he reappeared in the emergency room. "Your fellow with that bad disease is back. He broke his other hip," said the ER nurse over the phone. Again, we fixed his broken hip.

Two years later, I learned that he had died with his wife at his bedside.

Note: Creutzfeld-Jakob Disease is a rare, degenerative, invariably fatal brain disorder. It affects about one person in every one million people per year in the United States. This disease belongs to a family of human diseases known as the transmittable spongiform (appearance of the brain) encephalopathies. It occurs in those with no known risk, those with a family history, and exposure to brain or nerve tissue. This disease, when found in cows, is called, "mad cow disease." Reference: National Institute of Neurological Disorder

"WELL, HE COULD DIE."

It was a dumb thing.

It was a dumb thing trying out a horse for my daughter. My friend, Dr. Bob Jennings had a horse for sale. His daughter was going off to college and had outgrown her enthusiasm for riding. Anyway, he had a very nice mare for sale that was gaited and I was in the market for a horse.

I met him at a neighborhood stable where several locals boarded their horses. The horse was a gray dapple, with a black flowing mane, about fourteen hands high and might be just the one for my daughter.

I mounted her and after several turns in the inside ring, I had trouble with the left stirrup which seemed too long. Apparently, I leaned to the left to adjust it as the horse shied or made a sudden lunge and off I went onto the dirt, landing literally on my head with a sudden excruciating pain and numbness in my neck and right shoulder.

I dusted myself off, climbed back upon the animal and completed my assessment of the horse. "I'll talk to my daughter and let you know about our decision," I told my friend.

For days into weeks, I suffered pain in my neck and shoulder until I could hardly sleep at night and mild medicine did not relieve the pain. I was hesitant to take stronger medications as I was aware of some doctors that had treated themselves with tragic results of addiction or other complications from strong narcotics. I ventured to our hospital X-ray department and ordered a series of cervical films. I reviewed them with our radiologist. "Oh," he mumbled, "looks like something going on at C-5 and C-6 level but I'm not sure what."

For several more weeks I suffered and finally elected to take my films to Emory, where I had trained, for a definitive consultation. I pulled the films out of the folder and placed them on the view box in my friend and former professor's office. The two of us stared at the films. "Yep, something is going on, but it doesn't look like a fracture, just some blurring and maybe some bone erosion or replacement at the level of C-5 and C-6," he said.

We didn't have MRIs then, but Grady had an early, perhaps the first, C-Scan machine in Atlanta. "Let's get a scan," Tom suggested, "and we'll look at it together."

It was an experience to sit in the Grady waiting room with the rest of the Grady population as just another patient. I watched the slow movement of the technicians as they puttered about, obviously tired with too many folks to see. They seemed overwhelmed. I tried to remember what the old days were like in the department. I watched, not as a physician but as an ordinary Grady patient. I felt the

421

loneliness that patients must experience, wondering if the technicians, doctors and nurses really cared about me. Did they feel what I and my fellow patients felt?

Was I just one of the unidentified objects or one of the statistics calculated in the day's work? I wanted to see what it felt like to be among the crowd, just another number.

Back in Tom's office I said, "This is really hurting. I can't sleep at night and I worry if it is making me slow at work. It's hard to do my surgeries."

He pulled the C-scan films from the folder and remarked, "I'm still not sure what this is but I'll keep the films. My friend Dick Rothman is coming down from Philadelphia next week for a conference and I'll have him look at these." He slipped the films back into the folder and laid the folder among a pile of other films on his desk.

"You come back, and we'll get him to look at you, too. You know he's head of Orthopaedics at Penn."

I knew him by name. He had recently published the latest text on bone pathology and was well known in academic circles. He was a national specialist on bone tumor pathology.

The following week, I sat in a conference as my old professor and Rothman placed the X-rays up for review. Dr. Rothman, a lean fellow, younger than I had envisioned him, carefully viewed the films and worriedly said, "I think this patient has a chondrosarcoma or at least a similar lesion. Look, it seems to be eroding or seriously replacing C-5 and C-6."

I was sitting in the corner, not even noticed by the visiting professor. I couldn't believe this conversation and I blurted out, "Hey, those are my films and I don't think that's right." I had not been introduced as the patient, but simply as another surgeon to the visiting doctor.

To make a long story short, my wife and I had a consultation with the doctor a few days later. I wanted her to hear the whole story and the proposed exploratory surgery. (With all the updated technical studies now available, the term "exploratory surgery" is now rarely used.) I wanted her to share in the decisions.

My old professor dismissively told her what he thought should be done and explained the possible surgery. "Well," she inquired, "what might be the worst complication if this is done?"

He glanced at her and responded, "Well, he could die."

She was quiet, but I knew by her expression, she was not pleased. We were all friends, yet she was truly disturbed. I couldn't help but laugh and tried to assure her that he meant no harm. He was actually a serious and considerate guy.

"Oh my, that's just his way," I remarked. "His bedside manner is plain, objective, and not subtle, and by damn, he's the best spine surgeon I know."

After convincing her, that when in the operating room we were not there for chatty conversation, but to get my neck fixed. To get me better, to relieve the pain and allow me to work comfortably – we elected to have the surgery.

I did, however, call my good friend, John Whitehurst, a head and neck cancer surgeon, to assist in case Whitesides and Rothman were correct in the possible cancer diagnosis. John had recently left the Emory Clinic and gone out into private practice but was agreeable to coming to Emory to assist with the planned surgery.

Fortunately, the surgery went well. They explored my cervical spine through a right anterior neck incision, identified a benign neurolemoma tumor, extending from inside the spinal canal. It had apparently been damaged by the fall from the horse. My surgeons removed it and resected the neuroforamen (nerve window) relieving the nerve pressure. After surgery, John Whitehurst and Tom Whitesides assured my wife, "All is well. No bad cancer found."

My symptoms gradually abated. I was able to return to full work within a few weeks with some weakness in my right triceps muscle and a vague discomfort persisting in my arm and hand. I adapted to these changes and moved on.

My professor later wrote and published an article in a national surgery journal about the rare Neurolemoma spinal tumor syndrome.

I did not buy the horse I had "tried out" for my daughter.

SIBLINGS

"No, not possible…"

When I was in my mid-fifties my wife, Barbara and I planned a trip to Europe, but I realized that my passport had expired, and I would have to get it renewed. No problem, I thought, so I called and was told I would have to have a certified copy of my birth certificate to get a new passport. Again, I thought, no problem.

I had a printed "official birth" certificate required when I went on active military duty and I had a Social Security number, but I couldn't find the paperwork for the birth certificate. It was necessary to go to the Fulton County registrar across from Grady Hospital to get the copy of my birth certificate for the passport office.

At the department of records, the young lady handed me a certified copy. I folded it into an envelope and when I got home, I read it. It was strange information and I read it to my wife, "What does this 'foster' mother and 'foster' father mean?" I asked.

She looked the piece of paper over, frowned and calmly commented, "These were not your real parents."

"What can that mean?" I was astounded and confused. "Not possible," I muttered, "No, not possible."

A few days later, I called around and asked all my living relatives about the certificate. They were all mum. "Don't know anything about that," they all said. I remained persistent until Aunt Elizabeth, Dorothy's sister, finally confessed that the birth certificate was true and that I had been adopted as an infant. "Your mother told us before she died if we ever told, she would come back and haunt us," she said, "so we've never told you."

Eventually, they all confessed that they knew and that they thought it was better never to bring up the subject. They did confide that my mom had told them, "If he ever finds out, tell him that his natural mother was a nurse and his natural father was an Atlanta doctor, a surgeon."

How theatrical, I thought. And then I turned to my childhood friend Helen who confirmed the fact that her mother and my "foster" mother were dear friends and that each had adopted a child. Helen had been adopted by Margaret and her husband. Dorothy and Harvey had adopted me at about the same time. We both grew up playing together, not knowing we were adopted.

Through Helen's suggestion, I spoke to a lady at the Fulton County Courthouse who had helped her. There I obtained true copies of all the adoption papers. By further inquiries, after an appointment with a Fulton County judge, I got a copy of my original birth certificate. It gave me the true name of my birth mother. To my surprise the certificate described her as a graduate nurse, so the earlier tale was true. She had been a nurse.

Months later we traveled through South Carolina. We stopped in Greenwood, the home of my natural mother according to the birth certificate, and I carefully searched the telephone book for the "Lumley" name. Several were listed, one being a company. I drove by the company site and went inside the building and asked for Mr. Lumley. "He doesn't come in much anymore. His sons, young Harold and Tom, now run the business and they are not here today," the employee said.

We went back to our hotel and I nervously dialed the residence number. The housekeeper answered the phone, "Oh no, Mr. Lumley is lying down, but his wife is here."

I was concerned about talking to his wife, so I said I'd call back, and before I finished, the housekeeper said, "Oh my, Mr. Lumley, he's here now."

A strong, but elderly voice answered and identified himself. Now what was I to say? How was I going to approach this conversation? I made up a story. "My mother had an old friend in Greenwood many years ago and she said for me to call her friend if I was ever in the town."

"Oh, yes," he said, "Kathryn was my younger sister, but she passed away years ago."

For a moment I didn't know what to say. After a couple of innocuous comments, I asked, "Did Kathryn have any children?"

"Yes, she did, two daughters." He proceeded to tell me about them. When I inquired further, he called his wife, "Honey can you get the address book and give me Peggy and Dorothy's numbers?"

He described them and told me that Peggy lived in Atlanta. I was stunned and delighted to know that I had half-sisters, one in the Atlanta area. I thanked him without disclosing the true purpose of my call. I had no idea whether he ever knew of my existence or not and I certainly did not want to spring such a surprise on an elderly fellow.

For several months, I delayed following up on the call. But when my birthday arrived, I decided I must make contact with my sister. I sat down and sipped a glass of wine – maybe two – before I built up the courage to call, then I hesitantly dialed the number I had been given. *What shall I say and what will she think?* Would she think I was some imposter and that I was a fraud, looking to dupe someone? Would – or how could – they believe me, I wondered.

A woman answered the phone with a soft, "Hello?" I nearly hung up but waited a few seconds until she again said, "Hello?"

I cautiously introduced myself by my adopted name, described that I was a doctor and was trying to contact Peggy. She was silent. I wondered if she would be agreeable to talking to a complete stranger. Perhaps she would think this was some kind of prank call.

I explained that it was not an emergency. I was inquiring because there might be a possibility of a family relationship and that Mr. Lumley had given me her name. I felt that perhaps after I mentioned the old gentleman, she might think that this was a legitimate call. After some bland conversation, I hardly remember what we said, I interjected, "It is my understanding that we might be related."

There was a definite pause. Dead silence followed.

"Are you sitting down?" I asked, then paused again, "It is possible that you are my sister." The silence seemed interminable.

"How can that be?" she responded.

I cautiously said, "We may have the same parent."

"The same parent?"

"Yes. Kathryn Lumley," I softly responded, "the same mother."

We talked for a while about how I had discovered my birth mother and she said, "Well, my father left us and I first thought that maybe you could be his child, but it didn't occur to me that you would be my mother's child."

She explained that she and her sister and their mother had been abandoned when she was quite young. They had lost contact with their natural father. "I used to get birthday cards and gifts from his mother, my grandmother, but that stopped long ago."

"When we were a little older my mother married a dentist, whose wife had died many years before and we moved into his house. My mother had worked with him at the military hospital."

Our conversation ended pleasantly, and she said. "I must call my sister and let her know." We agreed to meet for dinner at a future date; thus, began a relationship with younger siblings that I had never dreamed existed.

A few weeks later we met at Peggy's home in Atlanta. I laid out the certified copies of the adoption papers on a table and she and her sister shuffled through the papers until they came to the end.

Both stared for a moment at the typed name and the signature. "Yes, that's our mom's signature," Peggy said quietly, running her finger over the signature. Dorothy nodded and glanced over at me, perhaps now convinced.

THE RIGHTEOUS MAN

"Somewhere in ancient history…"

Somewhere in ancient history is the tale of the old man searching the countryside, a lantern in hand, for a righteous man. During my thirties, I found that man but didn't realize it until he was gone.

In the early 1970s I built a house with a yard that was far too large for me to manage alone so I employed a man near our neighborhood to help me. Some would call him a gardener or yard man, but I came to know him as my true friend.

Ollis Williams was black, though his skin was not like most of the other black people I knew. He had a grayish tint to his skin and blue gray eyes. He was small in stature, lean and wiry, but big in heart. I hired him because our housekeeper was his friend. Ruby Nell said he was the most reliable Christian man she knew. I took her word and asked him if he would help me keep up the yard that I was trying to develop. "Yes, I will," he said.

"Great," I said and thanked him for taking on that responsibility.

Ollis was an expert. He knew more about plants than I would ever know and all the secrets that make plants and flowers and grass grow. It was not that I was lazy, maybe a little, but I had so few hours at home that I simply couldn't handle all the responsibilities of a big yard.

Little did I know when I contracted with this good man that I was getting a friend and someone with whom to share my innermost feelings. Many weekends we worked together in the yard, on our knees, digging and planting and when the time came, trimming in a professional manner. Ollis knew all the shrubs and trees and just what tender care each needed. I knew laboratory botany, for I had studied botany, but Ollis knew the living plants.

My lagniappe as we called it in Louisiana, was Ollis' friendship with my children. Many days my young children wandered around the yard, following him. He never minded. He would stop his work and sit and talk with them without complaint. He became their confidant. When they had problems, they would talk them over with him. My middle child, Allyson, would take her dog and escape to the treehouse that Ollis and I had built for them. There, Ollis would confront this child about her distress. She would sit and pout in her playhouse as he consoled her. He listened patiently. Soon her difficulties would be resolved. Perhaps he gave her some secret advice. After some time, she and her little dog would saunter back into the house.

Occasionally, I returned home from the hospital and found Ollis and my young son both gone and yard tools lying piled up in the yard. "Where are Ollis and Little Jerry?" I asked.

"Oh, Daddy, they've gone fishing," Laura, my oldest, would answer. We lived next to Lake Lanier in North Georgia.

Out of the wooded area, I would see two tired fishermen coming home with one or two little fishes. They were like Mark Twain's Huck Finn and Jim. Ollis taught my son all about lures, hooks and secrets for catching fish. Regrettably, I always had a hard time being patient or sitting still long enough to catch fish. Ollis, by his mere presence, instilled patience in my son that I could not. He was the surrogate father on this point.

I drove Ollis and Jerry down the highway to the Old Bait Shop and there Ollis instructed us which bait or lures to buy. Jerry would dig out his change and unroll his crumpled dollar or two, that he kept tightly rolled in his little pocket, and hand his allowance money to the storekeeper. With a bucket of bait and new lures or worms we would head back home for fishing time.

Ollis was a man's man. He graduated from high school at age seventeen and immediately volunteered and entered the United

States Navy during the Second World War. His ship was a cargo and ammunition carrier in the South Pacific. As a sailor, he served as the cabin steward to the ship's commander. His was the "best job on board," he claimed, "always with the Captain." He never mentioned much about the horrors of war. That was his modest style.

After the Second World War, he returned to a still segregated Georgia. During the forties, segregation remained an immutable fact of life in the South.

I wondered why he ever returned to North Georgia when the cities he had visited in the North and on the West Coast had so much more opportunity for a man like him. He had an education, was smart and had a winning personality. "It's home," he said softly.

He had many jobs and a good reputation in his work. He described to me his interesting racial background. His daddy was a white man-about-town, now deceased. Ollis often jokingly said that he had to go down to the "Purina feed store" where he visited with his "white cousins."

"What do you say to them?" I asked.

"Oh, I just call them 'cuzz' and we get along fine. We respect each other and talk about local stuff, politics and especially about the War, 'cause we've all been in it." He smiled broadly and we had a good laugh.

The only time I ever had a misunderstanding with Ollis, was when I returned home one evening and he had cut down what I must admit was a straggly old dogwood tree.

"Where is my dogwood?" I asked. He explained that he had orders from my wife and shook his head. I knew he loved dogwoods as much as I did. We didn't mention the dogwood again.

I was taught as a child that the wood from the dogwood tree was the wooden cross upon which Christ was crucified. The four white or pink petals of the blossoms represented Christ's out-stretched arms and the small red at the tip of each petal represented His blood. I was also told that the Lord caused the dogwood tree to be crooked so that it might never be used again to make a cross. Perhaps that's why I still love dogwoods.

430

Since Ollis was a Navy veteran he often went to the # 48 Veterans Hospital in Atlanta. He would present his symptoms to me, especially his joint aches and pains. I would examine him in the yard then we would go by the office and get X-rays. I would diagnose and describe his condition to him, but he would rarely go to our local hospital and preferred his veteran's hospital. "I'm covered at the VA," he said. I would call and talk to the VA doctors and send the X-rays with him when he made his appointments.

Some years later, I was out of town and returned home and learned that he had gone into the local hospital for some tests and while moving about his hospital room, had an unexpected heart attack or possible pulmonary embolus (blood clot to the lungs). He died suddenly, right there in his hospital room.

My friend was gone, and I didn't have a chance to say good-bye. I am grateful for his friendship and his memory. In Ollis, I found the "Righteous Man."

Note: The tale of the old man searching the countryside for the righteous man can be found in Diogenes the Cynic of Sinope, (412 BC – 323 BC) and Jeremiah 5: 1 – 4 (626 – 586 BC)

HER NAME WAS RUBY NELL

She had good advice and a strong honest personality.

We had not lived long in Gainesville when we built a new house. We elected to live in a neighborhood beside Lake Lanier. Our children were too young to be right on the water, so we selected a corner lot angled toward the lake. It was quite satisfactory.

Once we completed the house, with three children to manage, we needed some housekeeping assistance. Ruby Nell became a true member of our family as she helped care for our children. We in turn helped with her growing children.

Having Ruby Nell and Ollis was a double blessing. From her, my children learned integrity, and became stronger individuals by association. They could confide in Ruby Nell and Ollis about problems they might never divulge to us. She was honest and strong-willed and demanded respect from all. During times of domestic problems, she was a pillar to us – wise, determined and a real Christian in "thought and deed."

Occasionally, as in most families, interpersonal disagreements occurred resulted in her walking out or quitting, only to reappear a few days later as if nothing had happened. Usually we just smiled and went on with our normal home activities as most families do or should do.

She had a hard life as a single mom, but a good life. She raised intelligent and honorable children. At her funeral in 2014, my son and I drove to Gainesville. Together, with my cousin Bill Manus and his family, we heard the minister tell wonderful, deserved stories about her honesty, forthrightness, even to the point of often correcting the preacher. She "trucked no foolishness" and "didn't suffer fools."

She was a reader and a literal practitioner of the King James Bible. While attending my daughter's wedding in the Napa Valley, the weather turned cold and we suggested she wear slacks to warm her legs. She without hesitation announced, "In Isaiah it says, women shall not dress as men."* She quoted the chapter and verse and continued to dress "her way."

She was a wonderful person and we all still miss her.

Isaiah 3:16 and Deuteronomy 22: 5–12

TIGHT CHEST PAIN – AN EPIPHANY

"A moment of truth…"

Having a heart attack is not a hell of a lot of fun, but it is an education. On a hot late June afternoon, while working on my boat dock across the lake, my chest seemed to burst apart, and I began to have trouble breathing. *Well, damn!* I thought, I couldn't believe this was really happening to me. Yet I knew how I had warned so many patients, "If it's steady pain in your chest, not a sharp pain but a tight squeezing pain, beware: it's a heart attack. You can believe it!" There I was, miles away from the Emergency Room, with that tight squeezing feeling that felt like a tiger in my chest that wouldn't let go.

I knew I had to get to the hospital even though I had tried to rest, to count my pulse and to lie down. To lie down was to give up. To lie down was to die. *Damn*, I thought, *not here on my dock. I've got to get some help.* I knew I could not climb the steep hill to my lake cabin, so my wife Barbara drove our motorboat over the rough water, as I threw up over the side. We arrived at the shore, a couple of hundred feet from my house, climbed a small embankment to the house and called the ER at my hospital. "Who's on call for Dr. Stribling's and Jenning's cardiac group?" I asked.

"Dr. Neal," Miss Strickland, the nurse, replied, "and he's here in the ER."

"Let me talk to him," I asked.

"Come right in!" he said. "I'll wait for you here."

I hung up the phone. "I'm going to take a quick shower, then we'll go," I said to my wife.

"Oh no," she answered. "We're going now. Forget the shower."

My wife rushed me to the ER, and we parked in the ambulance lot closest to the ER. "You can't go in there," the thin, prickly ER receptionist yelled as we pushed through the ER swinging doors. "I need your insurance information."

"We think he's having a heart attack," my wife said to her.

I couldn't believe the hospital had hired such a dumb ninny. She chased after us waving her clipboard, her high heels clicking on the ER floor. "He may have a heart problem, but I need his insurance information first," she repeated.

Dr. Neal glared at me as I stumbled into the ER, short of breath and holding my chest. He reached out and grasped my wrist, attempting to count my pulse. "Get him in Room One," he ordered the nurse.

The nurse, Miss Strickland, looked at me. "He's sweaty and he looks gray, Dr. Neal," she said frantically.

"Hook up the EKG leads," Dr. Neal ordered. "Let's get the IVs going and give him some morphine now. Push a quarter grain. And give him some nitroglycerine."

"Yes, sir," the nurse responded as she laid me down on the stretcher, placed a blood pressure cuff on my arm while a second nurse started an IV in the other arm.

"It's hard to get a vein, his pressure is really low," the first nurse said to the other one as they unbuttoned my shirt and attached the sticky EKG leads to my chest. The machine began to buzz as the stylus needle rapidly moved and inked in the squiggly lines with the arrhythmic movement of the heart's muscle and electrical activity.

"Oh Hell," said Dr. Neal as he glanced at the strip of magic paper. It gave him the linear picture of an acute myocardial infarction and an irregular heart rate. "Get the heparin started, now," he blurted, "and get the TPA drawn up so we can bust his clot." (TPA stands for tissue plasminogen activator.)

Within a few minutes the morphine and the sublingual nitroglycerine had begun to relieve the dire chest pain.

"I'm better," I whispered to the nurse. It was so good to see Miss Strickland. She had once worked as a staff member in my office and later I had encouraged her to attend nursing school. She was the same nurse that years before had helped me with a

Creutzfeld-Jakob case. It was comforting to have friends caring for me on this tough adventure.

Once stabilized and relieved of the acute pain, and before sending me to the Intensive Care Unit, Dr. Neal appeared and opened the curtains to my ER cubicle. "What you need is a real doctor!" he chirped. I knew what my friend meant with that sly grin. He was the internist and to him I was merely a surgeon, someone who the internists had said, "Could barely read or write." I was a surgeon and this night I belonged to his crowd, the internists, "the real doctors."

EPIPHANY TO A SILVER LINING

"From a myocardial infarction to the Silver Valley..."

For five days, I remained in the Cardiac Intensive Care Unit. During that time, I had lots to think about. A myocardial infarction, or heart attack, is an avenue to an epiphany.

The first few days the medical staff scurried around me as if they thought I might be rolled out of the Unit under a heavy white sheet. It seemed like every few minutes someone was checking my blood pressure or sticking me and drawing blood. I was squeezed and stabbed constantly.

I had practiced surgery for over twenty-five years in a small North Georgia town and suddenly realized how delicate a life could be. *This can't happen to me,* I had thought. *Somebody else should be in this bed.* Well, I was wrong. I was in this bed and someone else held my life in their hands for the first time since I was an infant. It was apparent that I was no longer the Alpha dog.

There were younger guys out there trained just as well as me. At that point, I decided they could have it. Our town would still have good orthopaedic care. Sadly, I felt I would have to revise my whole life. House, property, and bank accounts seemed to have little value. I had not accumulated that much after sending three children to the best colleges I could afford and living the high life. All the accoutrements of success meant very little in the CICU. I thought, if they did roll me out under a crisp white sheet, it wouldn't be in a tuxedo, but in this tacky hospital gown, that didn't even cover my rear.

Thank goodness I'm a surgeon, I thought, or I might be frightened by the EKG monitor hanging up like a TV set in the corner of the room. *Damn, those squiggly lines represent my life.*

A heart catheterization by the young cardiologist, Dr. Ferguson, demonstrated an occlusion of the distal left main coronary artery. The vessel opened a bit after the heparin and "clot buster" dissolved the offending blood clot. "We can handle this heart problem medically," I was told. As a surgeon, I felt that more aggressive treatment was needed. A few days after release from the Hall County Hospital, I headed down to Emory University where I had trained, for a cardiac surgery consult.

I talked to my friend, Dr. Ellis Jones, who turned me over to his associate. "We need to do bypass surgery on you," Joe Craver said gruffly as he glanced at the heart catheter films.

"When?" I asked.

"Tomorrow," tall, husky Dr. Craver answered. "The guys that treated you did a whale of a good job. Just look at that left coronary. It's still nearly closed, and you may not be so lucky next time."

I reviewed the films with my son. "That left main coronary artery is still almost closed. That's the widow maker," I said to him.

"What are you going to do, Dad?" he asked.

"Doctor Craver is right. I'll stay. It is surgery tomorrow!"

Doctor Craver warned me, "You know this is the hospital July changeover with new interns and residents and I'll be off for a couple of days for the Fourth. I'll be up in North Georgia at my cabin, but I'll be in phone call distance if you need me."

"I would pick the scariest time of the medical year to have surgery," I muttered, "but I don't have much choice. It's now or never," and the odds seemed yet in favor of the definitive surgery.

EMORY HEART SURGERY

"The organ that keeps on giving. Maybe?"

The night before surgery, the hospital orderly came around and shaved me from the top of my chest to my ankles. Not a hair was left. "Now I know what a chicken feels like at the poultry plant," I said to him.

"Yes, sir, you do look kinda like a plucked chicken," he chuckled as he packed away his clippers and razors. He nodded and whispered, "Good luck tomorrow." In a moment he was gone.

Later in the evening, the young intern came by. He had just rotated to the chest service. I remembered the old doc at the Georgia Medical license table some thirty or so years past when he looked at my fresh medical diploma, at me, then at my pals, and commented to the old codgers nearby on the panel. "These boys just look younger and younger." He was right. "These boys just look younger and younger."

"We have two methods of stopping your heart at the surgery," the young intern explained. He paused. With great authority he continued, "In our series, when we stop the heart and you are on bypass, we either warm it with warm saline or cool it with cold saline, known as the chill method. Do you have a preference?"

I sat up, propped up on my elbows, and eyed him carefully. "Which does Dr. Craver prefer?" I inquired.

"I don't really know," he confessed. "I think he does both."

"Well, tell Dr. Craver to decide when he opens my chest to choose which- ever way he thinks is best at that moment. I trust his judgment," I said. *Another damn series,* I thought. Is medicine now simply a series of trials? "I'd rather not be in an arbitrary blind series," I added.

"Yes, sir, I'll do that. I'll tell him," he responded meekly. He looked over my chart, flipped his stethoscope from around his neck and quickly listened to my chest, moving the scope from the aortic area to the apex of the heart, and then he pulled the EKG paper strip from the chart, looked it over carefully, frowned and left. I wondered if he knew what the hell he was doing.

That night I had a lot to think about. An epiphany about mortality is a strong awakening. "Well," I said to my son, "I'm glad to be back at Emory. I'm among friends. And here, I'll get my heart fixed."

Emory University
Atlanta, Georgia, 1958 – 1959
(Photo by author)

In the CICU I had determined to change my lifestyle, end a difficult marriage, and start over if the Lord would let me.

A few weeks after surgery I returned to my office intending to gradually lessen my practice. A few months after the triple by-pass operation, I closed my surgery office and accepted a one-year contract in a non-surgical practice in Atlanta. It would be less strenuous work and allow me to completely recover.

A GENTLE VOICE FROM THE PAST

"Says she's an old friend?"

It was near the end of my Atlanta contract when the phone rang in my office on a day with too many patients to see. "I've got a person on the phone who says she would like to speak to you," announced my secretary.

Oh my, I thought, *I've more folks to see than I can possibly handle today.* "Get her name and I'll call her back at the end of office hours if it's not an emergency."

"She says she is an old friend," insisted my secretary.

"Yeah, I've got many old friends but why do they call me in the middle of office hours?" I impatiently said. "Okay, get her name and I'll get back to her."

My nurse interrupted me, "Doctor we'll never get through today, you know you are the only doctor in the office. We're way behind and the X-ray machine is slowing us down. It's barely working."

"Okay," I answered. "Just ask the lady's name."

"She says her name is Ellen. She's calling from Louisiana."

"Ellen who?"

My secretary told me her name and I stopped in my tracks. I had not heard that name or her voice in nearly forty years. The last time I heard her lovely voice was a winter night in Germany when I, not unlike the foggy night scene in the movie, Casablanca, in a flight suit strolled across the airfield through a dense fog and boarded a huge military plane and disappeared in that fog, headed back to the United States.

"Yes, I can answer that phone call right now," I whispered.

A Non-Surgical Practice

Practicing without surgery was no fun. I missed the operating room and I couldn't stand the way industrial medicine was practiced. In my opinion, it was a business run by entrepreneurs who only respected the bottom line. I felt they cared little for the physicians and staff and even less for the patients, but they seemed to love the insurance companies and the litigation lawyers.

Though I thoroughly enjoyed the physicians and office staff, I'd had enough of corporate medicine and didn't extend my one-year contract. The corporate executives were glad to see me out the door since I had such difficulty aligning myself with the insurance companies and litigating attorneys.

I was the patient's doctor. I couldn't change and that was that.

A JOURNEY TO REMEMBER

"Where's Idaho?"

In late fall, near the end of my office contract, while still working in the non-surgical practice, our secretary leaned through my office doorway, as was her custom, "There's a call for you, says he's from Montana."

"I don't know anyone in Montana," I answered. *Who would be calling from Montana* I wondered?

"Well, that's where he says he's from," she said. "It's from a hospital."

Hmmm, I thought, *maybe some patient referral or request for information on a prior patient.*

"Yes," I said into the phone without having any idea who might be on the other end of the line.

After giving me his name, in a strong voice he continued, "I'm a hospital administrator in Montana and we're looking for an orthopaedic surgeon to join another surgeon in our town." He named the town. We talked for a few minutes and he inquired if I might be interested.

I didn't hesitate for a moment, "Thanks for the offer, but I don't think so."

After a couple of minutes conversation, he asked, "Will it be okay if my brother, another hospital administrator, calls?"

"Sure, but I doubt if I'm interested," I said.

A week later my secretary announced, "We've got another call. It's from Idaho. Where's that? Is it near Iowa?"

"I don't know anyone in Idaho," I commented.

"My brother called you last week to see if you might move west to practice, so I'm calling to ask," the voice on the line said.

"In Idaho or Montana?" I asked.

"Oh, I'm in Idaho, not Montana," he replied.

We spoke for a few minutes and after telling him I was not interested, he said, "Hang on for just a moment. Let me turn you over to my secretary."

There was a click then a gentle voice said, "We have searched for someone to replace our surgeon who left to move back to Florida." She paused, "We've already gotten several recommendations about you, one from a neurosurgeon in nearby Coeur d'Alene. He used to practice in Atlanta and says he knows you well. We want you to simply come out here and visit us." Without hesitation she added, "We've already mailed you an airplane ticket on his recommendation to visit us next week, that's Thanksgiving weekend."

I couldn't believe this conversation. *How do they even know about me? Who is this neurosurgeon they mention?* I thought for a moment, *Why not?* I had no Thanksgiving plans. *No harm in looking.*

On the 1992 Thanksgiving weekend, I flew to Spokane, Washington, rented a car and drove over the snow-covered mountains to the little town of Kellogg, Idaho. I approached the town after dark. All I saw from the highway was glistening snow with a thousand tiny lights glowing and sparkling in the distance.

It was an enchanting drive through the cold clear night. The night's stillness was broken only by the sound of the snow crunching under the tires and rustling of trees dropping snow from the bending tree branches near the high mountain pass. The snow-covered trees were like a million puffs of winter, shimmering gently in the moonlight. I was smitten and at that moment decided to move west to Idaho.

Frozen road between Osborn and Kellogg, Idaho, 1994
(Photo by author)

I flew to Boise, Idaho, and met with members of the Idaho State Medical Board and soon my credentials were approved. I was issued a medical license to practice surgery in Idaho.

I had recovered from my heart issues and was ready to return to the operating room. I visited my former practice in Gainesville. I talked to a couple of other surgeons, collected my personal surgical instruments, and resisted the invitation to return. It was obvious that I would be in the same stressful grind that had nearly cost me my life.

I agreed on a contract with the small Shoshone County Hospital and Medical Center in Kellogg, Idaho. "You won't have to worry about the business end of a practice," the administrator said. "We'll handle all the office staff and management and you will be covered by the hospital insurance, both medical and liability."

The hospital was well-managed, and I ultimately served as the chief of surgery and, during my last year, served as medical and surgery chief of staff. We were the only hospital with an orthopaedic surgeon from Missoula, Montana, to the western border of Idaho. We served the towns of Kellogg, Osborn and Wallace (the last town west on Interstate 90 with a single traffic light) and the small towns west in Idaho as well as east into Montana. The area was known as the Silver Valley of the Great Northwest. Huge amounts of silver and lead ore had been produced from mining in this region since the 1800s. It was claimed that more silver ore had come from the Sunshine Mine than anywhere elsewhere in America.

I practiced there for three and a half years. It seemed for me a community of "newly found acquaintances" who had migrated, many from big cities, escaping to the small community of North Idaho. As one young lady, Joan said, "It was all providential that we should become a band of vagabonds and friends in the high mountain valley."

HYPERBARIC OXYGEN CHAMBER

"In a little town in northern Idaho…"

Dr. Fred Kramer, a surgeon on the Shoshone Hospital staff and former Air Force general surgeon, called to inquire if I would be interested in helping him set up a hyperbaric medicine program at the small Idaho hospital.

"I don't know much about that stuff," I answered. Though I had been in the Air Force, I had had no real occasion to use the pressure chamber and had, while on active duty thirty years before, referred our cases to larger military facilities that had the hyperbaric chambers. They were used primarily in the Navy for deep sea divers and, to a limited degree in the Air Force for altitude problems.

"Well, I ran a unit in the Air Force," he answered. "We not only used it for our altitude problems but also for our burn and other applicable surgical problems. My interest now is in using it for diabetic circulation problems and wound management."

"I'm open to any new promising management," I responded, just a little cautious.

Within a few weeks I was sent to Columbia, S.C., for the hyperbaric medicine program at the University of South Carolina Medical School. I completed the course, was certified to work under the supervision of Dr. Kramer for a period of time, and then was fully certified. We started out with a single patient chamber and later added chambers.

The chambers were heavy plexiglass cylinders with a door at one end and a sliding tray for the patient to be placed upon and slipped into the chamber. Oxygen at two to three times atmospheric pressure was then pumped into the chamber for variable lengths of time, usually an hour or less.

Though the idea of hyperbaric medicine was then questioned by many, we opened the first and only chamber, at the time, in northern Idaho and western Montana and treated patients for miles around. Our emphasis was on diabetic wound management. Along with the local fire department we treated cases of acute carbon monoxide poisoning.

Most patients receiving hyperbaric chamber treatment suffered from slow-healing wounds. If not carefully and meticulously managed these difficult wounds could result in the loss of lower limbs largely from diabetic gangrene or extreme circulatory disturbances of various conditions.

Our management was largely to preserve or prevent the loss of limbs as well as management of long-term soft tissue sores of various origins. The wounds were carefully and surgically cleaned and debrided to remove the necrotic, damaged or infected tissue. The patient was placed in the airtight oxygen chamber for the pre-determined time with treatments performed on daily or selected periods, depending on the severity of the problem. The theory of management was to give maximum oxygen under "hyperbaric pressure" to increase the absorbed oxygenation to the involved damaged tissues.

A nurse was trained to assist in the procedures. She became proficient and was able to take over much of the actual patient care. Though I originally had doubts about the theory of hyperbaric medicine and the procedure, I was fully pleased at the frequent good results with the limb-saving program. All patients did not improve, however. We believed the failed cases to be the most severe diabetics or those who failed in the rigorous management of follow-up care.

I debated that it might be the intense surgical debridement and careful wound care as much as the oxygenation that resulted in improvement.

The most delightful patient was a lady in her fifties, with a severe and nearly unmanageable (Type One) diabetes. She was first seen with bilateral lower extremity involvement and even after salvaging her leg for nearly a year she required a below the knee amputation. She bravely continued her care program until one day her husband announced, with tears in his eyes, that she had decided she had enough, and nature should take its course.

We reasoned with her yet understood her wishes. It was not for us to decide. We provided medications to relieve her pain for many weeks until her husband phoned to tell us she had passed away. She was one of the bravest patients I ever knew. She never complained and always presented with a smile.

We marveled at the admirers and speakers at her memorial service. She had contributed to society and her life was remarkably productive despite the limitations of her terminal disease. I shall always remember her smile and her bravery.

THAT SCRUFFY LITTLE KID

They're tougher in Idaho

He was a scruffy little seven or eight-year-old kid that I saw in the Emergency Room. The admitting nurse approached me with a serious and worried expression. "That little boy we brought back to the cast room has a bad hurt arm."

The little guy was sitting on the examining table in his dusty, blue baseball outfit holding a limp, angled right arm, wrapped in a heavy dusty white towel. His grim expression suggested a great deal of pain, but he was not crying. He emitted only a soft moan though he had tears flowing down his dirt stained cheeks.

I examined his arm, lifted it without moving the obvious fracture, splinted it on a wooden board and walked him to the X-ray department. The films demonstrated a severely displaced fracture of both bones of the forearm. "It's badly broken," I said to his dad standing nearby.

Despite the obvious pain, the little guy shed only silent tears. He was biting his lip and gritting his teeth to keep from making a sound.

"Buddy, we'll fix you right up," I said to him. I cleaned the arm with soapy water then iodine and an alcohol solution, drew up the Xylocaine (local anesthetic) and injected the medicine directly into the fracture site; still only a whimper.

Most kids would be yelling at this point but not this brave little man. I manipulated the now anesthetized fracture site and reduced and realigned the bones into good position. I then added the plaster cast. I split the cast with a loud vibrating saw down through the plaster and the soft cotton surrounding the arm and spread the cast a little bit to allow the expected swelling. Post-reduction films looked good.

446

He only nodded as he headed out of the ER with his dad rolling him in a wheelchair, his arm tucked close to his chest in a soft white sling resting on a plump pillow.

A week later follow up X-rays in the office showed satisfactory alignment. Several weeks later, the cast was ready to be removed. The little fellow did not whimper or flinch as I cut the hard cast again with the loud buzzing electric saw. Surprisingly, he never spoke the whole time I treated him.

A month later, he appeared for his final follow-up with his dad. The X-rays showed complete healing. "All done," I said to him and to his dad. The little guy jumped off the exam table and headed out the door. Then he stopped at the doorway looked up at me and with a shrug and a slight smile reached into his pants pocket and pulled out a little card and over his shoulder casually flipped it to me. "That's for you," he announced. Holding his dad's hand, he headed home.

I held the ragged worn card and glanced at the figure and read the bit of writing on the backside of the card. Stan Musial's faded picture was on the card.

The little guy's dad whispered from the door, "That's his favorite baseball card and he wanted you to have it, Doc."

HE HATED TO WEAR A TIE

There were others who went west. There were numerous new friends in the medical as well as the local community. Several were especially interesting.

"Stan, you'll have to dress better than that when you go out into practice. The patients expect it," his droll professor had said to him. Stan didn't know why he should dress any differently from when he was a resident physician on the wards at Case Western Reserve.

Medicine seemed so unnecessarily formal to Stan. He preferred blue jeans, T-shirts and sandals or at least casual loafers.

When he finished his medical residency, he was ready to go out into the world and "save it." He looked around the Detroit area and decided that it was just too big, too formal, too stifling. In his head, he kept hearing the tune, "Go west young man," so he did exactly that. He had gone to medical school in Iowa, but even that seemed too sophisticated to Stan.

Leaving the crowded metropolis of Detroit, he located Interstate 90 and drove westward. He stopped along the way and visited several hospitals, but they all wore dress shirts, ties and white coats.

Not for me, he mused. *Go further west,* his brain kept saying. *Not the Dakotas, not Montana, there is too much prairie,* he thought. *Bad omen. Wasn't that where Custer went?* Then there were those little towns with all that smelting ore. *Not sure,* he thought. He stopped at the Thousand Silver Dollar Café, just beyond Missoula and he was told, "gotta' go on to Idaho. Nothing here 'til you get past the Bitter Roots."

A few miles further down the road, after days of traveling, he drove his dusty car into Wallace, Idaho. Wallace had the last remaining red light on Interstate 90. It was a one red-light town.

"Nope, no hospital here. But there is a hospital a few miles down the highway, over at Kellogg," the scruffy, gray-bearded miner said as they shared the bar stools at the old Miner's Café.

Further along, he passed tall smokestacks that had once poured heavy destructive smoke from the smelters but were now still and smokeless.

He pulled off the Interstate among several small buildings. Up on a gradual rise, crowded just this side of the tall mountains he saw a low-slung 1950s Hill-Burton building with a lighted blue sign, Shoshone Medical Center. It was getting late. He found lodging at the musty Silver Horn Motel, just down the street.

"Just passing through?" the tall, red-headed woman at the motel desk asked.

"That depends," he answered.

A big black, long-haired mutt peered from under the counter and ambled toward Stan, now wagging its tail. He was eyeing the stranger. The lady gave Stan the room key and he stopped by the adjoining café-restaurant for a bite to eat. He could see the hospital from the restaurant window. As darkness descended, he found his room for the night. "I can check it out tomorrow," he whispered to himself.

The next morning, Stan wandered down the dark narrow hall to the motel restaurant. "What will you have?" the stout, middle-aged waitress asked as he took his seat by the window facing the road and the hospital building some hundred yards away. She reached in her apron and pulled out her order pad, flipped a couple of pages. She then pulled her pencil from her hair, licked the pencil point and prepared to write.

Stan looked over the menu. "What's the special of the house?"

She glared at him and thought, *Who's this wise guy. He doesn't look like any miner I've seen in these parts.* She bristled, "Why, we've got Russian eggs soufflé, Caviar, French and Dutch or Belgian pancakes or most anything you want," she snipped. "We got special blueberry syrup made just down the road, our own brand."

"I believe I'll have the eggs and the pancakes and that special syrup, you just mentioned."

"How about me pouring you a cup of our coffee, Honey?" she said, as she handed him a big mug.

"No coffee, just a tall orange juice and some hot tea later," he said as he glanced up at the waitress with a silly grin.

"Hot tea?" she smugly asked.

"Yeah," he answered, "hot tea with lemon."

"You got it coming, mister!" she answered and turned away, glancing back over her shoulder toward him, now smiling.

After breakfast Stan left the motel, sauntered down the main street by the Magic Burger Drive Inn, dodged the dangling Magic hanging sign along the road and a slow-moving weathered pickup. He crossed the street and headed for the Shoshone Medical Center.

He entered the visitor's front door and approached the information desk where a white haired, elderly volunteer was dusting off the desk and arranging the freshly cut sunflowers, the Black-eyed Susans. She glanced at him as he entered the glass door.

Stan looked around the Fifties-style glass-to-ceiling Mexican-tiled foyer and stepped up to the desk. "Could you tell me where the Administrator's office is?" he asked the lady.

"You mean Lang's office?" she inquired. Nobody ever asked for the Administrator's office. *This young fellow must be from somewhere else.* She wondered, where?

"Who's Lang?" Stan asked.

"Oh, he's the acting Administrator." She answered, now thinking the stranger might be looking for a job. They did need more cleaning folks on the night shift. This fellow looked like he was young and strong enough to do that.

"Where's the real Administrator?" Stan asked.

"Oh, I guess Lang is the real administrator, at least for now," she said. "Go down the hall on the left. His door is probably open."

"Thanks," he mumbled and nodded as he turned away to head toward the office.

There was no one at the secretary's desk as he stepped through the open office door. On the desk was a little sign that read, "Nancy, Secretary". He stood awkwardly by the desk, looking for someone to help him.

A voice from inside the inner office yelled out, "You looking for someone, fellow?"

Stan turned toward the inner office and approached the open door. Inside he saw a lean guy with long stringy gray hair in a ponytail and a waxed mustache. He wore blue jeans and a T-shirt and was leaning back with his boots up on the desk. He was reading the *Spokesman Review*, the Spokane morning paper and barely glanced up at the mute stranger.

"Come on in!" he blurted. "What can we do for you?"

"I'm looking for the hospital administrator," Stan responded.

"You're looking at him, at least for now," came the voice from behind the stretched-out newspaper.

"I'm Stan, Doctor Stan. —," the visitor answered.

"Well, I'm Lang, Administrator, anesthetist, all around handyman," the lean guy said as he jerked his cowboy boots from the desk and stood up to greet the visitor. He smiled graciously and extended his slender hand.

"Come on in and sit a spell. You want some coffee? We've got a new pot going."

"Nope, but I do want to talk to someone about the hospital," said Stan. He paused for a moment, "I'm surprised, you don't look like an Administrator!"

"What do you expect, a darn coat and tie?" answered Lang, "We don't wear coats and ties out here in Idaho, not unless it's to a wedding or funeral."

"Bingo!" shouted Stan, and then he quickly responded in a softer tone. "I'm here, and this is the place."

Lang was confused. He frowned, lifted his hand toward his lips in a quizzical, questioning manner, "You're here. What does that mean?"

"It means this is the place where I intend to practice medicine."

Lang looked at the stranger, in his blue jeans, T-shirt, and rusty tan jacket. He glanced down at Stan's outback shoes. He twisted his mustache, and with a grin gestured toward a chair, "Welcome Doctor, you'll do just fine. Have a seat!"

AFTER IDAHO

And after a long practice…

Idaho was cold, but wonderful. My little frame house on a ridge, allowed me, each winter morning, to look across my frozen snow-covered yard toward the snow-capped mountains. In spring, out back, I could gaze across a field of multi-colored wildflowers where the hill descended across the valley to the forest of the Great Northwest. It was like looking at a winter painting, snowy fields with a cottage in the distance and puffs of warm smoke coming from the stone chimney.

A close set of new friends seemed to appear, each with his or her own personality, and story: a couple of stock brokers hailing from California; a painter and his wife from Toronto; a couple from Washington State who had just opened the first McDonalds in North Idaho; a physician moved from Detroit; a cute couple who had opened a gift shop then she ran off with the carpenter who remodeled the building; an Episcopal minister who had retired but returned to serve the little Episcopal churches in Wallace and Kellogg; and a number of delightful local characters amalgamated into a close "set of vagabonds."

As was my wish, I found an Episcopal church in the town of Kellogg and another, a mission church in Wallace. I found few young folks, and all seemed to be my age or older. I approached one of the elderly ladies of the church and cautiously asked, "Where are the rest of the Episcopal members? There must be more?"

She grumbled, "Oh my, I guess they all died." I shook my head and wondered if I would fit in and what my fate might be with the diminishing Episcopal population.

The surgery practice was casual, almost no night calls. In the cold, cold snow of the Great Northwest folks go to bed early at night. The area was financially depressed because of the drop in the price of silver. The famous silver and lead mines of the Silver Valley had closed, and the young workers had moved away. Only years later did the mines reopen and recover some of the magic of the area's history.

Since we were taking care of the miners several of us from the hospital were invited to tour the remaining mines. "Sure," we said, "We'd like to go."

Our trip to the mine began with a lecture by the safety officer as what to expect deep down in the mine shaft. We each suited up with a heavy protective coat and a great leather belt and suspenders that held breathing emergency stuff. We added our special flashlights, water bottles, and other assorted things I don't remember, and finally our heavy boots and miner's helmets, each with its own light and face guard.

The gathering at the elevator at the top of the mine shaft caused me a bit of concern as I thought about all the miners ever trapped in the depths of mines and the devastating fire that this area once had some twenty years before. "Oh, don't worry, doc, we'll be fine, and you have us to look after you," the leader said.

We gathered, a couple of hospital administrators and doctors along with a regular crew that would be descending with us to replace a crew that had completed their hours in the depths of the mine. The elevator creaked and shook as it slowly then rapidly descended, I don't know how many feet to the floor of the mine. I never knew exactly how far down we went but it was a long way. One claimed we descended almost a mile.

On arriving at the bottom of our mine we were further instructed about the workings of the mine. It felt close and warm. A heated damp atmosphere filled the tunnel and further into the mine. *Getting close to Hell,* I thought. I could see that one of our members was beginning to feel closed in as he began to sweat. Our leader took him aside and whispered a few words to him and he seemed okay.

Along the way I picked up several raw bits of lead ore and stuffed them in my pockets until I felt weighted down and glad to have the suspenders holding up my heavy miner's pants. Several of the guys laughed at me for collecting but I continued. I knew I was likely never to return to this depth below the earth, ever.

We watched as the workers dug out the raw ore mixed with the clay and dirt placing it in their rolling carriers. The interior walls were lined with commercial heavy grade chain link fencing to prevent collapse of the walls and ceilings. I had wondered how they protected the mines but had never asked.

After we visited, perhaps an hour or so we gathered at the elevator shaft base awaiting the next elevator as the lights occasionally dimmed then brightened back up. To say it was eerie would be understating my feelings deep in the mine.

Our trip to the top took a bit longer than going down and upon reaching the top we all breathed deeply a sigh of relief at the fresh cool air.

Later back at my office a couple of the docs that had laughed at me wandered by and asked if they could have a bit of my ore to take to their children. I smiled and reminded them that they had laughed at me and I said, "You can get your share on your next trip down in the mine." I later relented and sent bits of my collection to their offices.

A few hours after my return to my office my nurse, Shelly appeared at the door, "Hey, we just got word from the ER that the mine had a cave in about an hour after you all left."

I swallowed carefully, and commented, "Oops, that could have been us involved down there."

A few miners were brought to the ER and one had a broken leg from the cave in, but the others were fine having had only a bad scare. Nevertheless, the mine closed for a day or two to clear the damage deep in the mine.

Nearby, north in the mountains there were a couple of old decayed boom towns. Murray, Mullan, and Pritchard were where miners had discovered gold that became part of the short-lived Coeur d'Alene Gold Rush. Wyatt Earp was in the area beginning in 1884 in Eagle, Idaho. Legend says a small chalkboard was once attached to Earp's saloon wall by the entrance, "Leave your guns at the door."

They say in 1882 miner A.J. Pritchard's mule kicked over a shiny stone and discovered valuable silver ore. For years the mountain in Kellogg was called "Jackass Mountain." Another story claims that a Noah Kellogg found an outcropping of Galena near Milo Gulch and this stimulated the mining boom in the area.

A new ski resort had recently opened on Silver Mountain. Some mornings we met at the base of the mountain and with hot chocolate and McDonalds' sausage biscuits, rode the gondola to the top and skied all day. Some days I could ski in the morning until noon then return to the base below, only a mile or so from my office, head to the hospital and see patients for the remainder of the day.

After three years in Idaho, I elected to join an acquaintance in Louisiana, the state where I had attended college. I came to that practice to help him. He had developed severe arthritis in his hands and could no longer perform the surgery required in his practice. I became the office's surgeon and stayed until I needed a surgical procedure myself, to open the lumen of one of my carotid arteries.

One day, in the operating room, I glanced at the scrub nurse and sighed, "I have done enough. I'm through."

"Oh, no," answered the sweet, young nurse as she frantically held a gut suture for the fascia layer, waiting for me to grasp it, "we've got to close the wound."

"My dear, I don't mean this minute. I mean, I've done enough surgery for a lifetime. I'm tired. I think it is time to quit."

Her blue eyes sparkled as she reached over her Mayo stand to prepare another needle. She gently tilted her head and through her surgical mask whispered, "Maybe so."

I thanked the surgical and ward staff of Our Lady of Lourdes and the Lafayette General Hospital for their good help. I had been impressed by the quality of care in each hospital. I advised my associate and delightful office staff that I would conclude my contract at its expiration date.

I had been out of medical school almost forty years. I had practiced surgery for more than thirty years. I was ready to stop while I could still do the work.

It had always been my philosophy to stop before I became too old or stuck in my ways or, worse, was "run off." I had experienced too many physicians and surgeons who practiced beyond their competence. I would not be one.

It would be hard to leave Cajun Louisiana, the great food, the fanciful music, and the fine folks, but it was time to retire.

My former wife had passed away earlier. I felt that it was time to begin a new life. I moved with my Irish Setter, Andrew, to the

New Orleans area to be closer to the young lady, Ellen Hunter, to whom I had been engaged nearly four decades before. At that time, she was a senior nursing student at Piedmont Hospital, and I was a young surgery intern at Grady. She was the lovely girl in Blue and White.

MANDEVILLE

I found Mandeville, Louisiana, to be the perfect small retirement town to enjoy life after many years of hard work. Living adjacent to Lake Pontchartrain, I found sailing again to my liking. My Irish setter, Andrew, was my faithful companion and shipmate. On arriving at the local harbor, he would rush to the boat slip and jump precariously from the dock onto the deck of my sailboat. He loved to stand elegantly at the bow with the wind blowing and tickling his nose held high. We spent many hours drifting and sometimes briskly sailing in the Louisiana breezes.

Andrew on board and ready to sail
Mandeville Boat Harbor, 2000

In nearby Madisonville I found the wonderful and historic Christ Episcopal Church and delightful folks. The convenience of the city of New Orleans offered all the amenities that anyone could want and brought back fond memories of long-gone college days. It was the perfect location.

LOUISIANA AND KATRINA

Since we lived across the lake from the city of New Orleans, when the hurricanes came, we left town, headed north for refuge in Oxford, Mississippi. There in the college town, famous for William Faulkner we felt safe and comfortable in the academic atmosphere of the University of Mississippi. There we had a couple of favorite little Italian restaurants, a great bookstore and a coffee shop that we enjoyed immensely.

At the end of August 2005, Hurricane Katrina, a category four or five storm, was predicted to hit land exactly in the New Orleans and southern Mississippi area. We closed the house, taped the windows to minimize the danger of shattered glass, selected food and drink from the refrigerator, especially the wine that we might need while away. We assumed that many restaurants would be shuttered. After closing the house tightly, we headed north to our safe haven for a few days to wait out the expected storm.

It was like a Biblical caravan leaving Louisiana. Cars crowded the highways, tanks filled up with fuel anticipating the storm. We called ahead and made reservations at our favorite Oxford motel. "Yes sir, we've got just one room left," the receptionist said.

When we arrived, families were already filling the lobby with sleeping bags and sacks of food and drink, staking out their sleeping sites. There was no place else for these folks to go.

Even far north from New Orleans the hurricane winds and torrential rains knocked out power and flooded areas around us. In our motel we stayed glued to the television as long as the power lasted, watching the city we loved being destroyed.

A day or so after the hurricane, we headed south toward our house, not knowing whether we would still have a home or not. All the gas stations were shut down far into southern Mississippi. Most electrical power was still out. Abandoned cars littered the side of the roads, all out of fuel. It was like seeing the discarded vehicles and personal belongings from the newsreels of a war zone.

As we neared Mandeville, we realized all the roads were closed. Work gangs and volunteers were cutting through the downed trees and obstructions, many with chain saws, cutting the paths into and through the towns.

We managed to get behind a Louisiana State patrol car. For some reason, perhaps by staying so close to the patrol car, we slipped through the blockades and physical obstructions, despite the warnings of live wires down and everywhere the trees piled up on the roads. We followed him closely, snaking through the streets, just close enough to get through before we could be stopped by the local police who flagged him on.

Only a few blocks from our house in Mandeville the patrol car turned off. We were left on our own. We entered a desolate, still steaming, ghost town. Everyone had evacuated and no one, as far as we could tell, had remained to weather the storm. We were eerily alone.

We approached the Lake causeway and, finding no police in the vicinity, we moved numerous road barriers and slipped into our neighborhood.

To our surprise, our house appeared intact. Only a few yards beyond our house the road was blocked by large pine trees, hackberry trees and scattered heavy tree limbs and branches.

The house across the street had a huge oak smashed through the front crushing the porch and on further notice we could see that the rear of the house was also damaged. Two houses away, a house had part of the rear gone and trees lay scattered in the back yard. The trees still standing were leafless, bare skeletons after Katrina had roared through. We could not see further down the street, but later learned that a few houses nearby had trees through the roofs with extensive damage, some destroyed.

We moved limbs and debris from the drive and drove into our own driveway. The house appeared completely intact. Small trees that had blown down fell away from the house.

We had left one car and miraculously a single limb had barely cracked the windshield. We entered the house cautiously and searched for any visible damage. On the exterior we found only a number of roof shingles absent, not enough to cause any water leaks as far as we could determine.

Though the power was off, the gas line was not shut off. There would be a functioning stove to prepare what food was available. We did not realize that the city had not shut the water down. We worried about possible contamination of the local water supply. We added Clorox to the water from our hydrant as well as boiling it. All we needed was to get sick from bad water.

A sultry, humid quiet filled the air. The only noise we heard until sundown were the loud chattering of chain saws in the distance cutting through the downed trees and road obstructions. After sundown all we heard were the chirping of the crickets who seemed to have weathered the storm undisturbed. The usually noisy, white plumed egrets that nested in the trees around our pond were nowhere to be seen or heard.

The heat was still miserable, despite the cold showers we took to get relief. We opened all the doors and toward midnight wandered out onto the second story porch and wondered at the stillness, the dark and the fantastic millions of twinkling stars. Despite the horror of the experience there was a woeful, yet soothing moment as we gazed at the galaxies in the heavens.

Since the power was off, we emptied the refrigerator and placed the contents in the garbage. We had only eggs and sardines and carrots to eat, so we boiled the eggs, ate the sardines from the can and ate the carrots raw, sipped on a bottle of wine, took another cold shower, and went to bed in the sweltering heat.

It was so unbearably hot that the following morning we decided we must leave; we couldn't stand another night.

All businesses were closed. Stores, service stations, and any hope of normal life seemed a long way off. Since the banks were closed, no cash machines worked. Fortunately, we had a little cash available. "We can't stay," we agreed, but how to get far away, we wondered.

"We can siphon gas from my Jeep and use the smaller car that won't use so much gas," I suggested.

However, as I attempted to insert surgical tubing that I found in an old medical bag, I learned that the Jeep had an anti-siphoning block in the pipe going to the gas tank. "Damn, no gas here," I said to Ellen. "We'll just have to try to find gas on the road."

I knew the power was off most everywhere so where would we find gas? It was a daring thought to consider driving away, but the small Mazda would give us better mileage of the two cars, so we chanced it.

We put a couple of pillows, blankets and flashlights in the car, packed a few items of clothes, filled a couple of water bottles (and of course collected a few bottles of wine), shut down the power to the house (should it be returned), shut off the gas, locked the doors and ventured East on Interstate #10.

We were well into Mississippi heading east when I began to panic as the gas gauge settled somewhere between one quarter full and empty. We turned off the interstate to several stations, but no gas. "No way to get it with no power," the lone station attendant volunteered, "The pumps are down, sorry."

At one station I noticed a faded, silver Lincoln at the far edge of the station lot. Beside the car was an old pickup with a lean, scruffy looking guy that seemed to be putting something into the Lincoln's gas tank. I wandered over and quietly asked, "You got some extra gas?"

"Yes, I got some more at home," he answered.

"You selling it?"

"Oh, yes, but I got to go back home and get more."

"How much you got?"

"About ten gallons left, I think."

How much you want for it," I asked

"How's thirty dollars?" he answered.

"Sold." I reached into my pocket and got a twenty and a ten and handed it to him, "Deal." I shook his hand. I wanted to be sure no one else offered him more.

He left the station in his truck. Shortly thereafter, a sheriff's car pulled into the station and a husky deputy climbed out. He tugged at his breeches, lifting his gun belt, took off his hat for a moment, rubbed his sweaty brow with a red rag, and began to ask around about someone illegally selling gas.

In a few minutes the tall, lanky farmer pulled up in his truck, got out and headed to the rear of his truck. I rushed over, "Hey, the sheriff is here and asking about someone selling illegal gas and we better not deal here."

The fellow looked undisturbed, and in a Mississippi Southern drawl said, "Lord, I can sell what I want to."

"Well, I'm not sure what that sheriff is up to or what he will do, because I'm not from here," I said, keeping my voice low.

He glanced over at the sheriff, nodded toward me and mumbled, "Follow me and we'll go to my place."

We got back into our car and followed him down a muddy road to his little farm. We entered his gravel drive and pulled up to a wooden shed, his barn. It turns out he was selling the gas he had for his farm tractor. There we got gas and when he finished, he said. "I got some extra you can have," and he handed me a red can with an extra gallon or two. I offered him an extra ten for the extra gas, but he wouldn't take it.

"No, sir, a deal's a deal," he said.

While we were talking, his little spotted white and brown dog jumped out of his truck and began sniffing my pants leg. He started to raise his hind leg and my first thought was, *If he pees on my pants then we just accept the bad with the good.* However, he finished his sniffing and trotted over beside his master.

"Hey, what's your dog's name?"

"His name is Susie," he answered as he picked up the skinny, little mutt and hugged him proudly.

I thanked him, shook his hand, and commented, "Good to do business with you, sir."

He nodded, "Now I can get some food. All my food from deer season got ruined in my freezer and we don't have much left in the house."

With a nearly full tank and a little extra we headed for Georgia where our relatives would shelter us for a few days.

A week or so later we returned to Louisiana. The devastation was still unbelievable, houses demolished and obviously un-repaired; businesses gone – wiped out; streets finally cleared yet in some places still littered with destroyed furnishings, old smelly refrigerators, abandoned cars, and rummaged dirty clothes, rubbish still everywhere. The odor was noticeably foul, unbelievable, and unbearable in some neighborhoods. The whole area smelled like the "morning after" in the gutters of the old French Quarter, even worse, a rank odor of death and destruction. *Will the community ever get this mess cleaned up?* I wondered.

The lakefront was more severely damaged with homes and businesses washed away or destroyed with remnants spread over a large portion of the lakefront. In the local Mandeville harbor where I kept a sailboat, we noted that many of the motor and sailboats had been lifted up onto the land by the surges of water beside the docks.

Some remained tilted with hull damage and some had floated back into their slips, some were sunk down in the shallow moorings.

We had barely been home a couple of hours when, after we cleared a portion of the yard, several husky young power workers entered our yard. They headed for a large electric transformer at the back of the property.

Pontchartrain – North Shore – Lake Front neighbors
"Though battered by Katrina in August 2005,
the survivors were unbroken."
(Photo by author)

A tall young man and his helper were driving some sort of a lift to the transformer. "Is it okay if we drive over the grass?" These guys were from the Oklahoma Power Company. We were to learn that many states had sent power workers to help New Orleans.

"When can we expect to have power?" I asked the tall worker.

With a chain saw strung over his shoulder he nodded and boasted, "We'll have you fixed up in about one hour, or two at the most."

I couldn't believe our luck. I mumbled, "Cool air finally."

"Yep, we'll get you all fixed up," he answered and returned to help his fellow worker as they were lifted by the truck bucket to service the transformer.

Before long, perhaps a week, the area was filled with out-of-state power company trucks and the independent guys out to make a buck fixing and cleaning. Money was slowly coming in from FEMA and the Red Cross, funds provided for victims, some receiving two thousand dollars cash from the Red Cross for immediate needs. The area was filled with helpers as well as vultures, overcharging and feeding off the ruin of the New Orleans storm.

Ellen and Jerry – Retired
Mandeville, Louisiana, 2005

POST KATRINA
Insurance adjuster

A few weeks after Katrina's ravaging storm, insurance agents arrived, spread out about the shoreline, and covered the devastated area. We called and requested an adjuster for our damage and made our claim for roof damage.

A husky, thirty-plus-year old young man arrived from the insurance carrier. After an appropriate greeting and brief interview, he climbed a steep, shaky ladder to the second story roof to survey the damage and give us our estimate. He yelled from high upon the ladder, "Well, folks, I think you are mighty lucky to have so little damage." I thought, *Isn't that just like an insurance adjuster!*

Upon returning to the yard he took out his clipboard and began his calculations and as we stood on the concrete patio under the upper story deck, our big Irish Setter began to sniff, and we heard a low growl.

Though our setter, generally a gentle dog, had a secure little fenced-in area, it was filled with downed limbs and debris. I had, during our clean-up efforts that day, temporarily tied him to a slender column supporting the deck. He suddenly stood between us and the insurance fellow and jerked loose from his tether. I never dreamed he was so protective.

Wide-eyed, the guy turned and like an Olympic sprinter with feet pounding the grass, headed for the far side of the yard and valiantly tried to scale the six-foot wooden fence separating our yard from our neighbors'. It was like an animated Disney cartoon watching him flee. We dared not laugh.

I managed to catch the dog before he grabbed the agent's breeches as he scurried up, hanging precariously onto the top ridge of the wooden fence.

Turning to my dog, Andrew, I jerked him back and directed him toward the gate of his enclosed area. Despite the downed limbs and brush I put him back in the little fences area.

With sweat pouring from his brow the agent returned to our side of the yard and carefully gauged his distance from the wild animal behind the dog fence.

As he ripped the forms from his clipboard and handed us his estimate, I whispered to Ellen, "That damn episode just cost us at least a thousand dollars."

FINALLY

After almost two years of ghastly slow cleanup and attempts to return New Orleans to normal we said, "We may not live long enough to see the city restored. It's just not coming back. It seemed that the city and area would never recover so depressed, we searched the Gulf shore for a new home. "What shall we do or where can we go?"

We passed through the destroyed Mississippi Gulf coast, searched the Alabama coast, across Mobile Bay to Fairhope, a literary town that we have since come to enjoy, and checked out other towns that were not severely damaged by Katrina. Heading further east we decided on the Atlanta arca, away from the hurricanes and to friends and relatives. Yes, we would head east to Atlanta, the city where I was born. It would be going home.

PEACHTREE CITY, GEORGIA

Though a native Atlantan, I think I really never heard of Peachtree City before the early 2000s. The town was started in 1959, now half a century ago by a group of young resourceful men that had imagined a designed town derived from the New Towns that grew up in England after the devastation of the Second World War.

I knew about Newnan, Fairburn, and Griffin and the small towns, College Park where as a child I had attended military school and

East Point where my family had often driven down to have ice-cream from a well-known ice cream shop on Main Street next to the railroad tracks, but never the little town developing further south in Fayette County. Why should I ever think about a town other than the city I loved, Atlanta!

During the last couple of years, we had visited Peachtree City where Ellen's brother, a former army officer had retired with his family. Our visits were always confusing as we had trouble with all the curvy streets and confusing names, Braelinn this and Braelinn that, and the numerous and different subdivisions in the planned community. Often lost we always found the local fire station for directions. It became a running joke as we attempted to hide our confusion when visiting. Finally, we decided we would consider Peachtree City as our next home. Ellen's sister-in-law found two potential houses and Ellen chose the single-story cluster home that has since served us well, located in a cul-de-sac with woods surrounding us as if we lived in a tree house.

"Are you getting a golf cart," everyone asked? "Oh no, we're not old enough for a cart." I hadn't played golf since military service, over a four of decades ago so there was little need for a cart, I thought. We would get bicycles and ride those until the small hills became too much for my cardiac situation.

Well, it is quiet and it's not the big city and doesn't have the glitzy big city lights, but we loved our new neighbors and the pleasant atmosphere of the town. Oh, and we were not too far from Atlanta and best of all a major airport was near so our collection of children could visit easily.

In PTC, I've found a church to my liking, wonderful folks associated with one of the best libraries I've ever experienced and several delightful writing groups that have allowed Ellen and me to each write.

Though celebrating more than twelve years, it seems we just moved here yesterday. We are beginning to look around for a retirement community but know that we really don't want to leave a town we now love.

AS TIME GOES BY

It has been many years since retirement and the moving back to Georgia feels as if I had never left. I've reconnected with many friends from childhood, have traveled a bit and set to writing a medical memoir for my medical school classmates, a military story of time served, and a life memoir for my grandchildren.

We have made many new friends and as time goes by, we lose some who have meant so much to us. Daily, I read the Atlanta Journal Constitution's obituary pages to see if any of my friends have left. I once asked my school pal, Jimmy Jenkins, who had gotten me interested in the obits, why he habitually read them. He answered, "To be sure I'm not in those pages." One day he was.

As friends depart, we often attend those last rites and celebrations of their lives. We muse over our lives and cheerfully recall each member of our group.

Not so long ago the special friend, Floyd Williams, who we depended on for much of the up to date information on our close classmates, going back to kindergarten, left us after an extended illness. At the Atlanta First Christian Church on Peachtree Street, several of us who had started school together in kindergarten, gathered during and after his funeral.

Danny Powers, a Georgia Tech graduate, spoke up and said, "You know, Floyd and I used to drop in at the Varsity after studying late at night, so why don't we go there?"

We've parked our cars in the huge parking lot, dodged the carhops, and entered the white and red trimmed building, Atlanta's famous Varsity at North Avenue and Spring Street.

The Varsity is just off I-85 and adjacent to the Georgia Tech campus, a place we all have frequented since childhood. It was opened in late 1920s by the late Mr. Frank Gordy.

We met at the ordering counter. "What'll-ya-have, what'll-ya-have?" the server, in his white and red paper hat and big smile, sings out. We nod, give our order, get our trays and collect our food and drink.

We're sitting at a long red shiny table emptying our trays, spreading out our naked dogs, our chili dogs, French fries, onion rings and PCs (plain chocolate milk over ice), Coca Colas and assorted other drinks.

On this day our thoughts drifted back to the days when we gathered here as children, high school students with our dates, and during college, some in convertibles and others in family cars. In those days the cars had running boards and the carhops would grab the door or roof as we entered the driveway and plant their feet securely on the running boards 'til we pulled into a parking slot. "What'll ya have, what'll ya have?" the familiar words, were chirped out by the carhops as they wrote down or memorized our orders.

"Two chili dogs, mustard and ketchup, one hamburger, with onions, but hold the cheese, and one plain bare-naked dog. Two Cokes "walking," one orange and one PC. Add two fries and two onion rings.'"

"Anything else?" the carhop would whisper.

"Yeah, change that plain dog to one with just ketchup, no mustard."

"Yes, sir, got it," and he would slap a cardboard square with a big number, his number on our windshield, and he was gone.

Today, we're not getting curb service, but are on an upper floor inside the main building that provides a panoramic view looking north toward Atlanta's tall buildings and the city we love.

"Yeah, Floyd would like to see us here at the old Varsity," one of our group, Harry, commented as we munched on our favorite Varsity chili dogs. "What in the world is better than being together again in Atlanta!"

CONCLUSION

There has been no fame and no fortune in my life. I have essentially lived the life I wanted, and I have made promises. I have tried to keep those promises and have asked only that I be allowed to live, as Sam Walter Foss wrote, *"...by the side of the road and be a friend to man."*

I believe I have been allowed that privilege.

The author,

JLW